VEST POCKET DICTIONARY
Second Edition

Katherine Soltis, Editor

Based on
**Webster's New World
Dictionary®**
of American English
Third College Edition

MACMILLAN • USA

Webster's New World™
Vest Pocket Dictionary, Second Edition
Copyright © 1994 by Simon & Schuster, Inc.

This book is based on and includes material from
Webster's New World Dictionary®, Third College Edition,
copyright © 1994.

Macmillan General Reference
A Simon & Schuster Macmillan Company
1633 Broadway
New York, NY 10019-6785

A Webster's New World™ Book

MACMILLAN is a registered trademark of Macmillan, Inc.
WEBSTER'S NEW WORLD DICTIONARY is a registered
trademark of Simon & Schuster, Inc.

Dictionary Editorial Offices:
New World Dictionaries
850 Euclid Avenue
Cleveland, Ohio 44114

Library of Congress Cataloging-in-Publication Data

Webster's New World vest pocket dictionary / Katherine Solt.
  editor. —2nd ed.
     p. cm.
  "Based on Webster's New World dictionary of American
  English, third college edition."
  "A Webster's New World book"—T.p. verso.
    ISBN 0-671-88993-1
    1. English language—Dictionaries. I. Soltis, Katherine.
  II. Webster's New World dictionary of American English. III.
  Title: Vest pocket dictionary.
    PE1628.W56377 1994
    423—dc20   94-5824
                                                      CIP

Database service and principal typesetting by
Lexi-Comp, Inc., Hudson, Ohio.
Manufactured in the United States of America

5 6 7 8 9 10   97 98 99 00 01 02

KEY TO PRONUNCIATION

	as in		*as in*
a	cat	ou	out
ā	ape	u	up
ä	cot	ʉ	fur
e	ten	ə	a *in* ago
ē	me		o *in* atom
i	fit	'	fertile (furt''l)
ī	ice	ch	chin
ō	go	ŋ	ring
ô	fall	sh	she
oi	oil	th	thin
oo	look	*th*	then
oo	tool	zh	measure

ABBREVIATIONS USED

a.	adjective	Mil.	military
abbrev.	abbreviated;	Mus.	music
	abbreviation	myth.	mythology
adv.	adverb	n.	noun
Ar.	archaic	Naut.	nautical
Biol.	biology	Obs.	obsolete
Br.	British	orig.	originally
c.	century	pl.	plural
Chem.	chemistry	Poet.	poetic
Col.	colloquial	prep.	preposition
con.	conjunction	pres.	present
Dial.	dialectal	pron.	pronoun
esp.	especially	pt.	past tense
etc.	et cetera	R.C.Ch.	Roman Catholic
fem.	feminine		Church
Fr.	French	Rom.	Roman
ft.	foot; feet	sing.	singular
Gr.	Greek	Sl.	slang
Gram.	grammar	Sp.	Spanish
in.	inch(es)	sp.	spelling; spelled
int.	interjection	spec.	specifically
L.	Latin	t.	tense
Math.	mathematics	Theol.	theology
mi.	mile(s)	v.	verb

Other abbreviations will be found on pages 182-185.

RULES FOR SPELLING

Words that end in a silent -e usually drop the -e when a suffix beginning with a vowel is added *[file—filing]*. However, before the suffixes -able and -ous, the -e is usually kept if it follows a soft c or g *[outrage—outrageous]*. The -e is usually kept when a suffix beginning with a consonant is added *[time—timely]*.

Words that end in a single consonant preceded by a single vowel usually double that consonant when a suffix beginning with a vowel is added, if: a) the word is a monosyllable *[sin—sinning]*, or b) the word has more than one syllable but is stressed on the last syllable *[refer—referring]*. If the final consonant is not preceded by a single vowel or, in American usage, if the last syllable is not stressed, the final consonant is usually not doubled *[hurl—hurling; travel—traveling]*.

Words that end in a double letter usually drop one letter when a suffix beginning with the same letter is added *[free—freest]*.

Words that end in -y preceded by a consonant usually change the -y to an i when a suffix that does not begin with i is added *[marry—married]*. If it follows a vowel, the -y is usually kept *[play—played]*.

Words that end in -ie change the -ie to a y when the suffix -ing is added *[lie—lying]*.

Words that end in -c usually take on a k when a suffix beginning with i or e is added *[picnic—picnicker]*.

Words containing ie or ei: The combination ei is usually used following the letter c and is always used to represent the sound (ā). In most other native English words the combination ie is used.

Note that the suffix -ful, unlike the adjective *full,* has only one l *[cupful]*.

Verbs ending in -cede and -ceed: Three common verbs *(exceed, proceed,* and *succeed)* end in -ceed. Most other verbs end in -cede.

RULES FOR FORMING PLURALS

Most nouns in English form the plural by adding -s or -es. When the singular noun ends in a sound that allows -s to be added and pronounced without the formation of a new syllable, -s is used *[book—books]*. When the singular noun ends in a sound such that -s cannot be joined to it and pronounced without the formation of an additional syllable, -es is used *[kiss—kisses; torch—torches]*.

The chief exceptions to this basic rule are listed below.

Words that end in -o usually form the plural by adding -es *[hero—heroes]*; however, some of them do so by adding -s *[solo—solos]*. There is no rule that deals with the distinction.

Some words that end in -f form the plural by changing the -f to v and adding -es *[wolf—wolves]*.

Words that end in -y preceded by a consonant usually form the plural by changing the -y to i and adding -es *[lady—ladies]*. If the -y is preceded by a vowel, they form the plural regularly, by adding -s *[day—days]*.

Some words form the plural by a vowel change. Among the commonest examples are *foot—feet; man—men; tooth—teeth; woman—women*.

Some words have special plurals to which none of the above general statements applies. Among them are words such as *alumna—alumnae; child—children; phenomenon—phenomena; radius—radii; sheep—sheep*.

A

a., *indefinite article* **1** one **2** each; any one

ard'vark' (ärd'-) *n.* African mammal that eats ants

a·back' *adv.*, *a.* [Ar.] back — **taken aback** surprised

ab'a·cus *n.* frame with beads for doing arithmetic

a·bal'o·ne *n.* sea mollusk

a·ban'don *v.* **1** give up entirely **2** to desert —*n.* lack of restraint

a·base' *v.* to humble

ab'bess *n.* woman who is head of a nunnery

ab'bot *n.* man who is head of a monastery

ab·bre'vi·ate' *v.* shorten, as a word —**ab·bre'vi·a'tion** *n.*

ABC *n.*, *pl.* **ABC's 1** *pl.* the alphabet **2** basics; rudiments

ab'di·cate' *v.* give up, as a throne

ab'do·men (*or* ab dō'-) *n.* part of the body between chest and pelvis

ab·duct' *v.* kidnap

a·bet' *v.* **a·bet'ted** to help, esp. in crime —**a·bet'tor, a·bet'ter** *n.*

ab·hor' *v.* **-horred'** shun in disgust, hatred, etc.

a·bide' *v.* **a·bode'** *or* **a·bid'ed 1** remain **2** [Ar.] reside **3** await **4** endure —**abide by** keep (a promise) or obey (rules)

a·bil'i·ty *n.*, *pl.* **-ties 1** a being able **2** talent

a'ble *a.* **1** having power (*to* do) **2** talented; skilled —**a'bly** *adv.*

ab·nor'mal *a.* not normal

a·board' *adv.*, *prep.* on or in (a train, ship. etc.)

a·bol'ish *v.* do away with

a·bom'i·na·ble *a.* **1** disgusting **2** very bad —**a·bom'i·na·bly** *adv.*

ab·o·rig'i·ne' (-rij'ə nē') *n.* first known inhabitant

a·bort' *v.* **1** have or cause to have a miscarriage **2** cut short (a flight, etc.), as because of equipment failure

a·bor'tion *n.* miscarriage, esp. one induced —**a·bor'tive** *a.*

a·bound' *v.* be plentiful

a·bout' *adv.* **1** around **2** near **3** in an opposite direction —*a.* nearly —*a.* astir —*prep.* **1** around **2** near to **3** just starting **4** concerning

a·bove' *adv.* **1** higher **2** earlier on a page —*prep.* **1** over **2** higher than —*a.* **1** mentioned above

a·breast' *adv.*, *a.* **1** side by side

a·bridge' *v.* shorten, as in wording; lessen —**a·bridg'ment** *n.*

a·broad' *adv.* **1** far and wide **2** outdoors **3** to or in foreign lands

a·brupt' *a.* **1** sudden **2** brusque; curt **3** steep

ab'scess' (-ses') *n.* inflamed, pus-filled area in body

ab'sent (*v.:* ab sent') *a.* **1** not present; away **2** lacking —*v.* keep (oneself) away —**ab'sence** *n.*

ab'sen·tee' *n.* absent person —*a.* of, by, or from one who is absent

ab'sent-mind'ed *a.* **1** not attentive **2** forgetful

ab'so·lute' *a.* **1** perfect **2** complete **3** not mixed; pure **4** certain; positive **5** real —**ab'so·lute'ly** *adv.*

ab·solve' *v.* to free from guilt, a duty, etc.

ab·sorb' *v.* **1** suck up **2** engulf wholly **3** interest greatly

ab·stain' *v.* do without; refrain

ab'sti·nence *n.* an abstaining from food, liquor, etc.

ab·stract' (*a. also, n. always:* ab' strakt') *a.* **1** apart from material objects; not concrete **2** theoretical —*v.* summarize —*n.* summary —**ab·strac'tion** *n.*

ab·surd' *a.* ridiculous

a·bun'dance *n.* more than is needed —**a·bun'dant** *a.*

a·buse' (-byōōz'; *n.:* -byōōs') *v.* **1** use wrongly **2** mistreat **3** berate —*n.* **1** wrong use **2** mistreatment **3** vile language

a·byss' *n.* deep or bottomless gulf

a·ca·dem'ic *a.* **1** of schools or colleges **2** of liberal arts **3** theoretical —**ac'a·dem'i·cal·ly** *adv.*

a·cad'e·my *n.*, *pl.* **-mies 1** private high school **2** school for special study **3** society of scholars, etc.

ac·cel'er·ate' *v.* **1** increase in speed **2** make happen sooner

ac'cent *n.* **1** stress on a syllable in speaking **2** mark showing this **3** distinctive way of pronouncing **4** rhythmic stress —*v.* emphasize

ac·cept' *v.* **1** receive willingly **2** approve **3** agree to **4** believe in —**ac·cept'a·ble** *a.* satisfactory

ac'cess' *n.* **1** right to enter, use, etc. **2** means of approach

ac·ces'so·ry *n.*, *pl.* **-ries 1** thing added for decoration **2** helper in a crime

ac'ci·dent *n.* **1** unexpected hap-

pening 2 mishap **3** chance —**ac'ci·den'tal** *a.*

ac'ci·dent-prone' *a.* likely or tending to be in or have accidents

ac·claim' *v.* greet with applause —*n.* great approval

ac·com'mo·date' *v.* **1** adjust **2** do a favor for **3** have room for; lodge —**ac·com'mo·da'tion** *n.*

ac·com'mo·dat'ing *a.* obliging

ac·com'pa·ny *v.* -nied **1** add to **2** go with **3** play music supporting a soloist —**ac·com'pa·ni·ment** *n.* —**ac·com'pa·nist** *n.*

ac·com'plice (-plis) *n.* partner in crime

ac·com'plish *v.* do; complete

ac·com'plished *a.* skilled

ac·cord' *v.* **1** agree **2** grant —*n.* agreement —**according to 1** consistent with **2** as stated by

ac·cor'di·on *n.* musical instrument with a bellows

ac·count' *v.* **1** give reasons (*for*) **2** judge to be —*n.* **1** *pl.* business records **2** worth **3** explanation **4** report —**on account of** because of —**on no account** never

ac·count'ing *n.* the keeping of business records —**ac·count'ant** *n.*

ac·cu'mu·late' *v.* pile up; collect —**ac·cu'mu·la'tion** *n.* —**ac'cu·mu·la·tive** *a.*

ac'cu·rate (-yər ət) *a.* exactly correct —**ac'cu·ra·cy** *n.* —**ac'cu·rate·ly** *adv.*

ac·cuse' (-kyōoz') *v.* **1** to blame **2** charge with doing wrong —**ac'cu·sa'tion** *n.*

ac·cus'tom *v.* make familiar by habit or use

ac·cus'tomed *a.* **1** usual; customary **2** used (*to*)

ace *n.* **1** playing card with one spot **2** expert

ac'e·ta·min'o·phen (ə sēt'ə min' ə fən) *n.* drug used to lessen fever or pain

ache (āk) *n.* dull, steady pain —*v.* have such pain

a·chieve' *v.* **1** do; accomplish **2** get by effort —**a·chieve'ment** *n.*

ac'id (as'-) *n.* **1** sour substance **2** chemical that reacts with a base to form a salt —*a.* **1** sour; sharp **2** of an acid —**a·cid'ic** *a.*

ac·knowl'edge *v.* **1** admit or recognize **2** to respond to (a greeting, etc.) **3** express thanks for —**ac·knowl'edg·ment** *n.*

ac'me (-mē) *n.* highest point

ac'ne (-nē) *n.* pimply skin

a'corn' *n.* nut of the oak

a·cous'tics (-kōos'-) *n.pl.* qualities of a room that affect sound —*n.* science of sound —**a·cous'tic, a·cous'ti·cal** *a.*

ac·quaint' *v.* **1** make familiar (*with*) **2** inform

ac·quaint'ance *n.* **1** personal knowledge **2** person one knows slightly

ac·quire' *v.* get as one's own

ac·qui·si·tion (ak'wə zish'ən) *n.* **1** an acquiring **2** something acquired

ac·quit' *v.* -quit'ted **1** declare not guilty **2** conduct (oneself)

a·cre (ā'kər) *n.* measure of land, 43,560 sq. ft. —**a'cre·age** *n.*

ac'ro·bat' *n.* performer on the trapeze, tightrope, etc. —**ac'ro·bat'ic** *a.*

a·cross' *adv.* from one side to the other —*prep.* **1** from one side to the other of **2** on the other side of **3** into contact with

a·cryl'ic (-kril'-) *a.* of certain synthetic fibers or resins used to make fibers, paints, etc.

act *n.* **1** thing done **2** a doing **3** a law **4** division of a play or opera —*v.* **1** perform in a play, etc. **2** behave **3** function **4** have an effect (*on*)

act'ing *a.* substitute

ac'tion *n.* **1** a doing of something **2** thing done **3** *pl.* behavior **4** way of working **5** lawsuit **6** combat

ac'ti·vate' *v.* make active

ac'tive *a.* **1** acting; working **2** busy; lively; agile —**ac·tiv'i·ty** *n.*, *pl.* -ties

ac'tor *n.* one who acts in plays —**ac'tress** *n.fem.*

ac'tu·al (-chōo-) *a.* existing; real

ac'u·punc'ture *n.* the practice of piercing the body with needles to treat disease or pain

a·cute' *a.* **1** sharp-pointed **2** shrewd **3** keen **4** severe **5** critical **6** less than 90°: said of angles

ad *n.* [Col.] advertisement

a·da'gio (-dä'jō) *a., adv. Mus.* slow(ly)

Ad'am's apple *n.* bulge in the front of a man's throat

a·dapt' *v.* fit or adjust as needed —**a·dapt'er, a·dapt'or** *n.*

add *v.* **1** join (*to*) so as to increase **2** increase **3** find the sum of **4** say further

ad'der *n.* small snake, sometimes poisonous

ad·dict' (n. ə dikt'; v.: ə dikt') *v.* give (oneself) up (*to* a habit) —*n.* one addicted, as to a drug —**ad·dic'**

tion n. —**ad·dic'tive** a.

ad·di'tion n. 1 an adding 2 part added —**ad·di'tion·al** a.

ad'dle v. make or become confused —**ad'dled** a.

ad·dress' (ə dres'; n.: also a'dres') v. 1 speak or write to 2 write the destination on (mail, etc.) 3 apply (oneself to) —n. 1 a speech 2 place where one lives

ad·e·noids' n.pl. growths in the throat behind the nose

ad·ept' (n.: ad'ept') a. highly skilled —n. an expert

ad'e·quate (-kwət) a. enough or good enough —**ad'e·qua·cy** n.

ad·here' v. 1 stick fast 2 give support (to)

ad·he'sive a. sticking —n. sticky substance, as glue

a·dieu' (ə dyōō') int. goodbye

ad·ja'cent a. near or next

ad'jec·tive (-tiv) n. word that qualifies a noun

ad·join' v. be next to

ad·journ' (-jurn') v. suspend (a meeting, etc.) for a time

ad·just' v. 1 alter to make fit 2 regulate 3 settle rightly —**ad·just'a·ble** a. —**ad·just'ment** n.

ad'-lib' [Col.] v. -**libbed'** improvise (words, etc.)

ad·min'is·ter v. 1 manage; direct 2 give; attend (to) —**ad·min'is·tra'tor** n.

ad'mi·ra·ble a. worth admiring

ad'mi·ral n. high-ranking naval officer

ad·mire' v. have high regard for —**ad·mi·ra'tion** n.

ad·mis'sion n. 1 an admitting 2 entrance fee 3 confession or concession

ad·mit' v. -**mit'ted** 1 let enter 2 concede or confess

ad·mon'ish v. 1 warn or advise 2 reprove mildly

a·do' n. fuss; trouble

a·do'be (-dō'bē) n. unburnt, sundried brick

ad'o·les'cence n. time between childhood and adulthood; youth —**ad'o·les'cent** a., n.

a·dopt' v. 1 take legally as one's child 2 take as one's own —**a·dop'tion** n. —**a·dop'tive** a.

a·dore' v. 1 worship 2 love greatly —**a·dor'a·ble** a.

a·dorn' v. decorate; ornament

a·droit' a. skillful and clever

a·dult' a. grown-up; mature —n. mature person, animal, or plant

a·dul'ter·ate v. make impure by adding things

a·dul'ter·y n. sexual unfaithfulness in marriage

ad·vance' v. 1 bring or go forward 2 pay before due 3 rise or raise in rank —n. 1 a move forward 2 pl. approaches to get favor —**in advance** ahead of time —**ad·vance'ment** n.

ad·van'tage n. 1 superiority 2 gain; benefit —**take advantage of** use for one's own benefit

ad·ven'ture n. 1 dangerous undertaking 2 exciting experience —**ad·ven'tur·er** n.

ad'verb' n. word that modifies a verb, adjective, or other adverb

ad'ver·sar·y n., pl. -**ies** foe; opponent

ad'ver·tise' v. tell about publicly to promote sales, etc. —**ad'ver·tis'ing** n.

ad'ver·tise'ment (or -vur'tiz-) n. public notice, usually paid for

ad·vice' n. opinion on what to do

ad·vise' v. 1 give advice (to) 2 offer as advice 3 inform —**ad·vis'or, ad·vis'er** n. —**ad·vi'so·ry** a.

ad'vo·cate (-kāt'; n.: -kət) v. support or urge —n. one who supports another or a cause

adz, adze n. axlike tool

aer'ate (er'-) v. expose to air

aer'i·al a. 1 of or like air 2 of flying —n. radio or TV antenna

aer·o'bic a. of exercise that conditions heart and lungs —n. pl. [sing. or pl. v.] aerobic exercises

aer'o·sol' a. using gas under pressure to dispense liquid or foam

aer'o·space' n. earth's atmosphere and outer space

a·far' adv. far away

af'fa·ble a. pleasant; sociable

af·fair' n. 1 matter; event 2 pl. business matters 3 amorous relationship of two people not married to each other

af·fect' v. 1 act on; influence 2 stir emotionally 3 like to wear, use, etc. 4 pretend to be or feel

af'fec·ta'tion n. 1 pretense 2 artificial behavior

af·fec'tion n. 1 fond feeling 2 disease

af'fi·da'vit n. sworn statement in writing

af·fil'i·ate (-āt'; n.: -ət) v. join as a member; associate —n. affiliated member —**af·fil'i·a'tion** n.

af·firm' v. assert or confirm

af·firm'a·tive a. affirming; positive —n. assent

af·flict' v. cause pain to; distress

af'flu·ence n. 1 plenty 2 riches

—af'flu·ent a.

af·ford' v. 1 have money enough for 2 provide

af·front' v., n. insult

a·float' a. 1 floating 2 at sea 3 current

a·foot' adv., a. 1 on foot 2 in motion; astir

a·fraid' a. 1 frightened 2 regretful

Af·ri·can-A·mer'i·can a., n. (of) a black American of African ancestry

aft adv. near the stern

af'ter adv. 1 behind 2 later —prep. 1 behind 2 in search of 3 later than 4 because of 5 in spite of 6 in imitation of 7 for —con. later than —a. later

af'ter·math' n. (bad) result

af'ter·noon' n. time from noon to evening

af'ter·ward adv. later: also afterwards

a·gain' adv. 1 once more 2 besides

a·gainst' prep. 1 opposed to 2 so as to hit 3 next to 4 in preparation for

ag'ate (-ət) n. hard semiprecious stone, often striped

age n. 1 length of time of existence 2 time of getting full legal rights 3 stage of life 4 old age 5 historical period —v. grow old or make old

a·ged (ā'jəd; 2: ājd) a. 1 old 2 of the age of

a'gen·cy n., pl. -cies 1 action or means 2 firm acting for another

a·gen'da n. list of things to be dealt with

a'gent n. 1 force, or cause of an effect 2 one that acts for another

ag'gra·vate' v. 1 make worse 2 [Col.] vex; annoy

ag·gres'sion n. unprovoked attack —ag·gres'sor n.

ag·gres'sive a. 1 quarrelsome 2 bold and active

a·ghast' (-gast') a. horrified

ag·ile (aj'əl) a. quick; nimble

ag'i·tate' (aj'-) v. 1 stir up 2 disturb 3 talk to arouse support (for) —ag'i·ta'tion n.

ag·nos'tic n. one who doubts the existence of God

a·go' adv., a. (in the) past

ag'o·ny n. great suffering

a·gree' v. 1 to consent 2 be in harmony or accord

a·gree'a·ble a. 1 pleasing 2 willing to consent

ag'ri·cul'ture n. farming

a·ground' adv., a. on or onto the shore, a reef, etc.

ah int. cry of pain, delight, etc.

a·head' adv., a. in front; forward; in advance

a·hoy' int. Naut. hailing call

aid v., n. help

aide n. 1 assistant 2 military officer assisting a superior

AIDS n. viral condition resulting in infections, cancer, etc.: usually fatal

ail v. 1 to pain 2 be ill

ail'ment n. chronic illness

aim v. 1 direct (a gun, blow, etc.) 2 intend —n. 1 an aiming 2 direction of aiming 3 intention; goal —aim'less a.

air n. 1 mixture of gases around the earth 2 appearance 3 pl. haughty manners 4 tune —v. 1 let air into 2 publicize —a. of aviation —on the air broadcasting on TV or radio

air conditioning n. controlling of humidity and temperature of air in a room, etc.

air'craft' n., pl. -craft' machine or machines for flying

air'field' n. field where aircraft can take off and land

air force n. aviation branch of a country's armed forces

air'line' n. air transport system or company: also air line

air'mail' n. mail transported by aircraft

air'plane' n. motor-driven or jet-propelled aircraft

air'port' n. airfield with facilities for repair, etc.

air'tight' a. too tight for air to enter or escape

air'y a. -i·er, -i·est 1 open to the air 2 flimsy as air 3 light; graceful 4 lighthearted

aisle (īl) n. passageway between rows of seats

a·jar' adv., a. slightly open

a·kim'bo adv., a. with hands on hips

a·kin' a. similar; alike

a' la mode' a. 1 in fashion 2 served with ice cream

a·larm' n. 1 signal or device to warn or waken 2 fear —v. to frighten

a·las' int. cry of sorrow, etc.

al·bi'no n., pl. -nos individual lacking normal coloration

al'bum n. blank book for photographs, stamps, etc.

al'che·my (-ka-) n. chemistry of the Middle Ages

al'co·hol' n. colorless, intoxicating liquid obtained from fermented grain, fruit, etc.

al·co·hol·ic *a.* of alcohol —*n.* one addicted to alcohol

al'cove *n.* recess; nook

ale *n.* kind of beer

a·lert' *a.* watchful; ready —*n.* an alarm —*v.* warn to be ready

al·fal'fa *n.* plant used for fodder, pasture, etc.

al'gae (-jē) *n.pl.* primitive water plants

al'ge·bra *n.* mathematics using letters and numbers in equations —**al'ge·bra'ic** *a.*

a·li·as (ā'lē as) *n.* assumed name —*adv.* otherwise named

al'i·bi' (-bī) *n., pl.* **-bis'** 1 plea that the accused was not at the scene of the crime 2 [Col.] any excuse —*v.* give an excuse

a·lien (āl'yən, ā'lē ən) *a.* foreign —*n.* foreigner

a·lign' (-līn') *v.* 1 line up 2 make agree —**a·lign'ment** *n.*

a·like' *a.* similar —*adv.* 1 similarly 2 equally

al'i·mo'ny *n.* money paid to support one's former wife

a·live' *a.* 1 living; in existence 2 lively —**alive with** teeming with

al'ka·li' (-lī') *n., pl.* **-lies'** or **-lis'** substance that neutralizes acids

all *a.* 1 the whole of 2 every one of 3 complete —*pron.* 1 [*pl. v.*] everyone 2 everything 3 every bit —*n.* a whole —*adv.* entirely

al·lege' *v.* declare, esp. without proof —**al'le·ga'tion** *n.*

al·le'giance (-jəns) *n.* loyalty, as to one's country

al'le·go'ry *n., pl.* **-ries** story in which things, actions, etc. are symbolic

al·le'gro (-le'-) *a., adv.* Mus. fast

al·ler'gy *n., pl.* **-gies** sensitive reaction to certain food, pollen, etc. —**al·ler'gic** *a.*

al·le'vi·ate' *v.* relieve; ease

al'ley *n., pl.* **-leys** 1 narrow street 2 bowling lane

al·li'ance *n.* 1 an allying 2 association; league

al·lied' *a.* 1 united by treaty, etc. 2 related

al'li·ga'tor *n.* large lizard like a crocodile

al·lot' *v.* **-lot'ted** 1 distribute in shares 2 assign

al·low' *v.* 1 to permit 2 let have 3 grant —**allow for** leave room, time, etc. for —**al·low'a·ble** *a.*

al·low'ance *n.* 1 thing allowed 2 amount given regularly

al'loy (*v.*: ə loi') *n.* metal mixture

—*v.* mix (metals)

all right *a.* 1 satisfactory 2 unhurt 3 correct —*adv.* yes

al·ly (ə lī'; *n.:* al'ī) *v.* **-lied'** unite; join —*n., pl.* **-lies** country or person joined with another

al'ma·nac' *n.* calendar with miscellaneous data

al·might'y *a.* all-powerful —**the Almighty** God

al'mond (ä'mənd, ôl'-) *n.* edible, nutlike, oval seed of a tree of the peach family

al'most' *adv.* very nearly

alms (ämz) *n.* money, food, etc. given to the poor

a·loft' *adv.* high up

a·lone' *a., adv.* with no other

a·long' *prep.* on or beside the length of —*adv.* 1 onward 2 together (*with*) 3 with one

a·loof' (-lōōf') *adv.* apart —*a.* cool and reserved

a·loud' *adv.* loudly

al'pha·bet' *n.* letters of a language, in the regular order

al·read'y *adv.* by or before the given time; previously

al'so *adv.* in addition; too

al'tar *n.* table, etc. for sacred rites, as in a church

al'ter *v.* change; modify

al'ter·nate (-nət; *v.:* -nāt') *a.* 1 succeeding each other 2 every other —*n.* a substitute —*v.* do, use, act, etc. by turns

al·though' *con.* in spite of the fact that

al'ti·tude' *n.* height, esp. above sea level

al'to *n., pl.* **-tos** lowest female voice

al'to·geth'er *adv.* wholly

a·lu·mi·num *n.* silvery, lightweight metal, a chemical element: also [Br.] **al'u·min'i·um**

a·lum'nus *n., pl.* **-ni'** (-nī') former student of a certain school or college —**a·lum'na** *n.fem., pl.* **-nae** (-nē)

al'ways *adv.* 1 at all times 2 continually

Alz·hei'mer's disease (älts'hī' mərz) *n.* disease causing degeneration of brain cells

am *v.* pres. *t.* of BE: used with *I*

am'a·teur (-char) *n.* 1 one who does something for pleasure, not pay 2 unskillful person

a·maze' *v.* astonish; surprise —**a·maze'ment** *n.*

am·bas'sa·dor *n.* top-ranking diplomatic official

am'ber *n.* 1 yellowish fossil resin 2 its color

am'bi·dex'trous *a.* using both hands with equal ease

am'bi·ence *n.* milieu; environment: also **am'bi·ance**

am·big'u·ous *a.* having two or more meanings; vague —**am·bi·gu'i·ty** *n., pl.* -**ties**

am·bi'tion *n.* 1 desire to succeed 2 success desired —**am·bi'tious** *a.*

am'ble *v.* move in an easy gait

am'bu·lance *n.* car to carry sick or wounded

am'bush' *n.* 1 a hiding for a surprise attack 2 the hiding place or group —*v.* to attack from hiding

a'men' *int.* may it be so!

a·mend' *v.* 1 to correct 2 improve 3 revise, as a law —**a·mend'ment** *n.*

a·mends' *n.pl.* a making up for injury, loss, etc.

a·men'i·ty *n., pl.* -**ties** 1 pleasantness 2 *pl.* courtesies 3 convenience: *often used in pl.*

am'e·thyst (-thist) *n.* purple quartz for jewelry

a'mi·a·ble *a.* good-natured; friendly

am'i·ca·ble *a.* friendly; peaceable

a·mid', a·midst' *prep.* among

a·miss' *adv., a.* wrong

am·mo'ni·a *n.* 1 acrid gas 2 water solution of it

am·mu·ni'tion *n.* bullets, gunpowder, bombs, etc.

am·ne'si·a (-zha) *n.* loss of memory

a·moe'ba (-mē-) *n., pl.* -**bas** or -**bae** (-bē) one-celled animal

a·mok' (-muk') *a., adv.* used chiefly in **run amok**, lose control and behave violently

a·mong', a·mongst' *prep.* 1 surrounded by 2 in the group of 3 to or for each of

a·mount' *v.* 1 add up (*to*) 2 be equal (*to*) —*n.* 1 sum 2 quantity

am'pere' (-pir') *n.* unit of electric current

am·phet'a·mine' (-mēn') *n.* drug used as a stimulant and to lessen appetite

am·phib'i·an *n.* 1 land-and-water animal, as the frog 2 land-and-water vehicle

am·phib'i·ous *a.* adapted to both land and water

am'ple *a.* 1 large 2 adequate; plenty —**am'ply** *adv.*

am'pli·fy' *v.* -**fied'** make stronger, louder, or fuller —**am'pli·fi·ca'tion** *n.* —**am'pli·fi'er** *n.*

am'pu·tate' *v.* to cut off, esp. by surgery

a·muse' *v.* 1 entertain 2 make laugh —**a·muse'ment** *n.*

amusement park *n.* entertainment area with rides, food, etc.

an *a., indefinite article* 1 one 2 each; any one

an'a·con'da *n.* large South American boa snake

an'al·ge'sic (-jē'zik) *n., a.* (drug) that eases pain

an'a·log' *a.* 1 of electronic equipment, recordings, etc. in which the signal responds to physical change 2 using hands, dials, etc. to show number amounts

an'a·logue' *n.* something analogous

a·nal'o·gy (-jē) *n., pl.* -**gies** similarity in some ways

a·nal'y·sis (-a sis) *n., pl.* -**ses'** (-sēz') 1 separation of a whole into its parts to find out their nature, etc. 2 psychoanalysis —**an'a·lyst** (-list) *n.* —**an'a·lyt'i·cal** *a.* —**an'a·lyze'** (-līz') *v.*

an'ar·chy *n.* 1 absence of government and law 2 great disorder —**an·ar'chic** *a.*

a·nat'o·my *n.* 1 science of plant or animal structure 2 structure of an organism

an'ces·tor *n.* person from whom one is descended

an·chor (aŋ'kər) *n.* 1 metal weight lowered from a ship to prevent drifting 2 one who anchors a newscast: also **an'chor·man'**, *pl.* -**men'**, or **an'chor·wom'an**, *pl.* -**wom'en**, or **an'chor·per'son** —*v.* 1 hold secure 2 coordinate and report (a newscast)

an'cho'vy (-chō'-) *n., pl.* -**vies** tiny herring

an·cient (ān'chənt, -shənt) *a.* 1 of times long past 2 very old

and *con.* 1 also 2 plus 3 as a result

an·dan'te (än dän'tā) *a., adv. Mus.* moderately slow

an'ec·dote' *n.* brief story

a·ne'mi·a *n.* deficiency of red blood cells —**a·ne'mic** *a.*

an·es·the'si·a (-zha) *n.* loss of the sense of pain, touch, etc.

an·es·thet'ic *n., a.* (drug, gas, etc.) that produces anesthesia —**an·es'the·tize'** *v.*

an'eu·rysm', an'eu·rism' (-yōō riz'əm) *n.* sac formed by swelling in an artery wall

a·new' *adv.* 1 once more 2 in a new way

an·gel (ān'jəl) *n.* messenger of God, pictured with wings and halo —**an·gel'ic** (an-) *a.*

an·ger *n.* hostile feeling; wrath

an·gle *n.* 1 space formed by two lines or surfaces that meet 2 point of view —*v.* 1 bend at an angle 2 fish with hook and line 3 use tricks to get something

an·gry *a.* **-gri·er, -gri·est** 1 feeling anger; enraged 2 stormy —**an·gri·ly** *adv.*

an·guish *n.* great pain, worry, or grief

an·i·mal *n.* 1 living organism able to move about 2 any four-footed creature —*a.* 1 of an animal 2 bestial

an·i·mate (-māt'; *a.:* -mət) *v.* 1 give life to 2 make lively —*a.* 1 living 2 lively —**an·i·mat'ed** *a.* —**an·i·ma'tion** *n.*

an·i·mos·i·ty *n.* strong hatred; ill will

an·ise (-is) *n.* plant whose seed is used as flavoring

an·kle *n.* joint connecting foot and leg

an·nex (ə neks'; *n.:* an'eks) *v.* attach or join to a larger unit —*n.* something annexed

an·ni·hi·late (-nī'ə-) *v.* destroy

an·ni·ver·sa·ry *n., pl.* **-ries** yearly return of the date of some event

an·nounce' *v.* make known; tell about —**an·nounc'er** *n.*

an·noy' *v.* to bother or anger —**an·noy'ance** *n.*

an·nu·al *a.* yearly —*n.* 1 plant living one year 2 yearbook

an·nu·i·ty *n., pl.* **-ties** investment yielding fixed annual payments

an·nul' *v.* **-nulled'** make null and void —**an·nul'ment** *n.*

a·node' *n.* positive electrode

a·noint' *v.* put oil on, as in consecrating

a·non' *adv.* 1 soon 2 at another time

a·non'y·mous *a.* with name unknown or withheld; unidentified

a·noph'e·les *n.* ailment characterized by lack of appetite for food

an·oth'er *a., pron.* 1 one more 2 a different (one)

an·swer (-sər) *n.* 1 thing said or done in return; reply 2 solution to a problem —*v.* 1 reply (to) 2 serve or suit 3 be responsible

ant *n.* small insect living in colonies

an·tag'o·nism' *n.* hostility

ant·arc'tic *a.* of or near the South Pole —*n.* antarctic region

an'te·lope' *n.* horned animal like the deer

an·ten'na *n., pl.* **-nae** (-ē) or **-nas** 1 feeler on the head of an insect, etc. 2 *pl.* **-nas** wire(s) for sending and receiving radio waves

an'them *n.* religious or patriotic choral song

an'ther *n.* pollen-bearing part of a stamen

an·thol'o·gy *n., pl.* **-gies** collection of poems, stories, etc.

an'thra·cite' *n.* hard coal

an·thro·pol'o·gy *n.* study of the races, customs, etc. of mankind

an·ti·bi·ot'ic (-bī-) *n.* substance produced by some microorganisms, able to kill or weaken bacteria

an·ti·bod'y *n., pl.* **-ies** substance produced in body to act against toxins, etc.

an'tic *n.* silly act; prank

an'ti·de·pres'sant *n.* drug that lessens medical depression

an'ti·dote' *n.* remedy to counteract a poison or evil

an'ti·his'ta·mine' (-mēn) *n.* drug used to treat allergies

an·tip'a·thy *n., pl.* **-thies** strong dislike

an'ti·per'spi·rant *n.* skin lotion, cream, etc. for reducing perspiration

an·tique' (-tēk') *a.* 1 of a former period 2 out-of-date —*n.* piece of furniture, etc. from earlier times

an·tiq'ui·ty (-tik'wə-) *n., pl.* **-ties** 1 ancient times 2 great age 3 ancient relic, etc.

an'ti·sem'i·tism' *n.* prejudice against Jews —**an'ti·sem'ite'** *n.* —**an'ti·se·mit'ic** *a.*

an'ti·sep'tic *a.* preventing infection by killing germs —*n.* antiseptic substance

an'ti·so'cial *a.* 1 not sociable 2 harmful to society

an'ti·tox'in *n.* serum that counteracts a disease

ant'ler *n.* branched horn of a deer, elk, etc.

an'to·nym' (-nim') *n.* word opposite in meaning

an'vil *n.* block on which to hammer metal objects

anx·ious (aŋk'shəs) *a.* 1 worried 2 eagerly wishing

an'y *a.* 1 one of more than two 2 some 3 every —*pron.* [*sing. or pl. v.*] any person(s) or amount —*adv.* at all

an'y·bod'y *pron.* anyone

an'y·how' *adv.* **1** in any way **2** in any case

an'y·one' *pron.* any person

an'y·thing' *pron.* any thing

an'y·way' *adv.* anyhow

an'y·where' *adv.* in, at, or to any place

a·or'ta (ā-) *n.* main artery leading from the heart

a·part' *adv.* **1** aside **2** away from (one) another **3** into pieces —*a.* separated

a·part'heid' (-pärt'tāt', -tid') *n.* strict racial segregation as practiced in South Africa

a·part'ment *n.* room or set of rooms to live in

ap'a·thy *n.* lack of feeling or interest —**ap'a·thet'ic** *a.*

ape *n.* large, tailless monkey —*v.* imitate

a'pex' *n.* highest point

a·piece' *adv.* to or for each

a·poc'a·lypse' (-lips') *n.* total devastation, as doomsday

ap'o·gee' *n.* point farthest from earth in a satellite's orbit

a·pol'o·gy *n., pl.* **-gies 1** expression of regret for a fault, etc. **2** defense of an idea, etc. —**a·pol'o·get'ic** *a.* —**a·pol'o·gize'** *v.*

A·pos'tle (-päs'al) *n.* **1** any of the disciples of Jesus [a-] leader of a new movement

a·pos'tro·phe (-fē) *n.* sign (') indicating: *a)* omission of letter(s) from a word *b)* possessive case

ap·pall', ap·pal' *v.* to dismay

ap'pa·ra'tus (-rat'as, -rāt'-) *n.* **1** tools, etc. for a specific use **2** complex device

ap·par'el *n.* clothes

ap·par'ent *a.* **1** obvious; plain **2** seeming —**ap·par'ent·ly** *adv.*

ap·peal' *n.* **1** request for help **2** attraction **3** request for rehearing by a higher court —*v.* **1** make an appeal **2** be attractive

ap·pear' (-pir') *v.* **1** come into sight **2** seem **3** come before the public —**ap·pear'ance** *n.*

ap·pen'dec'to·my *n., pl.* **-mies** surgical removal of the appendix

ap·pen'dix *n., pl.* **-dix·es** *or* **-di·ces'** (-də sēz') **1** extra material at the end of a book **2** small, closed tube attached to large intestine

ap'pe·tite' *n.* desire, esp. for food

ap'pe·tiz'ing *a.* stimulating the appetite; savory —**ap'pe·tiz'er** *n.*

ap·plaud' *v.* show approval, esp. by clapping the hands; praise

ap·plause' *n.* approval, esp. by clapping

ap'ple *n.* round, fleshy fruit

ap·pli'ance *n.* device or machine, esp. for home use

ap'pli·cant *n.* one who applies, as for a job

ap'pli·ca'tion *n.* **1** an applying **2** thing applied **3** formal request

ap·ply' *v.* **-plied' 1** to put on **2** put into use **3** devote (oneself) diligently **4** ask formally **5** be relevant —**ap'pli·ca·ble** *a.*

ap·point' *v.* **1** set (a time, etc.) **2** name to an office **3** furnish

ap·praise' *v.* estimate the value of —**ap·prais'er** *n.*

ap·pre'ci·ate' (-shē-) *v.* **1** value; enjoy **2** recognize rightly or gratefully —**ap·pre'ci·a'tion** *n.*

ap'pre·hend' *v.* **1** arrest **2** understand

ap'pre·hen'sive *a.* anxious

ap·pren'tice *n.* helper who is being taught a trade —*v.* to place as apprentice

ap·proach' *v.* **1** come nearer (to) **2** speak to —*n.* **1** a coming near **2** way of beginning **3** access

ap·pro'pri·ate' (-āt'; *a.:* -at) *v.* **1** take for one's own use **2** set (money) aside for some use —*a.* suitable —**ap·pro'pri·a'tion** *n.*

ap·prove' *v.* **1** consent to **2** have a favorable opinion (*of*) —**ap·prov'al** *n.*

ap·prox'i·mate' (-māt'; *a.:* -mət) *v.* be about the same as —*a.* nearly exact or correct

A'pril *n.* fourth month

a'pron *n.* garment to protect the front of one's clothing

apt *a.* **1** fitting; suitable **2** likely (*to*) **3** quick to learn

ap'ti·tude' *n.* **1** ability **2** quickness to learn

a·quar'i·um (-kwer'-) *n.* tank, etc. for keeping fish or other water animals

a·quat'ic (-kwät'-, -kwat'-) *a.* **1** living in water **2** taking place in water

aq'ue·duct' (ak'wə-) *n.* large pipe or channel bringing water from a distance

Ar'ab *n., a.* **1** (native) of Arabia **2** (one) of a people now scattered through lands around Arabia

ar'a·ble *a.* fit for plowing

ar'bi·ter *n.* judge; umpire

ar·bi·trar·y *a.* using only one's own reasoning or whim

ar·bi·trate' *v.* settle (a dispute) by using or being an arbiter

ar·bor *n.* place shaded by trees, shrubs, or vines

arc *n.* **1** curved line, as part of a circle **2** band of light made by electricity leaping a gap

ar·cade' *n.* **1** covered passage, esp. one lined with shops **2** row of arches on columns

ar·cane' *a.* secret or esoteric

arch *n.* curved support over an opening —*v.* form (as) an arch

ar·chae·ol'o·gy (-kē-) *n.* study of ancient peoples, as by excavation of ruins

ar·cha'ic (-kā'-) *a.* **1** out-of-date **2** now seldom used

arch·an'gel (ärk'-) *n.* angel of the highest rank

arch·bish'op (ärch'-) *n.* bishop of the highest rank

arch'er·y *n.* practice or sport of shooting with bow and arrow — **arch'er** *n.*

ar·chi·pel'a·go (-kə-) *n.*, *pl.* **-goes'** or **-gos'** chain of islands in a sea

ar·chi·tect' *n.* one who designs buildings

ar'chi·tec'ture *n.* science of designing and constructing buildings —**ar·chi·tec'tur·al** *a.*

ar'chives' (-kīvz') *n.pl.* public records or place to store them

arch'way' *n.* passage under an arch

arc'tic *a.* of or near the North Pole —*n.* arctic region

are *v.* pres. t. of BE: used with *you, we,* or *they*

ar'e·a *n.* **1** region **2** total surface, measured in square units **3** scope

a·re'na *n.* **1** center of amphitheater, for contests, etc. **2** area of struggle

ar·gue *v.* **1** give reasons (*for* or *against*) **2** dispute; debate —**ar'gu·ment** *n.* —**ar'gu·men·ta'tion** *n.* —**ar'gu·men'ta·tive** *a.*

a·rid (er'-) *a.* **1** dry **2** dull

a·rise' *v.* **a·rose', a·ris'en 1** get up; rise **2** come into being

ar·is·toc'ra·cy *n.* **1** government by an upper class minority **2** upper class —**a·ris'to·crat'** *n.*

a·rith'me·tic *n.* science of computing by numbers

ark *Bible* boat in which Noah survived the Flood

arm *n.* **1** one of two upper limbs of the human body **2** anything

like this **3** weapon **4** military branch **5** *pl.* coat of arms —*v.* provide with weapons —**arm in arm** with arms interlocked

ar'ma·ments *n.pl.* military forces and equipment

arm'chair' *n.* chair with supports for one's arms

ar'mi·stice *n.* truce

ar'mor *n.* protective covering

arm'pit' *n.* the hollow under the arm at the shoulder

ar'my *n., pl.* **-mies 1** large body of soldiers **2** any very large group

a·ro'ma *n.* pleasant odor

a·round' *adv., prep.* **1** in a circle (about) **2** on all sides (of) **3** to the opposite direction **4** [Col.] nearby

a·rouse' *v.* wake; stir up

ar·raign' (-rān') *v.* **1** bring to court for trial **2** accuse

ar·range' *v.* **1** put in a certain order **2** plan **3** adjust; adapt

ar·ray' *v.* **1** place in order **2** dress finely —*n.* **1** an orderly grouping **2** impressive display **3** finery

ar·rest' *v.* **1** stop or check **2** seize **3** seize and hold by law —*n.* an arresting

ar·rive' *v.* **1** reach one's destination **2** come —**ar·riv'al** *n.*

ar'ro·gant *a.* haughty; overbearing —**ar'ro·gance** *n.*

ar·row *n.* **1** pointed shaft shot from a bow **2** sign (←) to show direction

ar'se·nal *n.* place for making or storing weapons

ar'son *n.* crime of purposely setting fire to property

art *n.* **1** skill; craft **2** aesthetic work, as painting, sculpture, music, etc. **3** *pl.* academic studies **4** cunning; wile

ar·ter·y *n., pl.* **-ies 1** tube carrying blood from the heart **2** a main road

ar·thri'tis *n.* inflammation of joints —**ar·thrit'ic** *a.*

ar'ti·choke' *n.* **1** thistlelike plant **2** its flower head, cooked as a vegetable

ar'ti·cle *n.* **1** single item **2** separate piece of writing, as in a magazine **3** section of a document **4** any of the words *a, an,* or *the*

ar·tic'u·late' (-lāt'; *a.:* -lət) *v.* **1** speak clearly **2** join —*a.* **1** clear in speech **2** jointed: usually *ar·tic'u·lat'ed* —**ar·tic'u·la'tion** *n.*

ar'ti·fact' *n.* any object made by

human work

ar·ti·fi·cial a. 1 made by man; not natural 2 not genuine; affected —**ar·ti·fi·ci·al'i·ty** n.

ar·til'ler·y n. 1 mounted guns, as cannon 2 military branch using these

art'ist n. person with skill, esp. in any of the fine arts

ar·tis'tic a. 1 of art or artists 2 skillful —**art'ist·ry** n.

as adv. 1 equally 2 for instance —con. 1 in the way that 2 while 3 because 4 though — pron. that —prep. in the role of —as for (or to) concerning —as of on or up to (a certain point)

as·bes'tos n. fibrous mineral used in fireproofing

as·cend' v. go up; climb

as·cent' n. 1 an ascending 2 upward slope

as·cribe' v. assign or attribute

ash n. 1 often pl. grayish powder left from something burned 2 shade tree

a·shamed' a. feeling shame

a·shore' adv., a. to or on shore

a·side' adv. 1 on or to one side 2 away 3 apart —aside from except for

as'i·nine' n. stupid; silly

ask v. 1 call for an answer to 2 inquire of or about 3 request 4 invite

a·skew' (-skyoō'-) adv., a. awry

a·sleep' a. 1 sleeping 2 numb — adv. into sleep

asp n. poisonous snake

as·par'a·gus n. plant with edible green shoots

as'pect' n. 1 look or appearance 2 side or facet

as'pen n. poplar tree with fluttering leaves

as'phalt' n. tarlike substance used for paving, etc.

as·phyx'i·ate' (-fik'sē-) v. overcome by cutting down oxygen in the blood —**as·phyx'i·a'tion** n.

as'pi·ra'tion n. ambition

as·pire' v. be ambitious (to)

as'pi·rin n. drug that relieves pain or fever

ass n. 1 donkey 2 fool

as·sail' v. attack

as·sas'sin n. murderer

as·sas'si·nate' v. murder, esp. for political reasons

as·sault' n., v. attack

as·sem'ble v. 1 gather in a group 2 put together

as·sem'bly n., pl. -blies 1 an assembling 2 group 3 [A-] legislative body

as·sem'bly·man n., pl. -men member of a legislative assembly

as·sent' v., n. consent

as·sert' v. 1 declare 2 defend, as rights —**as·ser'tion** n.

as·sess' v. 1 set a value on for taxes 2 impose a fine, tax, etc.

as'set n. 1 valuable thing 2 pl. property, cash, etc.

as·sign' v. 1 designate 2 appoint 3 allot; give —**as·sign'ment** n.

as·sim'i·late' v. merge; absorb

as·sist' v., n. help; aid —**as·sist'ance** n. —**as·sist'ant** a., n.

as·so'ci·ate' (-āt'; n., a.: -ət) v. 1 join 2 connect in the mind 3 join (with) as a partner, etc. — n. partner, colleague, etc. —a. associated —**as·so'ci·a'tion** n.

as·sort'ed a. 1 miscellaneous 2 sorted

as·sort'ment n. variety

as·sume' v. 1 take on (a role, look, etc.) 2 undertake 3 take for granted 4 pretend to have —**as·sump'tion** n.

as·sure' v. 1 make sure; convince 2 give confidence to 3 promise 4 guarantee —**as·sur'ance** n. —**as·sured'** a.

as'ter·isk' n. sign (*) used to mark footnotes, etc.

a·stern' adv. at or toward the rear of a ship

as'ter·oid' n. any of the small planets between Mars and Jupiter

asth'ma (az'-) n. chronic disorder characterized by coughing, hard breathing, etc.

a·stir' adv., a. in motion

as·ton'ish v. fill with sudden surprise

as·tound' v. astonish greatly

a·stray' adv., a. off the right path

as·trin'gent n., a. (substance) contracting body tissue and blood vessels

as·trol'o·gy n. pseudoscience of effect of stars, etc. on human affairs —**as·trol'o·ger** n.

as'tro·naut' n. traveler in outer space

as'tro·nau'tics n. science of spacecraft and space travel

as'tro·nom'i·cal a. 1 of or in astronomy 2 huge, as numbers

as·tron'o·my n. science of the stars, planets, etc. —**as·tron'o·mer** n.

a·sy'lum n. 1 place of safety 2 institution for the mentally ill, aged, etc.

at prep. 1 on; in; near 2 to or

toward **3** busy with **4** in the state of **5** because of

a'the·ism' *n.* belief that there is no God —**a'the·ist'** *n.*

ath'lete' *n.* one skilled at sports requiring strength, speed, etc. — **ath·let'ic** *a.* —**ath·let'ics** *n.pl.*

at'las *n.* book of maps

at'mos·phere' *n.* **1** the air surrounding the earth **2** general feeling or spirit **3** [Col.] interesting effect produced by decoration, etc. —**at'mos·pher'ic** *a.*

at·oll (a'tôl') *n.* coral island surrounding a lagoon

at'om *n.* smallest particle of a chemical element, made up of electrons, protons, etc. —**a·tom'ic** *a.*

atomic (or **atom**) **bomb** *n.* bomb whose immense power derives from nuclear fission

atomic energy *n.* energy released from an atom in nuclear reactions

a·tone' *v.* make amends (*for*)

a·top' *adv., prep.* on the top (of)

a·tro'cious (-shəs) *a.* **1** cruel or evil **2** very bad

at·tach' *v.* **1** fasten; join **2** tie by devotion **3** seize by legal order

at·tack' *v.* **1** to fight or work against **2** undertake vigorously —*n.* **1** an attacking **2** fit of illness

at·tain' *v.* **1** to gain; achieve **2** arrive at —**at·tain'a·ble** *a.*

at·tempt' *v., n.* try

at·tend' *v.* **1** be present at **2** pay attention **3** go with —**attend to** take care of —**at·tend'ant** *n.*

at·tend'ance *n.* **1** an attending **2** number present

at·ten'tion *n.* **1** a giving heed **2** heed; notice **3** *pl.* kind acts

at'tic *n.* space just below the roof; garret

at·tire' *v.* clothe; dress up —*n.* clothes

at'ti·tude' *n.* **1** bodily posture **2** way of looking at things, or manner

at·tor'ney (-tur'-) *n., pl.* **-neys** lawyer: also **attorney at law**

at·tract' *v.* **1** draw to itself **2** make notice or like one —**at·trac'tion** *n.* —**at·trac'tive** *a.*

at·trib'ute (*n.:* a'trə byōōt') *v.* think of as belonging or owing (*to*) —*n.* characteristic

au'burn *a., n.* red-brown

auc'tion *n.* public sale in which items go to the highest bidder — *v.* sell at auction

au·da'cious *a.* **1** bold; reckless **2** insolent

au'di·ble *a.* loud enough to be heard —**au'di·bly** *adv.*

au'di·ence *n.* **1** group seeing or hearing a play, concert, radio or TV show, etc. **2** formal interview

au'di·o' *a.* of the sound portion of a TV broadcast

au'di·o·vis'u·al *a.* involving both hearing and sight

au'dit *v.* examine and check (accounts) —*n.* an auditing

au·di'tion *n.* a hearing to try out a singer, actor, etc. —*v.* try out in an audition

au'di·to'ri·um *n.* a hall for speeches, concerts, etc.

au'di·to'ry *a.* of hearing

aug·ment' *v.* increase

Au'gust *n.* eighth month

au·gust' *a.* imposing

aunt (ant, änt) *n.* **1** sister of one's parent **2** uncle's wife

au'ra *n.* radiance or air about a person or thing

aus·pi'cious (-pish'əs) *a.* favorable; of good omen

aus·tere' *a.* **1** strict **2** very plain; severe

au·then'tic *a.* true, real, genuine, etc. —**au·then·tic'i·ty** (-tis'-) *n.*

au'thor *n.* writer or originator

au·thor'i·tar'i·an *a.* enforcing or favoring strict obedience to authority

au·thor'i·ty *n., pl.* **-ties 1** power to command **2** *pl.* persons with such power **3** expert; reliable source

au'thor·ize' *v.* **1** give official approval to **2** empower

au'tism' *n.* mental state marked by disregard of external reality

au'to *n., pl.* **-tos** automobile

au·to·bi·og'ra·phy *n., pl.* **-phies** one's own life story written by oneself

au'to·graph' *n.* signature —*v.* write one's signature on

au'to·mat'ic *a.* **1** done without conscious effort **2** operating by itself —**au'to·mat'i·cal·ly** *adv.*

au'to·ma'tion *n.* automatic system of manufacture, as by electronic devices

au'to·mo·bile' *n.* passenger vehicle propelled by an engine, for use on streets and roads —**au'to·mo'tive** *a.*

au'top·sy *n., pl.* **-sies** examination of a corpse to find cause of death

au·tumn (ôt'əm) *n.* season after summer, when leaves fall

aux·il·ia·ry (ôg zil'yə rē) a. 1 helping 2 subsidiary —n. use or help

a·vail' v. be of use or help (to) —n. use or help

a·vail'a·ble a. that can be got or had —**a·vail'a·bil'i·ty** n.

av'a·lanche' n. great fall of rock, snow, etc. down a hill

av'a·rice (-ris) n. greed for money

a·venge' v. get revenge for

av'e·nue' n. 1 street 2 way to something; approach

av'er·age n. 1 sum divided by the number of quantities added 2 usual kind, amount, etc. —a. being the average —v. 1 figure the average of 2 do on the average

a·ver'sion n. dislike

a'vi·a'tion n. science or work of flying airplanes —**a'vi·a'tor** n.

av'id a. eager or greedy

av'o·ca'do (-kä'-) n., pl. **-dos** thick-skinned tropical fruit

a·void' v. keep away from; shun

av·oir·du·pois (av'ər də poiz') n. weight system in which 16 oz. = 1 lb.

a·vow' v. declare openly; admit

a·wait' v. wait for

a·wake' v. **a·woke'** or **a·waked'**, **a·waked'** or **a·wok'en** rouse from sleep —a. 1 not asleep 2 alert

a·wak'en v. rouse; awake

a·ward' v. give after judging —n. 1 decision, as by judges 2 prize

a·ware' a. conscious; knowing

a·way' adv. 1 to another place 2 aside 3 from one's keeping —a. 1 absent 2 at a distance

awe n. reverent fear and wonder

awe'some a. causing awe

aw'ful a. 1 terrifying; dreadful 2 bad —**aw'ful·ly** adv.

a·while' adv. for a short time

awk'ward a. 1 clumsy 2 uncomfortable 3 embarrassing

awl n. pointed tool for making holes in wood, etc.

awn'ing n. overhanging shade of canvas, metal, etc.

a·wry (ə rī') adv., a. 1 with a twist to a side 2 amiss

ax, axe n., pl. **ax'es** tool for chopping wood, etc.

ax'is n., pl. **ax'es'** (-ēz') straight line around which a thing rotates —**ax'i·al** a.

ax'le n. rod on which a wheel revolves

aye, ay (ī) adv., n. yes

a·za·lea (-zāl'yə) n. shrub with brightly colored flowers

az'ure (azh'-) a., n. sky blue

B

bab'ble v. 1 talk in a foolish or jumbled way 2 murmur —n. babbling talk or sound

ba·boon' n. ape with doglike snout

ba'by n., pl. **-bies** very young child; infant —a. 1 of, for, or like a baby 2 small or young

bach'e·lor n. unmarried man

back n. 1 rear or hind part 2 backbone 3 the reverse 4 football player behind the line —a. 1 at the rear 2 of the past 3 backward —adv. 1 at or to the rear 2 to a former time, place, etc. 3 in return —v. 1 move backward 2 support 3 provide a back for —**back down** retract an opinion, etc. —**back up** 1 support 2 move backward, etc.

back'board' n. Basketball board behind the basket

back'bone' n. 1 spinal column 2 courage; firmness

back'fire' n. faulty ignition in an engine —v. 1 have a backfire 2 go awry, as plans

back'ground' n. 1 the part behind, more distant, etc. 2 past events, causes, etc.

back'ward adv. 1 toward the back 2 with the back foremost 3 into the past Also **back'wards** —a. 1 turned to the rear or away 2 shy 3 retarded

ba'con n. cured meat from hog's back or sides

bac·te'ri·a n.pl., sing. **-ri·um** microorganisms causing diseases, fermentation, etc.

bad a. **worse**, **worst** 1 not good 2 spoiled 3 incorrect 4 wicked 5 severe —adv. [Col.] badly —n. anything bad —**bad'ly** adv.

badge n. pin or emblem worn to show rank, membership, etc.

badg'er n. burrowing animal

bad'min·ton n. game using rackets and a feathered cork

baf'fle v. puzzle; bewilder

bag n. 1 container made of fabric, paper, etc. 2 suitcase 3 purse —v. **bagged** 1 hang loosely 2 kill or capture 3 put into a bag —**bag'gy** a.

ba'gel (-gəl) n. hard bread roll like a small doughnut

bag'gage n. luggage

bail n. money left as security to free a prisoner until trial —v. 1 get freed by giving bail 2 dip out (water) from (a boat)

bait v. 1 torment, as by insults 2 put food on (a hook, etc.) as a lure —n. anything used as a lure

bake v. 1 cook by dry heat in an oven 2 harden by heat

bal'ance n. 1 instrument for weighing, with two pans 2 equilibrium 3 harmonious proportion 4 equality of or difference between credits and debits 5 remainder —v. 1 compare 2 offset; counteract 3 put, keep, or be in equilibrium 4 be equal 5 sum up or equalize the debits and credits of (an account)

bal'co·ny n., pl. **-nies** 1 platform projecting from an upper story 2 tier of theater seats above main floor

bald a. 1 lacking hair on the head 2 plain and frank

bale n. large bundle, as of raw cotton —v. make into bales

balk v. 1 stop and refuse to move 2 obstruct

ball n. 1 round object; sphere 2 round or oval object used in games 3 formal social dance 4 Baseball pitched baseball that is not a strike 5 [Sl.] good time

bal'lad n. 1 popular love song 2 folk song or poem telling a story

bal'last (-ast) n. heavy matter put in a ship, etc. to keep it steady

bal'le·ri'na n. woman ballet dancer

bal·let' (ba lā') n. intricate, formalized group dance

bal·loon' n. bag that rises when filled with light gas

bal'lot n. 1 paper marked in voting 2 voting —v. to vote

balm (bäm) n. fragrant healing ointment or oil

bam·boo' n. tropical grass with hollow, treelike stems

ban v. banned forbid —n. formal forbidding by authorities

ba·nan'a n. long tropical fruit with creamy flesh

band n. 1 strip of cloth, etc. as for binding 2 stripe 3 range of radio wave lengths 4 group of people 5 group of performing musicians

band'age n. cloth strip to bind an injury —v. bind with a bandage

ban·dan'na, ban·dan'a n. large, colored handkerchief

ban'dit n. robber; brigand

bang v., n. (make, or hit with a) loud noise

bangs n.pl. short hair worn across the forehead

ban'ish v. 1 to exile 2 dismiss

ban'jo n., pl. **-jos** or **-joes** stringed musical instrument with a circular body

bank n. 1 mound; heap 2 steep slope, as beside a river 3 row; tier 4 business handling savings, loans, etc. —v. 1 form a bank 2 put (money) in a bank 3 cover (a fire) to make last

bank'rupt' a. 1 legally declared unable to repay one's debts 2 lacking —v. make bankrupt

ban'ner n. 1 flag 2 long strip of cloth with writing, etc.

ban'quet n. formal dinner

ban'ter v. tease playfully

bap'tism' n. rite of admission into a Christian church by dipping in or sprinkling with water —**bap·tize'** v.

bar n. 1 long, narrow piece of wood, metal, etc. 2 oblong piece, as of soap 3 obstruction 4 band or strip 5 law court 6 legal profession 7 counter or place for serving liquor 8 Mus. a measure or vertical line marking it off —v. **barred** 1 obstruct; close 2 oppose 3 exclude

barb n. sharp, back-curving point —**barbed** a.

bar·bar'i·an (-ber'-) n. uncivilized person; savage

bar'ba·rous a. 1 uncivilized 2 crude; coarse 3 brutal

bar'be·cue' n. 1 animal roasted whole over open fire 2 picnic at which such meat is served —v. 1 roast whole 2 broil in spicy sauce (barbecue sauce)

bar'ber n. one who cuts hair, shaves beards, etc.

bare a. 1 naked 2 exposed 3 empty 4 mere —v. uncover —**bare'foot', bare'foot'ed** a., adv.

bare'ly adv. only just

bar'gain (-gan) n. 1 agreement or contract 2 item bought at a favorable price —v. haggle

barge n. flat-bottomed freight boar —v. enter abruptly (into)

bar'i·tone' n. male voice, or instrument, between tenor and bass

bark n. 1 outside covering of trees 2 sharp cry of a dog 3 sailing vessel —v. 1 utter a bark 2 scrape off the skin of

bar'ley n. cereal grain

bar mitz'vah (-va) n. religious ceremony for a Jewish boy when he becomes thirteen years old

barn n. farm building for livestock, storage, etc. —**barn'yard'** n.

bar'na·cle n. shellfish that clings to ships, etc.

ba·rom'e·ter n. instrument to measure atmospheric pressure

bar'on n. nobleman of lowest rank —**bar'on·ess** n.fem.

bar'racks n.pl. building(s) for housing soldiers

bar'rel n. 1 round, wooden container with bulging sides 2 tube of a gun

bar'ren a. 1 sterile 2 unproductive

bar'ri·cade' n. barrier for defense —v. block with a barricade

bar'ri·er n. fence, wall, or other obstruction

bar'tend'er n. person serving drinks at a BAR (n. 7)

bar'ter v. exchange (goods)

base n. 1 part that a thing rests on 2 basis 3 goal in some games 4 headquarters or a source of supply 5 substance reacting with an acid to form a salt —v. put on a base —a. 1 morally low 2 inferior

base'ball' n. 1 team game played with a bat and ball 2 the ball used

base'ment n. story just below the main floor

bash'ful a. socially timid; shy

bas'ic a. of or at the base; fundamental —**bas'i·cal·ly** adv.

ba'sin n. 1 wide, shallow container for liquid 2 a sink 3 bay, cove, etc. 4 area drained by a river

ba'sis n., pl. -ses' (-sēz') 1 base or foundation 2 main constituent

bas'ket n. 1 container made of interwoven strips 2 goal in basketball

bas'ket·ball' n. 1 team game with raised open nets through which a large ball must be tossed 2 this ball

bass (bās) n. 1 lowest male singing voice 2 singer or instrument with low range

bass (bas) n. perchlike fish

bas·soon' n. double-reed, bass woodwind instrument

bas'tard n. illegitimate child —a. 1 illegitimate 2 sham, not standard, etc. —**bas'tard·ize'** v.

baste v. 1 sew with loose, temporary stitches 2 moisten (a roast) with drippings, etc.

bas'tion (-chan) n. 1 part of a fort that juts out 2 any strong defense

bat n. 1 a club to hit a ball, as in baseball 2 nocturnal, mouselike, flying mammal —v. [Col.] 1 hit as with a bat 2 [Col.] blink etc. in one lot

batch n. quantity taken, made, etc. in one lot

bath n. 1 a washing of the body 2 water, etc. for bathing or soaking something 3 bathtub 4 bathroom

bathe (bāth) v. 1 give a bath to, or take a bath 2 put into a liquid 3 cover as with liquid

bath'room' n. room with a bathtub, toilet, etc.

bat mitz'vah (bät-) n. religious ceremony for a Jewish girl similar to bar mitzvah

ba·ton' n. 1 stick used in leading an orchestra, etc. 2 staff serving as a symbol of office

bat'ter v. 1 strike repeatedly 2 injure by hard use —n. 1 player at bat in baseball 2 mixture of flour, milk, etc. for making cakes

bat'ter·y n., pl. -ies 1 cell or cells providing electric current 2 set of artillery guns 3 pitcher and catcher in baseball 4 illegal beating of a person

bat'tle n., v. fight, esp. between armies —**bat'tler** n.

bawl v. 1 to shout 2 to weep noisily —**bawl out** [Sl.] scold angrily

bay n. 1 wide inlet of a sea or lake 2 alcove 3 recess in a wall, as for a window (**bay window**) 4 laurel tree 5 a) reddish brown b) horse of this color —v. bark or howl in long, deep tones

bay'o·net' n. blade attached to a rifle barrel

bay·ou (bī'ōō) n. marshy inlet or outlet of a lake

ba·zaar' (-zär') n. 1 Oriental market place 2 benefit sale for a club, etc.

be v. was or were, been 1 exist; live 2 occur 3 remain; continue Be is also an auxiliary verb

beach n. stretch of sandy shore

bead n. 1 small ball of glass, etc., pierced for stringing 2 pl. string of beads 3 drop or bubble

bea'gle n. small, short-legged hound

beak n. 1 bird's bill 2 any beaklike mouth part

beak'er n. broad glass container

beam n. 1 long, thick piece of timber, etc. 2 ship's greatest breadth 3 shaft of light 4 radiant look or smile 5 guiding radio signal —v. 1 radiate in a beam 2 smile warmly

bean n. 1 edible seed of some plants 2 pod of these

bear n. 1 large, heavy mammal with shaggy fur 2 rough, rude person —v. bore, borne or born 1 carry 2 have or show 3 give birth to 4 produce 5 permit of 6 endure —**bear out** confirm —**bear up** endure

beard n. 1 hair on a man's face 2 awn —**beard'ed** a.

bear'ing n. 1 way one carries oneself 2 relative position or direction 3 relation 4 ball, roller, etc. on which something turns or slides

beast n. 1 any large four-footed animal 2 brutal, gross person

beat v. beat, beat'en 1 strike repeatedly 2 punish by striking 3 mix by stirring 4 defeat 5 throb 6 flap (wings) 7 make (a path) by tramping —n. 1 a throbbing 2 habitual route 3 unit of musical rhythm —a. [Col.] tired —**beat'er** n.

beau'ti·ful (byōo'-) a. having beauty —**beau'ti·ful·ly** adv.

beau'ty n., pl. -ties 1 pleasing quality as in looks, sound, etc. 2 person or thing of beauty

bea'ver n. amphibious mammal with webbed hind feet

be·cause' con. for the reason that

be·come' v. -came', -come' 1 come to be 2 suit

be·com'ing a. right or suitable; attractive

bed n. 1 piece of furniture to sleep on 2 plot of soil for plants 3 flat bottom or foundation 4 layer

bed'clothes' n.pl. bedsheets, blankets, etc.

bed'rid'den a. confined to bed, as by long illness

bed'rock' n. 1 solid rock under soil 2 base or bottom

bed'room' n. sleeping room

bee n. 1 winged insect that makes honey 2 meeting of group, as to work together

beef n., pl. beeves or beefs 1 cow, bull, or steer 2 its meat

been v. pp. of BE

beep n. brief, shrill sound of a horn or electronic signal —v. make this sound

beer n. mildly alcoholic drink brewed from malt, hops, etc.

beet n. plant with edible red or

white root

bee'tle n. insect with hard front wings —v. jut out

be·fall' v. -fell', -fall'en happen (to)

be·fore' adv. 1 in front 2 till now 3 earlier —prep. 1 ahead of 2 in sight of 3 earlier than 4 rather than —con. earlier or sooner than

be·fore'hand' adv., a. ahead of time

beg v. begged 1 ask for (alms) 2 entreat

be·get' v. -got', -got'ten or -got' 1 to father 2 to cause

beg'gar n. 1 one who lives by begging 2 very poor person

be·gin' v. -gan', -gun' 1 start 2 originate —**be·gin'ner** n.

be·gin'ning n. 1 start 2 origin 3 first part

be·go'ni·a (-gōn'yə) n. plant with showy flowers

be·grudge' v. 1 envy the possession of 2 give reluctantly

be·half' n. support, side, etc. —in (or on) behalf of in the interest of

be·have' v. 1 conduct (oneself), esp. properly 2 act

be·hav'ior n. conduct

be·head' v. cut off the head of

be·hind' adv. 1 in the rear 2 slow; late 3 to the back —prep. 1 in back of 2 later or slower than 3 supporting —a. 1 that follows 2 in arrears

be·hold' v. -held' see; look at

beige (bāzh) n. grayish tan

be'ing n. 1 existence; life 2 one that lives

be·lat'ed a. too late

belch v. 1 expel stomach gas orally 2 eject with force

be·lief' n. 1 conviction; faith 2 trust 3 opinion

be·lieve' v. 1 take as true 2 have faith (in) 3 suppose; guess

be·lit'tle v. make seem little or unimportant

bell n. 1 hollow metal object that rings when struck 2 sound of a bell

bel·lig'er·ent (bə lij'-) a. warlike

bel'low v., n. roar or shout

bel'lows n., pl. -lows' collapsible device for producing a stream of air

bell pepper n. large, sweet red pepper

bel'ly n., pl. -lies 1 abdomen 2 stomach —v. -lied to bulge

be·long' v. have a proper place —**belong to** 1 be a part of 2 be owned by 3 be a member of

be·lov'ed (-luv'əd, -luvd') *a.*, *n.* dearly loved (person)

be·low' *adv.*, *a.* in or to a lower place; beneath —*prep.* lower than; beneath

belt *n.* 1 encircling band, as around the waist 2 distinct area —*v.* strike as with a belt

be·moan' *v.* lament

bench *n.* 1 long seat 2 worktable 3 seat for judges 4 status of a judge

bend *v.* **bent** 1 to curve, as by pressure 2 (make) yield 3 stoop —*n.* 1 a bending 2 bent part

be·neath' *adv.*, *a.* below; underneath —*prep.* 1 below; under 2 unworthy of

ben'e·dic'tion *n.* blessing

ben'e·fac'tor *n.* one who has given money or aid

ben'e·fi'cial (-fish'əl) *a.* producing benefits

ben'e·fi'ci·ar·y (or -fish'ər ē) *n.*, *pl.* **-ies** one receiving benefits, as from insurance

ben'e·fit *n.* 1 help or advantage 2 a show, etc. to raise money for a cause —*v.* 1 to help 2 profit

be·nign' (-nīn') *a.* 1 kindly 2 favorable 3 not malignant

bent *a.* 1 curved 2 determined (on) —*n.* inclination

be·queath' (-kwēth', -kwēth') *v.* 1 leave (property) to another by one's will 2 hand down —**be·quest'** *n.*

be·rate' *v.* scold severely

be·reave' *v.* **-reaved'** or **-reft'** 1 deprive 2 leave forlorn, as by death —**be·reave'ment** *n.*

be·ret' (-rā') *n.* flat, round, soft cap

berm *n.* ledge along the edge of a paved road

ber'ry *n.*, *pl.* **-ries** small, fleshy fruit with seeds

berth (burth) *n.* 1 ship's place of anchorage 2 built-in bed 3 position or job

be·seech' *v.* **-sought'** or **-seeched'** ask (for) earnestly; entreat —**be·seech'ing·ly** *adv.*

be·side' *prep.* 1 at the side of; near 2 as compared with 3 besides —*adv.* aside from —*adv.* besides

be·sides' *adv.* 1 in addition 2 else 3 moreover —*prep.* in addition to

best *a.* 1 most excellent 2 most suitable —*adv.* 1 in the best way 2 most —*n.* 1 best person, thing, etc. 2 the utmost —*v.*

outdo; beat —**all for the best** turning out to be good

be·stow' *v.* present as a gift (on or upon)

bet *n.* 1 agreement that the one proved wrong will pay something 2 thing so staked —*v.* **bet** or **bet'ted** 1 make a bet 2 stake in a bet —**bet'tor, bet'ter** *n.*

be·tray' *v.* 1 be disloyal to 2 deceive 3 seduce 4 reveal —**be·tray'al** *n.*

be·troth' (-trōth', -trôth') *v.* promise in marriage

bet'ter *a.* 1 more excellent 2 more suitable 3 improved —*adv.* 1 in a better way 2 more —*n.* 1 a superior 2 a better thing, etc. —*v.* to surpass or improve —**better off** in better circumstances —**get** (or **have**) **the better of** defeat or outwit —**had better** should

be·tween' *prep.* 1 in the space or time separating 2 involving 3 joining 4 in the common possession of 5 one of —*adv.* in the middle

bev'er·age *n.* drink

be·ware' *v.* guard against

be·wil'der *v.* confuse

be·witch' *v.* to enchant

be·yond' *prep.* 1 farther or later than; past 2 more than —*adv.* farther away

bi·as (bī'əs) *n.* 1 diagonal or slanting line 2 prejudice —*v.* to prejudice —**on the bias** diagonally

Bi'ble sacred book of Christians or of Jews —**bib'li·cal** *a.*

bib'li·og'ra·phy *n.*, *pl.* **-phies** list of writings on one subject or by one author

bi·car'bon·ate of soda *n.* baking soda

bick'er *v.*, *n.* quarrel

bi'cy·cle *n.* two-wheeled vehicle —*v.* ride a bicycle —**bi'cy·clist** *n.*

bid *v.* **bade** (bad) or **bid**, **bid'den** or **bid** 1 command or ask 2 tell 3 bid offer as a price —*n.* 1 amount bid 2 attempt

bide *v.* **bode** or **bid·ed**, **bid'ed** 1 stay 2 dwell 3 wait —**bide one's time** wait patiently for a chance

bi·en'ni·al *a.* 1 every two years 2 lasting two years —*n.* plant living two years

bier (bir) *n.* frame on which a coffin is put

big *a.* **big'ger**, **big'gest** 1 of great size 2 loud 3 important 4 noble

big·a·my n. crime of marrying again while still married

big·ot n. narrow-minded, intolerant person —**big·ot·ed** a.

bike n., v. [Col.] 1 bicycle 2 motorcycle

bill n. 1 statement of charges, as for goods 2 list of things offered 3 proposed law 4 piece of paper money 5 bird's beak —v. present a bill of charges to

bil·liards (-yərdz) n. game played with cue and three balls on a table with raised edges

bil·lion n. a thousand millions —**bil·lionth** a., n.

bil·lion·aire′ n. one having at least a billion dollars

bil·low n. 1 large wave 2 swelling mass, as of smoke

bi·month·ly a., adv. once every two months

bin n. box or enclosed space for storage

bi·na·ry a. 1 twofold 2 of a number system with only two digits

bind v. **bound** 1 tie together 2 to hold; restrain 3 encircle with (a belt, etc.) 4 bandage 5 put together (a book) with a cover 6 to obligate —**bind′er** n.

bi′o·de·grad′a·ble (-grād′-) a. readily decomposed by bacteria

bi·og′ra·phy n., pl. **-phies** one's life story written by another —**bi′o·graph′i·cal** a.

bi·ol′o·gy n. science of plants and animals —**bi′o·log′i·cal** a. —**bi·ol′o·gist** n.

birch n. 1 tree with smooth bark 2 its hard wood

bird n. warmblooded vertebrate with feathers and wings

birth n. 1 a being born 2 descent or origin 3 beginning —**give birth to** bring into being

birth′day′ n. day of birth or its anniversary

bis′cuit (-kit) n. 1 small bread roll 2 [Br.] cracker

bi·sex′u·al a. sexually attracted to both sexes —n. bisexual person

bish′op n. 1 clergyman heading a diocese 2 chessman moving diagonally

bi′son n., pl. **bi′son** shaggy, oxlike animal of North America

bit n. 1 mouthpiece on a bridle, for control 2 cutting part of a drill 3 small piece or amount 4 single digit in a binary number system 5 [Col.] short time —**bit**

by bit gradually

bitch n. female dog, fox, etc.

bite v. **bit**, **bit′ten** or **bit** 1 seize or cut as with the teeth 2 sting, as a bee 3 cause to smart 4 swallow a bait —n. 1 a biting 2 biting quality; sting 3 wound from biting 4 mouthful 5 [Col.] light meal

bit′ter a. 1 sharp to the taste 2 sorrowful, painful, resentful, etc. 3 harsh —**bit′ter·ly** adv.

bi·week′ly a., adv. once every two weeks

bi·zarre (bi zär′) a. odd; fantastic

black a. 1 of the color of coal; opposite to white 2 having dark skin 3 without light; dark 4 dirty 5 evil 6 sad —n. 1 black pigment 2 member of a dark-skinned people, or person having African ancestry —v. to blacken —**black′ness** n.

black′ber′ry n., pl. **-ries** 1 small, edible, dark fruit 2 bramble it grows on

black′bird′ n. bird the male of which is all black

black′board′ n. smooth surface for writing with chalk

black′en v. 1 make or become black 2 slander

black′mail′ n. money extorted on threat of disclosing something disgracing —v. (try to) get blackmail from

black′smith′ n. one who forges iron and shoes horses

blad′der n. sac that collects urine from the kidneys

blade n. 1 leaf of grass 2 cutting part of a knife, tool, etc. 3 flat surface, as of an oar

blame v. 1 accuse of being at fault 2 put the responsibility of (on) —n. 1 a blaming 2 responsibility for a fault —**be to blame** deserve blame

bland a. mild; soothing

blank a. 1 not written on 2 empty 3 utter —n. 1 (printed form with) space to be filled in 2 cartridge without a bullet

blan′ket n. 1 wool spread used as bed cover, etc. 2 a covering, as of snow —v. to cover

blare v. sound loudly

blas′phe·my (-fə mē) n., pl. **-mies** profane abuse of God —**blas·pheme′** (-fēm′) v.

blast n. 1 strong rush of air 2 loud sound of horn, etc. 3 explosion —v. 1 explode 2 to blight; wither

blaze n. 1 burst of flame 2 bright light 3 vivid display 4 outburst 5 white spot on an animal's face —v. 1 burn or shine brightly 2 mark (a trail)

bleach v. whiten —n. chemical that bleaches

bleak a. 1 unsheltered; bare 2 cheerless; gloomy

bleat n. cry of a sheep or goat —v. make this cry

bleed v. **bled** 1 lose blood 2 draw blood, air, etc. from

blem'ish v. mar; injure —n. defect; fault

blend v. 1 mix 2 shade into each other —n. 1 a blending 2 mixture

bless v. **blessed** or **blest** 1 make holy 2 ask divine favor for 3 make happy —**bless·ed** (bles'əd, blest) a. —**bless'ing** n.

blew v. pt. of BLOW

blight n. 1 insect, disease, etc. that destroys plants 2 anything that destroys —v. destroy; ruin

blind a. 1 without sight 2 lacking insight 3 having no outlet 4 not controlled by reason —n. 1 window shade 2 a decoy —**blind'ness** n.

blind'fold' v. cover the eyes of —n. cloth used for this

blink v. 1 wink rapidly 2 flash on and off —n. 1 a blinking 2 glimmer —**blink at** ignore

bliss n. great happiness

blis'ter n. fluid-filled skin swelling caused by a burn, etc.

bliz'zard n. severe snowstorm with high wind

bloat v. swell up

blob n. small drop or mass

bloc n. group united for a common purpose

block n. 1 solid piece 2 auction platform 3 obstruction 4 city square or street section 5 pulley in a frame 6 part taken as a unit —v. 1 obstruct 2 shape

block·ade' n. shutting off of a place by warships, etc. —v. subject to a blockade

blond a. 1 having light-colored hair and skin 2 light-colored Also **blonde** —n. blond man or boy —**blonde** n.fem.

blood n. 1 red fluid in the arteries and veins 2 lineage 3 kinship —**in cold blood** deliberately

blood'hound' n. large, keen-scented tracking dog

blood'shed' n. killing

blood'y a. **-i·er, -i·est** 1 of or

covered with blood 2 involving bloodshed 3 bloodthirsty

bloom n. 1 a flower 2 time of flowering 3 healthy glow —v. be in bloom

blos'som n., v. flower

blot n. spot or stain —v. **blot'ted** 1 to spot, as with ink 2 erase or cancel (out) 3 to dry with soft paper, etc. —**blot'ter** n.

blotch n. discolored spot

blouse (blous) n. shirtlike garment for girls

blow v. **blew, blown** 1 move, as (by) wind 2 force air out, as with the mouth 3 sound by blowing —n. 1 a blowing 2 gale 3 a hit 4 shock —**blow out** 1 extinguish 2 burst —**blow up** 1 inflate 2 explode

blow'torch' n. small, hot-flamed torch for welding

blub'ber n. whale fat

blue a. 1 of the color of the clear sky 2 gloomy —n. color of the clear sky

blue'ber'ry n., pl. **-ries** small, edible, bluish berry

blue'bird' n. small bird with blue back and wings

blue'jay' n. crested bird with a blue back

blue'jeans' n.pl. jeans of blue denim

blue'print' n. 1 photographic copy, white on blue, of architectural plans, etc. 2 any detailed plan —v. make a blueprint of

bluff v. mislead by a fake, bold front —a. rough and frank —n. 1 a bluffing 2 one who bluffs 3 steep bank

blu'ish a. somewhat blue

blun'der n. foolish mistake —v. 1 make a blunder 2 move clumsily

blunt a. 1 dull-edged 2 plain-spoken —v. make dull

blur v. **blurred** 1 to smudge 2 make or become indistinct —n. indistinct thing

blush v. redden, as from shame

blus'ter n. 1 blow stormily 2 speak noisily or boastfully —n. swaggering talk —**blus'ter·y** a.

boar n. wild hog

board n. 1 broad, flat piece of wood, etc. 2 meals provided regularly for pay 3 council —v. 1 cover (up) with boards 2 get on (a ship, train, etc.) 3 get meals regularly for pay

boast v. 1 talk with too much pride 2 take pride in —n. thing boasted of

boat n. watercraft, esp. a small one

boat·swain (bō′sən) n. petty officer directing deck work

bob n. 1 small hanging weight 2 float on a fishing line —v. **bobbed** move jerkily

bob·o·link′ n. songbird with a call like its name

bob′white′ n. small quail

bode v. 1 be an omen of 2 pt. of **BIDE**

bod·ice (bäd′is) n. snug upper part of a dress

bod′y n., pl. **-ies** 1 whole physical structure 2 trunk of a man or animal 3 main part 4 distinct mass or group 5 [Col.] person —**bod′i·ly** a., adv.

bog n. a small swamp —v. **bogged** sink (down) as in a bog

bog′gle v. 1 be startled or hesitate (at) 2 confuse

boil v. 1 bubble up into vapor by heating 2 be agitated 3 cook by boiling —n. 1 boiling state 2 pus-filled pimple

boil′er n. tank for making steam or storing hot water

bold a. 1 daring; fearless 2 impudent 3 sharp and clear

bo·lo′gna (-nē) n. type of smoked sausage

bol′ster (bōl′-) n. long pillow

bolt n. 1 flash of lightning 2 sliding bar that locks 3 threaded metal rod used with a nut 4 roll of cloth —v. 1 gulp (food) 2 rush out 3 fasten with a bolt 4 sift

bomb (bäm) n. 1 explosive device or missile 2 [Col.] complete failure —v. 1 attack with bombs 2 [Col.] be a failure

bom·bard′ v. attack as with artillery or bombs —**bom′bar·dier′** (-dir′) n.

bomb′er n. airplane designed for dropping bombs

bond n. 1 thing that binds or unites 2 binding agreement 3 interest-bearing certificate 4 surety against theft, etc. —v. 1 bind 2 furnish a BOND (n. 4) for

bond′age n. slavery

bone n. material of the skeleton or piece of this —**bone′less** a.

bon′fire n. outdoor fire

bon′go n., pl. **-gos** either of a pair of small drums struck with the hands

bon′net n. hat

bon′sai (-sī) n., pl. **-sai** dwarfed tree or shrub

bo′nus n. payment over the usual or required amount

bon′y a., **-i·er, -i·est** 1 (full) of bones 2 lean; thin

boo int., n., pl. **boos** sound made to show disapproval or to startle

book n. 1 a bound, printed work 2 a division of a long literary work 3 ledger —v. 1 to list in a book 2 to reserve, as rooms

book′keep′ing n. work of recording business transactions —**book′keep′er** n.

boom v. 1 make a deep, hollow sound 2 grow rapidly 3 promote —n. 1 deep sound 2 long beam on a derrick 3 spar at the foot of a sail 4 period of prosperity

boom′er·ang′ n. 1 Australian curved stick that returns to the thrower 2 scheme that backfires

boor n. rude person

boost v., n. [Col.] 1 push upward 2 support

boot n. outer covering for the foot and leg

booth n. small stall or enclosure

boo′ty n. plunder; spoils

bor′der n. 1 edge; margin 2 boundary —v. put or be a border on —a. near a border

bore v. 1 drill a hole (in) 2 weary by being dull —n. 1 inside or diameter of a tube 2 dull person or thing

bor′row v. 1 take on loan 2 adopt (an idea)

bos′om (booz′-) n. breast

boss n. 1 employer or supervisor 2 head politician —v. 1 supervise 2 [Col.] order about

bot′a·ny n. science of plants —**bo·tan′i·cal** a. —**bot′a·nist** n.

botch v. spoil; bungle

both a., pron. the two —con., adv. equally

both′er v. 1 annoy; worry 2 trouble (oneself) —n. trouble —**both′er·some** a.

bot′tle n. glass container for liquids —v. put into a bottle

bot′tom n. 1 lowest part; base; underside 2 basis or cause

bough (bou) n. tree branch

bought (bôt) v. pt. & pp. of BUY

bouil·lon (bool′yän) n. clear broth

boul′der (bōl′-) n. large rock

bou′le·vard′ (bool′a-) n. broad, tree-lined street

bounce v. 1 spring back on impact 2 make bounce 3 leap —n. a bouncing

bound v. 1 pt. & pp. of BIND 2

leap or bounce **3** be a limit or boundary to —*a.* **1** tied **2** certain (*to*) **3** obliged **4** with a binding **5** headed (*for*) **6** [Col.] determined —*n.* **1** a leap or bounce **2** boundary

bound·a·ry *n., pl.* **-ries** anything marking a limit

boun'ty *n., pl.* **-ties 1** generosity **2** gift or reward

bou·quet (bō kā′, bōō-) *n.* **1** bunch of flowers **2** aroma

bout *n.* **1** struggle; contest **2** spell or term

bow (bō) *n.* **1** curved stick strung with cord for shooting arrows **2** stick strung with horsehairs, for playing a violin, etc. **3** knot with broad loops

bow (bou) *v.* **1** bend down in respect **2** to submit **3** weigh (*down*) —*n.* **1** bending of the head or body **2** front part of a ship

bow'els (bou′-) *n.pl.* **1** intestines **2** depths

bowl (bōl) *n.* **1** hollow, rounded dish or part **2** amphitheater **3** ball for bowling —*v.* **1** roll (a ball) in bowling **2** move fast

bowl'ing *n.* game in which a ball is rolled along a wooden lane (**bowling alley**) at ten wooden pins

box *n.* **1** container made of wood, cardboard, etc. **2** an enclosed group of seats **3** blow with the hand **4** evergreen shrub: also **box'wood** —*v.* **1** put (*in*) or shut (*up*) as in a box **2** fight with the fists —**box'er** *n.*

boy *n.* male child —**boy'hood'** *n.* —**boy'ish** *a.*

boy'cott' *v.* refuse to deal with — *n.* a boycotting

bra *n.* woman's undergarment for supporting the breasts

brace *v.* **1** strengthen with supports **2** prepare for a shock **3** stimulate —*n.* **1** pair **2** clamp **3** supporting device **4** handle of a drilling tool (**brace and bit**) **5** either of the signs { }, for connecting lines, etc.

brace'let *n.* decorative band for the arm

brack'et *n.* **1** projecting support **2** either of the signs [ ], for enclosing words **3** classification —*v.* **1** support with brackets **2** enclose in brackets **3** classify together

brag *n., v.* bragged boast

braid *v.* **1** interweave strands of **2** trim with braid —*n.* **1** braided

strip

Braille, braille (brāl) *n.* system of printing for the blind, using raised dots

brain *n.* **1** mass of nerve tissue in the head **2** *pl.* intelligence — *v.* smash the brain of

brake *n.* **1** thicket **2** device to stop or slow a machine, etc. —*v.* stop or slow as with a brake

bram'ble *n.* prickly shrub

bran *n.* husks separated from grains of wheat, etc.

branch *n.* **1** limb of a tree **2** off-shoot or division **3** tributary stream **4** local unit of an organization —*v.* put forth branches —**branch off** diverge

brand *n.* **1** burning stick **2** owner's mark burned on cattle **3** iron used to brand **4** stigma **5** trademark **6** make or kind —*v.* mark with a brand

bran'dy *n., pl.* **-dies** liquor distilled from wine or fruit juice

brash *a.* rash or insolent

brass *n.* **1** alloy of copper and zinc **2** [often with pl. v.] coiled musical instruments, as the trumpet, tuba, etc. **3** [Col.] rude boldness **4** [Sl.] military officer

brat *n.* unruly child

brave *a.* full of courage

bra'vo (brä′-) *int., n., pl.* **-vos** shout of approval

brawl *v.* quarrel or fight noisily —*n.* noisy fight

breach *n.* **1** break in something; gap **2** violation of a promise, friendship, etc.

bread *n.* **1** baked food of flour dough **2** livelihood

breadth *n.* width or scope

break *v.* **broke, bro'ken 1** split apart; smash **2** make or become unusable **3** tame by force **4** make penniless **5** surpass (a record) **6** violate (a law) **7** interrupt **8** stop **9** make or become known —*n.* **1** a breaking **2** broken place **3** interruption **4** beginning (of day) **5** sudden change **6** a chance — **break in 1** enter forcibly **2** interrupt **3** train —**break off** stop abruptly

break'down' *n.* **1** mechanical failure **2** physical or mental collapse **3** analysis

break'fast (brek′-) *n.* first meal of the day

break'through' *n.* **1** act, place, etc. of breaking through resistance **2** important discovery

breast *n.* **1** milk-secreting gland

on a woman's body **2** upper front of the body **3** the emotions —*v.* to face bravely

breath (breth) *n.* **1** air taken into and let out of the lungs **2** easy breathing **3** life **4** slight breeze

breathe (brēth) *v.* **1** inhale and exhale **2** live **3** whisper **4** rest

breath'less *a.* panting

breech'es (brich'-) *n.pl.* knickers or trousers

breed *v.* **bred 1** bring forth (offspring) **2** produce **3** raise (animals) —*n.* **1** race; stock **2** type

breeze *n.* gentle wind —**breez'y** *a.*, **-i·er**, **-i·est**

brew *v.* **1** make (beer, etc.) **2** steep (tea, etc.) **3** form —*n.* beverage brewed —**brew'er** *n.*

bribe *n.* thing given or promised as an inducement, esp. to wrongdoing —*v.* offer or give a bribe to —**brib'er·y** *n.*

brick *n.* **1** building block of baked clay **2** any oblong piece

bride *n.* woman just married or about to be married —**brid'al** *a.*

bride'groom' *n.* man just married or about to be married

brides'maid' *n.* any of the bride's wedding attendants

bridge *n.* **1** structure for crossing a river, etc. **2** thing like a bridge in shape, etc. **3** mounting for false teeth **4** card game for two players of players

bri'dle *n.* **1** head harness for a horse **2** thing that restrains —*v.* **1** put a bridle on **2** curb

brief *a.* short; concise —*n.* summary, as of a law case —*v.* summarize the facts for

bright *a.* **1** shining; full of light **2** vivid **3** cheerful **4** mentally quick —**bright'en** *v.* —**bright'ly** *adv.* —**bright'ness** *n.*

bril'liant (-yant) *a.* **1** shining brightly **2** splendid **3** keenly intelligent —**bril'liance** *n.*

brim *n.* **1** top edge of a cup, etc. **2** projecting rim of a hat

brine *n.* **1** water full of salt **2** ocean —**brin'y** *a.*, **-i·er**, **-i·est**

bring *v.* **brought** cause to come or happen; fetch, get, lead to, etc. —**bring about** to cause —**bring forth** give birth to; produce —**bring off** accomplish —**bring out** reveal —**bring to** revive —**bring up 1** rear (children) **2** mention

brink *n.* edge, as of a cliff

brisk *a.* **1** quick; energetic **2** invigorating

bris·tle (bris'əl) *n.* short, stiff hair —*v.* **1** stiffen like bristles **2** stiffen with anger —**bris'tly** *a.*

britch'es *n.pl.* [Col.] breeches

brit'tle *a.* hard but easily broken

broad *a.* **1** wide **2** obvious **3** tolerant **4** extensive; general —**broad'en** *v.*

broad'cast' *v.* **-cast'** or **-cast'ed 1** spread widely **2** send by radio, TV, etc. —*n.* radio, TV, etc. program —**broad'cast'er** *n.*

broad'-mind'ed *a.* liberal

broc'co·li *n.* green-headed cauliflower

broil *v.* cook by direct heat

broil'er *n.* **1** pan or stove section for broiling **2** chicken fit for broiling

bro'ken *v.* pp. of BREAK —*a.* **1** fractured **2** not in working order **3** violated, as a vow **4** ruined **5** interrupted **6** imperfectly spoken **7** tamed

bron'to·saur (-sôr') *n.* large plant-eating dinosaur: also **bron'to·sau'rus**

bronze *n.* **1** alloy of copper and tin **2** reddish brown —*v.* make bronze in color

brooch (brōch, brōōch) *n.* large ornamental pin with a clasp

brood *n.* **1** birds hatched at one time **2** offspring —*v.* dwell on moodily

brook *n.* a small stream —*v.* endure or tolerate

broom *n.* **1** long-handled brush for sweeping **2** kind of shrub

broth *n.* clear soup

broth'er *n.* **1** male related to one by having the same parents **2** fellow member —**broth'er·hood'** *n.* —**broth'er·ly** *a.*

broth'er-in-law' *n.*, *pl.* **broth'ers-** **1** brother of one's spouse **2** sister's husband

brow *n.* **1** eyebrow **2** forehead **3** edge of a cliff

brown *a.* chocolate-colored **2** tanned; dark-skinned —*n.* brown color —*v.* to make or become brown

browse *v.* **1** feed on grass, etc. **2** to glance through pages

bruise *v.* injure and discolor (the skin) without breaking it —*n.* discolored injury of the skin

brunch *n.* [Col.] combined breakfast and lunch

brunt *n.* main impact

brush *n.* **1** device with bristles, wires, etc. for cleaning, painting, etc. **2** a brushing **3** skirmish **4** underbrush **5** sparsely settled land —v. 1 use a brush on 2 touch lightly 3 remove as with a brush —brush off dismiss

brusque (brusk) a. abrupt in manner —brusque'ly adv.

bru'tal a. savage, cruel, etc.

brute a. of or like an animal; cruel, stupid, etc. —n. 1 animal 2 brutal person —brut'ish a.

bub'ble n. globule of air or gas in a liquid —v. 1 rise in bubbles 2 gurgle —bub'bly a.

buck n. 1 male deer, goat, etc. 2 a bucking 3 [Sl.] dollar —v. 1 rear up, as to throw off (a rider) 2 [Col.] resist

buck'et n. container with a handle, for water, etc.; pail

buck'le n. clasp for fastening a belt, etc. —v. 1 fasten with a buckle 2 bend or crumple

bud n. small swelling on a plant, start of a leaf, shoot, or flower —v. bud'ded 1 put forth buds 2 begin to develop

budge v. move slightly

budg'et n. 1 plan adjusting expenses to income 2 estimated cost of operating, etc.

buff v. polish, as with soft leather —buffer n.

buf'fa·lo' n., pl. -loes or -los 1 wild ox 2 American bison

buff'er n. anything that lessens shock

buf'fet (-ət) n., v. blow; slap

buf·fet' (-fā') n. 1 cabinet for dishes, silver, etc. 2 food which guests serve themselves as from a buffet

buf·foon' n. a clown

bug n. 1 crawling insect, esp. when a pest 2 [Col.] germ 3 [Sl.] defect 4 [Sl.] tiny microphone

bug'gy n., pl. -gies 1 light, one-horse carriage 2 baby carriage

bu'gle (byoo'-) n. small, valueless trumpet —bu'gler n.

build v. built 1 make by putting together parts 2 create, develop, etc. —n. form or structure —build'er n.

build'ing n. structure

bulb n. 1 underground bud, as the onion 2 bulblike electric lamp —bul'bous a.

bulge n. outward swelling —v. swell out —bulg'y a.

bulk n. 1 size or mass, esp. if great 2 main part —v. have, or gain in, size or importance —a. not packaged —bulk'y a., -i-er, -i-est

bull n. 1 male bovine animal, or

male seal, elephant, etc. 2 edict of the Pope —a. male

bull'dog' n. heavily built dog with a stubborn grip

bul'let n. shaped metal piece to be shot from a gun

bul'le·tin n. 1 brief news item 2 regular publication of a group

bul·lion (bool'yən) n. gold or silver ingots

bul'ly n., pl. -lies one who hurts or threatens weaker people

bum'ble v. blunder or stumble

bum'ble-bee' n. large bee

bump v. collide (with) —n. 1 light collision 2 swelling —bump'y a., -i-er, -i-est

bump'er n. device, as on a car, for easing collisions

bun n. small bread roll

bunch n. cluster of similar things —v. gather; group

bun'dle n. 1 number of things bound together 2 package —v. 1 make into a bundle 2 hustle (off) —bundle up dress warmly

bun'gle v. do clumsily; spoil

bunk n. 1 built-in bed 2 [Col.] any narrow bed 3 [Sl.] empty talk —v. sleep in a bunk

bun'ny n., pl. -nies [Col.] rabbit

bunt Baseball v. to bat (a pitch) so it does not go beyond the infield —n. a bunted ball

buoy (boi, boo'ē) n. floating marker —v. 1 keep afloat 2 lift up in spirits

bur n. prickly seedcase

bur'den n. 1 load carried 2 thing hard to bear

bu·reau (byoor'ō) n., pl. -reaus' or -reaux' (-rōz') 1 chest of drawers 2 government department 3 office

bur'ger n. [Col.] hamburger or cheeseburger

bur'glar n. one who breaks into a building to steal —bur'gla·ry n., pl. -ries

Bur'gun·dy n. 1 kind of red wine 2 purplish red

bur'i·al n. burying of a dead body

bur'lap' n. coarse cloth of hemp, etc., used for bags

burn v. burned or burnt 1 be or set on fire 2 destroy or be destroyed by fire 3 hurt or be hurt by acid, friction, etc. 4 feel or make feel hot 5 be excited 6 [Sl.] cheat or trick —n. injury from fire, acid, etc.

burr n. 1 rough edge left on metal 2 trilling of r 3 bur

bur'ro n., pl. -ros donkey

bur'row n. hole dug by an animal

burst v. burst 1 come apart suddenly; explode 2 appear, enter, etc. suddenly 3 be too full —n. a bursting

bur'y v. -ied 1 put in a grave, tomb, etc. 2 cover; hide

bus n., pl. bus'es or bus'ses large motor coach

bush n. 1 low, woody plant 2 uncleared land

bush'el n. a dry measure equal to 4 pecks

busi'ness (biz'-) n. 1 commerce 2 commercial or industrial establishment; store, factory, etc. 3 occupation 4 rightful concern 5 matter; affair —**busi'ness·man**' n., pl. -**men**'

bust n. 1 sculpture of head and shoulders 2 woman's bosom

bus·tle (bus'əl) v. hurry busily —n. 1 a bustling 2 padding for the back of a skirt

bus'y a. -i·er, -i·est 1 active; at work 2 full of activity —**bus'i·ly** adv. —**bus'y·ness** n.

but prep. except —con. 1 yet 2 on the contrary 3 unless —adv. 1 only 2 merely

butch'er n. 1 one who kills and dresses animals for meat 2 one who sells meat 3 killer

but'ler n. head manservant

butt n. 1 thick end 2 stub 3 object of ridicule 4 large cask —v. 1 join end to end 2 ram with the head —**butt in(to)** [Sl.] meddle in

but'ter n. yellow fat churned from cream —v. spread with butter —**but'ter·y** a.

but'ter·cup' n. a small, bright-yellow flower

but'ter·fly' n., pl. -flies insect with four broad, colorful wings

but'ter·milk' n. sour milk left after churning butter

but'tocks n.pl. fleshy, rounded parts of the hips

but'ton n. 1 small disk for fastening a garment, etc. 2 button-like part —v. to fasten with buttons

but'tress n. 1 outer structure supporting a wall 2 a prop

buy v. bought 1 get by paying money, etc. 2 to bribe

buzz v. hum like a bee —n. buzzing sound

buz'zard n. 1 kind of large hawk 2 kind of vulture

by prep. 1 near; beside 2 during 3 not later than 4 through 5 past 6 for 7 according to —adv. 1 near 2 past —**by and by**

after a while —**by and large** in most respects

bye'-bye' n., int. goodbye

by'gone' a. past

by'pass' n. 1 road, pipe, etc. that gets around the main way 2 surgery or passage to route blood around a diseased part —v. 1 to detour around 2 ignore

by'stand'er n. one standing near but not taking part

byte (bit) n. string of bits: basic unit in computing

C

cab n. 1 taxicab 2 place in a truck, etc. where the operator sits

cab'bage n. vegetable with round head of thick leaves

cab'in n. 1 hut 2 a room on a ship, etc.

cab'i·net n. 1 case with drawers or shelves 2 [C-] body of official advisers

ca'ble n. 1 thick rope, often of wire 2 wire for carrying electric current —v. cabled, cabling, to send (a message) by cable

ca·boose' n. crew's car on a freight train

cache (kash) n. 1 place for hiding food, supplies, etc. 2 anything so hidden

cack'le v., n. (make) the shrill sound of a hen

cac'tus n., pl. -tus·es or -ti (-tī') spiny desert plant

ca·det' n. student at a military or naval school

Cae·sar'e·an (section) (sə zer'-) n. surgery to deliver a baby

ca·fe (ka fā') n. 1 restaurant 2 barroom

caf·e·te'ri·a n. a self-service restaurant

caf·feine, caf·fein (kaf'ēn') n. stimulant in coffee, tea, etc.

cage n. openwork structure, esp. for confining animals

ca'gey, ca'gy a. -gi·er, -gi·est [Col.] sly; cunning

ca·jole' v. coax or wheedle

Ca'jun, Ca'jan n. Canadian French native of Louisiana

cake n. 1 baked dough or batter of flour, eggs, sugar, etc. 2 solid, formed, usually flat mass —v. form into a hard mass

ca·lam'i·ty n., pl. -ties disaster

cal'ci·um n. chemical element in bone, limestone, etc.

cal'cu·late' v. 1 figure by arithmetic 2 estimate —**cal'cu·la'tion** n. —**cal'cu·la'tor** n.

cal'cu·lus n. branch of higher mathematics

cal·dron (kôl′drən) *n.* large kettle or boiler

cal′en·dar *n.* **1** table showing the days, weeks, and months of a year **2** schedule

calf *n.*, *pl.* **calves 1** young cow or bull **2** young elephant, seal, etc. **3** fleshy part of leg below the knee

cal′i·ber *n.* **1** diameter of a bullet, bore of a gun, etc. **2** quality

cal′i·co′ *n.* cotton cloth, usually printed

cal′is·then′ics *n.pl.* simple athletic exercises

call *v.* **1** say loudly; shout **2** summon **3** name **4** telephone **5** stop (a game) —*n.* **1** shout or cry **2** summons **3** demand **4** need **5** short visit —**call for 1** demand **2** come and get —**call off** cancel —**call on 1** visit briefly **2** ask (someone) to speak

cal·lig′ra·phy *n.* artistic handwriting —**cal·lig′ra·pher** *n.*

cal′lous *a.* **1** hardened **2** unfeeling —**cal′lous·ly** *adv.*

cal′lus *n.* hard, thickened place on the skin

calm *n.* stillness —*a.* still; tranquil —*v.* make or become calm

cal′o·rie, cal′o·ry *n.*, *pl.* **-ries** unit of heat or of the energy gotten from food

cam·cord′er *n.* portable videotape recorder and TV camera

cam′el *n.* beast of burden with a humped back

ca·mel′li·a (-mēl′ya) *n.* large, roselike flower

cam′e·o′ *n.*, *pl.* **-os′ 1** gem, etc. with figure carved on it **2** small role for notable actor

cam′er·a *n.* **1** device for taking photographs **2** TV device that first receives the images for transmission

cam′ou·flage′ (-ə fläzh′) *n.* disguising of potential targets in wartime

camp *n.* **1** place with tents, huts, etc., as for vacationers or soldiers **2** supporters of a cause —*v.* set up a camp —**camp′er** *n.*

cam·paign′ *n.* series of planned actions, as in war, an election, etc. —*v.* wage a campaign

cam′pus *n.* school or college grounds —*a.* of students

can *n.* metal container, as for foods —*v.* **canned** preserve (food) in cans or jars

ca·nal′ *n.* **1** artificial waterway **2** body duct

ca·nar′y *n.*, *pl.* **-ies** yellow songbird kept in a cage

can′cel *v.* **1** cross out **2** make invalid **3** abolish

can′cer *n.* **1** malignant tumor **2** a spreading evil —**can′cer·ous** *a.*

can·de·la′brum (-lä′-, -lā′-) *n.*, *pl.* **-bra** or **-brums** large, branched candlestick: also **can′de·la′bra**

can′did *a.* frank; honest

can′di·date′ *n.* one seeking office, etc. —**can′di·da·cy** *n.*

can′dle *n.* wax taper with a wick, burned for light

can′dy *n.*, *pl.* **-dies** confection of sugar or syrup —*v.* **-died** cook or preserve in sugar

cane *n.* **1** hollow, jointed stem, as of bamboo **2** walking stick **3** split rattan

ca′nine′ *a.* of or like a dog —*n.* dog

can′is·ter *n.* box or can for coffee, tea, etc.

can′ni·bal *n.* person who eats human flesh

can′non *n.*, *pl.* **-nons** or **-non** large mounted gun

can′not can not

ca·noe′ *n.* narrow, light boat moved with paddles —*v.* paddle or go in a canoe

ca·no′la (oil) *n.* cooking oil, from the seed of the rape plant

can′on *n.* **1** body of church laws **2** any law **3** official list **4** clergyman serving in a cathedral **5** musical round

can′on·ize′ *v.* name as a saint

can′o·py *n.*, *pl.* **-pies** covering hung over a bed, throne, etc.

can′ta·loupe′, can′ta·loup′ (-lōp′) *n.* sweet, juicy melon

can·teen′ *n.* **1** general store at an army post **2** soldier's water flask

can′ter *n.* easy gallop —*v.* go at this pace

can′tor *n.* liturgical singer in a synagogue

can′vas *n.* coarse cloth used for tents, sails, oil paintings, etc.

can′vass (-vəs) *v.* seek votes, opinions, etc. from —*n.* a canvassing —**can′vass·er** *n.*

can′yon *n.* narrow valley between high cliffs

cap *n.* **1** brimless hat, often with a visor **2** caplike cover —*v.* **capped 1** put a cap on **2** surpass

ca′pa·ble *a.* able; skilled —**capable of** able or likely to

ca·pac'i·ty n. 1 ability to contain or hold 2 volume 3 ability 4 position

cape n. 1 sleeveless coat fastened about the neck 2 land jutting into water

ca'per v. skip about playfully —n. 1 wild, foolish act 2 [Sl.] criminal act, esp. a robbery

cap·il·lar·y a. having a tiny bore, as a tube —n., pl. **-ies** tiny blood vessel

cap'i·tal a. 1 bringing or punishable by death 2 chief; main 3 excellent —n. 1 capital letter 2 city from which a state is governed 3 money or property owned or used in business 4 capitalists collectively 5 top of a column

cap'i·tal·ism' n. economic system in which the means of production and distribution are privately owned

cap'i·tal·ize' v. 1 convert into capital 2 use to advantage: with on 3 supply capital for 4 write with a capital letter

Cap'i·tol n. building where a legislature meets

cap'let n. medicinal tablet with a protective coating

cap'size' v. upset; overturn

cap'sule n. small case, as for a dose of medicine

cap'tain n. 1 leader 2 army officer above lieutenant 3 navy officer above commander 4 master of a ship —v. to head

cap'tion n. 1 title, as under a newspaper picture 2 TV or film subtitle

cap'ti·vate' v. fascinate

cap'tive a., n. (held) prisoner

cap'tor n. one who captures

cap'ture v. take by force, by surprise, etc. —n. a capturing or the thing captured

car n. 1 wheeled vehicle; esp., an automobile 2 elevator

ca·rafe' (-raf') n. bottle for water, coffee, etc.

car'a·mel (or kär'mal) n. 1 burnt sugar used to flavor 2 chewy candy

car'at n. 1 unit of weight for jewels 2 karat

car'a·van' n. group traveling together, as through a desert

car·bo·hy'drate n. compound of carbon, hydrogen, and oxygen, as sugar or starch

car'bon n. nonmetallic chemical element in all organic compounds: diamond and graphite

are pure carbon

car'bon·ate' v. charge with carbon dioxide —**car'bo·na'tion** n.

carbon di·ox'ide' n. odorless gas given off in breathing

carbon mon·ox'ide n. colorless, odorless, poisonous gas

car'bu·ret'or (-rāt'-) n. device in an engine for mixing air with gasoline

car'cass (-kəs) n. dead body of an animal

card n. 1 flat piece of stiff paper 2 postcard 3 playing card 4 pl. game played with cards 5 metal comb for wool, etc.

card'board' n. stiff paper

car'di·ac' a. of the heart

car'di·gan n. knitted jacketlike sweater

car'di·nal a. 1 chief; main 2 bright-red —n. 1 high Roman Catholic Church official 2 red American songbird

car·di·ol'o·gy n. branch of medicine dealing with the heart

care n. 1 worry 2 watchfulness 3 charge; keeping —v. 1 be concerned 2 wish (to do) —**care for** 1 love or like 2 look after —(in) **care of** at the address of —**take care of** 1 look after 2 protect —**care'free'** a. —**care'ful** a.

care'less a.

ca·reer' n. 1 full speed 2 progress through life 3 profession or occupation

ca·ress' v. touch lovingly —n. affectionate touch

car'go n., pl. **-goes** or **-gos** load carried by a ship, etc.

car'i·bou' (-bōō') n. North American reindeer

car'ni·val n. 1 festivity 2 kind of fair, with rides, etc.

car·niv'o·rous a. flesh-eating

car'ol n. (Christmas) song of joy —v. sing —**car'ol·er** n.

ca·rouse' v., n. (join in) a drinking party

carp n. freshwater fish

car'pen·ter n. construction worker who makes wooden parts —**car'pen·try** n.

car'pet n. heavy fabric for covering a floor —v. to cover as with a carpet

car pool n. group plan to rotate cars, going to and from work

car'riage n. 1 horsedrawn vehicle 2 posture 3 moving part that holds and shifts something

car'ri·er n. one that carries

car'rot n. plant with an edible, orange-red root

car'ry v. **-ried** 1 take to another place 2 lead, transmit, etc. 3 win (an election, etc.) 4 hold; support 5 bear (oneself) 6 keep in stock 7 cover a range —**be** (or **get**) **carried away** to become very emotional or enthusiastic —**carry out** (or **through**) to accomplish

car'ry-out' a. of prepared food sold to be eaten elsewhere

cart n. small wagon or vehicle with wheels, pushed or pulled by hand —v. carry in a vehicle

car'ti-lage n. tough, elastic skeletal tissue

car'ton n. cardboard box

car-toon' n. 1 drawing that is a caricature 2 comic strip 3 film of drawn figures that seem to move —**car-toon'ist** n.

car'tridge n. 1 cylinder holding the charge and bullet or shot for a firearm 2 small container for film, etc.

carve v. 1 make or shape by cutting 2 slice —**carv'er** n. —**carv'ing** n.

ca·sa'ba n. melon with a yellow rind

cas·cade' n. 1 waterfall 2 a shower —v. fall in a cascade

case n. 1 example or instance 2 situation 3 lawsuit 4 form of a noun, etc. showing its relation to neighboring words 5 container 6 protective cover —v. 1 put in a case 2 [Sl.] examine carefully —**in case** if —**in case of** in the event of

cash n. money on hand —v. give or get cash for

cash'ew n. kidney-shaped, edible nut

cash'ier' n. one in charge of cash transactions

cask n. barrel for liquid

cas'ket n. coffin

cas'se·role' n. covered dish for baking and serving

cast v. **cast** 1 throw 2 deposit (a vote) 3 mold 4 select (an actor) —n. 1 a throw 2 plaster form for broken limb 3 the actors in a play 4 type or quality 5 tinge —**cast about** search —**cast aside** (or **away** or **off**) discard

cas'ta·nets' n.pl. two hollow pieces clicked together in one hand in rhythm

caste (kast) n. class distinction based on birth, etc.

cast iron n. hard, brittle pig iron —**cast'-i'ron** a.

cas'tle n. large, fortified dwelling

cas'tor oil n. oil used as a laxative

cas'trate' v. remove the testicles of —**cas·tra'tion** n.

cas'u·al (kazh'-) a. 1 by chance 2 careless 3 nonchalant 4 informal

cat n. 1 small, soft-furred animal kept as a pet 2 any related mammal, as the lion

cat'a·log', cat'a·logue' n. complete list, as of library books

cat'a·lyst' (-list') n. substance that affects a chemical reaction but itself remains unchanged

cat'a·pult' n. device for throwing or launching

cat'a·ract' n. 1 large waterfall 2 opaque condition of eye lens

ca·tas'tro·phe (-fē) n. sudden great disaster

catch v. **caught** 1 capture 2 deceive 3 surprise 4 get 5 grab 6 understand 7 take or keep hold —n. 1 a catching 2 thing that catches or is caught —**catch on** 1 understand 2 become popular —**catch up** to overtake —**catch'er** n.

cat'e·chism' (-kiz'əm) n. list of questions and answers to teach religious beliefs

cat'e·go'ry n., pl. **-ries** any of a system of classes

ca'ter v. provide food, etc. for a party —**ca'ter·er** n.

cat'er·pil'lar n. larva of a butterfly, moth, etc.

ca·the'dral n. large church

cath'ode' n. 1 a negatively charged electrode 2 positive terminal of a battery

cath'o·lic a. 1 universal 2 liberal 3 [C-] Roman Catholic —n. [C-] member of the Roman Catholic Church —**Ca·thol'i·cism'** n.

cat'nip' n. plant like mint

CAT scan n. computerized photographic technique using X-rays

cat'sup (or kech'əp) n. ketchup

cat'tail' n. marsh plant with long, brown spikes

cat'tle n. 1 livestock (cows, bulls, steers, or oxen

Cau·ca·soid' (kô'kə soid') n., a. (member) of one of the major groups of human beings, loosely called the *white race*: also **Cau·ca·sian** (kô kā'zhən)

cau'cus n. political meeting to choose party candidates, etc.

caul'dron n. caldron

cau'li·flow'er n. hard, white head

of a cabbagelike plant

caulk (kôk) v. make watertight or airtight by filling cracks with a puttylike sealant

cause n. 1 thing bringing a result 2 motive 3 group movement with an aim 4 lawsuit —v. bring about

cau'tion n. 1 warning 2 prudence —v. warn —**cau'tious** a.

cav'a·lier' (-lir') n. 1 knight 2 gallant gentleman

cav'al·ry n., pl. **-ries** army troops on horses or in motorized vehicles

cave n. hollow place in the earth

cav'ern n. large cave —**cav'ern·ous** a.

cav'i·ar', cav'i·are' n. fish eggs eaten as a relish

cav'i·ty n., pl. **-ties** hole or hollow place

cay·enne' (kī-, kā-) n. ground hot red pepper

CD n. compact disc

cease v. to end; stop

cease'-fire' n. truce

ce'dar n. evergreen tree with fragrant wood

cede (sēd) v. give up; transfer

ceil'ing n. 1 inner roof of a room 2 upper limit

cel'e·brate' v. 1 to perform (a ritual) 2 commemorate with festivity 3 honor; praise

ce·leb'ri·ty n., pl. **-ties** 1 fame 2 pl. **-ties** famous person

cel'er·y n. plant with edible crisp stalks

cell n. 1 small room as in a prison 2 small unit of protoplasm 3 device for generating electricity chemically 4 unit of an organization —**cel'lu·lar** a.

cel'lar n. room(s) below ground under a building

cel·lo (chel'ō) n., pl. **-los** instrument like a large violin, held between the knees in playing —**cel'list** n.

cel'lu·lose' n. substance in plant cell walls, used in making paper, etc.

Cel'si·us a. of a thermometer on which 0° is the freezing point and 100° the boiling point of water

ce·ment' n. 1 mixture of lime, clay, and water, used for paving, in mortar, etc. 2 any adhesive

cem'e·ter·y n., pl. **-ies** place for burying the dead

cen'ser n. container in which incense is burned

cen'sor n. one who examines books, mail, etc. to remove things considered unsuitable —v. act as censor of

cen'sure n., v. blame

cen'sus n. official count of population

cent n. 100th part of a dollar; penny

cen·ten'ni·al n. 100th anniversary —a. of a centennial

cen'ter n. 1 middle point, esp. of a circle or sphere 2 any central place, thing, or person

cen'ti·grade' a. Celsius

cen'ti·me'ter n. 1/100 meter

cen'ti·pede' n. wormlike animal with many pairs of legs

cen'tral a. 1 in or near the center 2 main; chief

cen'tu·ry n., pl. **-ries** period of 100 years

ce·ram'ics n. the making of pottery, porcelain, etc. —n.pl. pottery, etc. —**ce·ram'ic** a.

ce're·al n. 1 grain used for food, as wheat, oats, etc. 2 food made from grain

cer·e·bel'lum n. lower rear part of the brain

cer'e·brum (or sə rē'-) n. upper, main part of the brain

cer·e·mo'ni·al a. ritual; formal

cer·e·mo'ny n., pl. **-nies** 1 set of formal acts; rite 2 rigid etiquette; formality

cer'tain a. 1 fixed; settled 2 sure; positive 3 specific, but unnamed 4 some —**cer'tain·ly** adv. —**cer'tain·ty** n.

cer·tif'i·cate (-kət) n. written statement testifying to a fact, promise, etc.

cer'ti·fy' v. **-fied'** 1 formally declare to be true, etc. 2 guarantee —**cer'ti·fi·ca'tion** n.

Cha·blis' (sha blē') n. dry white wine

chafe v. 1 make warm or sore by rubbing 2 be angry

chaff n. 1 threshed husks of grain 2 worthless stuff

cha·grin' (shə-) n. disappointment, humiliation, etc.

chain n. 1 flexible series of joined links 2 pl. fetters 3 connected series —v. restrain as with chains

chair n. 1 seat with a back 2 office of authority

chair'man n., pl. **-men** one who presides at a meeting —**chair'man·ship'** n. —**chair'per·son** n. —**chair'wom'an** n.fem., pl. **-wom·en**

cha·let (sha lā') n. cottage with

overhanging eaves

chalk (chôk) *n.* soft limestone for writing on a blackboard

chalk'board' *n.* blackboard

chal'lenge *n.* 1 demand for identification 2 a calling into question 3 call to a contest, etc. 4 anything calling for special effort —*v.* put a challenge to

cham'ber *n.* 1 room 2 *pl.* judge's office 3 assembly or council 4 part of a gun for the cartridge

cha·me'le·on (ka-) *n.* lizard able to change its color

champ *v.* chew or bite noisily

cham·pagne (sham pān') *n.* effervescent white wine

cham'pi·on *n.* 1 one who fights for a cause 2 winner of first place —**cham'pi·on·ship'** *n.*

chance *n.* 1 luck; fortune 2 risk 3 opportunity 4 possibility —*a.* accidental —*v.* 1 happen 2 risk

chan·de·lier (shan'də lir') *n.* hanging lighting fixture

change *v.* 1 to substitute 2 exchange 3 alter; vary —*n.* 1 alteration or variation 2 variety 3 money returned as overpayment 4 small coins

change of life *n.* menopause

chan'nel *n.* 1 bed of a river, etc. 2 wide strait joining two seas 3 any passage 4 official course of action 5 assigned frequency band, esp. in TV

chant *n.* song with several words to each tone —*v.* to utter in a chant

Cha·nu·kah (khä'noo kä') *n.* Hanuka

cha·os (kā'äs') *n.* complete disorder —**cha·ot'ic** *a.*

chap *v.* chapped become rough and red as from the cold

chap'el *n.* small church

chap·er·on (shap'ə rōn') *n.* older person in charge of unmarried people at social affairs

chap'lain (-lən) *n.* clergyman in the armed forces

chap'ter *n.* 1 main division of a book 2 branch of an organization

char *v.* charred scorch

char'ac·ter *n.* 1 letter or symbol 2 trait 3 kind or sort 4 personality 5 moral strength 6 person in a play, novel, etc.

char·ac·ter·is'tic *a.* typical; distinctive —*n.* distinguishing quality

char'coal' *n.* pieces of incompletely burned wood

charge *v.* 1 fill (*with*) 2 add electricity to 3 command 4 accuse 5 ask as a price 6 ask payment (*for*) 7 put as a debt 8 attack —*n.* 1 load 2 responsibility or care (*of*) 3 chemical energy in a battery 4 someone in one's care 5 command 6 accusation 7 a cost 8 debt 9 attack —**in charge (of)** in control (*of*)

char'i·ot *n.* ancient, horse-drawn, two-wheeled cart

char'i·ty *n., pl.* -ties 1 leniency in judging others 2 a helping those in need 3 institution for so helping —**char'i·ta·ble** *a.*

charm *n.* 1 words or thing supposed to have magic power 2 trinket on a bracelet, etc. 3 fascination; allure —*v.* 1 to use a magical charm on 2 to fascinate; delight —**charm'ing** *a.*

chart *n.* 1 map, esp. for navigation 2 graph, table, etc.

char'ter *n.* official paper licensing a new company, society, chapter, etc.

chase *v.* 1 follow in order to catch 2 drive away 3 decorate (metal) as by engraving —*n.* a chasing —**give chase** pursue

chasm (kaz'əm) *n.* deep crack in the earth's surface

chas·sis (chas'ē, shas'-) *n., pl.* -sis (-ēz) 1 frame, wheels, and motor of a car 2 frame, tubes, etc. of a radio or TV

chas·tise' (-tīz') *v.* 1 punish as by beating 2 scold sharply

chat *v.* **chat'ted;** *n.* talk in a light, informal way

chat'ter *v.* 1 talk much and foolishly 2 click together rapidly

chauf·feur (shō'fər) *n.* man hired to drive one's car

chau·vin·ism' (shō'-) *n.* 1 fanatical patriotism 2 unreasoning devotion to one's race, sex, etc.

cheap *a.* 1 low in price 2 of little value —*adv.* at a low cost

cheap'en *v.* make cheaper

cheat *n.* 1 fraud 2 swindler —*v.* deceive or practice fraud

check *n.* 1 sudden stop 2 restraint or restrainer 3 test of accuracy, etc. 4 mark (✓) used to verify 5 token to show ownership 6 bill, as at a restaurant 7 written order to a bank to pay money 8 pattern of squares 9 *Chess* threat to the king —*v.* 1 stop or restrain 2 test, verify, etc. 3 mark with a check 4 deposit temporarily —

check in register at a hotel, etc. —**check out** 1 officially leave a hotel, etc. 2 collect money owed in a supermarket, etc.

check'book' n. booklet of bank checks

check'er·board' n. board for checkers, with 64 squares

check'ers n. game like chess, for two players

check'up' n. medical examination

Ched'dar (cheese) n. a hard, smooth cheese

cheek n. 1 side of the face below the eye 2 [Col.] impudence

cheer n. 1 joy; gladness 2 shout of excitement, welcome, etc. —v. 1 fill with cheer 2 urge on, praise, welcome

cheer'ful a. 1 joyful 2 bright and attractive Also **cheer'y**

cheese n. solid food made from milk curds

chef (shef) n. head cook

chem'i·cal a. of, in, or by chemistry —n. substance used in or obtained by chemistry

chem'is·try n. science dealing with the composition, reactions, etc. of substances —**chem'ist** n.

che'mo·ther'a·py (kē'-) n. use of drugs in treating disease

cher'ish v. 1 hold or treat tenderly 2 keep in mind

cher'ry n., pl. **-ries** tree with small, red fruit

chess n. checkerboard game for two players using various pieces

chest n. 1 box with a lid 2 piece of furniture with drawers 3 front part of the body above the abdomen

chest'nut' n. 1 edible nut of a kind of beech 2 [Col.] trite joke

chew v. grind with the teeth — **chew'y** a., **-i·er, -i·est**

chick n. young chicken

chick'en n. hen or rooster, or its edible flesh

chide v. scold; rebuke

chief n. leader —a. main; most important —**chief'ly** adv.

chief'tain n. chief of a clan or tribe

child n., pl. **chil'dren** 1 infant 2 boy or girl before puberty 3 son or daughter —**with child** pregnant —**child'hood'** n.

child'birth' n. a giving birth to a child

child'ish a. silly; immature

chil'i n., pl. **-ies** 1 hot, dried pod of red pepper 2 spicy dish of beef, chilies, beans, etc.

chill n. 1 moderate coldness 2 body coldness with shivering 3 sudden fear —a. uncomfortably cool —v. make or become cool

chime n. usually pl. set of tuned bells —v. to sound as a chime

chim'ney n. passage for smoke from a furnace, etc.

chim·pan·zee' n. medium-sized African ape

chin n. face below the lips

chi'na n. dishes, etc. of fine porcelain

chink n. 1 crack 2 clinking sound —v. to clink

chip v. chipped break or cut off bits from —n. 1 fragment 2 place where bit is chipped off 3 small disk used in gambling 4 thin slice of food 5 microchip

chip'munk' n. small, striped squirrel

chirp v. make short, shrill sounds —n. such a sound

chis'el (chiz'-) n. tool for chipping wood, stone, etc. —v. 1 chip with a chisel 2 [Col.] swindle —**chis'el·er, chis'el·ler** n.

chit'ter·lings (chit'linz) n.pl. pig intestines, used for food: also **chit'lins** or **chit'lings**

chlo'ri·nate' (klôr'ə-) v. purify (water) with chlorine

chlo·rine (klôr'ēn') n. greenish gas, a chemical element

chlo'ro·phyll, chlo'ro·phyl' (-fil') n. green coloring in plants

choc'o·late n. 1 ground cacao seeds 2 drink or candy made with this 3 reddish brown

choice n. 1 selection 2 right to choose 3 the one chosen

choir (kwir) n. group of singers, esp. in a church

choke v. 1 stop the breathing of; suffocate 2 obstruct; clog

cho·les'ter·ol' (ka-) n. substance in animal fats, etc.

chomp v. to champ

choose v. chose, cho'sen 1 take; select 2 prefer; decide

chop v. chopped 1 cut by blows of sharp tool 2 cut in bits —n. 1 sharp blow 2 a slice from the rib or loin

chop'sticks' n.pl. two sticks used as eating utensils in some Asian countries

chop su·ey (sōō'ē) n. American-Chinese stew served with rice

cho·ral (kôr'al) a. of or for a choir or chorus

chord (kôrd) n. 1 straight line joining two points on an arc 2 three or more tones sounded together in harmony

chore n. daily task

cho·rus (kôr'əs) n. 1 group of singers or singers and dancers 2 music for group singing 3 refrain of a song

chow'der n. fish or clam soup with vegetables

chow mein (mān) n. American-Chinese stew served on fried noodles

chro'mo·some' n. any of the microscopic bodies carrying the genes of heredity

chron'o·log'i·cal a. in order of occurrence —**chro·nol'o·gy** n.

chrys'a·lis (kris'-) n. pupa or its cocoon

chrys·an'the·mum n. plant with ball-shaped flowers

chub'by a. plump

chuck v. 1 tap playfully 2 toss —n. 1 tap 2 toss 3 shoulder cut of beef

chuck'hole' n. rough hole in pavement

chuck'le v. laugh softly —n. soft laugh

chum [Col.] n. close friend —**chum'my** a.

chunk n. thick piece

church n. 1 building for public worship 2 religion or religious sect

churn n. device for making butter —v. 1 shake (cream) in a churn to make butter 2 stir about vigorously

chute (shōōt) n. inclined passage for sliding things

ci'der n. juice from apples

ci·gar' n. roll of tobacco leaves for smoking

cig'a·rette' n. tobacco cut fine and rolled in paper for smoking

cinch n. 1 saddle girth 2 [Sl.] thing easy to do

cin'der n. 1 tiny charred piece of wood, etc. 2 pl. ashes

cin'e·ma n. films collectively; the movies: with *the*

cin'na·mon n. brown spice from East Indian tree bark

ci·pher (sī'fər) n. 1 zero; 0 2 code 3 key to a code

cir'ca prep. about; approximately

cir'cle n. 1 closed, curved line always equidistant from the center 2 cycle 3 group with interests in common 4 extent; scope

cir'cuit (-kət) n. 1 boundary 2 regular, routine journey 3 theater chain 4 path for electric current

cir'cu·lar a. 1 round 2 round about —n. advertisement sent to many people

cir'cu·late' v. move or spread about —**cir'cu·la·to'ry** a.

cir'cu·la'tion n. 1 movement, as of blood through the body 2 distribution

cir'cum·cise' v. cut off the foreskin of

cir·cum'fer·ence n. distance around a circle, etc.

cir'cum·flex' n. pronunciation mark (^)

cir'cum·stance' n. 1 connected fact or event 2 pl. financial condition 3 ceremony —**under no circumstances** never

cir'cus n. a show with acrobats, animals, clowns, etc.

cite v. 1 summon by law 2 quote 3 mention as example 4 mention in praise —**ci·ta'tion** n.

cit'i·zen n. member of a nation by birth or naturalization —**cit'i·zen·ship'** n.

cit'rus n. orange, lemon, etc. —a. of these trees or fruits

cit'y n., pl. -ies large town

civ'ic a. of a city or citizens

civ'ics n. study of civic affairs and duties

civ'il a. 1 of citizens 2 polite 3 not military or religious

ci·vil'ian a., n. (of a) person not in armed forces

civ·i·li·za'tion n. 1 high social and cultural development 2 culture of a certain time or place

clad v. alt. pt. & pp. of CLOTHE

claim v. 1 demand as rightfully one's own 2 assert —n. 1 a claiming 2 right to something 3 thing claimed —**claim'ant** n.

clam n. hard-shelled, often edible, bivalve mollusk

clam'or n. 1 uproar 2 noisy demand —v. make a clamor

clamp n. device for clasping things together —v. fasten with a clamp

clan n. 1 group of related families 2 group with interests in common

clap v. **clapped** 1 make the sound of flat surfaces struck together 2 to strike together, as the hands in applauding

clap'board (klab'ərd) n. tapered board for siding

clar'i·fy' v. -**fied'** make or become clear

clar'i·net' n. single-reed, woodwind instrument —**clar'i·net'ist** n.

lash v. 1 collide noisily 2 disagree —n. a clashing

lasp n. 1 device to fasten things 2 an embrace 3 grip of the hand —v. 1 fasten 2 hold tightly

lass n. 1 group of like people or things; sort 2 social rank 3 group of students in school 4 grade or quality 5 [Sl.] excellence —v. classify —**class'mate'** n. —**class'room'** n.

clas'sic a. 1 most excellent 2 in the style of ancient Greece or Rome —n. a book, work of art, etc. of highest excellence

clas'si·cal a. 1 CLASSIC (a. 2) 2 of such music as symphonies, concertos, etc.

clas'si·fy' v. **-fied'** 1 arrange in classes 2 designate as secret

clause n. 1 part of a sentence, with a subject and verb 2 provision in a document

claw n. 1 sharp nail of an animal's or bird's foot 2 pincers of a lobster, crab, etc.

clay n. firm, plastic earth, used for pottery, etc.

clean a. 1 free from dirt 2 sinless 3 free from flaws 4 complete —adv. completely —v. make clean —**clean'er** n. —**clean'ly** (klēn'-) adv.

clean'ly (klen'-) a. **-li·er, -li·est** 1 having clean habits 2 always kept clean —**clean'li·ness** n.

cleanse (klenz) v. make clean or pure —**cleans'er** n.

clear a. 1 free from clouds 2 transparent 3 distinct 4 obvious 5 free from charges, guilt, obstruction, debt, etc. —adv. 1 in a clear way 2 completely —v. 1 make or become clear 2 pass or leap over 3 make as profit 4 to empty or unload 5 rid (the throat) of phlegm

cleave v. cleft or cleaved split; sever

cleave v. adhere; cling

cleav'er n. butcher's tool

clef n. musical symbol to indicate pitch

cleft a., n. split

clench v. close tightly

cler'gy n., pl. **-gies** ministers, priests, etc. collectively

cler'gy·man n., pl. **-men** minister, priest, etc. —**cler'gy·wom'an** n.fem., pl. **-wom'en**

cler'i·cal a. 1 of the clergy 2 of office clerks

clerk n. 1 office worker who keeps records, etc. 2 sales-person in a store

clev'er a. 1 skillful 2 intelligent

click n. slight, sharp sound —v. make a click

cli'ent n. 1 person or company for whom a lawyer, etc. acts 2 customer

cliff n. high, steep rock

cli'mate n. average weather conditions —**cli·mat'ic** a.

cli'max n. highest point, as of interest or excitement; culmination —v. bring to a climax —**cli·mac'tic** a.

climb v. go up; ascend 2 climbing —**climb'er** n.

clinch v. 1 fasten (a nail) by bending the end 2 settle (an argument, etc.)

cling v. clung 1 hold fast 2 stay near

clin'ic n. 1 place where medical specialists work as a group 2 outpatient department

clin'i·cal a. 1 of medical treatment, as in clinics 2 dispassionate

clip v. clipped 1 cut short 2 cut the hair of 3 [Col.] hit sharply 4 fasten together —n. 1 a clipping 2 [Col.] rapid pace 3 fastening device

cloak n. 1 loose, sleeveless outer garment 2 thing that conceals

clock n. device for measuring and showing time

clock'wise' adv., a. in the direction in which the hands of a clock rotate

clog n. 1 thing that hinders 2 heavy shoe —v. **clogged** 1 hinder 2 block up

clone n. exact genetic duplicate of an organism —v. produce as a clone

close (klōs) a. 1 confined 2 secretive 3 stingy 4 humid; stuffy 5 near together 6 intimate 7 thorough 8 nearly alike; nearly equal —adv. in a close way or position

close (klōz) v. 1 shut or stop up 2 end 3 come close, as to attack

clos'et n. small room for clothes, etc.

clot n. coagulated mass, as of blood —v. **clot'ted** coagulate

cloth (klôth) n. 1 fabric of cotton, wool, synthetics, etc. 2 tablecloth, dustcloth, etc.

clothe (klōth) v. **clothed** or **clad** 1 to put clothes on 2 provide with clothes

clothes n.pl. 1 clothing 2 bedclothes

cloth'ing n. wearing apparel; garments

cloud n. 1 mass of vapor in the sky 2 mass of smoke, dust, etc. 3 thing that darkens, etc.

clove n. 1 pungent spice 2 segment of a bulb

clo'ven a. split

clo'ver n. small forage plant with triple leaves

clown n. comic entertainer as in a circus —v. act like a clown

club n. 1 stick used as a weapon, or in games 2 social group or its meeting place 3 playing card marked with a ♣

cluck n. low, clicking sound made by a hen —v. make this sound

clue n. hint or fact that helps solve a mystery

clump n. 1 lump 2 cluster

clum'sy a. **-si·er, -si·est** awkward —**clum'si·ly** adv.

clus'ter n., v. group; bunch

clutch v. 1 snatch (at) 2 hold tightly —n. 1 pl. control 2 grip 3 device for engaging and disengaging an engine

clut'ter n., v. disorder

coach n. 1 big, four-wheeled carriage 2 railroad passenger car 3 bus 4 trainer of athletes, singers, etc. —v. be a coach (for)

co·ag'u·late' v. thicken; clot

coal n. 1 black mineral used as fuel 2 ember

coarse a. 1 made up of large particles 2 rough 3 vulgar

coast n. seashore —v. 1 slide down an incline 2 continue moving on momentum

coat n. 1 sleeved outer garment 2 natural covering 3 layer, as of paint —v. cover with a layer

coat'ing n. surface layer

coax v. urge or get by soothing words, etc.

cob'bler n. 1 shoemaker 2 fruit pie

co'bra n. poisonous snake of Asia and Africa

cob'web' n. spider web

co·caine', co·cain' n. drug used as a narcotic or anesthetic

cock n. 1 rooster 2 any male bird 3 faucet —v. 1 tilt 2 set hammer of (a gun) to fire

cock'er (spaniel) n. small spaniel with drooping ears

cock'roach' n. flat-bodied, dark insect, a kitchen pest

cock'tail' n. 1 mixed alcoholic drink 2 appetizer

co'coa (-kō) n. 1 powder made from roasted cacao seeds 2 drink made of this

co'co·nut', co'coa·nut' n. hard-shelled fruit of a palm tree, with edible white meat

co·coon' n. silky case of certain insect larvae

cod n. N Atlantic food fish

co'da n. Mus. end passage

cod'dle v. pamper

code n. 1 body of laws 2 set of principles 3 set of signals or symbols for messages

co·erce' (-urs') v. force; compel

co·ex·ist' v. exist together

cof'fee n. 1 drink made from roasted seeds of a tropical shrub 2 the seeds

cof'fin n. case in which to bury a dead person

cog'nac' (kōn'yak') n. brandy

cog'wheel' n. wheel rimmed with teeth, as in a gear

co·her'ent a. clear and intelligible

coif·fure (kwä fyoor') n. 1 headdress 2 hairstyle

coil v. to wind in a spiral —n. anything coiled

coin n. stamped metal piece, issued as money —v. 1 make into coins 2 make up (new word) —**coin'age** n.

co·in·cide' v. 1 occur at the same time 2 agree; match

co'i·tus n. sexual intercourse: also **co·i'tion**

coke n. 1 fuel made by removing gases from coal 2 [Sl.] cocaine

co'la n. carbonated soft drink with flavoring from the nut of an African tree

cold a. 1 low in temperature 2 feeling chilled 3 without feeling 4 unfriendly 5 [Col.] unprepared 6 [Col.] perfectly memorized 7 [Col.] unconscious —n. 1 absence of heat 2 common virus infection with sneezing, coughing, etc.

cold'blood'ed a. 1 having a body temperature that varies with the surroundings 2 cruel; callous

cole'slaw' n. salad made of shredded raw cabbage

col'ic n. sharp abdominal pain from the bowels —**col'ick·y** a.

col·lab'o·rate' v. 1 to work together 2 help the enemy

col·lage' (-läzh') n. bits of objects pasted onto a surface to make a work of art

col·lapse' v. 1 fall in or shrink 2

break down; fail 3 fold together —n. a collapsing

col'lar n. a band, or the part of a garment, around the neck

col'league' n. fellow worker; associate

col·lect' v. 1 gather together 2 get payment for 3 regain control (of oneself) —a., adv. with the receiver paying —**col·lect'i-ble, col·lect'a-ble** a. —**col·lec'tion** n. —**col·lec'tor** n.

col'lege n. 1 school of higher learning or special instruction 2 group with certain powers

col·lide' v. 1 come into violent contact 2 to conflict; clash

col'lie n. large, long-haired sheep dog

col·lo'qui·al (-kwē-) a. used in informal talk and writing

co·logne' (-lōn') n. scented liquid like diluted perfume

co'lon n. 1 mark of punctuation (:) 2 lower part of the large intestine

colo·nel (kur'nəl) n. officer above lieutenant colonel

col'o·ny n., pl. -nies 1 group of settlers from a distant land 2 land ruled by a distant country 3 community with common interests —**co·lo'ni·al** a. —**col'o·nist** n. —**col'o·nize'** v.

col'or n. 1 effect on the eyes of light waves of different wavelengths 2 pigment 3 complexion 4 pl. a flag 5 outward appearance 6 picturesque quality —v. 1 paint or dye 2 alter or distort 3 blush —**of color** not Caucasoid; spec., black —**col'or·ful** a. —**col'or·ing** n.

co·los'sal a. huge; immense

colt n. young male horse

col'umn (-əm) n. 1 slender upright structure 2 vertical section of printed matter 3 line of troops, etc. —**col'um·nist** n.

co'ma n. deep unconsciousness, as from injury

comb n. 1 flat, toothed object for grooming the hair 2 cockscomb 3 honeycomb —v. 1 groom with a comb 2 search

com'bat' (v.: also **kəm·bat'**) v., n. fight; struggle —**com·bat'ant** n.

com'bi·na'tion n. 1 a combining 2 combined things, groups, etc. 3 series of numbers dialed to open a lock

com·bine' (n.: **käm'bīn'**) v. join; unite —n. 1 machine for harvesting and threshing grain 2 commercial or political alliance

come v. **came, come** 1 move from "there" to "here" 2 arrive or appear 3 happen 4 result 5 become 6 amount (to) 7 extend

co·me'di·an n. actor who plays comic parts —**co·me'di·enne'** (-en') n.fem.

com'e·dy n., pl. -dies a humorous play, TV show, etc.

com'et n. mass of dust and gas in space, with a luminous tail

com'fort v. soothe in distress; console —n. 1 relief from distress 2 one that comforts 3 ease —**com'fort·a·ble** a.

com'ic a. 1 of comedy 2 funny: also **com'i·cal**

com'ma n. punctuation mark (,)

com·mand' v. 1 to order 2 to control 3 deserve and get —n. 1 an order 2 control 3 military force, etc. under someone's control

com·mand'ment n. command; law

com·mem'o·rate' v. honor the memory of

com·mence' v. begin

com·mence'ment n. 1 beginning 2 graduation ceremony of a school, etc.

com·mend' v. 1 entrust 2 recommend 3 to praise —**com·men·da'tion** n.

com'ment' n. 1 explanatory note 2 remark 3 talk —v. make comments

com'merce n. trade on a large scale

com·mer'cial (-shəl) a. 1 connected with commerce 2 done for profit —n. Radio & TV paid advertisement

com·mis'sion n. 1 authority to act 2 group chosen to do something 3 percentage of a sale allotted to the agent 4 military officer's certificate of rank —v. 1 give a commission to 2 authorize

com·mit' v. -mit'ted 1 put in custody 2 to pledge; bind

com·mit'tee n. group chosen to do something

com'mon a. 1 shared by all 2 general 3 usual; ordinary 4 vulgar 5 designating a noun that refers to any of a group

com'mon·wealth' n. 1 people of a state 2 democracy or republic

com·mu'ni·cate' v. 1 transmit; give or exchange (information) 2 be connected —**com·mu'ni·ca·ble** a. —**com·mu'ni·ca'tor** n.

com·mu'ni·ca'tion n. 1 a com-

com·mu·ni·cat·ing or means of doing this **2** message, etc.

com·mun·ion n. **1** a sharing or being close **2** group of the same religious faith **3** [C-] Holy Communion

com·mu·nism n. theory or system of ownership of the means of production by the community

com·mu·ni·ty n., pl. **-ties 1** body of people living in the same place **2** a sharing in common

com·mute v. **1** lessen (a punishment, etc.) **2** travel by train, etc. to and from work

com·pact (n., also a.: käm′pakt) a. **1** firmly packed **2** terse —n. **1** small case for face powder, etc. **2** agreement

compact disc (or **disk**) n. digital disc for recording music, etc.

com·pan·ion n. **1** comrade; associate **2** thing that matches or goes with another

com·pa·ny n., pl. **-nies 1** group of people associated for some purpose **2** [Col.] guest(s) **3** military unit

com·par·a·tive a. by comparison —n. the second degree of comparison of adverbs and adjectives

com·pare′ v. **1** liken (to) **2** examine for similarities or differences **3** to form the positive, comparative, and superlative degrees of (adjective or adverb) —**com·par′i·son** n.

com·part′ment n. section partitioned off

com′pass n. **1** instrument for drawing circles, etc. **2** range; extent **3** instrument for showing direction

com·pel′ v. **-pelled′** to force

com·pen·sate′ v. make up for; pay —**com′pen·sa′tion** n.

com·pete′ v. **1** vie; rival **2** take part (in a contest)

com′pe·tent a. **1** capable; able **2** adequate —**com′pe·tence** n.

com′pe·ti′tion (-tish′ən) n. **1** competing; rivalry **2** contest

com·plain′ v. **1** express pain, dissatisfaction, etc. **2** make an accusation —**com·plaint′** n.

com′ple·ment (-mənt; v.: -ment′) n. **1** that which completes **2** entirety —v. make complete —**com′ple·men′ta·ry** a.

com·plete′ a. **1** lacking no parts **2** finished **3** thorough; perfect —**com·plex′** (n., also a.: käm′

pleks′) a. **1** having two or more parts **2** complicated —n. **1** complex whole **2** mixed-up feeling about a thing

com·plex′ion (-plek′shən) n. **1** color or texture of the skin **2** nature; aspect

com′pli·cate′ v. make difficult or involved —**com′pli·cat′ed** a.

com′pli·ment (-mənt; v.: -ment′) n. **1** something said in praise **2** pl. respects —v. pay a compliment to

com′pli·men′ta·ry a. **1** giving praise **2** given free

com·pose′ v. **1** make by combining **2** put in proper form **3** write (a song, poem, etc.) **4** make calm —**com·posed′** a.

com·pos′er n. —**com′po·si′tion** (-zish′ən) n.

com′pound (n., also a.: käm′pound′) v. combine —n. **1** substance with combined elements **2** enclosed place —a. with two or more parts

com′pre·hend′ v. **1** understand **2** include —**com′pre·hen′si·ble** a. —**com′pre·hen′sion** n.

com·press′ (n.: käm′pres′) v. press tight —n. wet pad —**com·pres′sion** n.

com·prise′ v. consist of

com′pro·mise′ n. settlement made with concessions —v. **1** settle by compromise **2** make suspect

com·pul′sion n. a forcing or being forced —**com·pul′so·ry** a.

com·pute′ v. calculate; figure

com·put′er n. an electronic machine that rapidly calculates or correlates data —**com·put′er·i·za′tion** n. —**com·put′er·ize′** v.

com′rade′ (-rad′) n. **1** a close friend **2** associate

con adv. against

con·cave′ (or kän′kāv′) a. curved like the inside of a sphere

con·ceal′ v. hide

con·cede′ v. **1** admit as true **2** grant as a right

con·ceit′ n. **1** vanity; pride **2** fanciful notion

con·ceive′ v. **1** become pregnant **2** think of **3** understand

con′cen·trate′ v. **1** fix one's attention, etc. (on) **2** increase, as in density **3** concentrated substance —**con′cen·tra′tion** n.

con′cept′ n. idea; notion

con·cep′tion n. **1** a conceiving **2** concept

con·cern′ v. be related to; involve —n. **1** business **2**

con·cerned' *a.* 1 involved or interested 2 anxious

con·cern'ing *prep.* relating to

con'cert *n.* 1 agreement 2 musical performance

con·cer'to (-cher'-) *n., pl.* **-tos** composition for solo instrument(s) and orchestra

con·cise' *a.* short and clear; terse **—con·cise'ly** *adv.*

con·clude' *v.* 1 finish 2 decide 3 arrange **—con·clu'sion** *n.*

con·coct' *v.* prepare or plan

con·course' *n.* 1 a crowd; gathering 2 open space for crowds

con·crete' *a.* 1 real; actual 2 specific **—***n.* hard material made of sand, gravel and cement **—con·crete'ly** *adv.*

con·cur' *v.* **-curred'** 1 occur together 2 agree

con·cus'sion *n.* 1 jarring shock 2 brain injury from a blow

con·demn' (-dem') *v.* 1 disapprove of 2 declare guilty 3 to doom 4 take for public use 5 declare unfit

con·dense' *v.* 1 make or become denser 2 express concisely

con'di·ment *n.* seasoning

con·di'tion *n.* 1 prerequisite 2 state of being 3 healthy state 4 rank **—***v.* 1 to make healthy 2 make accustomed (*to*) **—con·di'tion·er** *n.*

con'dom *n.* covering for the penis, generally of rubber, worn during sexual intercourse

con·do·min'i·um *n.* separately owned unit in a multiple-unit dwelling: also **con'do'**

con·done' *v.* forgive or overlook

con'duct' (*v.*: kən dukt') *n.* 1 management 2 behavior **—***v.* 1 to lead 2 manage 3 to direct 4 behave (oneself) 5 transmit, as electricity **—con·duc'tion** *n.*

cone *n.* 1 pointed, tapered figure with circular base 2 woody fruit of evergreens

con·fed'er·a·cy *n., pl.* **-cies** league **—[C-]** South in the Civil War

con·fed'er·ate (-ət; *v.*: -āt') *a.* united; allied **—***n.* 1 an ally 2 accomplice **—***v.* unite; ally

con·fer' *v.* **-ferred'** 1 give 2 meet to discuss **—con'fer·ence** *n.*

con·fess' *v.* 1 admit (a crime) 2 affirm (a faith) 3 tell (one's sins) **—con·fes'sion** *n.*

con·fide' *v.* 1 trust (*in*) 2 share as a secret

con'fi·dence *n.* 1 trust 2 assurance 3 self-reliance 4 a sharing of a secret **—con'fi·dent** *a.*

con'fi·den'tial (-shal) *a.* 1 secret 2 entrusted with private matters

con·fine' (*v.*: kən fīn') *n.* limit: *used in pl.* **—***v.* 1 restrict 2 to shut up, as in prison

con·firm' *v.* 1 to strengthen 2 approve formally 3 prove to be true 4 admit to membership in a church **—con'fir·ma'tion** *n.*

con·fis'cate *v.* seize legally

con'flict' (*n.*: kän'flikt') *v.* be in opposition **—***n.* 1 a fight 2 sharp disagreement

con·form' *v.* 1 be in agreement 2 act according to rules, customs, etc. **—con·form'ist** *n.*

con·found' *v.* confuse

con·front' *v.* 1 face boldly 2 bring face to face **—con'fron·ta'tion** *n.* **—con'fron·ta'tion·al** *a.*

con·fuse' *v.* 1 mix up 2 bewilder **—con·fu'sion** *n.*

con·gen'ial *a.* friendly; agreeable **—con·ge'ni·al'i·ty** *n.*

con·gen'i·tal *a.* existing from birth

con·gest' *v.* fill too full, as with blood **—con·ges'tion** *n.*

con·grat'u·late *v.* rejoice with (a fortunate person)

con·grat'u·la'tions *n.pl.* expressions of pleasure over another's good luck, etc.

con'gre·ga'tion *n.* assembly of people, esp. for worship

con'gress *n.* 1 assembly 2 legislature, esp. **[C-]** of the U.S. **—con·gres'sion·al** *a.* **—con'gress·man** *n., pl.* **-men —con'gress·per'son** *n.* **—con'gress·wom'an** *n.fem., pl.* **-wom'en**

con'i·fer (kän'ə-, kō'nə-) *n.* cone-bearing tree

con'ju·gate *v.* give the inflectional forms of (a verb)

con·junc'tion *n.* 1 a joining together; union 2 an occurring together 3 word used to join words, clauses, etc.

con·jure *v.* 1 practice magic 2 entreat 3 cause to appear, etc. as by magic

con·nect' *v.* 1 join; link 2 show or think of as related

con·nec'tion *n.* 1 a connecting or being connected 2 thing that connects 3 relation

con·nive' *v.* 1 pretend not to look (*at* crime, etc.) 2 cooperate secretly in wrongdoing

con·nois·seur (kän'ə sur') *n.* expert, esp. in the fine arts

con·note' v. suggest in addition to the explicit meaning

con'quer (-kər) v. defeat; overcome —**con'quer·or** n. —**con'quest'** n.

con'science (-shəns) n. sense of right and wrong

con'sci·en'tious (-shē-) a. scrupulous; honest

con'scious (-shəs) a. 1 aware (of or that) 2 able to feel and think; awake 3 intentional

con'se·crate' v. 1 set apart as holy 2 devote

con·sec'u·tive a. following in order without a break

con·sent' v. agree —n. agreement or approval

con'se·quence' n. 1 a result 2 importance

con·serv'a·tive a. 1 opposed to change 2 cautious —n. conservative person

con·serve' v. keep from being damaged, lost, etc. —**con'ser·va'tion** n.

con·sid'er v. 1 think over 2 keep in mind 3 have regard for 4 believe to be —**con·sid'er·ate** (-ət) a. —**con·sid'er·a'tion** n.

con·sid'er·a·ble a. large or important

con·sid'er·ing prep. taking into account

con·sist' v. be made up (of)

con·sist'en·cy n., pl. -cies 1 thickness, as of a liquid 2 agreement 3 uniformity of action —**con·sist'ent** a.

con·sole' v. comfort; cheer up

con·sol'i·date' v. unite

con'so·nant n. letter for a breath-blocked sound, as p, t, l, etc. —a. in harmony

con·spic'u·ous a. 1 easy to see 2 outstanding

con·spire' v. join in a plot —**con·spir'a·cy** n.

con'sta·ble n. policeman

con'stant a. 1 not changing; fixed 2 faithful 3 continual —n. unchanging thing —**con'stan·cy** n. —**con'stant·ly** adv.

con'stel·la'tion n. group of fixed stars

con·stit'u·ent n. 1 necessary part 2 voter

con'sti·tu'tion n. 1 structure; makeup 2 basic laws of a government, etc., esp. [C-] of the U.S. —**con'sti·tu'tion·al** a.

con·strain' v. force or restrain

con·struct' v. build; devise

con·struc'tion n. 1 a constructing 2 structure 3 explanation

4 arrangement of words

con'sul n. government official in a foreign city looking after his country's business there

con·sult' v. 1 confer 2 ask the advice of 3 consider —**con·sult'ant** n. —**con'sul·ta'tion** n.

con·sume' v. 1 destroy 2 use up 3 eat or drink up

con·sump'tion n. 1 a consuming 2 using up of goods 3 amount used up 4 tuberculosis of the lungs

con·tact' n. 1 a touching 2 being in touch (with) 3 connection —v. 1 place in contact 2 get in touch with

contact lens n. tiny, thin lens worn on the eye to improve vision

con·tain' v. 1 have in it 2 be able to hold 3 restrain

con·tam'i·nate' v. make impure; pollute —**con·tam'i·na'tion** n.

con'tem·plate' v. 1 to watch intently 2 meditate 3 intend —**con'tem·pla'tion** n.

con·tem'po·rar'y n., a., pl. -ries (one) living in the same period

con·tempt' n. 1 scorn 2 disgrace 3 disrespect shown for a judge, etc.

con·tend' v. 1 struggle 2 compete 3 assert

con·tent' a. satisfied: also **con·tent'ed** —n. satisfaction

con'tent' n. 1 pl. all that is contained 2 meaning 3 capacity

con·test' (n.: kän'test') v. 1 to dispute; question 2 fight for —n. 1 struggle 2 race, game, etc. —**con·test'ant** n.

con'ti·nent n. large landmass —**con'ti·nen'tal** a.

con·tin'u·al a. 1 repeated often 2 continuous

con·tin'ue v. 1 keep on; go on 2 endure; last 3 resume 4 extend 5 postpone

con·tin'u·ous a. without interruption; unbroken

con·tort' v. twist out of shape

con'tour n. outline of a figure, land, etc. —v. shape to contour —a. made to fit the contour of something

con'tra·band' n. smuggled goods

con'tra·cep'tion n. prevention of human conception —**con'tra·cep'tive** a., n.

con'tract' (v. 2, 3: kən trakt') n. legally valid agreement —v. 1 undertake by contract 2 get; incur 3 shrink —**con·trac'tor** n.

con·trac'tion n. 1 a contracting

2 shortened form

con·tra·dict' v. say or be the opposite of —**con'tra·dic'tion** n.

con'tra·ry a. 1 opposed; different 2 perverse —n. the opposite

con·trast' (n.: kän'trast') v. 1 compare 2 show difference —n. striking difference when compared

con·trib·ute v. 1 give, esp. to a common fund 2 furnish (an idea, article, etc.) —**con'tri·bu'tion** n. —**con·trib'u·tor** n.

con·trite' a. remorseful

con·trol' v. **-trolled'** 1 regulate (finances) 2 direct 3 restrain —n. 1 authority 2 means of restraint 3 pl. regulating mechanism —**con·trol'ler** n.

con'tro·ver·sy n. debate or dispute —**con'tro·ver'sial** (-shal) a.

con·tu'sion n. a bruise

con·va·les'cence n. (period of) recovery after illness

con·vene' v. assemble; meet

con·ven'ience n. 1 a being convenient 2 comfort 3 thing that saves work, etc.

con·ven'ient a. easy to do, use, or get to; handy

con'vent n. community of nuns or their living place

con·ven'tion n. 1 an assembly 2 custom; usage

con'ver·sa'tion n. informal talk

con·verse' v.: kän'vərs) v. 1 to talk —a. opposite —n. 1 conversation 2 the opposite

con·vert' (n.: kän'vurt') v. change in form, use, etc. or in religion —n. person who has converted —**con·ver'sion** n.

con·vex' (or kän'veks') a. curved outward like the outside of a sphere

con·vey' v. 1 carry 2 transmit

con·vict' (n.: kän'vikt') v. prove or find guilty —n. prisoner serving a sentence

con·vic'tion n. 1 a being convicted 2 strong belief

con·vince' v. make feel sure

con·vulse' v. shake as with violent spasms —**con·vul'sion** n.

coo v. make the soft sound of a pigeon or dove —n. this sound

cook v. boil, bake, fry, etc. —n. one who cooks —**cook'er·y** n.

cook'ie, cook'y n., pl. **-ies** small, sweet, flat cake

cool a. 1 moderately cold 2 not excited 3 unfriendly 4 [Sl.] very good —n. cool place, time, etc. —v. make or become cool —**cool'ly** adv. —**cool'ness** n.

coop n. pen for poultry

co-op n. [Col.] a cooperative

co·op'er·ate, co·öp'er·ate v. to work together —**co·op'er·a'tion, co·öp'er·a'tion** n.

co·op'er·a·tive, co·öp'er·a·tive a. cooperating —n. collective, profit-sharing enterprise

co·or'di·nate, co·ör'di·nate (-nət; v.: -nāt') a. equally important —v. to harmonize; adjust —**co·or'di·na'tion, co·ör'di·na'tion** n.

cop n. [Sl.] policeman

cope v. deal (with) successfully

cop'i·er n. person who copies or machine that makes copies

cop'per n. reddish-brown metal, a chemical element

cop'y n., pl. **-ies** 1 thing made just like another 2 one of many books, etc. all alike —v. **-ied** 1 make a copy of 2 imitate

cop'y·right' n. exclusive rights over a book, song, etc.

cor'al n. 1 hard mass of sea animal skeletons 2 yellowish red

cord n. 1 thick string 2 wood pile of 128 cu. ft. 3 insulated electric wire —**cord'less** a.

cor'dial (-jal) a. friendly

cor'du·roy n. ribbed cotton fabric

core n. 1 central part, as of an apple 2 most important part —v. remove the core of

cork n. 1 light, thick bark of a certain oak 2 stopper

corn n. 1 grain 2 grain that grows on large ears with a hard core (**corn'cob'**); maize 3 [Col.] trite humor 4 horny thickening of the skin

cor'ne·a n. clear, outer layer of the eyeball —**cor'ne·al** a.

cor'ner n. 1 place where lines or surfaces meet 2 a region 3 monopoly —v. 1 put into a difficult position 2 get a monopoly in

cor'net' n. brass instrument like a trumpet

cor'nice (-nis) n. molding along the top of a wall, etc.

cor'o·nar'y a. of the arteries supplying the heart

cor'o·na'tion n. crowning of a sovereign

cor'o·ner n. official who investigates unnatural deaths

cor'po·ral n. lowest ranking noncommissioned officer

cor'po·ra'tion n. group given legal status of an individual —**cor'po·rate** a.

corps (kôr) *n.* 1 organized group 2 large military unit

corpse *n.* dead body

cor·ral' *n.* pen for horses, etc.

cor·rect' *v.* 1 make right 2 mark errors of 3 punish —*a.* right, true, etc. —**cor·rec'tion** *n.* —**cor·rect'ly** *adv.*

cor're·late' *v.* bring into mutual relation —**cor're·la'tion** *n.*

cor're·spond' *v.* 1 be similar or equal to 2 communicate as by letters —**cor're·spond'ence** *n.*

cor'ri·dor *n.* long hall

cor·rode' *v.* wear away; rust —**cor·ro'sion** *n.*

cor·rupt' *a.* 1 rotten 2 evil 3 taking bribes —*v.* to make or become corrupt —**cor·rupt'i·ble** *a.* —**cor·rup'tion** *n.*

cor·sage' (-säzh') *n.* small bouquet worn by a woman

cor'tex *n.*, *pl.* **-ti·ces'** (-tə sēz') outer layer of the brain, kidney, etc. —**cor'ti·cal** *a.*

cos·met'ic *n.*, *a.* (preparation) for enhancing beauty

cos'mic *a.* 1 of the cosmos; orderly 2 vast; huge

cos'mos (-məs, -mōs') *n.* the universe seen as an orderly system

cost *v.* cost require the payment, etc. of —*n.* 1 price 2 loss; sacrifice —**at all costs** by any means whatever

cost'ly *a.* **-li·er, -li·est** expensive

cos'tume' *n.* 1 the dress of a people, period, etc. 2 set of outer clothes for some purpose

cot *n.* folding bed

cot'tage *n.* small house

cot'ton *n.* 1 plant with head of soft, white fibers 2 thread or cloth from this —**cot'ton·y** *a.*

cot'ton·wood' *n.* poplar having seeds covered with cottony fibers

cot'y·le'don (kät'ə lēd''n) *n.* first leaf produced by a plant embryo

couch *n.* piece of furniture to lie on —*v.* put in words

cough (kôf) *v.* expel lung air in a loud burst —*n.* 1 a coughing 2 condition of frequent coughing

could *v.* pt. of CAN: *could* is also used to show slightly more doubt than *can*

couldn't could not

coun'cil *n.* an advisory, administrative, or legislative body —**coun'cil·man** *n.*, *pl.* **-men** —**coun'cil·wom'an** *n.fem.*, *pl.* **-wom·en**

coun'sel *n.* 1 advice 2 lawyer(s) —*v.* to advise —**coun'se·lor** *n.*

count *v.* 1 add up to get a total 2 name numbers in order 3 include or be included 4 consider 5 be important —*n.* 1 a counting 2 total number 3 each charge in an indictment 4 nobleman —**count on** rely on

coun'te·nance *n.* 1 a facial expression 2 face

count'er *n.* long table for displaying goods, serving food, etc. —*adv.*, *a.* contrary —*v.* oppose

coun'ter·clock'wise' *adv.*, *a.* like the hands of a clock moving in reverse

coun'ter·feit' (-fit') *a.* made in imitation with intent to defraud —*n.* fraudulent imitation —*v.* 1 make counterfeits 2 pretend

count'ess *n.* wife or widow of a count or earl

count'less *a.* too many to count

coun'try *n.*, *pl.* **-tries** 1 region 2 nation 3 rural area —*a.* rural —**coun'try·side'** *n.*

coun'ty *n.*, *pl.* **-ties** subdivision of a State

cou'ple *n.* 1 a pair 2 engaged, married, etc. man and woman 3 [Col.] a few —*v.* join together

cou'pon' (kōo'-, kyōo'-) *n.* certificate, ticket, etc. redeemable for cash or gifts

cour'age *n.* fearless or brave quality —**cou·ra'geous** *a.*

course *n.* 1 path or channel 2 direction taken 3 regular mode of action 4 series 5 separate part of a meal 6 a study or series of studies —*v.* run —**of course** 1 naturally 2 certainly

court *n.* 1 an open space surrounded by buildings or walls: also **court'yard'** 2 playing area 3 royal palace 4 family, advisers, etc. of a sovereign 5 courtship 6 *Law a)* judge(s) *b)* place where trials are held (also **court'room'**) —*v.* woo

cour'te·sy *n.*, *pl.* **-sies** polite behavior or act —**cour'te·ous** *a.*

court'-mar'tial *n.*, *pl.* **courts'-mar'tial** or **court'-mar'tials** trial by a military or naval court —*v.* try by such a court

cous'in *n.* child of one's uncle or aunt

cove *n.* small bay

cov'e·nant *n.* agreement; compact

cov'er *v.* 1 place something over 2 extend over 3 conceal 4 protect 5 include; deal with —*n.* thing that covers —**take cover** seek shelter —**cov'er·ing** *n.*

cov'et v. desire ardently (what belongs to another)

cow n. mature female of the ox, or of the elephant, seal, etc.

cow'ard n. one lacking courage —**cow'ard·ly** a., adv.

coy a. shy or pretending to be shy —**coy'ly** adv.

coy·o·te (kī ōt'ē, kī'ōt') n. small prairie wolf

co'zy a. -zi·er, -zi·est warm and comfortable; snug

crab n. 1 shellfish with eight legs and two pincers 2 complainer

crack v. 1 make a sudden, sharp breaking noise 2 break without separation of parts 3 [Sl.] make (a joke) 4 solve —n. 1 sudden, sharp noise 2 incomplete break 3 sharp blow 4 [Col.] try 5 [Sl.] gibe 6 [Sl.] form of cocaine

crack'er n. thin, crisp wafer

crack'le v., n. (make) a series of slight, sharp sounds

cra'dle n. baby's bed on rockers

craft n. 1 skill; art 2 slyness 3 pl. **craft** boat or aircraft

crafts'man n., pl. -men skilled workman —**crafts'man·ship** n.

craft'y a. -i·er, -i·est sly; cunning

cram v. **crammed** 1 to stuff 2 study hurriedly for a test

cramp n. 1 painful contraction of a muscle 2 pl. intestinal pain

cran'ber·ry n., pl. -ries sour, edible, red berry

crane n. 1 long-legged wading bird 2 machine for lifting heavy weights —v. stretch (the neck)

crank n. 1 handle for turning a shaft 2 [Col.] an eccentric —v. start or work by a crank

crap n. [Sl.] 1 nonsense 2 junk

craps n.pl. dice game

crash v. 1 fall, break, drop, etc. with a loud noise 2 fail 3 [Col.] get into uninvited —n. 1 loud noise 2 a crashing 3 failure, as of business 4 coarse linen

crate n. wooden packing case

cra'ter n. bowl-shaped cavity or pit, as of a volcano

crave v. ask or long for

crawl v. 1 move slowly with flat on the ground 2 creep 3 swarm with crawling things

cray'fish', craw'fish' n. shellfish like a small lobster

cray'on n. small stick of chalk, wax, etc. for drawing

craze v. make or become insane —n. fad

cra'zy a. -zi·er, -zi·est insane, mad, etc. —**cra'zi·ly** adv.

creak v., n. squeak

cream n. 1 oily part of milk 2 creamy cosmetic 3 best part —v. beat till smooth as cream

cream'y a., -i·er, -i·est

crease n. line made by folding —v. make a crease in

cre·ate' v. make; bring about —**cre·a'tion** n. —**cre·a'tive** a. —**cre·a'tor** n.

crea'ture n. living being, animal or human

cred'it n. 1 belief; trust 2 reputation 3 praise or source of praise 4 trust that one will pay later 5 completed unit of study

cre'do (krē'dō, krā'-) n., pl. -dos' creed

creed n. statement of belief

creek n. small stream

creep v. **crept** 1 go on hands and knees 2 go slowly or stealthily 3 grow along the ground, etc. —n. [Sl.] disgusting person

cre'mate' v. burn (a dead body)

crepe, crêpe (krāp; n. 2: also krep) n. 1 thin, crinkled silk, rayon, etc. 2 a thin pancake, rolled and filled

cres'cent n. shape of a quarter moon

crest n. 1 tuft on an animal's head 2 heraldic device 3 top; summit

crev'ice n. narrow crack

crew n. group of workers, as the seamen on a ship

crib n. 1 box for fodder 2 baby's small bed 3 wood shed for grain

crick'et n. 1 leaping insect 2 ball game played with bats and wickets

crime n. 1 an act in violation of a law 2 sin

crim'i·nal a. of crime —n. person guilty of crime

crim'son n. deep red

cringe v. 1 shrink back as in fear 2 to fawn

crin'kle v. to wrinkle or rustle

crip'ple v. disable

cri'sis n., pl. -ses' (-sēz') 1 turning point 2 crucial situation

crisp a. 1 brittle 2 clear 3 fresh; bracing

criss'cross' n. crossed lines —v. 1 mark with crisscross 2 move crosswise —adv. crosswise

crit'ic n. 1 judge of books, art, etc. 2 faultfinder

crit'i·cal a. 1 finding fault 2 of critics or their work 3 being a crisis —**crit'i·cal·ly** adv.

crit'i·cize' v. 1 judge as a critic 2

find fault (with) —**crit'i·cism'** *n.*

crit'ter *n.* [Dial.] creature

croak *v., n.* (to make) a deep, hoarse sound

cro·chet' (-shā') *v.* knit with one hooked needle

crock *n.* earthenware jar

croc'o·dile' *n.* large reptile of tropical streams

cro'cus *n.* small plant of the iris family

crois·sant (krə sänt') *n.* a crescent-shaped bread roll

crook *n.* 1 a bend or curve 2 [Col.] swindler

crook'ed *a.* 1 not straight 2 dishonest

croon *v.* sing in a soft tone

crop *n.* 1 saclike part of a bird's gullet 2 farm product, growing or harvested 3 group 4 riding whip

cro·quet' (-kā') *n.* game with hoops in the ground through which balls are hit

cro·quette' (-ket') *n.* small mass of meat, fish, etc. deep-fried

cross *n.* 1 upright post with another across it 2 figure of this, symbolic of Christianity 3 any affliction 4 mark made by intersecting lines, bars, etc. 5 hybrid —*v.* 1 place, go, or lie across 2 go (*over*) to the other side 3 intersect 4 draw a line across 5 thwart 6 interbreed —*a.* 1 lying or passing across 2 irritable —**cross'ing** *n.* —**cross'·ness** *n.*

cross'-coun'try *a.* across open country, as a race

cross'-eyed' *a.* having the eyes turned toward the nose

cross'wise' *adv.* across

crotch *n.* place where branches or legs fork

crouch *v., n.* stoop with legs bent low

crow *n.* 1 large, black bird with a harsh call 2 rooster's cry —*v.* 1 make a rooster's cry 2 exult

crowd *v.* to throng, press, cram, etc. —*n.* a mass of people

crown *n.* 1 head covering of a monarch 2 power of a monarch 3 top part, position, quality, etc. —*v.* 1 make a monarch of 2 honor 3 be atop 4 climax

cru'cial (-shəl) *a.* 1 decisive 2 trying

cru'ci·fix' *n.* representation of Jesus on the cross

cru'ci·fy' *v.* -**fied'** execute by suspending from a cross

crude *a.* 1 raw; unprocessed 2 rough or clumsy —**cru'di·ty,** **crude'ness** *n.*

cru'el *a.* causing suffering; pitiless —**cru'el·ty** *n.*

cruise *v.* travel about, as by ship —*n.* voyage

crumb *n.* small piece, as of bread; bit

crum'ble *v.* break into crumbs —**crum'bly** *a.,* **-bli·er,** **-bli·est**

crum'ple *v.* to crush into wrinkles

crunch *v.* chew or crush with a crackling sound —**crunch'y** *a.,* **-i·er,** **-i·est**

cru·sade' *v., n.* (to engage in) united action for some idea or cause —**cru·sad'er** *n.*

crush *v.* 1 press out of shape 2 pound into bits 3 subdue —*n.* 1 a crushing 2 crowded mass 3 [Col.] infatuation

crust *n.* 1 hard outer part of bread, earth, etc. 2 dry piece of bread

crutch *n.* support held under the arm to aid in walking

cry *v.* **cried** 1 utter loudly 2 sob; weep —*n., pl.* **cries** 1 a shout 2 entreaty 3 call of a bird, etc.

crypt (kript) *n.* underground (burial) vault

crys'tal *n.* 1 clear quartz 2 clear, brilliant glass 3 solidified substance with its molecules arranged symmetrically

cub *n.* young bear, lion, etc.

cube *n.* 1 a solid with six equal, square sides 2 product obtained by multiplying a number by its square —*v.* 1 get the CUBE (*n.* 2) of 2 cut into cubes —**cu'bic** *a.*

cuck·oo (kōo'kōo') *n.* brown, slender bird —*a.* [Sl.] crazy

cud *n.* food regurgitated by cattle and chewed again

cud'dle *v.* hold or lie close and snug —**cud'dly** *a.*

cue *n.* 1 signal to begin 2 hint 3 rod for striking a billiard ball —*v.* to signal

cuff *n.* 1 band or fold at the wrist of a sleeve or the bottom of a trouser leg 2 a slap

cull *v.* pick over; select

cul'prit *n.* one accused, or found guilty, of a crime

cult *n.* system of worship or group of worshipers

cul'ti·vate' *v.* 1 prepare (land) for crops 2 grow (plants) 3 develop, as the mind

cul'ture *n.* 1 animal or plant breeding 2 training of the mind, taste, etc. 3 civilization of a people or period —**cul'tur·al** a.

cum'ber·some a. unwieldy

cun'ning a. 1 sly; crafty 2 pretty —n. craft

cup n. small bowl with handle, for beverages —v. **cupped** shape like a cup —**cup'ful'** n., pl. **-fuls'**

cup·board (kub'ərd) n. cabinet for dishes, food, etc.

cup'cake' n. small cake

curb n. 1 chain or strap on a horse's bit for checking the horse 2 thing that restrains 3 edging along a street —v. to restrain

curd n. coagulated part of soured milk

cur'dle v. form curd

cure n. 1 a healing 2 remedy —v. 1 make well; heal 2 remedy 3 preserve (meat) —**cur'a·ble** a.

cur'few' n. evening deadline for being off the streets

cu'ri·ous a. 1 eager to know; inquisitive 2 strange

curl v. 1 twist (hair, etc.) into ringlets 2 curve around; coil —n. 1 ringlet of hair 2 any curling —**curl'er** n. —**curl'y** a., **-i·er**, **-i·est**

cur'rant n. 1 small, seedless raisin 2 sour berry

cur'ren·cy n., pl. **-cies** 1 money circulated in a country 2 general use; prevalence

cur'rent a. 1 of this day, week, etc. 2 commonly accepted or known —n. flow of air, water, electricity, etc.

cur'ry n. spicy powder or sauce —v. **-ried** brush the coat of (a horse, etc.)

curse v. **cursed** or **curst** 1 call or bring evil down on 2 swear (at) —n. 1 a cursing 2 evil or injury —**curs'ed** a.

cur'sive (-siv) a. of writing with joined letters

cur'sor n. movable indicator light on a computer screen

curt a. so brief as to be rude

cur·tail' v. cut short

cur'tain n. piece of cloth hung, as at a window, to decorate or conceal

curve n. line, surface, etc. having no straight part —v. form or move in a curve —**cur'va·ture** n.

cush'ion n. 1 pillow or pad 2 something absorbing shock

cus'tard n. pudding made with eggs, milk, and sugar

cus'to·dy n. 1 guarding; care 2 imprisonment —**cus·to'di·al** a.

cus'tom n. 1 usual or traditional practice; usage 2 pl. duties on imported goods —a. made to order: also **cus'tom-made'**

cus'tom·ar·y a. usual

cus'tom·er n. one who buys

cut v. **cut** 1 gash 2 pierce 3 sever 4 hew 5 reap 6 trim 7 pass across 8 reduce 9 [Col.] snub —n. 1 a cutting 2 part cut open or off 3 reduction 4 style 5 plate engraved for printing 6 insult 7 [Col.] share, as of profits —**cut and dried** dull; boring

cute a. [Col.] 1 clever 2 pretty or pleasing

cu'ti·cle (kyōōt'-) n. hardened skin, as at the base and sides of a fingernail

cut'let n. small slice of meat from the ribs or leg

cy'a·nide' n. poisonous white compound

cy'cle n. 1 complete round of regular events, or period for this 2 bicycle, tricycle, etc. —v. ride a bicycle, etc. —**cy'clic, cy·cli·cal** a. —**cy'clist** n.

cy'clone' n. storm with heavy rain and whirling winds

cyl'in·der n. round figure with two flat ends that are parallel circles —**cy·lin'dri·cal** a.

cym'bals n.pl. pair of round brass plates struck together for a ringing sound

cyn'ic n. one inclined to question goodness, sincerity, etc.

cy'press n. evergreen tree

cyst (sist) n. sac containing fluid or hard matter —**cyst'ic** a.

czar (zär) n. 1 Russian emperor 2 an autocrat

D

dab v. **dabbed** put on with light, quick strokes —n. soft or moist bit —**dab'ber** n.

dab'ble v. 1 splash in water 2 do something superficially: (with *in* or *at*) —**dab'bler** n.

dachs'hund (däks'ənd) n. small dog with a long body

dad n. [Col.] father: also **dad'dy**

daf'fo·dil' n. yellow flower

dag'ger n. 1 a short, sharp-pointed weapon 2 printed reference mark (†)

dai'ly a., adv. (done or happening) every day

dain'ty a. **-ti·er**, **-ti·est** 1 delicately pretty 2 fastidious —**dain'ti·ly** adv. —**dain'ti·ness** n.

dair'y n., pl. **-ies** place where milk, butter, etc. are made or sold —**dair′y·man** n., pl. **-men**

dai′sy n., pl. **-sies** flower with white rays around a yellow disk

dam n. 1 barrier to hold back flowing water 2 female parent of a horse, cow, etc. —v.

dammed keep back; confine

dam′age n. 1 injury; harm 2 pl. money paid for harm done —v. do damage to

damn v. **damned** condemn; declare bad, doomed, etc. —a., adv. [Col.] damned

damned a. 1 condemned 2 [Col.] outrageous —adv. [Col.] very

damp n. 1 moisture 2 mine gas —a. slightly wet; moist —v. 1 moisten 2 check or deaden

dance v. move in rhythm to music —n. 1 rhythmic movement to music 2 party or music for dancing —**danc′er** n.

dan·de·li·on n. common weed with yellow flowers

dan′druff n. little scales of dead skin on the scalp

dan′ger n. 1 liability to injury, loss, etc.; peril 2 thing that may cause injury, etc. —**dan′ger·ous** a.

dan′gle v. hang loosely

dap′ple a. spotted; mottled: also **dap′pled** —v. mottle

dare v. 1 have the courage (to) 2 challenge —n. a challenge —**dar′ing** a., n.

dare say think probable —**dar′ing** a., n.

dark a. 1 with little or no light 2 not light in color 3 gloomy 4 ignorant —n. a being dark —**dark′en** v. —**dark′ness** n.

dar′ling n., a. beloved

darn v. mend by sewing

dart n. 1 small pointed weapon for throwing 2 sudden movement —v. 1 smash 2 strike violently against 3 do hastily: (with off) 4 rush —n. 1 bit of something 2 short race 3 vigor 4 mark of punctuation (—)

da·ta (dāt′ə, dat′-) n. facts; information

da·ta·base n. large mass of organized data in a computer

date n. 1 time of an event 2 day of the month 3 social engagement 4 fruit of a tall palm —v. 1 mark with a date 2 belong to a particular time

daugh′ter n. female as she is related to her parents

daugh′ter-in-law′ n., pl. **daugh′ters-** wife of one's son

daunt v. 1 frighten 2 dishearten

daw′dle v. waste time; loiter

dawn v. 1 begin to be day 2 begin to be understood —n. 1 daybreak 2 beginning

day n. 1 period from sunrise to sunset 2 period of 24 hours, esp. from midnight to midnight 3 a period; era —**day′light′** n. —**day′time′** n.

day′break′ n. time of the first light in the morning

day care n. daytime care for children or adults —**day′-care′** a.

day′dream′ n. pleasant, dreamy thinking or wishing

daylight saving(s) time n. time one hour later than standard

daze v. 1 stun 2 dazzle

daz′zle v. overpower with light or brilliance

dea′con n. one who assists a minister

dead a. 1 not living 2 dull; inactive 3 complete —n. time of most cold, darkness, etc.

dead′en v. to dull

dead′line′ n. time limit

dead′lock′ n. standstill with equal forces opposed

dead′ly a. **-li·er, -li·est** 1 fatal 2 as or until death

deaf a. 1 unable to hear 2 unwilling to respond —**deaf′en** v.

deal v. **dealt** (delt) 1 distribute 2 have to do (with) 3 do business —n. transaction or agreement —**a good (or great) deal** 1 large amount 2 very much —**deal′er** n. —**deal′ing** n.

dear a. 1 much loved 2 esteemed 3 costly 4 earnest —n. darling

death n. 1 a dying or being dead 2 cause of death

death′ly a. characteristic of death —adv. extremely

de·bate′ v. argue in a formal way —n. formal argument

deb′it n. entry in an account of money owed —v. enter as a debit

de·bris′ (də brē′) n. broken, scattered remains; rubbish

debt (det) n. 1 something owed 2 state of owing

debt′or n. one owing a debt

de·but′ (dā bycō′, də-) n. 1 first public appearance, as of an actor 2 a formal introduction into society

dec′ade′ n. ten-year period

de·caf′fein·at·ed (-kaf′ə nāt′-) having its caffeine removed

de·cay' v. 1 fall into ruin 2 rot —n. a decaying; rot

de·cease' n. death

de·ceased' a. dead

de·ceit' n. 1 act of deceiving 2 deceiving quality —**de·ceit'ful** a.

de·ceive' v. make believe what is not true; mislead

De·cem'ber n. 12th month

de'cent a. 1 proper 2 respectable 3 adequate —**de'cen·cy** n.

de·cep'tion n. 1 a deceiving 2 illusion or fraud —**de·cep'tive** a.

de·cide' v. 1 settle by passing judgment 2 make up one's mind

de·cid'u·ous (-sij'ōō-) a. shedding leaves annually

dec'i·mal a. based on the number ten —n. a fraction with a denominator of ten or a power of ten, shown by a point (**deci·mal point**) before the numerator

de·ci'sion n. 1 a deciding 2 judgment 3 determination

deck n. 1 floor of a ship 2 pack of playing cards —v. adorn; trim

de·clare' v. 1 announce formally 2 say emphatically —**dec'la·ra'tion** n. —**de·clar'a·tive** a.

de·cline' v. 1 slope downward 2 lessen, as in force 3 refuse politely 4 Gram. give inflected forms of —n. 1 a failing, decay, etc. 2 downward slope

de·code' v. translate (a coded message) into plain language

de·com·pose' v. 1 break up into basic parts 2 rot

dé·cor, de·cor (dā kôr') n. decorative scheme

dec'o·rate' v. 1 adorn; ornament 2 give a medal to —**dec'o·ra'tive** a. —**dec'o·ra'tor** n.

de·coy' n. artificial bird, etc. used as a lure —v. lure

de·crease' (or dē'krēs') v. grow or make less or smaller —n. a decreasing

de·cree' n. official order; edict —v. -creed' order by decree

ded'i·cate' v. 1 set apart formally 2 devote 3 inscribe

de·duct' v. subtract or take away

de·duc'tion n. 1 a deducing or deducting 2 amount deducted 3 conclusion

deed n. 1 act 2 feat of courage, etc. 3 legal document transferring property

deep a. 1 extending far down, in, or back 2 hard to understand 3 involved (in) 4 of low pitch 5 intense —n. deep place

or part —adv. far down, etc.

deer n., pl. **deer** hoofed, cud-chewing animal, the male of which bears antlers

de·face' v. mar

de·fault' v., n. fail(ure) to do or pay as required

de·feat' v. 1 win victory over 2 frustrate —n. a defeating or being defeated

de'fect (v.: dē fekt') n. imperfection; fault —v. to desert

de·fend' v. 1 protect 2 support by speech or act 3 Law act for (an accused) —**de·fend'er** n.

de·fend'ant n. Law person sued or accused

de·fense' n. 1 a defending against attack 2 something that defends 3 defendant and his counsel —**de·fen'sive** a., n.

de·fer' v. -ferred' 1 postpone 2 to yield in opinion, etc.

de·fi'ance n. open resistance to authority —**de·fi'ant** a.

de·fi'cien·cy (-fish'ən-) n., pl. -cies shortage; lack —**de·fi'cient** a.

def'i·cit n. amount by which a sum of money is less than expected, etc.

de·fine' v. 1 mark the limits of 2 state the meaning of —**defi·ni'tion** n.

def'i·nite a. 1 having exact limits 2 explicit 3 certain

de·flate' v. 1 collapse by letting out air 2 lessen in amount, importance, etc. —**de·fla'tion** n.

de·for'est v. clear (land) of trees or forest —**de·for'est·a'tion** n.

de·form' v. mar the form of —**de·form'i·ty** n., pl. -ties

de·fraud' v. cheat

deft a. quick and skillful

de·fuse' v. 1 remove a fuse from 2 make less tense, etc.

de·fy' v. -fied' 1 resist openly 2 dare

de·gen'er·ate' (-āt'; a.: -at) v. lose normal or good qualities —a. deteriorated —**de·gen'er·a·cy** n. —**de·gen'er·a'tion** n.

de·gree' n. 1 successive step in a series 2 intensity, extent, etc. 3 rank given to a college graduate 4 unit of measure, as for angles, temperature, etc.

de·hu'man·ize' v. deprive of human qualities

de·hy'drate' v. remove water from —**de·hy·dra'tion** n.

deign (dān) v. condescend

de'i·ty n., pl. -ties god or goddess

de·ject'ed a. sad; depressed

de·lay' v. put off; postpone 1 make late; detain —n. a delaying

del'e·gate (-gət; v.: -gāt') n. representative —v. 1 appoint as delegate 2 entrust to another

del'e·ga'tion n. group of delegates

de·lete' v. take out (a word, etc.) —**de·le'tion** n.

de·lib'er·ate (-ãt'; a.: -ət) v. consider carefully —a. 1 done on purpose 2 not rash or hasty 3 unhurried —**de·lib'er·a'tion** n.

del'i·ca·cy n. 1 delicate quality 2 pl. **-cies** a choice food; dainty

del'i·cate a. 1 fine and lovely 2 fragile or frail 3 needing care 4 sensitive 5 considerate and tactful —**del'i·cate·ly** adv.

de·light' v. please greatly —n. great pleasure —**de·light'ful** a.

de·lin'quent a. 1 not obeying duty or law 2 overdue —n. one guilty of minor crimes —**de·lin'quen·cy** n.

de·lir'i·um n. 1 temporary mental illness 2 wild excitement

de·liv'er v. 1 set free; rescue 2 assist in birth 3 utter 4 hand over 5 distribute 6 strike or throw —**de·liv'er·ance** n.

del'ta n. 1 letter of Greek alphabet 2 soil deposit at a river mouth

de·lude' v. mislead

del'uge (-yōōj') n. 1 great flood 2 heavy rainfall

de·luxe' a. very good; elegant

dem'a·gogue, dem'a·gog (-gäg') n. one who appeals to prejudices, etc. to win power

de·mand' v. 1 ask for boldly 2 require —n. 1 strong request 2 requirement

de·mar·ca'tion n. boundary line

de·mean' v. degrade

de·mean'or n. behavior

de·mer'it n. 1 fault 2 mark for poor work, etc.

de·mise' (-mīz') n. death

de·moc'ra·cy n., pl. **-cies** 1 government in which the power is vested in all the people 2 equality of rights, etc. —**dem'o·crat'** n. —**dem'o·crat'ic** a. —**dem'o·crat'i·cal·ly** adv.

de·mol'ish v. destroy; ruin —**dem'o·li'tion** n.

de'mon n. devil; evil spirit

dem'on·strate' v. 1 prove 2 explain with examples 3 show the working of 4 show feelings publicly —**dem'on·stra'tion** n. —**dem'on·stra'tor** n.

de·mote' v. reduce in rank

den n. 1 animal's lair 2 haunt of thieves, etc. 3 small, cozy room

de·ni'al n. 1 a denying 2 contradiction

den'im n. coarse, twilled cotton cloth

de·nom'i·na'tion n. 1 a name 2 specific class or kind 3 religious sect —**de·nom'i·na'tion·al** a.

de·nom'i·na'tor n. term below the line in a fraction

de·note' v. 1 indicate 2 mean explicitly —**de·no·ta'tion** n.

de·nounce' v. 1 accuse publicly 2 condemn strongly

dense a. 1 packed tightly 2 thick 3 stupid —**dense'ly** adv.

dent n. slight hollow made in a surface by a blow

den'tal a. of the teeth

den'tist n. one who cares for and repairs teeth —**den'tis·try** n.

den'ture n. often pl. set of artificial teeth

de·ny' v. 1 declare untrue 2 refuse to give, accept, etc.

de·o'dor·ize' v. counteract the odor of —**de·o'dor·ant** n., a.

de·part' v. 1 leave 2 die 3 deviate (from) —**de·par'ture** n.

de·part'ment n. 1 division 2 field of activity

de·pend' v. 1 be determined by something else 2 rely, as for support —**de·pend'ence** n. —**de·pend'ent** a., n.

de·pend'a·ble a. reliable

de·pict' v. 1 represent by drawing, etc. 2 describe

de·plore' v. be sorry about

de·port' v. 1 behave (oneself) 2 expel (an alien)

de·pos'it v. 1 place for safekeeping 2 give as partial payment 3 set down —n. something deposited —**de·pos'i·tor** n.

de'pot (-pō) n. 1 warehouse 2 train or bus station

de·prave' v. make morally bad

de·pre'ci·ate' (-shē-) v. 1 lessen in value 2 belittle

de·press' v. 1 press down 2 sadden 3 lower in value, etc. —**de·pres'sant** a., n. —**de·pressed'** a.

de·pres'sion n. 1 a depressing 2 hollow place 3 dejection 4 period of reduced business and prosperity

de·prive' v. take away or withhold from —**dep'ri·va'tion** n.

depth n. 1 distance from the top or back 2 deepness 3 profundity 4 pl. deepest part

dep·u·ty *n., pl.* **-ties** substitute or agent

de·rail *v.* run off the rails

de·range *v.* 1 upset or disturb 2 make insane

der·e·lict *a.* 1 abandoned 2 negligent —*n.* thing or person abandoned as worthless

de·ride *v.* to ridicule —**de·ri'sion** (-rizh'ən) *n.*

de·rive *v.* 1 take or get (*from*) 2 deduce 3 originate 4 trace to a source —**der·i·va'tion** *n.*

der·ma·tol'o·gy *n.* study of the skin and its diseases

de·rog'a·to·ry *a.* detracting; disparaging

der·rick *n.* 1 machine for moving heavy objects 2 framework for drilling, as over an oil well

de·scend' (-send') *v.* 1 move down 2 come from earlier times 3 derive 4 make a sudden attack (on) —**de·scent'** *n.*

de·scend·ant *n.* offspring of a certain ancestor

de·scribe' *v.* 1 picture in words; tell about 2 trace the outline of —**de·scrip'tion** *n.* —**de·scrip'tive** *a.*

de·sert' *v.* abandon —*n. often pl.* reward or punishment —**de·ser'tion** *n.*

des'ert *n.* arid, sandy region

de·serve' *v.* be worthy of) —**de·serv'ing** *a.*

de·sign' *v.* 1 to plan 2 contrive —*n.* 1 plan; scheme 2 purpose 3 a pattern —**de·sign'er** *n.*

des'ig·nate *v.* 1 to point out; specify 2 appoint

de·sire' *v.* wish or long for; want —*n.* 1 a wish 2 thing wished for 3 sexual appetite —**de·sir'a·ble** *a.* —**de·sir'a·bly** *adv.*

de·sist' *v.* stop; cease

desk *n.* writing table

des'o·late (-lət, *v.;* -lāt') *a.* 1 lonely; forlorn 2 uninhabited 3 laid waste —*v.* make desolate

de·spair' *v.* lose hope —*n.* loss of hope

des'per·ate *a.* 1 reckless from despair 2 serious

de·spise' *v.* to scorn 2 loathe

de·spite' *prep.* in spite of

de·spon'den·cy *n.* loss of hope; dejection —**de·spond'ent** *a.*

des'pot *n.* tyrant —**des·pot'ic** *a.*

des·sert' *n.* sweet dish ending a meal

des·ti·na'tion *n.* place to which one is going

des'ti·ny *n., pl.* **-nies** (one's) fate

des'ti·tute *a.* needy

de·stroy' *v.* 1 tear down; demolish 2 ruin 3 kill

de·stroy'er *n.* fast warship

de·struc'tion *n.* ruin —**de·struc'tive** *a.*

de·tach' *v.* unfasten and remove —**de·tach'a·ble** *a.*

de·tail' (*or* dē'tāl) *v.* 1 tell minutely 2 *Mil.* choose for a special task —*n.* 1 minute account 2 small part 3 *Mil.* special task

de·tain' *v.* 1 keep in custody 2 delay —**de·ten'tion** *n.*

de·tect' *v.* discover (thing hidden, etc.) —**de·tec'tor** *n.*

de·tec'tive *n.* one who investigates crimes, etc.

de·ter' *v.* **-terred'** keep someone from an action

de·ter'gent *a., n.* cleansing (substance)

de·te'ri·o·rate (-tir'ē-) *v.* make or become worse

de·ter'mi·na'tion *n.* 1 firm intention 2 firmness of purpose

de·ter'mine *v.* 1 set limits to 2 decide; resolve 3 to find out exactly —**de·ter'mined** *a.*

de·test' *v.* hate —**de·test'a·ble** *a.*

de'tour' *n.* 1 (use) an indirect or alternate road

de·tract' *v.* take something desirable (*from*) —**de·trac'tor** *n.*

det'ri·ment *n.* damage; harm —**det'ri·men'tal** *a.*

de·val'ue *v.* lessen the value of

dev·as·tate *v.* destroy; ravage

de·vel'op *v.* 1 grow, improve, expand, etc. 2 work out by degrees 3 treat (film) to make the picture visible —**de·vel'op·ment** *n.* —**de·vel'op·men'tal** *a.*

de'vi·ant *n., a.* (person) deviating from social norms

de'vi·ate *v.* turn aside; diverge

de·vice' *n.* 1 a plan or scheme 2 mechanical contrivance 3 a design

dev'il *n.* 1 evil spirit; esp., [*often* D-] Satan 2 wicked or reckless person —*v.* 1 to season (food) highly 2 tease —**dev'il·ish** *a.*

de'vi·ous *a.* roundabout

de·vise' *v.* 1 to plan 2 bequeath by will

de·vote' *v.* 1 dedicate 2 apply to a purpose

de·vot'ed *a.* 1 dedicated 2 loyal

de·vo'tion *n.* 1 a devoting 2 *pl.* prayers 3 loyalty

de·vour' *v.* 1 eat up hungrily 2 take in eagerly

de·vout' *a.* pious or sincere

dew *n.* atmospheric moisture

condensing on cool surfaces at night —**dew'y** *a.*, **-i·er**, **-i·est**

di·a·be·tes (-bēt'ēz, -is) *n.* disease marked by excess sugar in the blood and urine —**di·a·bet'ic** *a.*

di·ag·no·sis *n.* identifying of a disease —**di·ag·nos'tic** *a.*

di·ag·o·nal *a.* slanting between opposite corners —*n.* a diagonal line

di·a·gram *n.*, *v.* sketch, plan, etc. to help explain

di·al *n.* 1 face of a clock, meter, etc. for indicating some variable 2 rotating disk, or numbered buttons, on a telephone

di·a·lect *n.* form of speech peculiar to a region, group, etc.

di·a·logue *n.* conversation

di·am·e·ter *n.* 1 straight line through the center of a circle, etc. 2 its length

di·a·mond (dī'mənd, dī'ə-) *n.* 1 precious gem of great brilliance 2 figure shaped like ◇ 3 baseball field

di·a·per (dī'pər, dī'ə-) *n.* cloth worn about a baby's crotch —*v.* to put a diaper on

di·a·phragm (-fram') *n.* 1 wall of muscle between chest and abdomen 2 vibrating disk producing sound waves 3 vaginal contraceptive

di·ar·rhe·a (-rē'ə) *n.* very loose bowel movements

di·a·ry *n.*, *pl.* **-ries** daily record of personal notes

dice *n.pl.*, *sing.* **die** small, spotted cubes, used in gambling —*v.* cut into cubes

dic'tate' *v.* 1 speak (something) for another to write down 2 command —**dic·ta'tion** *n.*

dic·ta'tor *n.* an absolute ruler; tyrant —**dic'ta·to'ri·al** *a.*

dic'tion *n.* 1 choice of words 2 enunciation

dic'tion·ar'y *n.*, *pl.* **-ies** book of words alphabetically listed and defined

did *v.* pt. of DO

die *v.* **died** 1 stop living 2 to end 3 [Col.] wish very much —*n.* 1 sing. of DICE 2 device for molding, stamping, etc.

die·sel (dē'zəl, -səl) *n.* [often D-] internal-combustion engine that burns fuel oil

di'et *n.* 1 one's usual food 2 special food taken as for health

dif'fer *v.* 1 to be different or unlike 2 disagree

dif'fer·ence *n.* 1 a being unlike 2 distinguishing characteristic 3 disagreement 4 amount by which two quantities differ

dif'fer·ent *a.* 1 not alike 2 distinct 3 unusual

dif'fi·cult' *a.* hard to do, learn, deal with, etc. —**dif'fi·cul·ty** *n.*, *pl.* **-ties**

dig *v.* **dug** 1 turn up (soil), as with a spade 2 make or get by digging

di·gest' (*v.*: di jest') *n.* summary —*v.* 1 to change (food) in the stomach, etc. so that it can be absorbed 2 absorb mentally —**di·gest'i·ble** *a.* —**di·ges'tion** *n.*

dig'it (dij'-) *n.* 1 any number from 0 to 9 2 a finger or toe

dig'i·tal *a.* 1 of a digit 2 showing time, temperature, etc. in a row of digits 3 designating a recording method in which sounds or images are converted into electronic bits 4 of a computer processing data by electronic means

dig'ni·ty *n.* 1 worthiness 2 high repute; honor 3 calm stateliness

dike *n.* embankment to hold back the sea, etc.

di·lem'ma *n.* perplexing situation

dil'i·gent *a.* careful and industrious —**dil'i·gence** *n.*

di·lute' *v.* weaken as by mixing with water —**di·lu'tion** *n.*

dim *a.* **dim'mer**, **dim'mest** not bright or clear

dime *n.* silver coin equal to ten cents

di·men'sion *n.* 1 any measurable extent 2 *pl.* measurement in length, breadth, and, often, height

dim'ple *n.* small, natural hollow, as on the cheek

din *n.* confused clamor

dine *v.* 1 eat dinner 2 give dinner to

din'er *n.* 1 railroad car for serving meals 2 restaurant built like this

ding *n.* sound of a bell: also **ding'-dong'**

din·ghy (diŋ'gē) *n.*, *pl.* **-ghies** small boat

din·gy (din'jē) *a.* **-gi·er**, **-gi·est** dirty; shabby

din'ner *n.* chief daily meal

di'no·saur *n.* huge extinct reptile

dint *n.* force: now chiefly in **by dint of**

di'o·cese (-sis, -sēz') *n.* district headed by a bishop

dip v. **dipped 1** plunge into liquid for a moment **2** scoop up **3** sink or slope down —n. **1** a dipping **2** sauce into which food may be dipped **3** downward slope

di·plo·ma n. certificate of graduation from a school

di·plo·ma·cy n. **1** the conducting of relations between nations **2** tact —**dip'lo·mat'** a.

dire a. **1** dreadful; terrible **2** urgent

di·rect' a. **1** straight **2** frank **3** immediate **4** exact —v. **1** manage; guide **2** order **3** aim —adv. in a direct way —**di·rect'ly** adv. —**di·rec'tor** n.

di·rec'tion n. **1** management; guidance **2** pl. instructions **3** an order **4** the point one faces or moves toward

di·rec'to·ry n., pl. **-ries** book of names and addresses of a specific group

dirt n. **1** dust, filth, etc. **2** earth; soil

dirt'y a. **-i·er, -i·est 1** soiled **2** obscene **3** mean **4** unfair **5** rough —**dirt'i·ness** n.

dis·a'ble v. make unable or unfit; cripple —**dis·a·bil'i·ty** n., pl. **-ties**

dis·ad·van'tage n. drawback; handicap; detriment

dis·ad·van'taged a. poor

dis·a·gree' v. **1** differ **2** quarrel **3** give distress: with with

dis·ap·pear' v. **1** go out of sight **2** cease being —**dis·ap·pear'ance** n.

dis·ap·point' v. spoil the hopes of

dis·ap·prove' v. **1** have an unfavorable opinion **2** reject

dis·arm' v. **1** remove weapons from **2** make friendly —**dis·ar'ma·ment** n.

dis·as'ter n. sudden misfortune; calamity —**dis·as'trous** a.

dis·burse' v. pay out

disc n. **1** disk **2** phonograph record, etc.

dis·card' (n.: dis'kärd') v. throw away —n. thing discarded

dis·cern' v. perceive —**dis·cern'i·ble** a.

dis·charge' (n.: dis'chärj') v. **1** dismiss **2** unload **3** shoot **4** emit **5** do (a duty) —n. a discharging or thing discharged

dis·ci'ple n. follower; pupil

dis'ci·pline n. **1** orderly training or conduct **2** punishment —v. **1** train; control **2** punish —**dis'ci·pli·nar'y** a.

dis·close' v. to reveal

dis·col'or v. to stain; tarnish

dis·com'fort n. lack of comfort or cause of this

dis'con·nect' v. to separate

dis'con·tent' n. dissatisfaction

dis'con·tin'ue v. to stop

dis'count (v.: also dis kount') v. **1** deduct, as from a price **2** disregard in part or entirely —n. deduction

dis·cour'age v. **1** deprive of hope or confidence **2** dissuade **3** work against

dis'course n. talk or formal lecture —v. to talk

dis·cour'te·ous a. impolite —**dis·cour'te·sy** n.

dis·cov'er v. **1** be the first to find, see, etc. **2** find out —**dis·cov'er·y** n., pl. **-ies**

dis·cred'it v. **1** disbelieve **2** cast doubt on **3** disgrace —n. **1** doubt **2** disgrace

dis·creet' a. careful; prudent

dis·crete' a. separate; distinct

dis·crim'i·nate v. **1** distinguish **2** show partiality —**dis·crim'i·na'tion** n.

dis·cuss' v. talk or write about —**dis·cus'sion** n.

dis·dain' v., n. scorn

dis·ease' n. (an) illness —**dis·eased'** a.

dis'en·chant' v. disillusion

dis'en·gage' v. disconnect

dis'en·tan'gle v. extricate

dis·fig'ure v. spoil the looks of; mar —**dis·fig'ure·ment** n.

dis·grace' n. shame; dishonor —v. to bring shame upon —**dis·grace'ful** a.

dis·guise' v. make unrecognizable —n. thing, as clothing or makeup, used for disguising

dis·gust' n. sickening dislike; loathing —v. cause disgust in

dish n. **1** plate, etc. for food **2** kind of food

dis·hon'est a. not honest —**dis·hon'es·ty** n.

dis·hon'or n., v. shame; disgrace

dis·il·lu'sion v. **1** to free from illusion **2** make disappointed

dis'in·fect' v. kill bacteria in

dis·in'te·grate' v. separate into parts; break up

dis·in'ter·est·ed a. **1** impartial **2** indifferent

disk n. **1** thin, flat, circular thing **2** thin plate for storing computer data **3** disc

disk·ette' n. floppy disk

dis·like' v., n. (have) a feeling of not liking

dis·lodge' v. force from its place

dis·loy'al a. not loyal —**dis·loy'al·ty** n.

dis'mal a. dreary

dis·may' v. make afraid; daunt —n. loss of courage

dis·mem'ber v. tear apart

dis·miss' v. 1 request or allow to leave 2 discharge 3 set aside —**dis·miss'al** n.

dis·mount' v. 1 get off 2 take from its mounting

dis'o·bey' v. refuse or fail to obey —**dis'o·be'di·ence** n.

dis·or'der n. 1 confusion 2 commotion 3 ailment —v. to cause disorder in —**dis·or'der·ly** a.

dis·or'gan·ize' v. throw into confusion —**dis·or'gan·i·za'tion** n.

dis·own' v. refuse to acknowledge as one's own

dis·patch' (n. 2, 3: also dis'pach') v. 1 send 2 finish quickly 3 kill —n. 1 speed 2 message 3 news story —**dis·patch'er** n.

dis·pense' v. 1 deal out 2 prepare and give out —**dispense with** do without —**dis'pen·sa'tion** n. —**dis·pens'er** n.

dis·perse' v. scatter

dis·place' v. 1 move from its usual place 2 replace

dis·play' v. to show; exhibit —n. exhibition

dis·please' v. annoy; offend

dis·pose' v. 1 arrange 2 incline mentally —**dispose of** 1 settle 2 get rid of —**dis·pos'a·ble** a. —**dis·pos'al** n. —**dis'po·si'tion** n.

dis·pro·por'tion n. lack of proportion

dis·prove' v. prove false

dis·pute' v., n. 1 debate 2 quarrel —**in dispute** not settled

dis·qual'i·fy' v. -fied' make ineligible —**dis·qual'i·fi·ca'tion** n.

dis·re·gard' v. ignore —n. lack of attention

dis·re·spect' n. lack of respect

dis·rupt' v. break up; disorder —**dis·rup'tion** n. —**dis·rup'tive** a.

dis·sat'is·fy' v. -fied' make discontented

dis·sect' (or di'sekt') v. 1 cut apart so as to examine 2 analyze closely —**dis·sec'tion** n.

dis·sent' v. disagree —n. difference of opinion

dis'si·pate' v. 1 vanish or dispel 2 squander

dis·solve' v. 1 melt 2 pass or make pass into solution 3 break up 4 end 5 disappear or make disappear

dis'tance n. 1 length between two points 2 aloofness 3 faraway place

dis'tant a. 1 far apart; remote 2 aloof

dis·taste' n. dislike

dis·tend' v. swell

dis·tinct' a. 1 not alike 2 separate 3 definite

dis·tinc'tion n. 1 a keeping distinct 2 quality that differentiates 3 fame; eminence

dis·tin'guish v. 1 perceive or show a difference 2 classify 3 make famous —**dis·tin'guish·a·ble** a. —**dis·tin'guished** a.

dis·tort' v. 1 twist out of shape 2 misrepresent —**dis·tor'tion** n.

dis·tract' v. 1 divert (the mind, etc.) 2 confuse 3 derange

dis·tress' v., n. pain, trouble, worry, etc.

dis·trib'ute v. 1 deal out 2 spread out 3 arrange

dis'trict n. 1 division of a state, etc. 2 region

dis·trust' n. lack of trust

dis·turb' v. 1 break up the quiet or settled order of 2 make uneasy 3 interrupt —**dis·turb'ance** n.

ditch n. channel dug out for drainage, etc. —v. [Sl.] get rid of

dit'to mark n. mark (") in lists showing the item above is to be repeated: also **dit'to,** pl. **-tos**

dive v. **dived** or **dove, dived** 1 plunge into water 2 plunge suddenly or deeply —n. 1 sudden plunge 2 [Col.] cheap saloon

di·verge' v. 1 branch off 2 deviate

di·verse' a. 1 different 2 varied

di·ver'si·ty n. variety

di·vert' v. 1 turn aside (from) 2 amuse

di·vide' v. 1 separate into parts 2 apportion 3 Math. separate into equal parts by a divisor —n. ridge —**di·vis'i·ble** (-viz'-) a.

div'i·dend' n. 1 number to be divided 2 sum divided among stockholders, etc.

di·vine' a. 1 of God or a god 2 supremely good —n. clergyman

di·vin'i·ty n. 1 a being divine 2 pl. **-ties** a god

di·vi'sion n. 1 a dividing 2 thing that divides 3 segment, group, etc. 4 section of an army corps

di·vi'sor n. number by which the dividend is divided

di·vorce' n. 1 legal dissolution of a marriage 2 separation —v. separate from, as by divorce

di·vor·cée' (-sā') *n.* divorced woman —**di·vor·cé'** (-sā') *n.masc.*

diz'zy *a.* **-zi·er, -zi·est** 1 giddy; confused 2 causing dizziness

DNA *n.* basic material of chromosomes that transmits hereditary pattern

do *v.* **did, done** 1 perform (an action) 2 finish 3 cause 4 deal with as required 5 have as one's work 6 get along 7 be adequate *Do* is also an auxiliary verb — **do's** (or **dos**) **and don'ts** [Col.] things permitted and things forbidden —**do'er** *n.*

dock *n.* 1 landing pier; wharf 2 water between piers 3 place for the accused in a courtroom —*v.* 1 bring or come to a dock 2 cut short 3 deduct from

doc'tor *n.* 1 person with the highest degree from a university 2 physician or surgeon

doc'trine *n.* something taught, as a religious tenet

doc'u·ment *n.* written record relied on as evidence —*v.* to support by documents

dodge *v.* 1 move quickly aside 2 avoid; evade

do'do *n.* 1 large extinct bird 2 [Sl.] stupid person

doe *n.* female deer, rabbit, etc.

does (duz) *v.* pres. t. of DO: used with *he, she,* or *it*

dog *n.* 1 domesticated animal of the wolf family 2 mean fellow

dog'ged *a.* stubborn

dog'ma *n.* strict doctrine

dog'wood' *n.* tree with pink or white flowers

dole *n.* money paid to the unemployed by the government: with *the* —*v.* give (*out*) sparingly

doll *n.* child's toy made to resemble a person

dol'lar *n.* U.S. monetary unit, equal to 100 cents

dol'ly *n., pl.* **-lies** 1 [Col.] doll 2 low, wheeled frame for moving heavy objects

dol'phin *n.* sea mammal with a beaklike snout

dolt *n.* stupid person

do·main' *n.* 1 territory under one ruler 2 field of activity

dome *n.* large, round roof

do·mes'tic *a.* 1 of home or family 2 of one's country 3 tame —*n.* a maid, cook, etc. — **do·mes'ti·cal·ly** *adv.*

do·mes'ti·cate' *v.* to tame

dom'i·nate' *v.* 1 rule or control 2 to rise high above —**dom'i-**

nance *n.* —**dom'i·nant** *a.*

do·min'ion *n.* 1 rule; power 2 governed territory

dom'i·noes', dom'i·nos' *n.* game with tiles marked with dots

don *v.* **donned** put on (clothes)

do'nate' *v.* give; contribute —**do·na'tion** *n.*

done (dun) *v.* pp. of DO

don'key *n., pl.* **-keys** horselike animal with long ears

do'nor *n.* one who donates

doom *n.* 1 a judgment 2 fate 3 ruin —*v.* 1 condemn 2 destine to a tragic fate

door *n.* 1 movable panel for closing an entrance 2 entrance, with or without a door: also **door'way'**

dope *n.* 1 [Col.] narcotic 2 [Col.] information 3 [Col.] stupid person —*v.* to drug

dor'mant *a.* 1 sleeping 2 quiet; inactive

dor'mer *n.* an upright window structure in a sloping roof

dor'mi·to'ry *n., pl.* **-ries** 1 room with many beds 2 building with many bedrooms Also **dorm**

dose *n.* amount of medicine taken at one time —*v.* to give doses to —**dos'age** *n.*

dot *n.* tiny mark or round spot

dote *v.* be too fond

dou'ble *a.* 1 of or for two 2 twice as much or as many — *adv.* twofold or twice —*n.* 1 twice as much or as many 2 a duplicate 3 *Baseball* hit putting the batter on second —*v.* 1 make or become double 2 fold 3 duplicate 4 turn backward 5 serve two purposes, etc.

double bass (bās) *n.* largest, deepest-toned instrument of violin family

dou'ble-cross' *v.* [Col.] to betray

dou'bly *adv.* twice

doubt (dout) *v.* 1 be uncertain about 2 to disbelieve —*n.* 1 wavering of belief 2 uncertainty —**no doubt** certainly

dough (dō) *n.* 1 thick mixture of flour, liquid, etc. for baking 2 [Sl.] money

dough'nut' *n.* small, fried cake, usually ring-shaped

douse (dous) *v.* 1 thrust into liquid 2 drench 3 [Col.] extinguish (a light)

dove (dōv) *v.* alt. pt. of DIVE

dove (duv) *n.* kind of pigeon

down *adv.* 1 to or in a lower place, state, etc. 2 to a later time 3 in cash 4 in writing —*a.*

1 descending **2** in a lower place **3** gone, paid, etc. down **4** discouraged —*prep.* down toward, into, along, etc. —*v.* put down —*n.* **1** descent **2** misfortune **3** soft feathers or hair **4** *pl.* high, grassy land

down'cast' *a.* **1** directed downward **2** sad

down'fall' *n.* sudden fall, as from power

down'heart'ed *a.* sad

down'hill' *adv., a.* down a slope; downward

down'right' *adv.* thoroughly —*a.* **1** utter **2** plain

down'spout' *n.* pipe for carrying rainwater from roof gutter

down'stairs' *adv., a.* to or on a lower floor or floors —*n.* lower floor or floors

down'-to-earth' *a.* sensible

down'town' *n.* city's business district

down'ward *adv., a.* toward a lower place, etc.

doze *v., n.* sleep; nap

doz'en *n.* set of twelve

drab *a.* drab'ber, drab'best dull

draft *n.* **1** drink **2** rough sketch of a writing **3** plan **4** current of air **5** written order for money **6** selection for compulsory military service **7** depth of water a ship displaces —*v.* **1** select to serve **2** make a plan, outline, etc. for —*a.* drawn from a cask

drag *v.* **dragged 1** pull or be pulled with effort, esp. along the ground **2** search (a river bottom, etc.) as with a net **3** pass slowly

drag'on *n.* large, mythical reptile breathing out fire

drag'on-fly' *n., pl.* **-flies'** long insect with two wings

drain *v.* **1** draw off (liquid, etc.) gradually **2** empty **3** exhaust, as energy **4** flow off —*n.* channel; pipe

dra'ma *n.* **1** a play **2** art of writing and staging plays

dra·mat'ic *n.* **1** of drama **2** vivid, exciting, etc.

dram'a·tize' *v.* **1** make into a drama **2** regard or show in a dramatic manner

drape *v.* cover or hang as with cloth in loose folds —*n.* curtain: *usually used in pl.*

drap'er·y *n., pl.* **-ies** curtain

dras'tic *a.* severe; harsh

draught (draft) *n., v., a.* draft

draw *v.* **drew, drawn 1** pull **2** attract **3** inhale **4** take out; get

5 come; move **6** write (a check) **7** deduce **8** stretch **9** make (lines, pictures, etc.) as with a pencil

draw'bridge' *n.* bridge that can be raised

drawer (drôr) *n.* **1** sliding box in a table, etc. **2** *pl.* underpants

drawl *n.* slow, prolonged manner of speech —*v.* to speak with a drawl

dread *v.* await with fear or distaste —*n.* fear —**dread'ful** *a.*

dream *n.* **1** images, etc. seen during sleep **2** fond hope —*v.* **dreamed** or **dreamt** (dremt) have dreams

drear'y *a.* **-i·er, -i·est** dismal

dredge *n.* apparatus for scooping up mud, etc. as in deepening channels —*v.* **1** enlarge with a dredge **2** gather (*up*) as with a dredge **3** sprinkle with flour

drench *v.* soak

dress *v.* **1** clothe **2** adorn **3** treat (a wound, etc.) **4** prepare (a fowl, etc.) by skinning, etc. —*n.* **1** clothes **2** woman's garment

dress'er *n.* chest of drawers with a mirror

dress'ing *n.* **1** bandages, etc. **2** salad sauce **3** stuffing for roast fowl

drift *v.* be carried along, as by a current —*v.* **1** snow, etc. driven into a heap **2** trend **3** meaning

drill *n.* **1** tool for boring **2** systematic training **3** seeding machine **4** coarse, twilled cloth —*v.* **1** bore with a drill **2** train systematically —**dril'er** *n.*

drink *v.* **drank, drunk** swallow (liquid) —*n.* **1** liquid for drinking **2** alcoholic liquor

drip *v.* **dripped** fall or let fall in drops —*n.* a dripping

drive *v.* **drove, driv·en** (driv'-) **1** force to go, do, pierce, etc. **2** operate, or go in, a vehicle —*n.* **1** trip in a vehicle **2** paved road **3** energy **4** urge **5** campaign —**drive at** to mean —**driv·er** *n.*

drive'way' *n.* path for cars

driz'zle *v., n.* rain in fine, mistlike drops

droll *a.* quaintly amusing

drone *n.* **1** male honeybee **2** constant hum —*v.* **1** to hum **2** talk monotonously

drool *v.* drip saliva

droop *v.* **1** sink or bend down **2** lose vitality —*n.* a drooping

drop *n.* **1** small, round mass, as of falling liquid **2** tiny amount

3 sudden fall **4** distance down —v. **dropped 1** fall or let fall **2** to send **3** utter (a hint, etc.) —**drop in** visit —**drop out** stop taking part —**drop'per** n.

drop'let n. very small drop

drop'out n. student who leaves school before graduating

drought (drout) n. spell of dry weather

drown v. **1** die or kill by suffocation in water **2** muffle (sound, etc.): with out

drowse v. be sleepy; doze — **drows'y** a., -i-er, -i-est

drudge n. one who does hard or dull work —v. do such work

drug n. **1** medicinal substance **2** narcotic

drug'gist n. pharmacist —**drug' store'** n.

drum n. **1** hollow form covered with a membrane and used as a percussion instrument **2** container, as for oil **3** eardrum —v. **drummed** beat as on a drum — **drum'mer** n.

drunk v. pp. of DRINK —a. overcome by alcohol —n. [Sl.] drunken person —**drunk'ard** n.

drunk'en a. intoxicated

dry a. **dri'er, dri'est 1** not wet **2** lacking rain **3** thirsty **4** not sweet **5** matter-of-fact **6** dull —v. **dried** to make or become dry —**dry'ly** adv.

dry'-clean' v. to clean (garments) with a solvent instead of water —**dry cleaner** n.

dry ice n. carbon dioxide in a solid state

du'al a. **1** of two **2** double

dub v. **dubbed 1** confer a title upon **2** insert (dialogue, etc.) in film soundtrack

duch'ess n. duke's wife

duck n. **1** flat-billed, webfooted swimming bird **2** cloth like canvas but lighter —v. **1** dip under water briefly **2** bend suddenly, as to avoid a blow **3** [Col.] avoid

duck'ling n. young duck

duct n. tube or channel for fluid

due a. **1** owed **2** suitable **3** expected to arrive —adv. exactly —n. anything due —**due to 1** caused by **2** [Col.] because of

due bill n. receipt for money paid, exchangeable for goods, etc. only

du'el n. planned formal fight between two armed persons

du-et' n. musical composition for two performers

duke n. nobleman next in rank to a prince —**duke'dom** n.

dul'ci-mer (-sə-) n. stringed musical instrument

dull a. **1** stupid **2** sluggish **3** boring **4** not sharp **5** not bright —v. make or become dull —**dul'ly** adv.

du'ly adv. properly

dumb a. **1** unable to talk **2** silent **3** [Col.] stupid

dum'my n., pl. **-mies 1** humanlike figure for displaying clothes **2** imitation **3** [Sl.] stupid person —a. sham

dump v. **1** unload in a heap **2** throw away —n. a place for dumping rubbish

dump'ling n. **1** piece of boiled dough **2** crust filled with fruit

dump truck n. truck with tilting container for unloading

dun a. dull grayish-brown —v. **dunned** to demand money owed

dunce n. stupid person

dune n. hill of drifted sand

dung n. animal excrement

dun'geon (-jən) n. dark underground prison

dunk v. **1** dip (food) into coffee, etc. **2** Basketball thrust (the ball) into the basket

dupe n. person easily tricked —v. deceive

du'pli-cate (-kət; v.: -kāt') a. **1** double **2** exactly alike —n. exact copy —v. **1** make a copy **2** make happen again —**du'pli-ca'tion** n. —**du'pli-ca'tor** n.

du'ra-ble a. lasting a long time

du-ra'tion n. time that a thing continues or lasts

du-ress' n. coercion

dur'ing prep. **1** throughout **2** in the course of

dusk n. evening twilight

dust n. finely powdered matter, esp. earth —v. **1** sprinkle with powder **2** wipe dust from — **dust'y** a., -i-er, -i-est

du'ty n., pl. **-ies 1** respect owed, as to parents **2** sense of obligation, justice, etc. **3** thing one must do **4** tax, as on imports

dwarf n. unusually small being or thing —v. **1** stunt in growth **2** make seem small —a. stunted

dwell v. **dwelt** or **dwelled** make one's home

dwin'dle v. decrease

dye n. coloring matter in solution —v. **dyed** to color with a dye —**dy'er** n.

dy-nam'ic a. **1** of energy **2** energetic; forceful

dy·na·mite' n. powerful explosive —v. blow up with dynamite

dy·nas·ty n., pl. **-ties** family line of rulers

dys·func'tion n. abnormal functioning —**dys·func'tion·al** a.

dys·lex'i·a n. impairment of reading ability

E

each a., pron. every one of two or more —adv. apiece

ea'ger a. keenly desiring

ea'gle n. large bird of prey with sharp vision

ear n. 1 organ of hearing 2 sense of hearing 3 attention 4 grain-bearing spike of a cereal plant

ear'drum' n. thin membrane inside the ear

earl n. Br. nobleman

ear'ly adv., a. **-li·er, -li·est** 1 near the beginning 2 before the expected or usual time

earn v. 1 receive for one's work 2 get as deserved 3 gain as profit

ear'nest a. serious or sincere

earn'ings n.pl. 1 wages 2 profits, interest, etc.

ear'ring n. ear ornament

earth n. 1 the planet we live on 2 land 3 soil

earth'quake' n. a shaking of the crust of the earth

ease n. 1 comfort 2 poise 3 facility —v. 1 to comfort 2 relieve 3 facilitate 4 shift carefully

ea'sel n. a stand to hold an artist's canvas

eas'i·ly adv. 1 with ease 2 without a doubt

east n. 1 direction in which sunrise occurs 2 region in this direction —[E—] the Orient —a., adv. in, toward, or from the east —**east'er·ly** a., adv. —**east'ern** a. —**east'ern·er** n. —**east'ward** a., adv. —**east'wards** adv.

eas'y a. **-i·er, -i·est** 1 not difficult 2 without worry, pain, etc. 3 comfortable 4 not stiff 5 not strict 6 unhurried —adv. [Col.] easily

eat v. **ate, eat'en** 1 chew and swallow (food) 2 wear away, corrode, etc. 3 make by eating

eaves n.pl. projecting edge of a roof

ebb n. 1 flow back toward the sea: said of the tide 2 decline

ec·cen'tric (ek sen'-) a. 1 hav-

ing its axis off center 2 odd in conduct —n. eccentric person

ec·cle'si·as'ti·cal a. of the church or clergy

ech·o (ek'ō) n., pl. **-oes** repetition of a sound by reflection of sound waves —v. 1 resound 2 repeat

e·clipse' n. the obscuring of the sun by the moon, or of the moon by the earth's shadow —v. surpass

e·col'o·gy n. science dealing with organisms in their environment —**e·co·log'i·cal** a.

ec·o·nom'ic (or ē'kə-) a. 1 of the management of income, expenditures, etc. 2 of economics

ec·o·nom'i·cal a. thrifty

ec·o·nom'ics n. science that deals with the production, distribution, and use of wealth —**e·con'o·mist** n.

e·con'o·my n., pl. **-mies** 1 management of finances 2 thrift 3 system of producing and consuming wealth

ec'o·sys'tem (or ē'kō-) n. community of animals, plants, etc.

ec·sta·sy n., pl. **-sies** overpowering joy —**ec·stat'ic** a.

edge n. 1 blade's cutting side 2 brink 3 border 4 [Col.] advantage —v. 1 put an edge on 2 move sideways —**on edge** tense

ed'i·ble a. fit to be eaten

ed'it v. 1 revise, select, etc. (writing) for publication 2 be in charge of (a newspaper, etc.) 3 prepare (film, etc.) by cutting, etc. —**ed'i·tor** n.

e·di'tion n. 1 form in which a book is published 2 total copies of a book, etc. published at one time

ed'i·to'ri·al n. article in a newspaper, etc. stating the opinions of the editor or publisher —a. of an editor —**ed'i·to'ri·al·ize'** v.

ed'u·cate' v. develop the knowledge, skill, etc. of by schooling —**ed'u·ca'tion** n.

eel n. snakelike fish

ee·rie (ir'ē) a. **-ri·er, -ri·est** mysterious; uncanny —**ee'ri·ly** adv.

ef·fect' n. 1 a result 2 influence 3 meaning 4 pl. belongings —v. bring about —**in effect** 1 actually 2 in operation

ef·fec'tive a. 1 producing a desired result 2 in operation

ef·fi'cient a. effective with a minimum of effort, expense, etc. —**ef·fi'cien·cy** n.

ef'fort n. 1 use of energy to do

something 2 attempt

egg n. 1 oval body from which young of birds, fish, etc. are hatched 2 ovum —v. to urge on

egg'plant' n. large, purple, pear-shaped vegetable

e'go n. 1 the self 2 conceit

e'go·ism' n. 1 selfishness 2 conceit —**e'go·ist** n. —**e·go·is'tic** a.

e'go·tism' n. 1 excessive reference to oneself 2 conceit —**e'go·tist** n. —**e·go·tis'tic, e·go·tis'ti·cal** a.

eight a., n. one more than seven —**eighth** a., n.

eight'een' a., n. eight more than ten —**eight'eenth'** a., n.

eight'y a., n., pl. -ies eight times ten —**eight'i·eth** a., n.

ei'ther (ē'-, ī'-) a., pron. one or the other (of two) —con. connecting word used with or —adv. any more than the other

e·ject' v. throw out; expel

eke (ēk) v. barely manage to make (a living): with out

e·lab'o·rate' (-rāt'; a.: -rət) v. add details —a. in great detail

e·las'tic a. springing back to shape —n. band, etc. with rubber in it —**e·las·tic'i·ty** (-tis'-) n.

e·late' v. make proud, happy, etc.

el'bow' n. joint between the upper and lower arm

eld'er a. older —n. 1 older person 2 church official 3 shrub with dark berries

eld'er·ly a. somewhat old

eld'est a. oldest

e·lect' v. select, esp. by voting —**e·lec'tion** n.

e·lec'tive a. 1 filled by election 2 optional

e·lec'tor n. 1 qualified voter 2 member of the electoral college —**e·lec'tor·al** a.

e·lec'tric, e·lec'tri·cal a. of, charged with, or worked by electricity

e·lec·tri'cian (-trish'ən) n. one who installs and repairs electrical apparatus

e·lec·tric'i·ty (-tris'-) n. 1 form of energy with magnetic, chemical, and radiant effects 2 electric current

e·lec'tri·fy v. -fied' 1 equip for the use of electricity 2 thrill

e·lec'tro·cute' v. kill by electricity —**e·lec'tro·cu'tion** n.

e·lec'trode' n. terminal of an electric source

e·lec'tro·mag'net n. soft iron core made magnetic by an electric current

e·lec'tron' n. negatively charged particle in an atom —**e·lec'tron'ic** a.

electronic mail n. messages sent to and from computer terminals, as by telephone lines

e·lec'tron'ics n. science dealing with the action of electronics

el'e·gant a. tastefully luxurious

el'e·ment n. 1 natural environment 2 basic part or feature 3 Chem. substance that cannot be separated into different substances except by nuclear disintegration —**the elements** wind, rain, etc. —**el·e·men'tal** a.

el'e·men'ta·ry a. of fundamentals; introductory

elementary school n. school of the first six (or eight) grades

el'e·phant n. huge, thick-skinned mammal with a long trunk and ivory tusks

el'e·vate' v. 1 raise 2 raise in rank 3 elate

el·e·va'tion n. 1 high place 2 height, as above sea level

el'e·va'tor n. 1 suspended cage for hoisting or lowering goods or people 2 warehouse for grain

e·lev'en a., n. one more than ten —**e·lev'enth** a., n.

elf n., pl. **elves** small fairy

el'i·gi·ble a. qualified —n. eligible person —**el·i·gi·bil'i·ty** n.

e·lim'i·nate' v. 1 remove 2 excrete —**e·lim·i·na'tion** n.

e·lite (ā lēt') n. best or most powerful part of a group

elk n. large deer

el·lip'sis n. 1 omission of a word or words 2 mark (...) showing this

elm n. tall shade tree

e·lon'gate v. lengthen

e·lope' v. run away to marry

el'o·quent a. vivid or forceful in expression —**el'o·quence** n.

else a. 1 different; other 2 in addition —adv. 1 otherwise 2 if not

else'where' adv. in or to some other place

e·lu'sive a. hard to grasp; baffling

e'mail' n. electronic mail

em'a·nate' v. come or issue

e·man'ci·pate' v. set free —**e·man'ci·pa'tion** n.

em·balm' (-bäm') v. preserve (a dead body)

em·bank'ment n. bank of earth, etc. as to keep back water

em·bar'go n., pl. -goes legal restriction of commerce or shipping

em·bark' v. 1 go aboard a ship 2 begin; start

em·bar'rass v. cause to feel self-conscious

em'bas·sy n., pl. **-sies** staff or headquarters of an ambassador

em·bed' v. **-bed'ded** set firmly (in)

em·bel'lish v. 1 decorate 2 add details, often untrue

em'ber n. glowing piece of coal or wood

em·bez'zle v. steal (money entrusted)

em'blem n. visible symbol; sign

em·bod'y v. **-ied** 1 give form to 2 include —**em·bod'i·ment** n.

em·brace' v. 1 hug lovingly 2 adopt, as an idea 3 include —n. an embracing

em·broi'der v. ornament with needlework —**em·broi'der·y** n., pl. **-ies**

em·bry·o' (-brē-) n., pl. **-os'** animal or plant in earliest stages of development —**em·bry·on'ic** a.

em'er·ald n. green jewel

e·merge' v. come out; appear

e·mer'gen·cy n., pl. **-cies** sudden occurrence demanding quick action

em'i·grate' v. leave one country to settle in another —**em'i·grant** a., n. —**em'i·gra'tion** n.

em'i·nent a. prominent or high

e·mit' v. **e·mit'ted** 1 send out; discharge 2 utter —**e·mis'sion** n. —**e·mit'ter** n.

e·mo'tion n. strong feeling, as of love, fear, anger, etc.

em'pa·thy n. ability to share another's feelings

em'per·or n. ruler of an empire —**em'press** n.fem.

em'pha·sis n., pl. **-ses'** (-sēz') stress; importance 2 stress on a syllable

em'pha·size' v. to stress

em'pire' n. group of countries under one sovereign

em·ploy' v. 1 use 2 keep busy 3 hire or have as workers

em·ploy·ee' (-ē) n. person working for another for pay

em·ploy'er n. one who employs others for pay

em·ploy'ment n. 1 an employing or being employed 2 work; occupation

emp'ty a. **-ti·er, -ti·est** 1 with nothing or no one in it 2 worthless —v. **-tied** 1 make or become empty 2 pour out

en·a'ble v. make able

en·act' v. 1 pass, as a law 2 act out

en·am'el n. 1 glassy coating fused to metal 2 white coating of teeth 3 hard, glossy paint

en·chant' v. charm; delight

en'chi·la'da (-lä'-) n. tortilla rolled with meat inside

en·cir'cle v. surround

en·close' v. 1 surround; shut in 2 insert in an envelope —**en·clo'sure** n.

en·code' v. put (a message) into code

en'core' (än'-) int. again! —n. song, etc. added by demand

en·coun'ter v. 1 meet unexpectedly 2 fight —n. 1 unexpected meeting 2 fight

en·cour'age v. 1 give courage or hope to 2 help

en·cy·clo·pe'di·a n. book or set of books on one or all branches of knowledge

end n. 1 last part; finish 2 destruction 3 tip 4 purpose —v. finish; stop —a. final —**end'ing** n.

en·dan'ger v. put in danger

en·deav'or (-dev'-) v. try hard —n. earnest attempt

end'less a. 1 eternal; infinite 2 lasting too long 3 with the ends joined to form a ring

en·dorse' v. 1 sign on the back of (a check) 2 approve

en·dow' v. 1 provide with some quality 2 give money to

en·dure' v. 1 stand (pain, etc.) 2 tolerate 3 last

en'e·my n., pl. **-mies** person or nation hostile to another; foe

en'er·gy n., pl. **-gies** 1 vigor; power 2 capacity to do work —**en'er·get'ic** a.

en·force' v. 1 impose by force 2 make people obey (a law) —**en·force'ment** n. —**en·forc'er** n.

en·gage' v. 1 bind by a promise of marriage 2 involve oneself 3 hire 4 attract and hold 5 enter into conflict with 6 interlock; mesh —**en·gaged'** a.

en·gine n. 1 a machine using energy to develop mechanical power 2 locomotive

en·gi·neer' n. 1 one trained in engineering 2 locomotive driver

en·gi·neer'ing n. practical use of sciences in industry, building, etc.

Eng'lish a., n. (of) the people or language of England

en·grave' v. cut (designs) on a metal plate, etc.), as for printing —**en·grav'er** n. —**en·grav'ing** n.

en·hance' v. make greater

en·joy' v. 1 get pleasure from 2 have the use of —**enjoy oneself** have a good time —**en·joy'a·ble** a. —**en·joy'ment** n.

en·large' v. make larger

en·light'en v. to free from ignorance, prejudice, etc.

en·list' v. 1 enroll in an army, etc. 2 engage in a cause

en·mi·ty n. ill will

e·nor'mi·ty n., pl. –ties 1 great wickedness 2 outrageous act

e·nor'mous a. huge; vast

e·nough' a., adv. as much as is needed —n. amount needed

en·rage' v. put into a rage

en·rich' v. make rich(er)

en·roll' v. put or be put in a list, as a member, etc. —**en·roll'ment** n.

en·sem·ble (än sem') n. 1 total effect 2 costume of matching parts 3 group of musicians playing together

en'sign (-sin; n. 2: -san) n. 1 flag 2 lowest-ranking navy officer

en·slave' v. make a slave of

en·tail' v. make necessary

en·tan'gle v. trap; confuse

en'ter v. 1 come or go in 2 put in a list, etc. 3 join 4 begin

en'ter·prise n. 1 important undertaking 2 energy and boldness

en'ter·tain' v. 1 amuse 2 act as host to 3 consider, as an idea —**en'ter·tain'er** n.

en·thrall' v. fascinate

en·thu'si·asm' n. eager interest —**en·thu'si·as'tic** a.

en·tice' v. tempt

en·tire' a. complete; whole —**en·tire'ly** adv. —**en·tire'ty** n.

en·ti'tle v. 1 give a title to 2 give a right to

en'trails n.pl. inner organs; spec., intestines

en'trance (v.: en trans') n. 1 act of entering 2 door, gate, etc. 3 permission to enter —v. to delight

en·treat' v. ask earnestly

en·tree (än'trā') n. main dish

en·trust' v. assign the care of (to)

en'try n., pl. –tries 1 entrance 2 item in a list, etc. 3 contestant

e·nu'mer·ate' v. name one by one —**e·nu'mer·a'tion** n.

e·nun'ci·ate' v. 1 to state 2 pronounce (words) clearly

en·ve·lope' n. covering, esp. for a letter

en·vi'ron·ment n. surroundings

—**en·vi'ron·men'tal** a.

en'voy (än'-, en'-) n. 1 messenger 2 diplomatic official

en'vy n. 1 discontent and ill will over another's advantages, etc. 2 object of such feeling —v. feel envy toward —**en'vi·ous** a.

en'zyme (-zim') n. a catalyst formed in body cells

ep'ic n. long poem about a hero's deeds —a. heroic

ep'i·cen'ter n. focal point, as of an earthquake

ep·i·dem'ic n. a. (disease) that spreads rapidly

ep·i·der'mis n. outermost layer of the skin

ep'i·lep'sy n. disease marked by convulsive fits, etc. —**ep·i·lep'tic** a., n.

ep'i·logue' (-lôg') n. part added at the end of a novel, play, etc.

e·pis'co·pal a. of or governed by bishops

ep'i·sode' n. incident

e·pis'tle (-pis'al) n. 1 letter 2 [E-] Bible letter of an Apostle

ep'i·taph' n. inscription on a tomb

ep'i·thet' n. word or phrase characterizing a person, etc.

ep'och (-ak) n. period marked by certain events —**ep'och·al** a.

ep·ox'y n. resin used in strong glues, enamels, etc.

e'qual a. of the same quantity, value, rank, etc. —n. person or thing that is equal —v. be, or do something, equal to —**equal to** capable of —**e·qual'i·ty** n. —**e'qual·ize'** v. —**e'qual·ly** adv.

e·quate' v. treat, regard, or express as equal

e·qua'tion n. 1 an equating 2 equality of two quantities as shown by the equal mark

e·qua'tor n. imaginary circle around the earth, equidistant from the North and South Poles —**e'qua·to'ri·al** a.

e'qui·dis'tant a. equally distant

e'qui·lib'ri·um n. state of balance

e'qui·nox' n. time when the sun crosses the equator, making night and day of equal length everywhere

e·quip' v. -quipped' fit out, as for an undertaking —**e·quip'ment** n.

eq'ui·ta·ble a. fair; just

e·quiv'a·lent a. equal in quantity, meaning, etc.

e·quiv'o·cal a. 1 purposely ambiguous 2 doubtful

e'ra n. period of time

e·rase' v. rub out, as writing —**e·ras'er** n. —**e·ras'a·ble** a.

e·rect' a. upright —v. 1 construct; build 2 set upright —**e·rec'tion** n.

e·rode' v. wear away —**e·ro'sion** n.

e·rot'ic a. causing sexual feelings or desires

err (ur, er) v. 1 be wrong 2 violate a moral code

er'rand n. short trip to do a thing

er·rat'ic a. irregular; odd

er·ro'ne·ous a. wrong

er'ror n. 1 mistake; blunder 2 mistaken belief

e·rupt' v. 1 burst forth 2 break out in a rash —**e·rup'tion** n.

es·ca·la·tor n. moving stairway on an endless belt

es·ca·pade' n. reckless adventure or prank

es·cape' v. 1 get free 2 slip away from —n. act or means of escape

es·ca·role' n. plant with leaves used in salads

es·cort' (v.: es kôrt') n. person(s) accompanying another to protect, honor, etc. —v. go with as an escort

es'pi·o·nage ('-näzh') n. a spying

es·pouse (e spouz') v. 1 marry 2 support (an idea or cause)

es·pres'so n. coffee made by forcing steam through ground coffee beans

es·say' (n.: es'ā) v. to try —n. 1 a try 2 short personal writing on one subject —**es'say·ist** n.

es'sence n. 1 basic nature 2 substance in concentrated form 3 perfume

es·sen'tial (-shəl) n., a. (something) necessary

es·tab'lish v. 1 set up; fix 2 to found 3 prove

es·tate' n. 1 one's possessions 2 piece of land with a residence

es·teem' v. value highly —n. high regard

es'ti·mate' (-mat'; n.: -mət) v. figure roughly, as size or cost —n. 1 rough calculation 2 opinion —**es'ti·ma'tion** n.

es'tu·ar'y (-tyŏŏ-, -chŏŏ-) n., pl. -ies wide mouth of a river

et cet'er·a and so forth: abbrev. **etc.**

etch v. put a design on metal plates or glass with acid, often for making prints —**etch'ing** n.

e·ter'nal a. 1 everlasting 2 forever the same

e·ter'ni·ty n. 1 a being eternal 2 endless time

e'ther n. an anesthetic

eth'ic n. 1 ethics 2 particular moral standard or value

eth'ics n.pl. moral standards; system of morals

eth'nic a. of any of the many peoples of mankind —n. member of a nationality group in a larger community

et'i·quette (-kət) n. social forms; good manners

é'tude' (ā'-) n. Mus. instrumental piece stressing a technique

et'y·mol'o·gy n., pl. -gies 1 origin of a word 2 study of word origins

eu'lo·gy n., pl. -gies praise

eu'phe·mism' n. mild word replacing an offensive one

eu'tha·na'si·a (-nā'zhə) n. painless death to end suffering

e·vac'u·ate' v. 1 make empty 2 to discharge (excrement) 3 remove 4 withdraw (from)

e·vade' v. avoid by deceit, indirect answer, etc. —**e·va'sion** n.

e·val'u·ate' v. find the value of

e·van'ge·list n. 1 [E-] Gospel writer 2 revivalist preacher —**e·van'ge·lism'** n.

e·vap'o·rate' v. 1 change into vapor 2 condense by heating 3 vanish —**e·vap'o·ra'tion** n.

eve n. 1 [Poet.] evening 2 evening before a holiday 3 time just before

e'ven a. 1 flat; level 2 constant; uniform 3 calm 4 equal 5 divisible by two 6 exact —adv. 1 indeed 2 exactly 3 still —v. make or become even —even if though —e'ven·ly adv.

eve'ning n. end of day and beginning of night

e·vent' n. 1 an occurrence 2 sports contest in a series

e·ven'tu·al a. final

ev'er adv. 1 always 2 at any time 3 at all

ev'er·green' n., a. (tree or plant) having green leaves all year

ev'er·y a. 1 each of a group 2 all possible —**every other** each alternate —**ev'er·y·bod'y, ev'er·y·one'** pron. —**ev'er·y·thing'** pron. —**ev'er·y·where'** adv.

ev'er·y·day' a. 1 daily 2 usual; common

e·vict' v. put (a tenant) out by law —**e·vic'tion** n.

ev'i·dence n. 1 sign; indication 2 proof —v. make evident

ev'i·dent *a.* easy to see; clear

e'vil *a.* 1 morally bad 2 harmful —*n.* wickedness —**e'vil·ly** *adv.*

e·voke' *v.* call forth; produce

ev·o·lu'tion *n.* 1 an evolving 2 theory that all species developed from earlier forms

e·volve' *v.* develop gradually; unfold

ewe (yōō) *n.* female sheep

ex·act' *a.* strictly correct; precise —**ex·act'ly** *adv.*

ex·ag'ger·ate' *v.* make seem greater than it really is; overstate —**ex·ag'ger·a'tion** *n.*

ex·alt' *v.* 1 raise in dignity 2 praise 3 fill with joy

ex·am'ine *v.* 1 inspect 2 test by questioning

ex·am'ple *n.* 1 sample 2 a warning 3 illustration 4 model

ex'ca·vate' *v.* 1 make a hole in 2 unearth 3 dig out —**ex'ca·va'tion** *n.* —**ex'ca·va'tor** *n.*

ex·ceed' *v.* 1 go beyond (a limit) 2 surpass

ex·cel' *v.* **-celled'** be better than

ex'cel·lent *a.* unusually good

ex·cept' *prep.* leaving out; but —*v.* exclude

ex·cep'tion *n.* 1 person or thing excluded 2 case to which a rule does not apply 3 objection

ex'cerpt' *n.* passage selected from a book, etc.

ex·cess' (or ek'ses') *n.* 1 more than is needed 2 surplus —*a.* extra —**ex·ces'sive** *a.*

ex·change' *v.* 1 to trade; barter 2 to interchange —*n.* 1 an exchanging 2 thing exchanged 3 place for exchanging

ex'cise' (*v.:* ek siz') *n.* tax on certain goods within a country: also **excise tax** —*v.* cut out

ex·cite' *v.* 1 make active 2 arouse; stir the feelings of —**ex·cit'a·ble** *a.* —**ex·cite'ment** *n.*

ex·claim' *v.* utter sharply —**ex'cla·ma'tion** *n.*

ex·clude' *v.* keep out or shut out —**ex·clu'sion** *n.*

ex·clu'sive *a.* 1 not shared 2 snobbish —**ex·clu'sive·ly** *adv.*

ex'com·mu'ni·cate' *v.* expel from communion with a church

ex'cre·ment *n.* waste material from the bowels

ex·cuse' (ek skyōoz'; *n.:* ek skyōos') *v.* 1 apologize for 2 overlook (an offense or fault) 3 release from a duty, etc. 4 let leave 5 justify —*n.* 1 apology 2 something that excuses 3 pretext —**ex·cus'a·ble** *a.*

ex'e·cute' *v.* 1 carry out; do 2 put to death legally 3 make valid (a will, etc.)

ex·ec'u·tive *a.* 1 having to do with managing 2 administering laws, etc. —*n.* one who administers affairs

ex·empt' *v.,a.* free(d) from a rule or obligation

ex'er·cise' *n.* 1 active use 2 activity to develop the body, a skill, etc. 3 *pl.* program, as at a graduation ceremony —*v.* 1 use 2 do or give exercises 3 exert

ex·ert' *v.* put into action

ex·hale' *v.* breathe out

ex·haust' *v.* 1 use up 2 drain 3 tire out —*n.* discharge from an engine —**ex·haus'tion** *n.*

ex·hib'it (eg zib'-) *v.,n.* show; display —**ex·hib'i·tor** *n.*

ex'hi·bi'tion (ek'sə-) *n.* 1 a (public) showing 2 that which is shown

ex·hume' *v.* dig out of the earth

ex'ile' *n.* 1 a prolonged, often enforced, living away from one's country 2 person in exile

ex·ist' *v.* 1 be 2 occur 3 live —**ex·ist'ence** *n.*

ex'it *n.* a (way of) leaving

ex'o·dus *n.* departure

ex·ot'ic *a.* 1 foreign 2 strangely beautiful, etc.

ex·pand' *v.* 1 spread out 2 enlarge —**ex·pan'sion** *n.*

ex·panse' *n.* wide extent

ex·pect' *v.* 1 look for as likely or due 2 [Col.] suppose —**ex'pec·ta'tion** *n.*

ex'pe·di'tion *n.* 1 a journey, as for exploration 2 those on such a journey

ex·pel' *v.* **-pelled'** 1 force out 2 dismiss by authority

ex·pend' *v.* spend; use up

ex·pend'i·ture *n.* 1 spending of money, time, etc. 2 amount spent

ex·pense' *n.* 1 cost 2 *pl.* charges met with in one's work, etc.

ex·pen'sive *a.* high-priced

ex·pe'ri·ence *n.* 1 a living through an event 2 thing one has done or lived through 3 skill gotten by training, work, etc. —*v.* have experience of

ex·per'i·ment *n.,v.* test to discover or prove something —**ex·per'i·men'tal** *a.*

ex'pert *a.* very skillful —*n.* one with great skill or knowledge in a field

ex·pire' *v.* 1 die 2 end 3 e'

ex·plain' v. 1 make plain or understandable 2 account for —**ex·pla·na'tion** n.

ex·plic'it a. clearly stated; definite

ex·plode' v. 1 burst noisily 2 discredit —**ex·plo'sion** n.

ex'ploit' (v.: eks ploit') n. bold deed —v. use to advantage

ex·plore' v. 1 investigate 2 travel in (a region) for discovery —**ex·plo·ra'tion** n.

ex·plo'sive a. of or like an explosion —n. substance that can explode

ex·po'nent n. 1 interpreter 2 example or symbol 3 Math. symbol at upper right showing times as a factor

ex·port' (n.: eks'pôrt') v. send (goods) to another country for sale —n. something exported

ex·pose' v. 1 lay open, as to danger 2 reveal 3 to subject photographic film to light —**ex·po'sure** n.

ex·po·si'tion n. 1 explanation 2 public exhibition

ex·press' v. 1 put into words 2 reveal; show 3 symbolize —a. 1 explicit 2 exact 3 fast and direct —adv. by express —n. an express train, bus, delivery service, etc.

ex·pres'sion n. 1 an expressing or way of expressing 2 certain word or phrase 3 look, etc. that shows how one feels

ex·pul'sion n. an expelling or being expelled

ex'qui·site a. 1 beautiful, delicate, etc. 2 very keen

ex·tend' v. 1 prolong 2 expand 3 stretch forth 4 offer

ex·ten'sion n. 1 an extending 2 an addition

ex·tent' n. 1 size 2 scope 3 vast area

ex·te'ri·or a. on or from the outside —n. the outside

ex·ter'mi·nate' v. to destroy entirely —**ex·ter'mi·na'tion** n.

ex·ter'nal a. 1 on or from the outside 2 superficial

ex·tinct' a. no longer existing or active

ex·tol' v. -tolled' praise highly

ex·tort' v. get (money) by threats, etc. —**ex·tor'tion** n.

ex'tra a. more than expected; additional —n. extra person or thing —adv. especially

ex·tract' (n.: eks'trakt') v. 1 pull out 2 get by pressing, distilling, etc. 3 select —n. something

extracted —**ex·trac'tion** n.

ex·tra·or'di·nar'y (ek strôr'-) a. very unusual

ex·trav'a·gant a. 1 excessive 2 wasteful —**ex·trav'a·gance** n.

ex·treme' a. 1 utmost 2 final 3 excessive or drastic 4 radical —n. extreme degree, state, etc.

ex·u'ber·ant a. 1 very healthy and lively 2 luxuriant

ex·ult' v. rejoice greatly

eye n. 1 organ of sight 2 vision 3 a look 4 attention —v. eyed look at

eye'brow' n. bony arch over the eye, or the hair on this

eye'lash' n. hair on the edge of the eyelid

eye'let n. small hole, as for a hook, cord, etc.

eye'lid' n. either of two folds of flesh that cover and uncover the eyeball

F

fa'ble n. 1 brief tale having a moral 2 untrue story

fab'ric n. cloth

fab'u·lous a. 1 fictitious 2 incredible 3 [Col.] wonderful

face n. 1 front of the head 2 (main) surface 3 appearance 4 dignity —v. 1 turn, or have the face turned, toward 2 confront —**fa'cial** (-shal) a.

fac'et (fas'-) n. 1 a surface of a cut gem 2 aspect

fac·ile (fas'al) a. 1 easy 2 superficial

fa·cil'i·ty n., pl. -ties 1 ease or skill 2 pl. things that help do something 3 building, etc. for some activity

fac·sim'i·le (-lē) n. exact copy

fact n. 1 actual happening 2 truth —**in fact** really

fac'tor n. 1 causal element 2 Math. any of the quantities multiplied together

fac'to·ry n., pl. -ries building in which things are manufactured

fac'ul·ty n., pl. -ties 1 natural power or aptitude 2 staff of teachers

fad n. passing fashion

fade v. 1 (make) lose color or strength 2 die out

Fahr·en·heit' (fer'ən hīt') a. of a thermometer on which the boiling point of water is 212°, the freezing point 32°

fail v. 1 fall short 2 weaken 3 become bankrupt 4 not succeed 5 neglect 6 not pass a test or course

fail·ing n. 1 failure 2 fault — prep. lacking

faint a. 1 weak, dim, etc. 2 weak and dizzy —n. state of temporary unconsciousness —v. fall into a faint —**faint'ness** n.

fair a. 1 beautiful 2 blond 3 clear and sunny 4 just 5 according to the rules 6 average —adv. in a fair way —n. exposition with exhibits, amusements, etc. —**fair'ly** adv. —**fair'ness** n.

fair'y n., pl. **-ies** tiny imaginary being in human form, with magic powers

faith n. 1 unquestioning belief, esp. in religion 2 particular religion 3 loyalty

faith'ful a. 1 loyal 2 exact

fake v., n., a. sham

fal'con n. hawk trained to hunt —**fal'con·ry** n.

fall v. fell, fall'en 1 to drop or descend 2 tumble 3 occur —n. 1 a falling 2 autumn 3 overthrow or ruin 4 amount of what has fallen 5 pl. a waterfall —**fall out** quarrel —**fall through** fail

fal'la·cy n., pl. **-cies** 1 false idea; error 2 false reasoning

false a. 1 not true 2 lying 3 unfaithful 4 not real —**fal'si·ty** n.

fal'ter v. 1 stumble 2 stammer 3 waver

fame n. great reputation

fa·mil'iar a. 1 friendly; intimate 2 too intimate; presumptuous 3 closely acquainted (with) 4 well-known —**fa·mil'i·ar'i·ty** n.

fam'i·ly n., pl. **-lies** 1 parents and their children 2 relatives 3 lineage 4 group of related things

fam'ine (-in) n. 1 widespread food shortage 2 starvation

fa'mous a. having fame

fan n. 1 device to move air for cooling, etc. 2 [Col.] enthusiastic supporter —v. fanned 1 blow air toward 2 stir up 3 spread (out)

fa·nat'ic a. too enthusiastic or zealous: also **fa·nat'i·cal** —n. fanatic person

fan'cy n., pl. **-cies** 1 playful imagination 2 notion, whim, etc. 3 a liking —a. **-ci·er, -ci·est** 1 extravagant 2 elaborate 3 of superior quality —v. **-cied** 1 imagine 2 be fond of 3 suppose —**fan'ci·ful** a.

fan'fare' n. 1 blast of trumpets 2 showy display

fang n. long, pointed tooth

fan·tas'tic a. 1 unreal 2 grotesque 3 extravagant

fan'ta·sy n., pl. **-sies** 1 fancy 2 illusion; reverie 3 fantastic poem, play, etc.

far a. far'ther, far'thest distant —adv. 1 very distant 2 very much —**by far** very much

far'a·way' a. distant

fare v. get along —n. 1 transportation charge 2 paying passenger 3 food

fare·well' (a.: fer'wel') int. goodbye —a., n. parting (wishes)

farm n. land used to raise crops or animals —v. 1 cultivate (land) 2 let out (work or workers) on contract —**farm'er** n.

farm'house' n. —**farm'ing** n.

far'sight'ed a. 1 planning ahead 2 seeing far objects best

far'ther a. 1 more distant 2 additional —adv. 1 at or to a greater distance or extent 2 in addition

far'thest a. most distant —adv. at or to the greatest distance

fas'ci·nate' v. hold spellbound; captivate —**fas'ci·na'tion** n.

fas·cism (fash'iz'əm) n. militaristic dictatorship —**fas'cist** n., a.

fash'ion n. 1 kind; sort 2 manner 3 current style

fast a. 1 firm 2 loyal 3 unfading 4 rapid; quick 5 of loose morals —adv. 1 firmly 2 rapidly —v. abstain from food —n. period of fasting

fas'ten (fas'ən) v. 1 attach 2 make secure; fix —**fas'ten·er** n.

fat a. fat'ter, fat'test plump —n. oily animal substance

fa'tal a. causing death

fate n. 1 power supposedly making events inevitable 2 one's lot in life 3 outcome 4 death; ruin

fa'ther n. 1 male parent 2 founder; creator 3 Christian priest —v. beget, found, etc. — [F-] God —**fa'ther·hood'** n. —**fa'ther·ly** a.

fa'ther-in-law' n., pl. **fa'thers-in-law'** father of one's wife or husband

fath·om (fath'əm) n. Naut. six feet —v. understand

fa·tigue' (-tēg') n. weariness —v. to weary

fau'cet n. device with valve to draw liquid from a pipe

fault n. 1 flaw 2 error 3 blame —**fault'less** a.

fau'na n. the animals of a certain region

fa′vor n. 1 approval 2 partiality 3 kind act 4 small gift —v. 1 show favor toward 2 resemble Also, Br. sp., **fa′vour** —**in favor of** approving —**fa′vor·a·ble** a.

fa′vor·ite a., n. preferred (one)

fawn v. 1 show affection as by licking hands: said of a dog 2 flatter servilely —n. baby deer

fax n. 1 electronic sending of pictures, print, etc., as over telephone lines 2 device for such sending —v. send by fax

fear n. 1 anxious anticipation of danger, pain, etc. 2 awe —v. 1 be afraid (of) 2 be in awe (of) —**fear′ful** a. —**fear′less** a.

feast n. 1 religious festival 2 banquet —v. 1 have a feast (for) 2 delight

feat n. bold and daring deed

feath′er n. 1 one of the outgrowths covering a bird 2 kind

fea′ture n. 1 pl. form of the face or its parts 2 special part, article, etc. 3 main attraction

Feb′ru·ar·y (-rōō-, -yōō-) n. second month

fed′er·al a. 1 of a union of states under a central government 2 of the central government, esp. [F-] of the U.S.

fed′er·a′tion n. union of states or groups; league

fee n. charge for some service or right

fee′ble a. weak; not strong

feed v. **fed** 1 give food to 2 supply as fuel, material, etc. 3 gratify —v. eat —n. fodder

feel v. **felt** 1 touch 2 have a feeling (of) 3 be aware of 4 believe 5 be or seem to be 6 grope —n. 1 sense of touch 2 way a thing feels

feel′ing n. 1 sense of touch 2 sensation 3 an emotion 4 pl. sensitiveness 5 sympathy 6 opinion

feign (fān) v. 1 make up (an excuse) 2 pretend

fe′line a. of or like a cat —n. a cat

fell v. 1 pt. of FALL 2 knock down 3 cut down

fel′low n. 1 an associate 2 an equal 3 a mate 4 man or boy

fel′on n. criminal

felt n. fabric made of fibers pressed together

fe′male a. 1 designating or of the sex that bears offspring 2 feminine —n. female person or animal

fem′i·nine (-nin) a. of or like

women or girls; female

fem′i·nism′ n. movement to win equal rights for women —**fem′i·nist** n., a.

fence n. 1 barrier of posts, wire, etc. 2 dealer in stolen goods —v. 1 enclose with a fence 2 fight with swords or foils as a sport —**fenc′er** n.

fend v. turn aside: with off —**fend for oneself** manage by oneself

fend′er n. a guard over an automobile wheel

fern n. nonflowering plant with fronds

fe·ro′cious (-shəs) a. savage; fierce —**fe·roc′i·ty** n.

fer′ric, fer′rous a. of iron

fer′ry v. -**ried** take across a river, etc. in a boat —n., pl. -**ries** boat used for ferrying

fer′tile (furt′'l) a. 1 producing abundantly 2 able to produce young, fruit, etc. —**fer·til′i·ty** n.

fer′til·ize′ v. 1 make fertile 2 spread fertilizer on 3 make fruitful by introducing a male germ cell —**fer′til·i·za′tion** n.

fer′til·iz′er n. manure, chemicals, etc. to enrich the soil

fes′ti·val n. time or day of celebration

fes·tiv′i·ty n., pl. -**ties** 1 gaiety 2 pl. things done in celebration

fetch v. 1 go after and bring back; get 2 sell for

fe′tus n. unborn young

feud (fyōōd) n. deadly quarrel, as between families

feu′dal·ism′ n. medieval system with lords, vassals, and serfs

fe′ver n. abnormally high body temperature —**fe′ver·ish** a.

few a. not many —pron., n. a small number

fi·an·cé (fē′än sā′) n. man to whom one is engaged —**fi′an·cée′** (-sā′) n.fem.

fib n. petty lie —v. **fibbed** tell a fib

fi′ber n. 1 threadlike part(s) forming organic tissue 2 threadlike part(s) used for weaving, etc. —**fi′brous** a.

fick′le a. tending to change one's mind

fic′tion n. literary work(s) with imaginary characters and events

fic·ti′tious (-tish′əs) a. imaginary

fid′dle n. [Col.] violin

field n. 1 piece of open land, esp. one for crops, grazing, etc. 2 expanse 3 area for athletic event 4 sphere of knowledge or

activity 5 all contestants

fiend (fēnd) *n.* 1 devil 2 [Col.] addict —**fiend'ish** *a.*

fierce *a.* 1 savage; wild 2 violent

fi'er·y *a.* **-i·er, -i·est** 1 flaming, hot, etc. 2 ardent

fi·es'ta (fē-) *n.* festival

if'teen' *a., n.* five more than ten —**fif'teenth'** *a., n.*

fifth *a.* preceded by four others —*n.* 1 one after the fourth 2 one of five equal parts 3 fifth of a gallon

if'ty *a., n., pl.* **-ties** five times ten —**fif'ti·eth** *a., n.*

ig *n.* sweet, chewy fruit with seed-filled pulp

ight *n., v.* **fought** struggle; battle; contest —**fighter** *n.*

ig'ure *n.* 1 outline; shape 2 person 3 likeness of a person or thing 4 illustration 5 design 6 a number 7 sum of money —*v.* 1 compute 2 be conspicuous 3 [Col.] predict —**figure out** solve

ile *n.* 1 container for keeping papers in order 2 orderly arrangement of papers, etc. 3 line of persons or things 4 ridged tool for scraping, etc. —*v.* 1 put papers, etc. in order 2 move in a file 3 smooth or grind with a file

fi·let (fi lā') *n., v.* fillet

fil'i·bus·ter *n.* obstruction of a bill in a legislature, as by a long speech

ill *v.* 1 make or become full 2 put into or hold (a job or office) 3 supply things ordered —*n.* anything that fills —**fill in** 1 make complete 2 substitute

fil·let (fi lā') *n.* boneless piece of fish or meat —*v.* to bone (fish, etc.)

filling *n.* thing used to fill something else

fil'ly *n., pl.* **-lies** young mare

film *n.* 1 thin coating 2 flexible cellulose material used in photography 3 *a)* series of pictures flashed on a screen in rapid succession so that things in them seem to move *b)* story in this form —*v.* make a FILM (*n.* 3)

fil'ter *n.* thing used for straining out particles, etc. from a fluid, etc.

filth *n.* 1 foul dirt 2 obscenity —**filth'y** *a.,* **-i·er, -i·est**

fin *n.* winglike, membranous organ on a fish

fi'nal *a.* 1 last 2 conclusive —**fi'nal·ly** *adv.* —**fi'nal·ize'** *v.*

fi·nance' (*or* fī'nans') *n.* 1 *pl.*

funds 2 science of managing money matters —*v.* supply money for —**fi·nan'cial** *a.*

finch *n.* small songbird

find *v.* **found** 1 come upon; discover 2 learn 3 recover (a thing lost) 4 decide

fine *a.* 1 excellent 2 not heavy or coarse 3 sharp 4 discriminating 5 very well —*n.* money paid as a penalty —*v.* cause to pay a fine

fin'ger *n.* any of the parts (five with the thumb) at the end of the hand —*v.* to handle —**fin'ger·nail'** *n.* —**fin'ger·tip'** *n.*

fin'ish *v.* 1 to end 2 complete 3 use up 4 perfect; polish —*n.* 1 last part; end 2 polish or perfection 3 way a surface is finished

fi'nite' *a.* having limits

fiord (fyôrd) *n.* sea inlet bordered by steep cliffs

fir *n.* evergreen tree

fire *n.* 1 flame 2 thing burning 3 ardor 4 discharge of guns —*v.* 1 make burn 2 shoot (a gun, etc.) 3 discharge from a job —**on fire** burning —**under fire** under attack —**fire'proof'** *v., a.*

fire'arm' *n.* rifle, pistol, etc.

fire'fight'er *n.* one who fights fires —**fire'fight'ing** *n.*

fire'fly' *n.* winged beetle with a glowing abdomen

fire'man *n., pl.* **-men** firefighter

firm *a.* 1 solid 2 fixed; stable 3 strong and steady —*v.* make firm —*n.* business company

first *a., adv.* before any others —*n.* 1 first one 2 beginning

first'-class' *a.* of the highest quality

first'-rate' *a.* excellent

fish *n., pl.* **fish;** for different kinds, **fish'es** coldblooded animal with gills and fins, living in water —*v.* 1 to catch fish 2 angle (*for*) —**fish'er·man** *n., pl.* **-men** —**fish'er·y** *n., pl.* **-ies**

fis·sion (fish'ən) *n.* a splitting apart

fist *n.* clenched hand

fit *v.* **fit'ted** *or* **fit** 1 be suitable to 2 be the proper size, etc. (for) 3 adjust to fit 4 equip —*a.* **fit'ter, fit'test** 1 suited 2 proper 3 healthy —*n.* 1 way of fitting 2 seizure as of coughing 3 outburst —**fit'ness** *n.*

five *a., n.* one more than four

fix *v.* 1 fasten or set firmly 2 determine 3 adjust or repair 4 prepare (food, etc.) 5 [Col.] influence by bribery, etc. —*n.* 1

[Col.] predicament 2 [Sl.] clear understanding —**fixed** a.

fix'ture n. any of the attached furnishings of a house

flag n. 1 cloth with colors or designs, used as a national symbol, etc. 2 iris (flower) —**flag' pole', flag'staff'** n.

fla'grant a. glaringly bad

flail n. implement used to thresh grain by hand —v. 1 use a flail 2 beat

flair n. aptitude; knack

flake n. 1 soft, thin mass 2 chip —**flak'y** a., **-i-er, -i-est**

flam·boy'ant a. showy

flame n. tongue(s) of fire; blaze —v. burst into flame

fla·min'go n. pink, long-legged wading bird

flam'ma·ble a. easily set on fire

flank n. 1 side of an animal between the ribs and the hip 2 side of anything

flan'nel n. soft, napped cloth of wool, etc.

flap n. 1 flat, loose piece 2 motion or sound of a swinging flap —v. flutter

flare v. 1 blaze up 2 spread outward —n. 1 bright, unsteady blaze 2 brief, dazzling signal light 3 sudden outburst 4 a spreading outward

flash v. 1 send out a sudden, brief light 2 sparkle 3 move suddenly —n. 1 sudden, brief light 2 an instant 3 bit of late news

flash'light' n. portable electric light

flask n. kind of bottle

flat a. **flat'ter, flat'test** 1 smooth and level 2 broad and thin 3 lying spread out 4 absolute 5 without taste or sparkle 6 dull; lifeless 7 emptied of air 8 Mus. below true pitch —adv. in a flat way —n. 1 flat surface or part 2 deflated tire 3 Mus. note (b) step below another: symbol (b) 4 apartment —**flat'ten** v.

flat'ter v. 1 praise insincerely 2 gratify the vanity of

flaunt (flônt) v. show off

fla'vor n. taste of a substance

flaw n. defect —**flawed** a. — **flaw'less** a.

flax n. plant with fibers that are spun into linen thread

flea n. small jumping insect that is parasitic

flee v. fled flee escape swiftly, as from danger

fleet n. 1 group of warships

under one command 2 an similar group, as of truck planes, etc. —a. swift

flesh n. 1 tissue between th skin and bones 2 pulp of fruit and vegetables 3 the body

flex'i·ble a. 1 easily bent; pliabl 2 adaptable

flick n. light, quick stroke — strike, throw, etc. with such stroke

flick'er v. move, burn, or shin unsteadily

fli'er n. 1 aviator 2 handbill o leaflet

flight n. 1 act or power of flyin 2 distance flown 3 group o things flying together 4 trip b airplane 5 set of stairs 6 a flee ing —**flight'less** a.

flim'sy a. **-si-er, -si-est** 1 easil broken 2 trivial

flinch v. draw back, as from blow

fling v. throw with force —n. 1 flinging 2 [Col.] a try 3 [Col.] brief love affair

flint n. a hard quartz

flip v. **flipped** toss with a quick jerk —a. [Col.] flippant

flip'pant a. frivolous and disre spectful —**flip'pan·cy** n.

flirt v. 1 play at love 2 trifle —n one who plays at love

flit v. **flit'ted** move lightly and rapidly

float n. 1 thing that stays on th surface of a liquid 2 flat, deco rated vehicle in a parade —v. 1 stay on the surface of a liquid 2 drift gently in air, etc. 3 put into circulation, as a bond issue

flock n. group, esp. of animals

floe n. large sheet of floating ice

flog v. **flogged** beat, thrash, or whip

flood n. 1 overflowing of water on land 2 great outpouring

floor n. 1 bottom surface of a room, etc. 2 story in a building 3 permission to speak

flop v. **flopped** 1 move, drop, or flap about clumsily 2 [Col.] fail —n. a flopping —**flop'py** a.

floppy (disk) n. small, flexible computer disk

flo'ra n. the plants of a region

flo'rist n. one who grows or sells flowers

floun'der v. struggle or speak clumsily —n. kind of edible flat-fish

flour n. a powdery substance ground from grain

flour'ish v. 1 thrive 2 be in

one's prime **3** brandish —*n.* **1** contrast

sweeping motion or stroke **2** fanfare

low *v.* **1** move as water does **2** move smoothly **3** proceed **4** hang loose —*n.* a flowing or thing that flows

lower *n.* **1** petals and pistil of a plant **2** a plant grown for its blossoms **3** best part —*v.* **1** to produce blossoms **2** become its best

lu *n.* influenza

lue *n.* shaft in a chimney

luffy *a.* -**i-er**, -**i-est** soft and light

luid *a.* **1** able to flow **2** not fixed —*n.* liquid or gas

lu-o-res-cent (floor es'ənt) *a.* giving off cool light

lu-o-rine (floor'ēn') *n.* yellowish gas, a chemical element

lur'ry *n.*, *pl.* -**ries 1** gust of wind, rain, or snow **2** sudden commotion

lush *v.* **1** to redden in the face **2** start up from cover, as a bird **3** wash out —*n.* a blush; glow —*a.* **1** well-supplied **2** level (*with*) **3** direct

lus'ter *v.* make confused

flute *n.* tubelike wind instrument

flut'ter *v.* wave, move, or beat rapidly or irregularly —*n.* **1** a fluttering **2** confusion

fly *v.* **flew** *or* (*v.* **5**) **flied, flown** *or* (*v.* **5**) **flied 1** move through the air by using wings **2** wave or float in the air **3** move swiftly **4** flee **5** hit a fly in baseball **6** travel in or pilot (aircraft) —*n.*, *pl.* **flies 1** flap concealing buttons, etc. in a garment **2** baseball batted high **3** winged insect

fly'er *n.* flier

foal *n.* young horse

foam *n.* **1** bubbly mass on liquids **2** spongy mass of rubber, plastic, etc. —*v.* form foam

fo'cus *n.*, *pl.* -**cus-es** *or* -**ci'** (-sī') **1** point where rays of light meet **2** adjustment of lens distance for clear image **3** center of activity —*v.* **1** bring into focus **2** concentrate —**fo'cal** *a.*

fod'der *n.* coarse food for cattle, horses, etc.

foe *n.* enemy

fog *n.* **1** thick mist **2** mental confusion —*v.* **fogged** make or become foggy —**fog'gy** *a.*, -**gi-er**, -**gi-est** —**fog'gi-ness** *n.*

foil *v.* thwart —*n.* **1** thin fencing sword **2** thin sheet of metal **3** one that enhances another by

fold *v.* **1** double (material) over **2** intertwine **3** wrap up —*n.* **1** folded layer **2** pen for sheep

fo'li-age *n.* plant leaves

folk *n.*, *pl.* **folk** *or* **folks** people —*a.* of the common people

folk'lore' *n.* beliefs, legends, etc. of a people

fol'low *v.* **1** come or go after **2** go along **3** take up (a trade) **4** result (from) **5** obey **6** pay attention to **7** understand —**fol'low-er** *n.*

fol'ly *n.*, *pl.* -**lies** foolish state, action, belief, etc.

fond *a.* loving; tender —**fond of** liking —**fond'ly** *adv.*

food *n.* substance taken in by an animal or plant to enable it to live and grow

fool *n.* **1** silly person **2** dupe —*v.* **1** be silly or playful **2** trick

fool'ish *a.* silly; unwise

foot *n.*, *pl.* **feet 1** end part of the leg, on which one stands **2** bottom; base **3** measure of length, 12 inches —**on foot** walking

foot'ball' *n.* **1** team game played on a field with an inflated leather ball **2** this ball

foot'note' *n.* note at the bottom of a page

for *prep.* **1** in place of **2** in the interest of **3** in favor of **4** with the purpose of **5** in search of **6** meant to be received, used, etc. **7** with respect to **8** because of **9** to the extent or duration of —*con.* because

for-bear' *v.* -**bore'**, -**borne'** refrain (from) **2** control oneself

for-bid' *v.* -**bade'** (-bad') *or* -**bad'**, -**bid'den** not permit; prohibit

force *n.* **1** strength; power **2** coercion **3** effectiveness **4** organized group, as an army —*v.* **1** make do something; compel **2** break open **3** impose, produce, etc. by force —**force'ful** *a.*

ford *n.* shallow place in a river —*v.* cross at a ford

fore *adv.*, *a.*, *n.* (in or toward) the front part —*int.* Golf warning shout

fore'bear' *n.* ancestor

fore'cast' *v.* -**cast'** *or* -**cast'ed** predict —*n.* prediction

fore-close' *v.* take away the right to redeem (a mortgage)

fore'fa'ther *n.* ancestor

fore'fin'ger *n.* finger nearest the thumb

fore-gone' *a.* previous

fore'head' *n.* part of the face above the eyebrows

for'eign (-in) *a.* 1 of or from another country 2 not characteristic —**for'eign·er** *n.*

fore'man *n., pl.* -men 1 man in charge of workers 2 chairman of a jury

fore'most' *a., adv.* first

fore'run'ner *n.* person or thing foretelling another

fore·see' *v.* -saw', -seen' see or know beforehand

fore'sight' *n.* 1 power to foresee 2 prudence

fore'skin' *n.* fold of skin over the end of the penis

for'est *n.* tract of land covered with trees

for'est·ry *n.* science of the care of forests —**for'est·er** *n.*

fore·tell' *v.* -told' predict

for·ev'er *adv.* 1 for all time 2 at all times

fore·warn' *v.* warn beforehand

fore'wom'an *n., pl.* -wom'en woman serving as a foreman

fore'word' *n.* preface

for'feit (-fit) *n.* penalty —*v.* lose as a penalty

forge *n.* 1 furnace for heating metal to be wrought 2 smith's shop —*v.* 1 shape by heating and hammering 2 counterfeit (a signature) 3 advance slowly

for'ger·y *n., pl.* -ies 1 crime of forging documents, signatures, etc. 2 anything forged

for·get' *v.* -got', -got'ten or -got' 1 be unable to remember 2 neglect —**for·get'ful** *a.*

for·give' *v.* -gave', -giv'en give up wanting to punish; pardon —**for·give'ness** *n.* —**for·giv'ing** *a.*

for·go' *v.* -went', -gone' do without

fork *n.* 1 pronged instrument for lifting 2 place of branching

for·lorn' *a.* 1 abandoned 2 wretched; miserable

form *n.* 1 shape; figure 2 mold 3 style; customary behavior 4 document to be filled in —*v.* 1 to shape 2 develop (habits) 3 constitute —**form'less** *a.*

for'mal *a.* 1 according to custom, rule, etc. 2 stiff; prim 3 for use at ceremonies

for'mat' *n.* general arrangement, as of a book

form'er *a.* 1 of the past 2 being the first mentioned

for'mu·la *n., pl.* -las or -lae (-lē') 1 fixed expression or rule 2 set of symbols expressing a mathematical rule, chemical compound, etc. —**for'mu·late'** *v.*

for·sake' *v.* -sook', -sak'e abandon; desert

fort *n.* fortified place for militar defense

forth *adv.* 1 forward 2 out; int view

for'ti·fy' *v.* -fied' to strengthen enrich, etc.

fort'night' *n.* two weeks

for'tress *n.* fortified place

for'tu·nate *a.* lucky

for'tune *n.* 1 luck; fate 2 goo luck 3 wealth

for'ty *a., n., pl.* -ties four time ten —**for'ti·eth** *a., n.*

fo'rum *n.* meeting for public dis cussion

for'ward *a.* 1 at, to, or of the front 2 advanced 3 bold —*adv* ahead: also **for'wards** —*v.* promote 2 send on

fos'sil *n.* hardened plant or ani mal remains, as in rock

fos'ter *v.* 1 bring up 2 promote —*a.* in a family but not by birt or adoption

foul *a.* 1 filthy 2 stormy 3 out side the rules or limits 4 very bad —*n.* foul hit, blow, etc. —*v.* 1 make filthy 2 entangle 3 make a foul

found *v.* 1 pt. & pp. of FIND 2 establish —**found'er** *n.*

foun·da'tion *n.* 1 establishment or basis 2 base of a wall, house, etc. 3 philanthropic fund or institution

foun'tain *n.* 1 spring of water 2 jet of water or basin for it 3 source

four *a., n.* one more than three —**fourth** *a., n.*

four'score' *a., n.* eighty

four'teen' *a., n.* four more than ten —**four'teenth'** *a., n.*

fowl *n.* 1 any bird 2 domestic bird, as the chicken

fox *n.* small, wild, doglike animal

frac'tion *n.* 1 part of a whole, as $\frac{3}{4}$, $\frac{1}{2}$, etc. 2 small part

frac'ture *n.* a break, esp. in a bone —*v.* to break; crack

frag·ile (fraj'əl) *a.* easily broken

frag'ment *n.* 1 part broken away 2 incomplete part

fra'grant *a.* sweet-smelling

frail *a.* 1 fragile 2 delicate or weak —**frail'ty** *n., pl.* -ties

frame *v.* 1 make, form, build, etc. 2 enclose in a border —*n.* 1 framework 2 framing border or case 3 mood

frame'work' *n.* supporting or

basic structure

frank a. outspoken; candid

frank'furt·er n. smoked link sausage; wiener

fran'tic a. wild with anger, worry, etc. —**fran'ti·cal·ly** adv.

fra·ter'nal a. 1 brotherly 2 of a fellowship society

fra·ter'ni·ty n., pl. **-ties** 1 brotherliness 2 college social club for men 3 group with like interests

fraud n. 1 a cheating or tricking; dishonesty 2 hypocrite; cheat

fray n. quarrel or fight —v. make or become ragged

freak n. abnormal animal or plant —a. abnormal

freck'le n. small brown spot on the skin

free a. **fre'er, fre'est** 1 not under another's control 2 loose, clear, unrestricted, etc. 3 without cost —adv. 1 without cost 2 in a free way —v. **freed** make free

free'dom n. 1 independence 2 liberty 3 ease of movement 4 a right

freeze v. **froze, fro'zen** 1 to change into, or become covered with, ice 2 make or become very cold 3 kill or damage by cold 4 fix (prices, etc.) at a set level

freight n. 1 goods transported 2 transportation of goods or its cost 3 train for freight

French fries n.pl. potatoes cut in strips and fried in deep fat

French horn n. brass musical instrument with a coiled tube

fren'zy n., pl. **-zies** wild excitement —**fren'zied** a.

fre'quen·cy n., pl. **-cies** 1 frequent occurrence 2 number of times anything recurs in a given period

fre'quent (v.: frē kwent') a. 1 occurring often 2 constant —v. go to habitually

fresh a. 1 not spoiled, stale, worn out, etc. 2 new 3 refreshing 4 not salt: said of water

fresh'man n., pl. **-men** first-year student in high school or college

fresh'wa·ter a. living in water that is not salty

fret v. **fret'ted** to worry —n. 1 worry 2 ridge on fingerboard of banjo, guitar, etc.

fric'tion n. 1 rubbing of one object against another 2 conflict —**fric'tion·al** a.

Fri'day n. sixth day of the week

friend n. 1 person one knows well and likes 2 ally

friend'ly a. **-li·er, -li·est** kindly;

helpful

fright n. sudden fear

fright'en v. 1 make afraid 2 drive (away) by fright

fright'ful a. 1 causing fright 2 disgusting

frig'id a. very cold

fringe n. border, as of loose threads

frit'ter v. waste (money, etc.) bit by bit —n. small fried cake

frock n. 1 dress 2 robe

frog n. 1 leaping web-footed animal 2 braided loop

from prep. 1 beginning at 2 out of 3 originating with 4 out of the possibility, reach, etc. of 5 as not being like 6 because of

frond n. fern or palm leaf

front n. 1 forward part 2 first part 3 land along a street, ocean, etc. 4 outward behavior —a. of or at the front —v. to face —**front'age** n. —**fron'tal** a.

fron'tier n. 1 border of a country 2 new or unexplored field

frost n. 1 temperature causing freezing 2 frozen dew or vapor —v. cover with frost or frosting

frost'ing n. 1 icing 2 dull finish on glass

froth n., v. foam —**froth'y** a., **-i·er, -i·est**

frown v. 1 contract the brows 2 look with disapproval (on) —n. a frowning

fru'gal a. thrifty or sparing

fruit n. 1 pulpy, edible product of a plant or tree 2 result; product —**fruit'ful** a. —**fruit'less** a.

fry v. **fried** cook in hot fat or oil

fudge n. soft candy made of butter, sugar, etc.

fu'el n. thing burned for heat or power —v. supply with or get fuel

fu'gi·tive n. one who has fled from the law, etc.

ful·fill' v. **-filled'** carry out or complete, as a promise or duty —**ful·fill'ment** n.

full a. 1 containing all there is space for 2 having much in it 3 complete 4 ample —n. greatest amount, extent, etc. —adv. 1 completely 2 exactly —**full'y** adv.

full'-time' a. of work, etc. using all one's regular working hours

fum'ble v. grope or handle clumsily —n. a fumbling

fume n. offensive smoke or vapor

fun n. 1 lively play; merry time 2 source of gaiety

func′tion n. 1 special or typical action, use, duty, etc. 2 formal ceremony or social affair —v. do its work —**func′tion·al** a.

fund n. 1 supply; store 2 money set aside for a purpose 3 pl. ready money

fun′da·men′tal a., n. basic (thing)

fun′da·men′tal·ism′ n. religious beliefs based literally on the Bible —**fun′da·men′tal·ist** n., a.

fu′ner·al n. ceremonies for burial or cremation

fun′gus n., pl. **-gi′** (-jī′, -gī′) or **-gus·es** n. any of the mildews, molds, mushrooms, etc. —**fun′gous** a.

fun′nel n. 1 slim tube with a cone-shaped mouth 2 ship's smokestack

fun′ny a. **-ni·er, -ni·est** 1 amusing 2 [Col.] odd

fur n. soft, thick hair on an animal —**fur′ry** a., **-ri·er, -ri·est**

fu′ri·ous a. full of fury

fur′long n. ⅛ of a mile

fur′nace n. structure in which heat is produced

fur′nish v. 1 put furniture into 2 supply

fur′ni·ture n. chairs, beds, etc. in a room, etc.

fur′row n. 1 groove made in the ground by a plow 2 deep wrinkle —v. make furrows in

fur′ther a. 1 additional 2 more distant —adv. 1 to a greater extent 2 in addition 3 at or to a greater distance —v. to promote —**fur′ther·more′** adv. besides

fur′thest a. most distant —adv. at or to the greatest distance or extent

fu′ry n. 1 wild rage 2 violence

fuse v. melt (together) —n. 1 wick that is lighted to set off an explosive 2 safety device that breaks an electric circuit when the current is too strong —**fu′sion** n.

fuss n. nervous, excited state v. bustle about or worry over trifles —**fuss′y** a., **-i·er, -i·est**

fu·tile (fyoot′l) a. useless

fu′ture a. that is to be or come —n. 1 time that is to come 2 what is going to be; prospects

fuzz n. loose, light particles; fine hairs —**fuzz′y** a., **-i·er, -i·est**

G

ga′ble n. triangular wall enclosed by the sloping ends of a roof

gadg′et (gaj′-) n. small mechanical device

gag v. **gagged** 1 retch or cause to retch 2 keep from speaking as with a gag —n. 1 something put into the mouth to prevent speech 2 joke

gai′e·ty n. 1 cheerfulness 2 merriment

gai′ly adv. 1 merrily 2 brightly

gain n. 1 increase 2 profit —v. 1 earn 2 win 3 get as an addition or advantage 4 reach 5 make progress

gait n. manner of walking or running

gal n. [Col.] girl

ga′la a. festive —n. festival

gal′ax·y n., pl. **-ies** very large group of stars —**ga·lac′tic** a.

gale n. 1 strong wind 2 outburst, as of laughter

gal′lant a. 1 brave and noble 2 polite to women

gal′le·on n. large Spanish ship of 15th-16th centuries

gal′ler·y n., pl. **-ies** 1 covered walk 2 outside balcony 3 theater balcony 4 place for art exhibits

gal′ley n., pl. **-leys** 1 ancient sailing ship with oars 2 ship's kitchen

gal′lon n. four quarts

gal′lop n. fastest gait of a horse —v. go or make go at a gallop

gal′lows n., pl. **-lows** or **-lows·es** structure for hanging condemned persons

ga·losh′es n.pl. high overshoes

gam′ble v. 1 play games of chance for money 2 take a risk 3 bet —n. risk; chance

gam′bol v., n. frolic

game n. 1 amusement or sport with competing players 2 wild animals hunted for sport —v. gamble —a. 1 plucky 2 ready (for) 3 [Col.] lame

gam′ut n. the entire range, esp. of a musical scale

gan′der n. male goose

gang n. group working or acting together

gan′grene′ n. decay of body tissue from lack of blood supply

gang′ster n. member of a gang of criminals

gap n. 1 opening or break 2 blank space

ga·rage′ n. shelter or repair shop for automobiles, etc.

garb n. clothing; style of dress

gar′bage n. waste parts of food

gar′den n. 1 plot for flowers,

vegetables, etc. 2 fertile area 3 public park —v. make, or work in, a garden —**gar'den·er** n.

gar'gle v. rinse the throat —n. liquid for gargling

gar'land n. wreath of flowers, leaves, etc.

gar'lic n. strong-smelling plant bulb, used to season

gar'ment n. piece of clothing

gar'ner v. gather and store

gar'net n. deep-red gem

gar'nish v. decorate (food) —n. decoration for food

gar'ret (gar'-) n. attic

gar'ter n. elastic band to hold up a stocking

gas n. 1 fluid substance that can expand; vapor: some gases are used as fuel 2 gasoline —v.

gassed attack with gas

gash v. cut deep into —n. deep cut

gas'o·line n. liquid fuel from petroleum

gasp v. catch the breath with effort —n. a gasping

gate n. 1 hinged door in a fence or wall 2 number of paid admissions

gate'way n. entrance with a gate

gath'er v. 1 bring or come together; collect 2 infer 3 draw into pleats —n. a pleat —**gath'er·ing** n.

gaud'y a. -i·er, -i·est showy but tasteless —**gaud'i·ly** adv.

gauge (gāj) n. 1 standard measure 2 device for measuring —v. 1 to measure 2 to estimate

gaunt a. haggard; thin

gauze n. loosely woven material

gav'el n. chairman's small mallet

gawk v. stare stupidly

gay a. 1 joyous and lively 2 bright 3 homosexual

gaze v. look steadily; stare —n. steady look

ga·zelle' n. swift antelope

gear n. 1 equipment 2 system of toothed wheels that mesh 3 such a wheel

gear'shift' n. device for changing transmission gears

gel (jel) n. jellylike substance

gel'a·tin n. jellied substance extracted from bones, hoofs, vegetables, etc.

geld (geld) v. castrate (a horse, etc.) —**geld'ing** n.

gem n. precious stone

gen'der n. classification of words as masculine, feminine, or neuter

gene n. unit of heredity in chromosomes

gen'er·al a. 1 of or for all 2 widespread 3 usual 4 not specific —n. high-ranking army officer —**in general** usually

gen'er·ate' v. cause to be; produce —**gen'er·a·tive** a.

gen'er·a'tion n. 1 production 2 all persons born about the same time 3 average time (30 years) between generations

gen'er·a'tor n. machine for changing mechanical into electrical energy

ge·ner'ic a. 1 inclusive; general 2 of a genus

gen'er·ous a. 1 giving readily; unselfish 2 ample

gen'e·sis n. origin —[G-] first book of the Bible

ge·net'ics n. study of heredity —**ge·net'ic** a. —**ge·net'i·cist** n.

gen'i·al (jēn'-) a. kindly; amiable —**ge'ni·al'i·ty** n.

ge'nie n. 1 magic spirit that can be summoned 2 jinni

gen'i·tals n.pl. external sex organs —**gen'i·tal** a.

gen·ius (jēn'yas) n. 1 great mental or creative ability 2 person having this

gen·teel' a. (overly) polite, refined, etc.

gen'tile' (-tīl') a., n. [also G-] non-Jewish (person)

gen'tle a. 1 mild; moderate 2 kindly; patient —**gent'ly** adv.

gen'tle·man n., pl. -men 1 well-bred, courteous man 2 any man: polite term

gen'u·ine (-in) a. 1 real; true 2 sincere

ge'nus n., pl. **gen'er·a** or sometimes **ge'nus·es** class; kind, esp. in biology

ge·o·des'ic a. of a dome with a gridlike framework

ge·og'ra·phy n. science of the earth's surface, climates, plants, animals, etc. —**ge·og'ra·pher** n. —**ge'o·graph'i·cal** a.

ge·ol'o·gy n. science of the earth's crust and of rocks and fossils —**ge·o·log'i·cal** a. —**ge·ol'o·gist** n.

ge·om'e·try n. branch of mathematics dealing with plane and solid figures —**ge'o·met'ric**, **ge'o·met'ri·cal** a.

ge·ra'ni·um n. plant with showy flowers

ger'bil n. small rodent

germ n. 1 microscopic, disease-causing organism 2 seed, bud, etc. 3 origin

ger'mi·nate' v. sprout, as from a seed —**ger'mi·na'tion** n.

ger·on·tol'o·gy (jer'-) n. study of aging —**ger·on·tol'o·gist** n.

ger'ry·man'der (jer'-) v. divide (voting area) unfairly to benefit one party

ger'und (jer'-) n. verbal noun ending in -ing

ges'ture n. movement of part of the body, to express ideas, feelings, etc. —v. make gestures

get v. got, got or got'ten 1 come to have; obtain 2 come, go, or arrive 3 bring 4 make or become 5 [Col.] a) be obliged to (with have or has) b) possess c) baffle d) understand —**get along** manage —**get away** escape —**get by** [Col.] survive; manage —**get over** recover from —**get together** 1 assemble 2 [Col.] reach an agreement —**get up** rise (from sleep, etc.)

gey'ser (gī'zər) n. gushing hot spring

ghost n. supposed disembodied spirit of a dead person

gi'ant n. person or thing of great size, strength, etc. —a. like a giant

gib'bon (gib'-) n. small, slender, long-armed ape

gibe (jīb) v., n. taunt

gib'let (jib'-) n. edible internal part of a fowl

gid'dy a. -di·er, -di·est 1 dizzy 2 frivolous —**gid'di·ness** n.

gift n. 1 a present 2 a giving 3 natural ability

gift'ed a. talented

gi·gan'tic a. huge

gig'gle v. laugh in a nervous, silly way —n. such a laugh

gild v. gild'ed or gilt 1 to cover with a layer of gold 2 make better than it is

gill (gil; n. 2: jil) n. 1 breathing organ of a fish 2 ¼ pint

gilt n. surface layer of gold

gin n. 1 an alcoholic liquor 2 machine for separating cotton from the seeds

gin'ger n. spice from the root of a tropical herb

gi·raffe' n. large African animal with a very long neck

gird'er n. large beam for supporting a floor, etc.

gir'dle n. 1 a belt 2 light, flexible corset

girl n. female child or young woman —**girl'ish** a.

gist (jist) n. main point

give v. gave, giv'en 1 hand over; deliver 2 cause to have 3 produce 4 utter 5 perform 6 bend, etc. from pressure —n. a bending, etc. under pressure —**give out** 1 make public 2 distribute 3 become worn out —**give up** 1 relinquish 2 stop

giv'en a. 1 bestowed 2 accustomed 3 stated

giz'zard n. muscular second stomach of a bird

gla'cier (-shər) n. large mass of ice moving slowly down a slope

glad a. glad'der, glad'dest 1 happy 2 causing joy 3 pleased

glade n. clearing in a forest

glad'i·o'lus n. plant with tall spikes of funnel-shaped flowers: also **glad'i·o'la**

glam'our, glam'or n. bewitching charm

glance v. 1 strike and go off at an angle 2 look briefly —n. a glimpse

gland n. body organ that secretes a substance

glare v. 1 shine with a dazzling light 2 stare fiercely —n. 1 dazzling light 2 fierce stare 3 glassy surface, as of ice

glass n. 1 hard, brittle substance, usually transparent 2 a drinking vessel, mirror, etc. made of this 3 pl. eyeglasses or binoculars

glaze v. 1 furnish with glass 2 give a glossy finish to 3 cover with a sugar coating

gleam n. 1 faint glow of light 2 brief show, as of hope —v. send out a gleam

glee n. joy —**glee'ful** a.

glen n. secluded valley

glide v. to move or descend smoothly and easily

glim'mer v., n. (give) a faint, flickering light

glimpse n. brief, quick view

glis·ten (glis'ən) v., n. sparkle

glit'ter v., n. sparkle

glitz n. [Col.] gaudy showiness —**glitz'y** a., -i·er, -i·est

gloat v. feel or show malicious pleasure

globe n. 1 ball-shaped thing 2 the earth, or a model of it

gloom n. 1 darkness 2 dark place 3 sadness

glo'ry n., pl. -ries 1 great praise or fame 2 splendor 3 heavenly bliss —v. -ried exult (in)

gloss n. 1 surface polish 2 explanation; footnote —**gloss'y** a., -i·er, -i·est

glos'sa·ry n., pl. -ries list of diffi-

glove n. 1 covering for the hand with sheaths for the fingers 2 padded mitt for boxing

glow v. 1 give off bright or steady light 2 be elated 3 be bright with color —n. 1 bright or steady light 2 brightness, warmth, etc.

glue n. thick, adhesive liquid —v. stick together as with glue

glut'ton n. one who eats too much —**glut'ton·ous** a.

gnash (nash) v. grind (the teeth) together

gnat (nat) n. small insect

gnaw (nô) v. 1 wear away by biting 2 torment —**gnaw'ing** a.

gnome (nōm) n. dwarf

gnu (nōō, nyōō) n. African antelope

go v. went, gone 1 move along; pass or proceed 2 depart 3 work, as a clock 4 be or become 5 fit or suit 6 belong in a place —n. 1 a success 2 [Col.] energy 3 [Col.] a try —**go off** explode —**go out** 1 be extinguished 2 go to social affairs, etc. —**go over** 1 examine 2 do again —**go through** 1 endure 2 search —**go under** fail —**let go** release one's hold

goad n. 1 pointed stick 2 spur —v. urge on

goal n. 1 place where a race, trip, etc. ends 2 end striven for 3 place to put the ball or puck to score

goal'keep'er n. player guarding a goal: also **goal'ie** or **goal'tend'er**

goat n. cud-chewing horned animal

gob'ble n. cry of a male turkey —v. 1 make this cry 2 eat greedily —**gob'bler** n.

gob'let n. stemmed glass

gob'lin n. evil spirit

God monotheistic creator and ruler of the universe —n. [g-] any divine being —**god'dess** n.fem. —**god'like** a.

god'child' n. the person (**god'daugh'ter** or **god'son'**) that a godparent sponsors

god'par'ent n. spiritual sponsor (**god'fa'ther** or **god'moth'er**) of an infant, esp. at baptism

go'ing n. 1 departure 2 degree of ease in traveling

goi'ter, goi'tre n. enlargement of the thyroid gland

gold n. 1 yellow precious metal, a chemical element 2 money; wealth 3 bright yellow —a. of gold —**gold'en** a.

gold'en·rod' n. plant with long, yellow flower clusters

gold'fish' n. small yellowish fish, kept in ponds, etc.

golf n. outdoor game in which a small ball is driven, with special clubs, into holes —**golf'er** n.

gon'er n. person sure to die, be ruined, etc.

gong n. metal disk that resounds loudly when struck

good a. **bet'ter, best** 1 having proper qualities 2 beneficial 3 of moral excellence 4 enjoyable, happy, etc. 5 considerable —n. 1 worth or virtue 2 benefit

good'bye', good'-bye' int., n. farewell: also written **good'by'** or **good'-by'**

good'-na'tured a. pleasant

goods n.pl. 1 personal property 2 wares 3 fabric

goof [Sl.] n. 1 a blunder 2 stupid or silly person —v. 1 to blunder 2 waste time: with off

goose n., pl. **geese** 1 long-necked water bird like a large duck 2 silly person

go'pher n. burrowing rodent

gore n. 1 clotted blood 2 tapered cloth inserted to add width —v. 1 pierce as with a tusk 2 insert gores in

gorge n. deep, narrow pass —v. eat or stuff greedily

go·ril'la n. largest of the apes, native to Africa

gos'pel n. 1 [often G-] teachings of Jesus and the Apostles 2 belief proclaimed as true

gos'sip n. 1 one who chatters about others 2 such idle talk

gouge (gouj) n. 1 chisel for cutting grooves 2 such a groove —v. 1 scoop out as with a gouge 2 [Col.] overcharge —**goug'er** n.

gourd (gôrd, goord) n. 1 bulb-shaped fruit of a trailing plant 2 its dried shell hollowed out for use

gour·met (goor mā', gôr-) n. judge of fine foods and drinks

gov'ern v. 1 control 2 influence; determine

gov'ern·ment n. 1 control; rule 2 system of ruling 3 those who rule —**gov'ern·men'tal** a.

gov'er·nor n. 1 one who governs; esp., head of a State 2 device to control engine speed automatically

gown n. 1 woman's dress 2 long

robe, as for a judge

grab v. **grabbed** snatch suddenly

grace n. **1** beauty of form, movement, etc. **2** favor; good will **3** delay granted for payment due **4** prayer of thanks at a meal **5** God's love for man —v. **graced** dignify or adorn — **grace'ful** a. **—grace'ful·ly** adv.

gra'cious (-shəs) a. kind, polite, charming, pleasing, etc.

grade n. **1** degree in a scale of rank or quality **2** slope **3** any of the school years through the 12th **4** mark or rating, as on a test —v. **1** classify; sort **2** give a GRADE (n. 4) to **3** make (ground) slope or level

grad'u·al a. little by little

grad'u·ate (-ət; v: -āt') n. one who has completed a course of study at a school or college —v. **1** give a diploma to (a graduate) **2** become a graduate **3** mark with degrees for measuring

graft n. **1** shoot, etc. of one plant inserted in another to grow **2** transplanting of skin, etc. **3** dishonest gain of money by public officers —v. insert (a graft)

grain n. **1** seed of wheat, corn, etc. **2** cereal plants **3** particle, as of salt or sand **4** smallest unit of weight **5** natural markings on wood, leather, etc.

gram n. metric unit of weight (⅕ of an ounce)

gram'mar n. system of speaking and writing a language —**gram·mat'i·cal** a.

grand a. great in size, beauty, importance, etc.; imposing, splendid, etc. —n. [Sl.] a thousand dollars

grand'child' n. child (**grand'-daugh'ter** or **grand'son'**) of one's son or daughter

gran'deur (-jər, -dyoor) n. great size, beauty, etc.; splendor

grand'par'ent n. parent (**grand'-fa'ther** or **grand'moth'er**) of one's father or mother

gran'ite (-it) n. very hard crystalline rock

gran·o'la n. breakfast cereal of oats, honey, nuts, etc.

grant v. **1** consent to or give **2** concede —n. something granted **—take for granted** consider as a fact

grape n. small, round fruit growing in clusters

grape'fruit' n. large citrus fruit with a yellow rind

graph n. a diagram that shows changes in value

graph'ic a. **1** vivid; in lifelike detail **2** of the arts of drawing, printing, etc.

graph'ite' n. soft, black carbon in pencils, etc.

grasp v. **1** grip; seize **2** comprehend —n. **1** a grip **2** control **3** power to grasp

grass n. **1** green plant grown for lawns **2** cereal plant **3** pasture

grass'hop'per n. leaping insect with long hind legs

grate v. **1** form into particles by scraping **2** rub with a harsh sound **3** irritate —n. **1** frame of bars to hold fuel **2** framework of bars over an opening

grate'ful a. thankful

grat'i·fy' v. **-fied'** please **2** indulge —**grat'i·fi·ca'tion** n.

grat'ing n. GRATE (n. 2)

grat'i·tude' n. thankful appreciation

gra·tu'i·ty n., pl. **-ties** gift of money for a service

grave a. **1** serious **2** solemn —n. **1** burial place, esp. a hole in the ground

grav'el n. bits of rock

grave'yard' n. cemetery

grav'i·ty n. **1** seriousness **2** weight **3** Physics force of mutual attraction between masses; esp., the pull on bodies toward earth's center

gra'vy n., pl. **-vies** juice from cooking meat

gray n. mixture of black and white —a. **1** of this color **2** dreary —**gray'ish** a.

graze v. **1** feed on growing grass, etc. **2** rub lightly in passing

grease n. **1** melted animal fat **2** thick oily lubricant —v. put grease on —**greas'y** a., **-i·er, -i·est**

great a. much larger, more, or better than average

Great Dane n. large, strong dog with short hair

greed n. excessive desire, as for wealth —**greed'y** a., **-i·er, -i·est**

green n. **1** color of grass **2** pl. leafy vegetables **3** smooth turf —a. **1** of the color green **2** unripe **3** inexperienced

green'house' n. heated glass building for growing plants

greet v. address, meet, or receive in a certain way

gre·nade' n. small bomb usually thrown by hand

grey n., a. Br. sp. of GRAY

grey'hound' n. swift dog

grid n. 1 GRATE (n. 2) 2 network of crossed lines, as on a map

grief n. deep sorrow

grieve v. be or make sad

grill n. 1 framework on which to broil 2 restaurant serving grilled foods —v. 1 broil 2 question relentlessly

grim a. **grim'mer, grim'mest** 1 fierce 2 hideous; ghastly

grime n. sooty dirt —**grim'y** a., **-i-er, -i-est**

grin v. **grinned** smile broadly — n. such a smile

grind v. **ground** 1 crush into bits 2 sharpen, smooth, etc. by friction 3 rub harshly 4 work by cranking —n. hard task

grip n. 1 firm hold 2 handclasp 3 a handle 4 a valise —v. **gripped** hold firmly

grit n. 1 rough bits of sand, etc. 2 obstinate courage

groan v., n. (utter) a deep sound of pain, etc.

gro'cer n. storekeeper who sells food, etc.

gro'cer·y n., pl. **-ies** 1 store of a grocer 2 pl. goods sold by a grocer

groin n. fold where the abdomen joins either thigh

groom n. 1 man who tends horses 2 bridegroom

groove n. 1 narrow furrow 2 channel 3 routine —v. make a groove in

grope v. feel or search about blindly

gross (grōs) a. 1 flagrant 2 coarse 3 total —n. 1 overall total 2 pl. gross twelve dozen

gro·tesque' (-tesk') a. 1 distorted 2 absurd

ground v. 1 pt. & pp. of GRIND 2 set or keep on the ground 3 base 4 instruct (in) —n. 1 land; earth 2 pl. tract of land 3 often pl. cause or basis 4 background 5 pl. dregs

ground'hog' n. woodchuck

group n. persons or things gathered or classed together —v. form a group

grouse n. game bird

grove n. small group of trees

grov·el (gruv'-, gräv'-) v. 1 crawl abjectly 2 behave humbly

grow v. **grew, grown** 1 develop 2 increase 3 become 4 raise (crops) —**grow up** to mature

growl n. rumbling sound, as of an angry dog —v. make this sound

grown'-up' (n.: -up') a., n. adult

growth n. 1 a growing 2 something that grows

grub v. **grubbed** 1 dig or dig up 2 work hard —n. 1 wormlike larva, esp. of a beetle 2 [Sl.] food

grub'by a. **-bi-er, -bi-est** dirty; untidy

grudge n. resentment or a reason for this

grue'some a. causing loathing and horror

grum'ble v. mutter in discontent

grunt v., n. (utter with) the deep sound of a hog

guar·an·tee' (gar'-) n. 1 pledge to replace something sold if faulty 2 assurance 3 pledge or security for another's debt or obligation —v. 1 give a guarantee for 2 assure

guard (gärd) v. 1 protect; defend 2 keep from escape 3 take precautions (against) —n. 1 a person or thing that guards 2 careful watch

guard'i·an n. 1 one legally in charge of a minor, etc. 2 custodian

gu·ber·na·to'ri·al a. of a governor or governor's office

guer·ril'la (ga-) n. fighter who makes raids behind enemy lines

guess (ges) v. 1 estimate; judge 2 suppose —n. judgment

guest n. 1 one entertained at another's home, etc. 2 paying customer, as at a hotel —a. 1 for guests 2 performing by invitation

guide v. 1 show the way to 2 control —n. person or thing that guides —**guid'ance** n.

guild (gild) n. association to promote mutual interests

guile (gīl) n. deceit

guilt n. 1 fact of having committed an offense 2 painful feeling that one has done a wrong

guilt'y a. **-i-er, -i-est** having or showing guilt —**guilt'i·ly** adv.

guin·ea pig (gin'ē) n. small rodent used in experiments

guise (gīz) n. assumed or false appearance

gui·tar' n. musical instrument usually with six strings plucked or strummed —**gui·tar'ist** n.

gulch n. deep narrow valley

gulf n. 1 ocean area partly enclosed by land 2 wide chasm 3 vast separation

gull n. 1 gray and white seabird 2 dupe —v. cheat

gul'ly n., pl. **-lies** narrow ravine

gulp v. swallow greedily or hastily —n. a gulping

gum n. 1 sticky substance from some plants 2 an adhesive 3 flesh around the teeth

gun n. weapon for shooting projectiles —v. **gunned** 1 to shoot or hunt with a gun 2 to increase the speed of (an engine)

gun'pow'der n. explosive powder used in guns, etc.

gur'gle n. bubbling sound —v. make this sound

gu'ru n. Hindu spiritual advisor or teacher

gush v. 1 flow copiously 2 talk too emotionally —n. a gushing

gust n. 1 sudden rush of air 2 sudden outburst

gut n. 1 intestine 2 cord made of intestines 3 pl. [Col.] courage

gut'ter n. channel to carry off rain water, etc.

guy n. 1 guiding rope 2 [Sl.] boy or man

gym (jim) n. [Col.] gymnasium

gym·na'si·um n. place for physical training and sports

gym·nas'tics n.pl. v 1 exercises for the muscles 2 sport employing acrobatics, etc. —**gym'nast'** n. —**gym·nas'tic** a.

Gyp'sy n., pl. **-sies** [also **g-**] one of a wandering people

gy'ro·scope' n. wheel mounted in a ring and spinning rapidly, used as a stabilizer

H

ha'be·as cor'pus n. writ requiring a court to decide the legality of holding a prisoner

hab'it n. 1 costume 2 custom 3 fixed practice

hab'i·tat' n. natural living place

ha·bit'u·al (-bich'ōō-) a. 1 done by habit 2 constant 3 usual

hack v. 1 chop roughly 2 cough harshly —n. 1 gash 2 harsh cough 3 vehicle for hire 4 old, worn-out horse 5 a literary drudge

hack'er n. 1 unskilled golfer 2 talented amateur computer user

had'dock n. small ocean fish used as food

hag n. ugly old woman

hag'gard a. having a wasted, worn look; gaunt

hai'ku' (hī'-) n. three-line Japanese poem

hail n. 1 greeting 2 frozen raindrops 3 shower of or like hail —int. shout of greeting, etc. —v.

cheer 2 shout to 3 pour down (like) hail

hair n. 1 threadlike outgrowth from the skin 2 growth of these, as on the head —**split hairs** quibble —**hair'y** a., **-i'er**, **-i'est**

hale a. healthy; robust

half n., pl. **halves** either of the two equal parts of a thing —a. 1 being a half 2 partial —adv. 1 to the extent of a half 2 partially

half'heart'ed a. with little enthusiasm or interest

half'way' a. 1 midway between points 2 partial —adv. to the halfway point

hal'i·but n. large flounder

hall n. 1 public building with offices 2 large room for meetings, shows, etc. 3 vestibule 4 passageway

hal·le·lu'jah, hal·le·lu'iah (-ya) int., n. praise (to) God

hal'low v. make or regard as holy

hal·lu·ci·na'tion n. apparent perception of sights, etc. not really present —**hal·lu'ci·nate'** v.

hall'way' n. corridor

ha'lo n. ring of light

halt v. 1 to stop 2 to limp 3 hesitate —n. a stop

halve (hav) v. 1 divide into halves 2 reduce to half

ham n. 1 upper part of a hog's hind leg 2 [Col.] amateur radio operator

ham'burg'er n. 1 ground beef 2 cooked patty of such meat, often in a bun Also **ham'burg**

ham'let n. small village

ham'mer n. tool with a metal head for pounding —v. pound, drive, shape, etc. as with a hammer

ham'mock n. bed of canvas, etc. swung from ropes

ham'per v. hinder; impede —n. large basket

hand n. 1 end of the arm beyond the wrist 2 side or direction 3 active part 4 handwriting 5 applause 6 help 7 hired worker 8 pointer on a clock 9 cards held by a player in a card game —a. of, for, or by the hand —v. give as with the hand —**on hand** available —**hand'ful** n.

hand'book' n. compact book of instructions or facts

hand'cuff' n. one of a pair of shackles for the wrists

hand'gun' n. firearm held with one hand, as a pistol

hand'i·cap' n. 1 difficulty or

advantage given to some contestants to equalize their chances 2 hindrance 3 physical disability —v. -capped' hinder

hand'i·craft n. work calling for skill with the hands

hand·ker·chief (haŋ'kər chif') n. small cloth for wiping the nose

han'dle n. part of tool, etc. by which it is held —v. 1 touch, lift, etc. with the hand 2 manage 3 deal with 4 deal in; sell

hand'some adv. 1 good-looking in a manly or impressive way 2 sizable 3 gracious

hand'writ'ing n. writing done by hand —**hand'writ'ten** a.

hand'y a. -i·er, -i·est 1 nearby 2 easily used 3 clever with the hands —**hand'i·ly** adv.

hang v. hung or (v. 3) hanged 1 to attach or be attached from above 2 attach so as to swing freely 3 kill by suspending from a rope above the neck 4 attach to walls 5 droop —**hang on** 1 keep hold 2 persevere —**hang up** 1 end a telephone call 2 delay

hang'ar n. aircraft shelter

Ha·nu·ka (hä'noo kä') n. Jewish festival

hap'haz·ard a. not planned; random —adv. by chance

hap'pen v. 1 take place 2 occur by chance 3 have the luck or occasion

hap'py a. -pi·er, -pi·est 1 showing pleasure or joy 2 lucky 3 apt —**hap'pi·ly** adv.

ha·rangue' (-raŋ') v., n. (to address in) a noisy or scolding speech

ha·rass (hə ras', har'əs) v. trouble or attack constantly

har'bor n. protected inlet for ships —v. 1 to shelter 2 hold in the mind

hard a. 1 firm or solid 2 powerful 3 difficult to do, understand, etc. 4 harsh —adv. 1 with energy 2 with strength 3 firmly

hard'heart'ed a. cruel

hard'ly adv. 1 barely 2 not likely

hard'ship' n. thing hard to bear, as poverty, pain, etc.

hard'ware' n. 1 metal articles, as tools, nails, etc. 2 electronic equipment

hard'y a. -di·er, -di·est 1 bold and resolute 2 robust

hare n. rabbit, esp. one of the larger kind

ha·rem (her'əm) n. 1 quarters

for the women in a Muslim's house 2 these women

hark v. [Poet.] listen

harm n., v. hurt; damage

har·mon·i·ca n. small wind instrument held to the mouth

har'mo·nize' v. 1 be, sing, etc. in harmony 2 bring into harmony

har'mo·ny n. 1 pleasing agreement of parts 2 agreement in ideas, action, etc. 3 pleasing combination of musical tones —**har·mo'ni·ous** a.

har'ness n. straps, etc. for hitching a horse to a wagon, etc. —v. 1 put a harness on 2 control for use

harp n. stringed musical instrument played by plucking

har·poon' n. barbed shaft for spearing whales

har'row (har'-) n. frame with spikes or disks for breaking up plowed land

harsh a. 1 rough to the ear, eye, taste, etc. 2 cruel or severe

har'vest n. 1 a season's crop or the gathering of it 2 season for this —v. reap

has'sle n. [Col.] annoying or troubling situation —v. [Sl.] annoy; harass

has'sock n. firm cushion used as a footstool, etc.

haste n. hurry or rush

hast'y a. -i·er, -i·est done with haste —**hast'i·ly** adv.

hat n. head covering, often with a brim

hatch v. 1 bring or come forth from (an egg) 2 contrive (a plot) —n. hatchway or its lid

hatch'et n. short ax

hate v. dislike strongly —n. strong dislike: also **ha'tred**

hate'ful a. deserving hate

haugh·ty (hôt'ē) a. -ti·er, -ti·est scornfully proud

haul v. 1 pull; drag 2 transport by truck, etc.

haunch n. hip, rump, and upper thigh

haunt v. 1 visit often 2 recur often to —n. place often visited

haunt'ed a. supposedly frequented by ghosts

have v. had 1 hold; possess 2 experience 3 hold mentally 4 get; take 5 beget 6 engage in 7 cause to do, be, etc. 8 permit 9 be forced —**Have** is also an auxiliary verb —**have to do with** deal with

ha'ven n. shelter; refuge

hav'oc n. great destruction

hawk n. bird of prey —v. 1 peddle (goods) in the streets 2 clear the throat

hay n. grass, clover, etc. cut and dried —**hay'stack'** n.

haz'ard n. 1 chance 2 risk; danger 3 obstacle on a golf course —v. to risk —**haz'ard·ous** a.

haze n. 1 mist of fog, smoke, etc. 2 vagueness —**ha'zy** a., **-zi·er, -zi·est**

he pron. 1 the male mentioned 2 anyone

head n. 1 part of the body above or in front of the neck 2 mind 3 top or front part 4 leader 5 crisis 6 poise —a. 1 chief 2 at the head —v. 1 to lead 2 set out; go —**head off** intercept

head'ache' n. pain in the head

head'ing n. title; caption

head'light' n. light at the front of a vehicle

head'line' n. title of newspaper article —v. feature

head'long' a., adv. 1 with the head first 2 rash(ly)

head'quar'ters n.pl. center of operations; main office

heal v. cure or mend

health n. 1 soundness of body and mind 2 physical condition —**health'ful** a. —**health'y** a., **-i·er, -i·est**

heap n. v. pile; mass

hear v. **heard** 1 receive (sounds) through the ear 2 listen to 3 be told —**not hear of** not permit

hear'ing n. 1 ability to hear 2 chance to be heard

hearse (hurs) n. vehicle to carry a body to the grave

heart n. 1 organ that circulates the blood 2 vital part 3 love, sympathy, courage, etc. 4 figure shaped like ♥ —**by heart** from memory

heart'en v. encourage

hearth (härth) n. 1 floor of a fireplace 2 home

heart'y a. **-i·er, -i·est** 1 cordial 2 vigorous 3 strong and healthy 4 nourishing —**heart'i·ly** adv.

heat n. 1 hotness, or the perception of it 2 strong feeling 3 single race, etc. in a series 4 sexual excitement in animals —v. to make or become hot

heath'er (heth'-) n. low plant with purple flowers

heave v. **heaved** or **hove** 1 lift, or lift and throw, with effort 2 make (a sigh) with effort 3 rise and fall in rhythm 4 retch or vomit —n. act of heaving

heav'en Theol. the place where God and the angels are —n. 1 pl. sky 2 state of bliss —**heav'en·ly** a.

heav'y a. **-i·er, -i·est** 1 weighing much 2 very great, intense, etc. 3 sorrowful

heav'y-du'ty a. made to withstand hard use

heck'le v. annoy with questions, taunts, etc. —**heck'ler** n.

hec'tic a. rushed, frenzied, etc.

hedge n. dense row of shrubs

hedge'hog' n. porcupine

heed n. careful attention —v. pay heed (to) —**heed'ful** a.

heel n. 1 back part of the foot 2 part of shoe, etc. at the heel —v. 1 furnish with heels 2 follow closely 3 lean to one side, as a ship

heif'er (hef'-) n. young cow

height n. 1 highest point or degree 2 distance from bottom to top 3 altitude 4 pl. high place

height'en v. make or become higher, greater, etc.

heir (er) n. one who inherits another's property, etc. —**heir'ess** n.fem.

heir'loom' n. a possession handed down in a family

hel'i·cop'ter n. aircraft with a horizontal propeller above the fuselage

he'li·um n. very light, nonflammable gas, a chemical element

hell Theol. place of torment for sinners after death —n. state of evil or great suffering

hel·lo' int. exclamation of greeting

helm n. 1 tiller or wheel to steer a ship 2 control

hel'met n. protective head covering of metal, etc.

help v. 1 give assistance (to); aid 2 to remedy 3 avoid 4 serve —n. 1 aid; assistance 2 remedy 3 one that helps 4 hired helper(s)

hem v. **hemmed** 1 fold the edge of and sew down 2 surround or confine 3 clear the throat audibly —n. hemmed edge —**hem and haw** hesitate in speaking

hem'i·sphere' n. 1 half a sphere 2 any of the halves (N or S, E or W) of the earth

hem'or·rhage' ('-ər ij') n. heavy bleeding —v. bleed heavily

hemp n. tall plant with fibers used to make rope, etc.

hen n. female of the chicken or

certain other birds

hence *adv.* 1 from this place or time 2 therefore

her *pron.* objective case of SHE —*a.* of her

her'ald *n.* 1 messenger 2 forerunner —*v.* foretell

herb (urb, hurb) *n.* nonwoody plant, now esp. one used as seasoning or in medicine —**herb'al** (hur'bal, ur'-) *a.*

herd *n.* cattle, etc. feeding or living together —*v.* form into a herd or group

here *adv.* 1 in, at, or to this place 2 at this point; now —*n.* this place

here·af'ter *adv.* from now on —*n.* state after death

he·red'i·tar·y *a.* of, or passed down by, heredity or inheritance

he·red'i·ty *n.* passing on of characteristics to offspring or descendants

here·in' *adv.* in this place, matter, writing, etc.

her'e·sy (her'-) *n.*, *pl.* -sies unorthodox opinion or religious belief —**her'e·tic** *n.*

her'it·age *n.* tradition, etc. handed down from the past

her'mit *n.* one who lives alone in a secluded place

her'ni·a *n.* rupture, as of the abdominal wall

he·ro (hir'ō) *n.*, *pl.* -roes 1 brave, noble person, esp. a man 2 central male character in a story —**he·ro'ic** *a.* —**her·o·ine** (her'ō in') *n.fem.* —**her'o·ism** *n.*

her'o·in *n.* narcotic

her'on *n.* wading bird

her'ring *n.* food fish of the Atlantic

hers *pron.* that or those belonging to her

her·self' *pron.* intensive or reflexive form of SHE

hes'i·tate' *v.* 1 feel unsure; waver 2 pause

het·er·o·sex'u·al *a.* of or having sexual desire for those of the opposite sex —*n.* heterosexual person

hex'a·gon' *n.* figure with six angles and six sides —**hex·ag'o·nal** *a.*

hi'ber·nate' *v.* spend the winter in a sleeplike state

hic'cup *n.* muscle spasm that stops the breath —*v.* have a hiccup

hick'o·ry *n.*, *pl.* -ries 1 hardwood tree 2 its nut

hide *v.* hid, hid'den or hid 1 put,

or be, out of sight 2 keep secret —*n.* animal skin or pelt

hid'e·ous *a.* very ugly

hi'er·o·glyph'ics (hī'ər ə glif'-, hī'rə glif'-) *n.pl.* picture writing, as of the ancient Egyptians

high *a.* 1 tall 2 to, at, or from a height 3 above others in rank, size, cost, etc. 4 raised in pitch; shrill 5 elated 6 [Sl.] drunk or influenced by drugs —*adv.* in or to a high level, etc. —*n.* 1 high level, degree, etc. 2 the gear arrangement giving greatest speed —**high'ly** *adv.*

high school *n.* school from grades 10 (or 9) through 12

high'way' *n.* main road

hike *v.*, *n.* 1 (take) a long walk 2 [Col.] increase

hi·lar'i·ous *a.* very funny or merry —**hi·lar'i·ty** *n.*

hill *n.* mound of land —**hill'y** *a.*, -i·er, -i·est

hilt *n.* handle of a sword, dagger, etc.

him *pron.* objective case of HE

him·self' *pron.* intensive or reflexive form of HE

hind *a.* back; rear

hin'der *v.* keep back; stop or thwart —**hin'drance** *n.*

hinge *n.* joint on which a door, etc. swings

hint *n.* slight indication —*v.* give a hint

hip *n.* part between the upper thigh and the waist

hip·po·pot'a·mus *n.*, *pl.* -mus·es or -mi' (-mī') large, thick-skinned animal of Africa

hire *v.* pay for the services or use of —*n.* amount paid in hiring

his *pron.* that or those belonging to him —*a.* of him

His·pan'ic *n.* Spanish-speaking Latin American living in U.S.

hiss *n.* prolonged *s* sound —*v.* 1 make this sound 2 disapprove of by hissing

his·to·ry *n.*, *pl.* -ries study or record of past events —**his·to'ri·an** *n.* —**his·tor'i·cal**, **his·tor'ic** *a.*

hit *v.* hit 1 come against with force; bump 2 give a blow (to); strike 3 affect strongly 4 come (*on* or *upon*) —*n.* 1 a blow 2 collision 3 successful song, play, etc. —**hit'ter** *n.*

hitch *v.* 1 move with jerks 2 fasten with a hook, knot, etc. —*n.* 1 a tug; jerk 2 hindrance 3 kind of knot

hith'er *adv.* to this place

hive *n.* 1 colony of bees or its

shelter 2 *pl.* skin allergy with raised, itching patches

hoard *n.* hidden supply —*v.* accumulate and store away (money, etc.) —**hoard'er** *n.*

hoarse *a.* sounding rough and husky

hoax *n.* a trick; practical joke

hob'by *n., pl.* **-bies** pastime activity —**hob'by·ist** *n.*

hock'ey *n.* team game played on ice skates

hoe *n.* garden tool with a thin blade on a long handle —*v.* **hoed** cultivate with a hoe

hog *n.* 1 pig 2 [Col.] greedy person —*v.* **hogged** [Sl.] take all of

hoist *v.* raise, esp. with a crane, etc. —*n.* apparatus for lifting

hold *v.* **held** 1 keep in the hands 2 keep in a certain position 3 keep back 4 occupy 5 have (a meeting, etc.) 6 contain 7 regard 8 remain unyielding —*n.* 1 grip 2 [Col.] strong influence 3 ship's interior below deck

hole *n.* 1 hollow place 2 burrow 3 an opening, tear, etc.

hol'i·day *n.* 1 religious festival 2 work-free day, usually set aside by law

hol'ler *v., n.* [Col.] shout

hol'low *a.* 1 having a cavity within it 2 concave; sunken 3 insincere 4 deep-toned and dull —*n.* 1 cavity 2 small valley —*v.* make or become hollow

hol'ly *n.* evergreen shrub with red berries

hol·o·caust (häl'ə kôst') *n.* great destruction, esp. of people or animals by fire

hol'ster *n.* leather pistol case

ho'ly *a.* **-li·er, -li·est** 1 sacred 2 sinless 3 deserving reverence or worship

hom'age (häm'-, äm'-) *n.* anything done to show honor or respect

home *n.* 1 place where one lives 2 household or life around it —*a.* 1 domestic 2 central —*adv.* 1 at or to home 2 to the target —**home'less** *a.* —**home'made'** *a.*

home'ly *a.* **-li·er, -li·est** 1 simple 2 plain; ugly

home run *n. Baseball* hit by which the batter scores a run

home'stead' *n.* 1 a home and its grounds 2 public land granted as a farm

home'ward *adv., a.* toward home

hom'i·cide' *n.* 1 a killing of one

person by another 2 one who kills another —**hom'i·ci'dal** *a.*

ho·mog·e·nize' ('-mäj'-) *v.* make uniform throughout

hom'o·graph' *n.* word with same spelling as another but having a different meaning

ho'mo·sex'u·al *a.* of or having sexual desire for those of the same sex —*n.* homosexual person

hone *v.* sharpen

hon'est (än'-) *a.* 1 not cheating, stealing, or lying; upright 2 sincere or genuine 3 frank and open —**hon'es·ty** *n.*

hon'ey *n.* sweet, syrupy substance made by bees (**hon'ey·bees'**)

hon'ey·moon' *n.* vacation for a newly married couple

honk *n.* 1 call of a wild goose 2 sound of an auto horn —*v.* make this sound

hon'or (än'-) *n.* 1 high regard 2 good reputation 3 adherence to right principles 4 glory or credit 5 [H-] title of certain officials 6 something showing respect 7 source of respect or fame —*v.* 1 treat with respect or high regard 2 confer an honor on 3 accept as valid

hood *n.* 1 covering for the head and neck 2 cover over an automobile engine 3 [Sl.] hoodlum

hoof *n., pl.* **hoofs** or **hooves** horny covering on the feet of cattle, horses, etc.

hook *n.* 1 bent piece of metal used to catch or hold something; spec., one for catching fish 2 sharp curve or curving motion —*v.* catch, fasten, hit, etc. with a hook

hoop *n.* large, circular band

hoot *n.* 1 cry an owl makes 2 shout of scorn —*v.* utter a hoot or hoots

hop *v.* **hopped** leap on one foot, or with all feet at once —*n.* 1 a hopping 2 [Col.] a dance 3 *pl.* dried cones of a vine, used to flavor beer, etc.

hope *n.* 1 trust that what is wanted will happen 2 object of this —*v.* want and expect

horde *n.* a crowd; pack

ho·ri'zon *n.* line where sky and earth seem to meet

hor'i·zon'tal *a.* 1 parallel to the horizon 2 level

hor'mone' *n.* substance that is formed by a gland and stimulates an organ

horn n. 1 bonelike growth on the head of a cow, etc. 2 brass musical instrument —**horned** a.

hor'net n. large wasp

hor'o·scope n. chart of the zodiac used by astrologers

hor·ren'dous a. horrible

hor'ri·ble a. 1 causing horror 2 [Col.] very bad, ugly, etc.

hor'rid a. horrible

hor'ri·fy v. **-fied** 1 make feel horror 2 [Col.] shock greatly

hor'ror n. 1 strong fear or dislike 2 cause of this

horse n. large animal domesticated for pulling loads, carrying a rider, etc.

horse'pow'er n. unit of power output, as of engines

hor'ti·cul'ture n. art of growing flowers, fruits, etc.

ho·san'na int., n. shout of praise to God

hose n. 1 pl. **hose** stocking 2 flexible tube to convey liquids

hos'pice (-pis) n. shelter for travelers, sick, poor, etc.

hos'pi·tal n. place of medical care for sick and injured —**hos'pi·tal·ize'** v.

host n. 1 man who entertains guests 2 great number

hos'tage n. person held as a pledge

host'ess n. 1 woman who acts as a host 2 woman in charge of seating in a restaurant

hos'tile (-tal) a. 1 of or like an enemy 2 unfriendly

hot a. **hot'ter, hot'test** 1 high in temperature; very warm 2 spicy; peppery 3 angry, violent, eager, etc. 4 close behind

ho·tel' n. place with rooms, food, etc. for travelers

hound n. breed of hunting dog

hour n. 1 1/24 of a day; 60 minutes 2 a certain time —**hour'ly** a., adv.

house (v.: houz) n. 1 building to live in 2 family 3 building for specified use 4 business firm 5 legislative assembly —v. cover, shelter, lodge, etc.

house'hold' n. 1 all those living in one house 2 home and its affairs

house'keep'er n. a woman who manages a home

house'work' n. work of cleaning, cooking, etc. in a house

hous'ing (houz'-) n. 1 shelter or lodging; houses 2 enclosing frame, box, etc.

hov'er (huv'-) v. 1 flutter in the air near one place 2 linger close by

how adv. 1 in what way 2 in what condition 3 why 4 to what extent

how·ev'er adv. 1 by whatever means 2 to whatever degree —con. nevertheless

howl v. 1 long, wailing cry of a wolf, dog, etc. 2 similar cry, as of pain —v. 1 utter a howl 2 laugh in scorn, mirth, etc.

hub n. 1 center of a wheel 2 center of activity, etc.

hud'dle v. 1 to crowd close together 2 draw (oneself) up tightly

hue n. color; tint

hug v. **hugged** 1 embrace 2 keep close to —n. embrace

huge a. very large; immense

hu'la n. native Hawaiian dance

hull n. 1 outer covering of a seed or fruit 2 main body of a ship

hum v. **hummed** 1 sing with closed lips 2 make a low, steady murmur —n. this sound

hu'man a. of or like a person or people —n. a person: also **human being** —**hu'man·ly** adv.

hu·mane' a. kind, merciful, etc.

hu·man·i·tar'i·an n. one devoted to promoting the welfare of humanity

hu·man'i·ty n. 1 a being human or humane 2 the human race

hu'man·ize' v. make human or humane

hu'man·kind' n. people

hum'ble a. 1 not proud; modest 2 lowly; unpretentious —v. to make humble —**hum'bly** adv.

hu'mid a. damp; moist

hu·mid'i·fy' v. **-fied'** make humid

hu·mil'i·ate' v. lower the pride or dignity of; mortify

hu·mil'i·ty n. humbleness

hum'ming·bird' n. tiny bird·able to hover

hu'mor n. 1 comical quality, talk, etc. 2 ability to see or express what is funny 3 mood 4 whim —**hu'mor·ist** n. —**hu'mor·ous** a.

hump n. rounded bulge

hu'mus n. dark soil made up of decayed leaves, etc.

hunch v. arch into a hump —n. 1 a hump 2 feeling not based on facts

hun'dred a., n. ten times ten —**hun'dredth** a., n.

hun'ger n. 1 need or craving for food 2 strong desire —v. feel hunger (for) —**hun'gry** a., **gri-**

er, -gri·est —**hun′gri·ly** *adv.*
hunk *n.* [Col.] large piece
hunt *v.* 1 search out (game) to catch or kill 2 search; seek 3 chase —*n.* a chase or search
hur′dle *n.* 1 frame for jumping over in a race 2 obstacle
hurl *v.* throw with force or violence —**hurl′er** *n.*
hur·rah′ *int., n.* shout of joy, approval, etc.: also **hur·ray′**
hur′ri·cane′ *n.* violent storm from the tropics
hur′ry *v.* **-ried** —*n.* move, act, etc. with haste; rush —*n.* rush; haste
hurt *v.* **hurt** 1 cause pain or injury to 2 damage 3 offend 4 have pain —*n.* pain, injury, or harm —**hurt′ful** *a.*
hus′band *n.* married man
hus′band·ry *n.* 1 thrifty management 2 farming
hush *v.* make or become silent —*n.* silence; quiet
husk *n.* dry covering of some fruits and seeds —*v.* remove the husk from
husk′y *a.* **-i·er, -i·est** 1 hoarse 2 big and strong —*n.* [also H-] arctic dog used for pulling sleds
hus′tle (-al) *v.* 1 shove roughly 2 move, work, etc. quickly or energetically —*n.* a hustling
hut *n.* shedlike cabin
hy′brid *n.* offspring of two animals or plants of different species, etc.
hy′drant *n.* large pipe with a valve for drawing water from a water main
hy′dro·e·lec′tric *a.* of the production of electricity by water power
hy′dro·gen *n.* colorless gas, the lightest chemical element
hydrogen bomb *n.* very destructive atomic bomb
hy′dro·pho′bi·a *n.* rabies
hy·e′na *n.* wolflike animal of Africa and Asia
hy′giene′ (-jēn′) *n.* set of principles for health
hy′gi·en′ic (-jē en′-, -jen′-) *a.* 1 of hygiene or health 2 sanitary
hymn (him) *n.* song of praise, esp. a religious one
hym′nal *n.* book of hymns: also **hymn′book′**
hy′phen *n.* mark (-) used between parts or syllables of a word
hyp·no′sis *n.* sleeplike state in which one responds to the hypnotist's suggestions
hyp′no·tize′ *v.* induce hypnosis

in —**hyp′no·tism′** *n.* —**hyp′no·tist** *n.*
hyp′o·crite′ (-krit′) *n.* one who pretends to have a virtue, feeling, etc. he or she does not have
hy′po·der′mic *a.* injected under the skin —*n.* syringe and needle for giving hypodermic injections
hy·pot′e·nuse′ (-nōōs′) *n.* side of right-angled triangle opposite the right angle
hy·poth′e·sis *n.* tentative explanation
hys·te′ri·a *n.* outbreak of wild emotion —**hys·ter′i·cal** *a.*

I

I *pron.* person speaking or writing
ice *n.* 1 water frozen solid by cold 2 frozen dessert of fruit juice, sugar, etc. —*v.* 1 change into ice 2 cool with ice 3 cover with icing —**iced** *a.*
ice′berg′ *n.* great mass of ice afloat in the sea
ice cream *n.* frozen cream dessert
ice skate *n.* shoe with a metal runner for gliding on ice —**ice′skate′** *v.*
i′ci·cle *n.* hanging stick of ice
ic′ing *n.* sweet, soft coating for cakes; frosting
i′con *n.* sacred image or picture
i′cy *a.* **i′ci·er, i′ci·est** 1 full of or covered with ice 2 very cold
i·de′a *n.* 1 mental conception; a thought or belief 2 a plan or scheme
i·de′al *n.* 1 conception of something in its perfect form 2 perfect model —*a.* thought of as, or being, an ideal —**i·de′al·ly** *adv.*
i·de′al·ism′ *n.* conception of, or striving for, an ideal —**i·de′al·ist** *n.* —**i′de·al·is′tic** *a.*
i·den′ti·cal *a.* the same
i·den′ti·fy′ *v.* **-fied′** 1 show to be a certain one 2 associate closely (with) —**i·den′ti·fi·ca′tion** *n.*
i·den′ti·ty *n., pl.* **-ties** 1 state or fact of being the same 2 individuality
id′i·om *n.* 1 set phrase with a special meaning 2 usual way of expression in words —**id′i·o·mat′ic** *a.*
id′i·ot *n.* foolish or stupid person
i′dle *a.* 1 useless 2 baseless 3 not busy or working 4 lazy —**i′dler** *n.* —**i′dly** *adv.*
i′dol *n.* image or object worshiped or adored

if con. 1 in case that 2 although 3 whether —**as if** as it would be if

ig'loo' n., pl. **-loos'** Eskimo hut made of snow blocks

ig·nite' v. 1 set fire to 2 catch on fire

ig·ni'tion n. 1 an igniting 2 electrical system for igniting the gases in an engine

ig'no·rant a. 1 showing lack of knowledge 2 unaware

ig·nore' v. pay no attention to

ill a. worse, worst 1 bad 2 sick —n. an evil or disease —adv. worse, worst 1 badly 2 scarcely

il·le'gal a. against the law

il·le·git'i·mate a. 1 born of unwed parents 2 contrary to law, rules, etc.

il·lit'er·ate a. unable to read —n. illiterate person

ill'-man'nered a. impolite; rude

il·log'i·cal a. not logical

ill'-tem'pered a. irritable

il·lu'mi·nate' v. 1 light up 2 explain 3 decorate

il·lu'sion n. 1 false idea 2 misleading appearance

il·lus'trate' v. 1 explain, as by examples 2 furnish (books, etc.) with pictures —**il·lus·tra'tion** n. —**il·lus·tra'tor** n.

im'age n. 1 a representation, as a statue 2 reflection in a mirror, etc. 3 mental picture; idea 4 copy —v. reflect

i·mag'i·nar'y a. existing only in the imagination

i·mag'i·na'tion n. 1 power to form mental pictures or ideas 2 thing imagined —**i·mag'i·na·tive** a.

i·mag'ine v. 1 conceive in the mind 2 suppose

im·be·cile (-səl) n. 1 foolish or stupid person

im'i·tate' v. 1 copy or mimic 2 resemble —**im·i·ta'tion** n., a. —**im'i·ta'tor** n.

im·mac'u·late a. 1 perfectly clean 2 without a flaw 3 pure; sinless

im'ma·ture' a. not fully grown or developed —**im'ma·tu'ri·ty** n.

im·meas'ur·a·ble a. boundless; vast —**im·meas'ur·a·bly** adv.

im·me'di·ate a. 1 closest 2 instant 3 direct —**im·me'di·ate·ly** adv.

im·mense' a. vast; huge —**im·men'si·ty** n.

im·merse' v. 1 plunge into a liquid 2 engross

im'mi·grate' v. enter a country,

etc. in order to settle there —**im' mi·gra'tion** n.

im·mo'bile (-bəl) a. not moving or movable —**im·mo'bi·lize'** v.

im·mod'er·ate a. without restraint; excessive

im·mod'est a. indecent

im·mor'al a. not moral; esp., unchaste —**im·mo·ral'i·ty** n.

im·mor'tal a. 1 living forever 2 having lasting fame —n. immortal being —**im·mor·tal·i·ty** n.

im·mune' a. exempt from or protected against something bad, as a disease, etc. —**im·mu'ni·ty** n. —**im'mu·ni·za'tion** n. —**im'mu·nize'** v.

immune system n. system protecting body from disease by producing antibodies

imp n. 1 young demon 2 mischievous child

im·pact' n. (force of) a collision

im·pact'ed a. describing a tooth lodged tight in jaw

im·pair' v. make worse, less, etc.

im·part' v. 1 give 2 tell

im·par'tial a. fair; just

im·pa'tient a. annoyed because of delay, etc. —**im·pa'tience** n.

im·peach' v. try (an official) on a charge of wrongdoing —**im· peach'ment** n.

im·pede' v. hinder

im·ped'i·ment n. thing that impedes; spec., a speech defect

im·pel' v. **-pelled'** 1 drive forward 2 force

im·per'a·tive a. 1 necessary; urgent 2 of the mood of a verb expressing a command

im·per'fect a. 1 not complete 2 not perfect

im·per·fec'tion n. 1 a being imperfect 2 fault

im·pe'ri·al (-pir'ē-) a. of an empire, emperor, or empress

im·per'son·al a. 1 without reference to any one person 2 not existing as a person

im·per'son·ate' v. 1 assume the role of 2 mimic

im·per'ti·nent a. 1 not relevant 2 insolent —**im·per'ti·nence** n.

im·pet'u·ous (-pech'-) a. impulsive; rash —**im·pet·u·os'i·ty** n.

im·plant' (n.: im'plant') v. 1 plant firmly 2 insert surgically —n. implanted organ, etc.

im'ple·ment n. tool or instrument —v. put into effect

im'pli·cate' v. show to be a party to a crime, etc.

im'pli·ca'tion n. 1 an implying or implicating 2 something

im·plic'it (-plis-) *a.* **1** implied **2** absolute

im·plode' *v.* burst inward

im·plore' *v.* beseech

im·ply' *v.* **-plied'** hint; suggest

im·po·lite' *a.* discourteous

im·port' (*n.:* im'pôrt) *v.* **1** bring (goods) into a country **2** signify —*n.* **1** thing imported **2** meaning **3** importance

im·por'tant *a.* **1** having much significance **2** having power or authority —**im·por'tance** *n.*

im·pose' *v.* put on (a burden, tax, etc.) —**im·po·si'tion** *n.*

im·pos'si·ble *a.* that cannot be done, exist, etc. —**im·pos'si·bil'i·ty** *n., pl.* **-ties**

im·pos'tor *n.* cheat pretending to be what he is not

im'po·tent (-pə-) *a.* lacking power; helpless —**im'po·tence** *n.*

im·pound' *v.* seize by law

im·prac'ti·cal *a.* not practical

im·pre'cise' *a.* not precise; not clear, etc.

im·preg'nate' *v.* **1** make pregnant **2** saturate

im·press' (*n.:* im'pres') *v.* **1** to stamp **2** affect the mind or emotions of **3** to fix in the memory —*n.* an imprint —**im·pres'sive** *a.*

im·pres'sion *n.* **1** a mark **2** effect produced on the mind **3** vague notion

im·pri·ma'tur (-mät'ər) *n.* permission, esp. to publish

im'print' (*n.:* im'print') *v.* mark or fix as by pressing —*n.* **1** a mark; print **2** characteristic effect

im·pris'on *v.* put in prison

im·prob'a·ble *a.* unlikely

im·promp'tu' *a., adv.* without preparation; offhand

im·prop'er *a.* not proper

im·prove' *v.* make or become better or more valuable

im'pro·vise' *v.* **1** compose and perform without preparation **2** make or do with whatever is at hand —**im'pro·vi·sa'tion** *n.*

im·pru'dent *a.* rash; indiscreet

im'pu·dent (-pyoō-) *a.* insolent

im'pulse' *n.* **1** driving force; impetus **2** sudden inclination to act —**im·pul'sive** *a.*

im·pure' *a.* **1** dirty **2** immoral **3** adulterated —**im·pu'ri·ty** *n., pl.* **-ties**

in *prep.* **1** contained by **2** wearing **3** during **4** at the end of **5** with regard to **6** because of **7** into —*adv.* to or at the inside

in·au'gu·rate' (-ô'gyə-) *v.* **1** formally induct into office **2** begin; open —**in·au'gu·ral** *a.*

in'born' *a.* present at birth; natural

in·can·des'cent *a.* **1** glowing with heat **2** shining

in·car'nate (-nat) *a.* in human form; personified

in·cen'di·ar'y *a.* **1** causing fires **2** stirring up strife

in·cense' (*v.:* in sens') *n.* **1** substance burned to produce a pleasant odor **2** this odor —*v.* enrage

in·cen'tive *n.* motive or stimulus

in·ces'sant *a.* constant

inch *n.* measure of length, $\frac{1}{12}$ foot

in'ci·dence *n.* range of occurrence or effect

in'ci·dent *n.* event

in'ci·den'tal *a.* **1** happening along with something more important **2** minor

in·cin'er·a'tor *n.* furnace for burning trash

in·ci'sion (-sizh'ən) *n.* **1** a cutting into **2** a cut; gash

in·ci'sor (-zər) *n.* any of the front cutting teeth

in·cite' *v.* urge to action

in·clem'ent *a.* stormy

in·cline' (*n.:* in'klīn') *v.* **1** lean; bend; slope **2** tend **3** have a preference **4** influence —*n.* a slope —**in'cli·na'tion** *n.*

in·clude' *v.* have or take in as part of a whole; contain —**in·clu'sion** *n.*

in'come' *n.* money one gets as wages, salary, rent, etc.

in·com'pa·ra·ble *a.* beyond comparison; matchless

in·com'pe·tent *a., n.* (one) without adequate skill or knowledge

in'com·plete' *a.* lacking a part or parts; unfinished

in'con·spic'u·ous *a.* attracting little attention

in·con'ti·nent *a.* unable to control one's natural functions

in'con·ven'ience *n.* **1** lack of comfort, etc. **2** inconvenient thing —*v.* cause bother, etc. to —**in'con·ven'ient** *a.*

in·cor'po·rate' *v.* **1** combine; include **2** merge **3** form (into) a corporation

in·crease' (*n.:* in'krēs') *v.* make or become greater, larger, etc. —*n.* **1** an increasing **2** amount of this

in·cred'i·ble *a.* too unusual to be

believed

in·cred'u·lous (-krej'-) *a.* showing doubt —**in'cre·du'li·ty** *n.*

in·crim'i·nate' *v.* involve in, or make appear guilty of, a crime

in'cu·bate' *v.* sit on and hatch (eggs) —**in'cu·ba'tion** *n.*

in'cu·ba'tor *n.* 1 heated container for hatching eggs 2 similar device in which premature babies are kept

in·cum'bent *a.* resting (*on* or *upon* one) as a duty —*n.* holder of an office, etc.

in·cur' *v.* **-curred'** bring upon oneself

in·debt'ed *a.* 1 in debt 2 owing gratitude

in·deed' *adv.* certainly —*int.* exclamation of surprise, doubt, sarcasm, etc.

in·del'i·ble *a.* that cannot be erased, washed out, etc.

in·dent' *v.* 1 to notch 2 space in from the regular margin —**in'den·ta'tion** *n.*

in·den'ture *v.* bind by a contract to work for another

in'de·pen'dent *a.* not ruled, controlled, supported, etc. by others —**in'de·pen'dence** *n.*

in'de·struct'i·ble *a.* that cannot be destroyed

in'dex' *n., pl.* **-dex·es** or **-di·ces'** (-di sēz') 1 the forefinger: also **index finger** 2 indication 3 alphabetical list of names, etc. in a book showing pages where they can be found

in'di·cate' *v.* 1 point out; show 2 be a sign of —**in·di·ca'tive** *a.* —**in'di·ca'tor** *n.*

in·dict' (-dīt') *v.* charge with a crime —**in·dict'ment** *n.*

in·dif'fer·ent *a.* 1 neutral 2 unconcerned 3 of no importance 4 fair, average, etc.

in·dig'e·nous (-dij'-) *a.* native

in'di·gent *a.* poor; needy

in'di·ges'tion *n.* difficulty in digesting food

in·dig'nant *a.* angry at unjust or mean action —**in'dig·na'tion** *n.*

in'di·go' *n.* 1 blue dye 2 deep violet-blue

in'di·vid'u·al (-vij'-) *n.* single person, thing, or being —*a.* 1 single 2 of, for, or typical of an individual

in'do·lent (-də-) *a.* idle; lazy

in'door' *a.* being, belonging, done, etc. in a building

in'doors' *adv.* in or into a building

in·duce' *v.* 1 persuade 2 bring

on; cause —**in·duce'ment** *n.*

in·duct' *v.* 1 install in an office, a society, etc. 2 bring into the armed forces —**in·duct·ee'** *n.*

in·dulge' *v.* 1 satisfy a desire 2 gratify the wishes of

in·dus'tri·al *a.* having to do with industries or people working in industry

in·dus'tri·ous *a.* working hard and steadily

in'dus·try *n., pl.* **-tries** 1 steady effort 2 any branch of manufacture or trade

in·ept' *a.* 1 unfit 2 foolishly wrong 3 awkward

in·ert' *a.* 1 unable to move or act 2 dull; slow 3 without active properties

in·er'ti·a (-sha) *n.* tendency of matter to remain at rest, or to continue moving in a fixed direction

in·ev'i·ta·ble *a.* certain to happen —**in·ev'i·ta·bil'i·ty** *n.*

in'ex·pe'ri·enced *a.* lacking experience or skill

in·fal'li·ble *a.* never wrong

in'fant *n.* baby —*a.* 1 of infants 2 in an early stage —**in'fan·cy** *n.* —**in'fan·tile'** *a.*

in'fan·try *n.* soldiers trained to fight on foot

in·fat'u·ate' (-fach'ōō-) *v.* inspire with unreasoning passion

in·fect' *v.* make diseased —**in·fec'tion** *n.*

in·fec'tious *a.* 1 caused by microorganisms in the body 2 tending to spread to others

in·fer' *v.* **-ferred'** conclude by reasoning —**in'fer·ence** *n.*

in·fe'ri·or (-fir'ē-) *a.* 1 lower in space, order, status, etc. 2 poor in quality —**in·fe'ri·or'i·ty** *n.*

in·fest' *v.* overrun in large numbers

in'fi·del'i·ty *n.* unfaithfulness

in'fi·nite (-nit) *a.* 1 lacking limits; endless 2 vast

in·fin'i·tive *n.* form of a verb without reference to person, tense, etc.

in·fin'i·ty *n.* unlimited space, time, or quantity

in·firm' *a.* weak; feeble

in·flame' *v.* 1 excite 2 make red, sore, and swollen —**in·flam·ma'tion** *n.* —**in·flam'ma·to'ry** *a.*

in·flam'ma·ble *a.* flammable

in·flate' *v.* make swell out, as with gas

in·fla'tion *n.* 1 an inflating 2 increase in the currency in circulation resulting in a fall in its value and a rise in prices

in·flect' v. **1** vary the tone of (the voice) **2** change the form of (a word) to show tense, etc.

in·flict' v. cause to suffer (a wound, punishment, etc.)

in·flu·ence n. **1** power to affect others **2** one with such power —v. have an effect on

in·flu·en·za n. acute, contagious viral disease

in·form' v. give information (to)

in·for·mal' a. **1** not following fixed rules **2** casual; relaxed —**in·for·mal·i·ty** n., pl. **-ties**

in·for·ma'tion n. news or knowledge imparted

in·fra·struc·ture n. basic installations and facilities, as roads

in·fu'ri·ate' v. enrage

in·gen'ious (-jēn'-) a. clever; resourceful —**in·ge·nu'i·ty** n.

in·gest' v. take (food, drugs, etc.) into the body

in·got (in'gət) n. mass of metal cast as a bar, etc.

in·gre'di·ent n. component part of a mixture

in·hab'it v. live in

in·hal'ant n. medicine, etc. to be inhaled

in·hale' v. breathe in

in·her'ent (-hir'-, -her'-) a. inborn; natural; basic

in·her'it v. **1** receive as an heir **2** have by heredity —**in·her'it·ance** n.

in·hu'man a. cruel, brutal, etc. — **in'hu·man'i·ty** n.

in·i·tial (i nish'əl) a. first —n. first letter of a name

in·i'ti·ate' v. **1** begin to use **2** teach the fundamentals to **3** admit as a new member

in·ject' v. **1** force (a fluid) into tissue, etc. with a syringe, etc. **2** throw in; insert —**in·jec'tion** n.

in·jure v. do harm to; hurt

in·ju·ry n., pl. **-ries** harm or wrong

in·jus'tice n. **1** being unjust **2** unjust act

ink n. colored liquid for writing, printing, etc. —v. mark or color with ink —**ink'y** a., **-i·er, -i·est**

ink'ling n. hint or notion

in·land a., adv. in or toward a country's interior

in·let' n. narrow strip of water going into land

in'mate' n. one kept in a prison, hospital, etc.

inn n. hotel or restaurant

in·nate' a. inborn; natural

in'ner a. **1** farther in **2** more secret

inner city n. crowded or blighted central section of a city

in'ner·most' a. **1** farthest in **2** most secret

in'no·cent a. **1** without sin **2** not guilty **3** harmless **4** artless —**in'no·cence** n.

in'no·va'tion n. new method, device, etc. —**in'no·va'tor** n.

in·oc'u·late' v. inject a vaccine so as to immunize —**in·oc'u·la'tion** n.

in·or·gan'ic a. not living; not animal or vegetable

in'put' n. **1** what is put in, as power into a machine or data into a computer **2** opinion or advice —v. feed (data) into a computer —**in'put'ter** n.

in·quire' v. **1** ask; question **2** investigate (into) —**in·quir'y** (in'kwə rē, in kwir'ē) n., pl. **-ies**

in·quis'i·tive (-kwiz'-) a. asking many questions; prying

in·sane' a. **1** mentally ill; crazy **2** of or for insane people —**in·san'i·ty** n.

in·scribe' v. mark or engrave (words, etc.) on —**in·scrip'tion** n.

in'sect' n. small animal with six legs, as a fly

in·se·cure' a. **1** not safe **2** anxious **3** not firm

in·sert' (n.: in'surt') v. put into something else —n. a thing inserted —**in·ser'tion** n.

in'set' v. set in —n. something inserted

in'side' n. inner side or part —a. **1** internal **2** secret —adv. **1** within **2** indoors —prep. in

in'sight' n. understanding of a thing's true nature

in·sig'ni·a n.pl. badges, emblems, etc., as of rank or membership

in·sin·cere' a. deceptive or hypocritical —**in·sin·cer'i·ty** n.

in·sin'u·ate' v. **1** hint; imply **2** to get in artfully

in·sist' v. **1** demand strongly **2** maintain a stand

in·som'ni·a n. abnormal inability to sleep —**in·som'ni·ac'** n.

in·spect' v. **1** look at carefully **2** examine officially —**in·spec'tion** n. —**in·spec'tor** n.

in·spire' v. **1** stimulate, as to a creative effort **2** arouse (a feeling) **3** inhale —**in·spi·ra'tion** n.

in·stall' v. **1** put formally in office **2** establish in a place **3** fix in place for use

in·stall'ment n. any of the several parts of a payment, magazine serial, etc.

in·stance n. 1 example 2 occasion

in·stant a. 1 immediate 2 quick to prepare —n. moment

in·stead' adv. in place of the other

in·sti·gate' v. urge on to an action; incite —**in·sti·ga'tor** n.

in·still', in·stil' v. put in gradually; implant

in·stinct' n. 1 inborn tendency to do a certain thing 2 knack

in·sti·tute' v. establish —n. organization for promoting art, science, etc.

in·sti·tu'tion n. 1 establishment 2 established law, custom, etc. 3 institute —**in·sti·tu'tion·al** a.

in·struct' v. 1 teach 2 direct —**in·struc'tion** n. —**in·struc'tive** a. —**in·struc'tor** n.

in·stru·ment n. 1 means; agent 2 tool or device for doing exact work 3 device producing musical sound

in·su·late' v. 1 protect with a material to prevent the loss of electricity, heat, etc. 2 set apart —**in·su·la'tion** n.

in·su·lin n. pancreatic hormone used to treat diabetes

in·sult' (v.: in sult') n. act or remark meant to hurt the feelings —v. subject to an insult

in·sur·ance (-shoor'-) n. 1 an insuring 2 contract whereby a company guarantees payment for a loss, death, etc. 3 amount for which a thing is insured

in·sure' v. 1 make sure 2 protect 3 get or give insurance on

in·te·ger n. whole number

in·te·grate' v. 1 form into a whole; unify 2 desegregate

in·tel·lect'u·al a. 1 of the intellect 2 needing or showing high intelligence —n. one with intellectual interests

in·tel·li·gence n. 1 ability to learn, or solve problems 2 news; information —**in·tel·li·gent** a.

in·tend' v. 1 to plan 2 to mean

in·tense' a. 1 very strong, great, deep, etc. 2 very emotional —**in·ten'si·ty** n.

in·ten·sive a. 1 thorough 2 Gram. emphasizing

in·tent' a. firmly fixed in attention or purpose —n. purpose; intention

in·ten'tion n. thing intended or planned; purpose

in·ter' (-tur') v. **-terred'** bury

in·ter·act' v. to act on one another —**in·ter·ac'tion** n.

in·ter·cept' v. seize or interrupt on the way —**in·ter·cep'tion** n.

in·ter·change' v. 1 exchange 2 alternate

in·ter·course' n. 1 dealings between people, countries, etc. 2 sexual union

in·ter·de·pend'ence n. mutual dependence

in·ter·est (in'trist) n. 1 feeling of curiosity or concern 2 thing causing this feeling 3 share in something 4 welfare; benefit 5 group with a common concern 6 (rate of) payment for the use of money —v. have the interest or attention of

in·ter·fere' v. 1 come between; intervene 2 meddle

in·te'ri·or n. 1 inner 2 inland 3 private —n. 1 interior part 2 domestic affairs of a country

in·ter·jec'tion n. 1 an interjecting 2 thing interjected 3 Gram. exclamation

in·ter·lock' v. lock together

in·ter·me'di·ate (-at) a. in the middle; in between

in·ter·mis'sion n. interval, as between acts of a play

in·tern' n. doctor in training at a hospital

in·ter'nal a. 1 inner 2 within a country

internal medicine n. diagnosis and nonsurgical treatment of disease

in·ter·na'tion·al a. 1 among nations 2 for all nations

in·tern·ist n. doctor specializing in internal medicine

in·ter'pret v. explain or translate —**in·ter'pre·ta'tion** n. —**in·ter'pret·er** n.

in·ter'ro·gate' (-ter'-) v. question formally —**in·ter'ro·ga'tion** n.

in·ter·rupt' v. 1 break in on (talk, etc.) 2 obstruct

in·ter·sect' v. 1 divide by passing across 2 cross each other

in·ter·state' a. between or among states of a country

in·ter·val n. 1 space between things 2 time between events 3 difference in musical pitch

in·ter·vene' v. 1 come or be between 2 come in so as to help settle something

in·ter·view' n. meeting of people, as to confer, ask questions, etc.

in·ti·mate' (-māt'; a., n.: -mət) v. hint —a. 1 most personal 2 very familiar —n. an intimate friend —in·tim·i·da·cy n., pl. -cies

in·tim·i·date' v. make afraid as with threats

in·to prep. 1 toward and within 2 to the form, state, etc.

in·tox·i·cate' v. 1 make drunk 2 excite greatly —in·tox·i·cant n.

in·tra·mu·ral a. among members of a school or college

in·tran·si·tive a. not taking a direct object, as some verbs

in·tra·ve·nous a. into or within a vein

in·tri·cate (-kət) a. hard to follow because complicated

in·trigue' (-trēg') v. 1 to plot secretly 2 excite the curiosity of —n. 1 secret plot 2 secret love affair

in·tro·duce' v. 1 insert 2 bring into use 3 make acquainted with 4 give experience of 5 begin —in·tro·duc·tion n.

in·trude' v. force oneself upon others without welcome —in·trud'er n. —in·tru·sion n.

in·tu·i·tion n. immediate knowledge of something without conscious reasoning

in·vade' v. enter forcibly, as to conquer —in·vad'er n.

in·va·lid n. one who is ill or disabled

in·val·id a. not valid, sound, etc.

in·vent' v. 1 produce (a new device) 2 think up —in·ven'tor n.

in·ven·tion n. 1 an inventing 2 power of inventing 3 something invented —in·ven'tive a.

in·ven·to·ry n., pl. -ries complete list or stock of goods

in·verse (or in'vurs') a. inverted; directly opposite —n. inverse thing

in·vert' v. 1 turn upside down 2 reverse —in·ver'sion n.

in·ver·te·brate (-brət) n., a. (animal) having no backbone

in·vest' v. 1 install in office 2 furnish with authority 3 put (money) into business, etc. for profit —in·ves'tor n.

in·ves·ti·gate' v. search (into); examine —in·ves'ti·ga'tor n.

in·vig'or·ate' v. enliven

in·vis·i·ble a. not visible or not evident —in·vis'i·bil'i·ty n.

in·vite' v. 1 ask to come somewhere or to do something 2 request 3 give occasion for

in·voice' n. itemized list of goods or services provided; bill

in·voke' v. call on (God, etc.) for help, etc.

in·vol'un·tar·y a. 1 not done by choice; unintentional 2 not consciously controlled

in·volve' v. 1 complicate 2 draw into difficulty, etc. 3 include 4 require 5 occupy the attention of —in·volve'ment n.

in·ward a. 1 internal 2 directed toward the inside —adv. 1 toward the inside 2 into the mind or soul —in'ward·ly adv.

i'o·dine' n. chemical element used in medicine, etc.

i·on n. (ī'ən, -än') n. electrically charged atom or group of atoms

ire n. anger; wrath

ir·i·des'cent a. showing a play of rainbowlike colors

i'ris n. 1 colored part of the eye, around the pupil 2 plant with sword-shaped leaves and showy flowers

irk v. annoy; tire out

i·ron (ī'ərn) n. 1 strong metal that is a chemical element 2 device used for smoothing wrinkles from cloth 3 pl. iron shackles 4 golf club with metal head —a. 1 of iron 2 strong —v. press with a hot iron

i·ro·ny (ī'rə nē) n., pl. -nies 1 expression in which what is meant is the opposite of what is said 2 event that is the opposite of what is expected —i·ron'ic a.

ir·ra'di·ate' v. 1 expose to X-rays, ultraviolet rays, etc. 2 shine; radiate

ir·ra'tion·al a. lacking reason or good sense

ir·reg'u·lar a. 1 not conforming to rule, standard, etc. 2 not straight or uniform —ir·reg'u·lar'i·ty n.

ir·rel'e·vant a. not to the point

ir·re·sist'i·ble a. that cannot be resisted

ir·re·spon'si·ble a. lacking a sense of responsibility

ir·rev'er·ent a. showing disrespect —ir·rev'er·ence n.

ir'ri·gate' v. 1 supply with water by means of ditches, etc. 2 wash out (a body cavity) —ir'ri·ga'tion n.

ir'ri·ta·ble a. easily irritated or angered —ir'ri·ta·bil'i·ty n.

ir'ri·tate' v. 1 to anger; annoy 2 make sore —ir'ri·tant a., n. —ir'ri·ta'tion n.

is v. pres. t. of BE: used with he, she, or it

Is·lam (is'läm', iz'-) n. Muslim religion —Is·lam'ic a.

is'land n. land mass surrounded

by water —is'land·er n.

isle (il) n. small island

i'so·late' v. place alone

is'sue n. 1 result 2 offspring 3 point under dispute 4 an issuing or amount issued —v. 1 emerge 2 result 3 put out; give out 4 publish

isth·mus (is'mas) n. strip of land connecting two larger bodies of land

it pron. the animal or thing mentioned *It* is also used as an indefinite subject or object

i·tal'ic a., n. (of) type in which the letters slant upward to the right —**i·tal'i·cize'** v.

itch n. 1 tingling of the skin, with the desire to scratch 2 restless desire —v. have an itch

i'tem n. 1 article; unit 2 bit of news

its a. of it

it·self' pron. intensive or reflexive form of IT

i'vo·ry n. 1 hard, white substance in elephants' tusks, etc. 2 creamy white

i'vy n., pl. **i'vies** climbing evergreen vine

J

jab v., n. **jabbed** punch or poke

jack n. 1 device to lift something 2 playing card with picture of male royal attendant 3 *Naut.* small flag 4 electric plug-in receptacle

jack'al n. wild dog of Asia or Africa

jack'et n. 1 short coat 2 outer covering

jack'knife' n. large pocketknife

jade n. 1 hard, green stone 2 worn-out horse —v. tire or satiate —**jad'ed** a.

jag'ged a. having sharp points; notched or ragged

jag'uar (-wär) n. animal like a large leopard

jail n. prison for short-term confinement —v. to put or keep in a jail —**jail'er, jail'or** n.

ja·la·pe·ño (hä'lä pän'yō) n. Mexican hot pepper

jam v. **jammed** 1 cram; stuff 2 crush or crowd 3 wedge tight — n. 1 a jamming 2 [Col.] a difficult situation 3 spread made by boiling fruit and sugar

jamb (jam) n. side post of a doorway

jan'i·tor n. one who takes care of a building —**jan'i·to'ri·al** a.

Jan'u·ar'y n. first month

jar v. **jarred** 1 make a harsh sound 2 jolt —n. 1 jolt 2 wide-mouthed container

jaun·dice (jôn'dis) n. disease that turns the skin, eyeballs, etc. yellow

jaun'ty a. **-ti·er, -ti·est** easy and carefree

jav'e·lin n. light spear thrown in contests

jaw n. either of the two bony parts that hold the teeth

jaw'bone' n. lower bone of jaw

jay n. 1 bird of the crow family 2 bluejay

jazz n. popular American music with strong rhythms

jeal'ous (jel'-) a. 1 resentfully suspicious or envious 2 watchful in guarding

jeans n.pl. trousers or overalls of twilled cotton cloth

jeep n. small, rugged, orig. military automobile

jeer v. ridicule —n. derisive comment

jel'ly n., pl. **-lies** 1 soft, gelatinous food made from cooked fruit syrup 2 gelatinous substance

jel'ly·fish' n. jellylike sea animal with tentacles

jeop'ard·ize' (jep'-) v. to risk; endanger

jerk n. 1 sharp pull 2 muscular twitch 3 [Sl.] disagreeable person —v. 1 move with a jerk 2 twitch —**jerk'y** a., **-i·er, -i·est**

jer'ky n. dried strips of meat

jer'sey n. 1 soft, knitted cloth 2 pl. **-seys** upper garment of this

jest v., n. 1 joke 2 ridicule

jet v. **jet'ted** 1 shoot out in a stream 2 travel by jet airplane —n. 1 liquid or gas in such a stream 2 spout that shoots a jet 3 jet-propelled airplane 4 black mineral

jet lag n. fatigue, etc. from adjusting to jet travel over great distances

jet propulsion n. propulsion by means of gases from a rear vent —**jet'-pro·pelled'** a.

jew'el n. 1 gem 2 small gem used as a watch bearing

jew'el·er, jew'el·ler n. one who deals in jewelry

jew'el·ry n. jewels, or ornaments with jewels

jibe v. 1 shift a sail, or the course, of a ship 2 [Col.] be in accord 3 to gibe —n. a gibe

jig n. 1 lively dance 2 device to

guide a tool

jin'gle v. make light, ringing sounds —n. 1 jingling sound 2 light verse

jin·ni' n., pl. **jinn** supernatural being in Muslim folklore

jive n. [Sl.] foolish or insincere talk —v. [Col.] be in accord; jibe

job n. 1 a piece of work 2 employment; work

jock'ey n. racehorse rider

joc'u·lar a. joking; full of fun

jog v. jogged 1 nudge; shake 2 move at a slow, steady, jolting pace —n. 1 nudge 2 jogging pace 3 part that changes direction sharply, as in a road

jog'ging n. steady trotting as exercise —**jog'ger** n.

join v. 1 to connect; unite 2 become a part or member (of)

joint n. 1 place where two things are joined 2 one of the parts of a jointed whole 3 [Sl.] any building, esp. a cheap bar —a. 1 common to two or more 2 sharing with another —**out of joint** 1 dislocated 2 disordered

joke n. 1 anything said or done to arouse laughter 2 thing not to be taken seriously —v. make jokes

jol'ly a. -li·er, -li·est merry —**jol'li·ness** n. —**jol'li·ty** n.

jolt v., n. 1 jar; jerk 2 shock or surprise

jos'tle (-al) v. shove roughly

jot n. very small amount —v. **jot'ted** write (down) briefly

jour'nal n. 1 diary 2 record of proceedings 3 a newspaper or magazine 4 book for business records 5 part of an axle, etc. that turns in a bearing

jour'nal·ism' n. newspaper writing and editing —**jour'nal·ist** n.

jour'ney n. a trip —v. to travel

joust (joust, just) n., v. fight with lances on horseback

jo'vi·al a. merry; jolly

jowl n. 1 cheek 2 pl. fleshy, hanging part under the jaw

joy n. gladness; delight —**joy'ful** a. —**joy'ous** a.

ju'bi·lant a. rejoicing

ju'bi·lee' n. 1 a 50th or 25th anniversary 2 time of rejoicing

judge v. 1 hear and decide cases in a law court 2 determine the winner 3 appraise or criticize 4 think; suppose —n. one who judges

judg'ment n. 1 a deciding 2 legal decision 3 opinion 4 ability to make wise decisions

ju·di'cial (-dish'əl) a. of judges, courts, etc.

ju·di'ci·ar·y a. of judges or courts —n., pl. **-ries** 1 part of government that administers justice 2 judges collectively

ju'do n. kind of Japanese wrestling used for self-defense

jug n. container for liquids, with a small opening and a handle

jug'gle v. 1 do tricks with (balls, etc.) 2 handle in a tricky way —**jug'gler** n.

jug'u·lar (vein) n. either of two large veins in the neck

juice n. liquid from fruit or cooked meat —**juic'y** a., -i·er, -i·est

Ju·ly' n. seventh month

jum'ble v. n. (mix into) a confused heap

jum'bo a. very large

jump v. 1 spring from the ground, etc. 2 leap or make leap over 3 move or change suddenly 4 rise or raise suddenly, as prices —n. a jumping 1 distance jumped 3 sudden move or change

jump'er n. sleeveless dress worn over a blouse, etc.

junc'tion n. 1 a joining 2 place where things join

June n. sixth month

jun'gle n. dense forest in the tropics

jun'ior a. 1 the younger: written **Jr.** 2 of lower rank, etc. —n. high school or college student in the next-to-last year

ju'ni·per n. small evergreen with berrylike cones

junk n. 1 old metal, paper, etc. 2 Chinese ship with flat bottom 3 [Col.] worthless thing(s); rubbish —v. [Col.] to discard; scrap

junk'ie n., pl. **-ies** [Sl.] narcotics addict

jun'ta (hoon'-, jun'-) n. military group seizing political power

ju'rist n. an expert in law

ju'ror n. member of a jury

ju'ry n., pl. **-ries** group of people chosen to give a decision, esp. in a law case

just a. 1 right or fair 2 righteous 3 well-founded 4 correct; exact —adv. 1 exactly 2 only 3 barely 4 a very short time ago 5 [Col.] quite; really

jus'tice n. 1 a being just 2 reward or penalty as deserved 3 the upholding of what is just 4 a judge

jus'ti·fy v. -fied 1 show to be

just, right, etc. **2** free from blame —**jus'ti·fi·ca'tion** n.

jut v. **jut'ted** stick out

jute n. strong fiber used to make burlap, rope, etc.

ju've·nile (-nīl', -nəl) a. **1** young; immature **2** of or for juveniles —n. child or young person

K

kan'ga·roo' n. leaping marsupial of Australia

kar'at n. one 24th part of (pure gold)

ka·ra·te (-rät'ē) n. self-defense by blows with side of open hand

kay'ak' (kī'-) n. Eskimo canoe

keel n. center piece along the bottom of a ship

keen a. **1** sharp **2** piercing **3** perceptive; acute **4** eager **5** intense —**keen'ly** adv.

keep v. kept **1** fulfill; observe **2** protect; take care of **3** preserve **4** retain **5** continue **6** hold and not let go **7** refrain —n. food and shelter —**keep'er** n.

keg n. small barrel

kelp n. brown seaweed

ken'nel n. **1** doghouse **2** often pl. place where dogs are bred or kept

ker'chief (-chif) n. **1** cloth worn around the head or neck **2** handkerchief

ker'nel n. **1** grain or seed **2** soft, inner part of a nut or fruit pit

ker'o·sene', ker'o·sine' n. oil distilled from petroleum

ketch'up n. thick sauce of tomatoes, spices, etc.

ket'tle n. **1** pot used in cooking **2** teakettle

key n. **1** device for working a lock **2** lever pressed in operating a piano, typewriter, etc. **3** thing that explains, as a code **4** controlling factor **5** mood or style **6** low island **7** Mus. scale based on a certain note —a. controlling —**key in** input (data) with a keyboard

key'board' n. row(s) of keys of a piano, computer terminal, etc.

key'stone' n. central, topmost stone of an arch

kha·ki (kak'ē) a., n. yellowish-brown (uniform)

kib·butz' (-boots') n., pl. -but·zim' (-boo tsēm') Israeli collective farm

kick v. **1** strike (out) with the foot **2** recoil, as a gun **3** [Col.]

complain —n. **1 a** kicking **2** [often pl.] [Col.] thrill

kid n. **1** young goat **2** leather from its skin: also **kid'skin' 3** [Col.] child —v. **kid'ded** [Col.] tease, fool, etc. —**kid'der** n.

kid'nap' v. **-napped'** seize and hold a person, esp. for ransom —**kid'nap'per** n.

kid'ney n., pl. **-neys** the urine-forming organ

kill v. **1** make die; slay **2** destroy **3** spend (time) idly —n. **1 a** killing **2** animal(s) killed

kiln (kil, kiln) n. oven for baking bricks, etc.

kil'o·gram' n. 1,000 grams

kil'o·me'ter (or ki läm'ət ər) n. 1,000 meters

kil'o·watt' n. 1,000 watts

kilt n. skirt worn by men of Northern Scotland

kin n. relatives; family

kind n. sort; variety —a. gentle, generous, etc. —**in kind** in the same way —**kind of** [Col.] somewhat —**kind'ly** a., adv.

kin'der·gar'ten n. class or school for children about four to six years old

kind'heart'ed a. kind

kin'dle v. **1** set on fire **2** start burning **3** excite

kin'dling n. bits of wood, etc. for starting a fire

kin'dred n. relatives; kin —a. related or similar

king n. **1** male ruler of a state **2** playing card with a king's picture **3** chess piece that has to be captured

king'dom n. country ruled by a king or queen

kink n., v. curl or twist

kiss v. caress with the lips in affection or greeting —n. **1** act of kissing **2** kind of candy

kit n. **1** set of tools, etc. **2** box or bag for it

kitch'en n. place for preparing and cooking food

kite n. **1** kind of hawk **2** light frame covered with paper, tied to a string, and flown in the wind

kit'ten n. young cat: also **kit'ty**

knack n. special ability

knack·wurst (näk'wurst') n. thick, spicy sausage

knap'sack' n. bag to carry supplies on the back

knave n. dishonest person; rogue

knead (nēd) v. press and squeeze

knee n. joint between thigh and lower leg

kneel v. **knelt** or **kneeled** rest on the bent knee or knees

knick'knack' n. small, showy article

knife n., pl. **knives** sharp cutting blade set in a handle

knight n. 1 medieval chivalrous soldier 2 British man holding honorary rank 3 chessman like a horse's head

knit v. **knit'ted** or **knit** 1 make by looping yarn with needles 2 draw or grow together

knob n. round handle

knock v. 1 hit; strike; rap 2 make a pounding noise 3 [Col.] find fault with —n. 1 hit; blow 2 a pounding noise —**knock out** make unconscious

knoll (nōl) n. little hill; mound

knot n. 1 lump in tangled thread, etc. 2 a tying together of string, rope, etc. 3 small group 4 hard lump in wood where a branch has grown 5 one nautical mile per hour

know v. **knew, known** 1 be informed (about) 2 be aware (of) 3 be acquainted with

knowl'edge (nä'lij) n. things known or learned

knuck'le n. joint of a finger

ko·a'la (-ä'-) n. tree-dwelling marsupial of Australia

ko'sher a. fit to eat according to Jewish dietary laws

L

lab n. [Col.] laboratory

la'bel n. card, etc. marked and attached to an object to show its contents, etc. —v. 1 attach a label to 2 classify as

la'bor n. 1 work 2 task 3 all workers 4 process of childbirth —v. 1 work hard 2 move with effort

lab'o·ra·to·ry (lab'rə-) n., pl. **-ries** place for scientific work or research

la'bor·er n. a worker; esp., an unskilled worker

labor union n. association of workers to further their interests

lace n. 1 string used to fasten together parts of a shoe, etc. 2 openwork fabric woven in fancy designs —v. 1 fasten with a lace 2 intertwine

lac'er·ate (las'-) v. tear jaggedly

lack n. state of not having enough or any —v. have little or nothing of

lac·quer (lak'ər) n. a varnish, often like enamel

lac'y a. **-i·er, -i·est** of or like lace

lad n. boy; youth

lad'der n. series of rungs framed by two sidepieces for climbing up or down

lad'en a. 1 loaded 2 burdened

la'dle n. long-handled, cuplike spoon for dipping

la'dy n., pl. **-dies** 1 well-bred, polite woman 2 any woman

lag v. **lagged** fall behind —n. 1 a falling behind 2 amount of this

la·goon' n. 1 shallow lake joined to a larger body of water 2 water inside an atoll

laid v. pt. & pp. of **LAY**

lain v. pp. of **LIE** (recline)

lair n. animal's den

lake n. large inland body of water

la'ma (lä'-) n. Buddhist priest or monk in Tibet

La·maze (lə mäz') n. training program in natural childbirth

lamb (lam) n. 1 young sheep 2 its flesh as food

lame a. 1 crippled 2 stiff and painful 3 poor; ineffectual

la·ment' v. feel or show deep sorrow for —**lam'en·ta·ble** a.

lam'i·nate' v. form of or into thin layers —**lam'i·nat·ed** a.

lamp n. 1 device for producing light 2 such a device set in a stand

lance n. 1 long spear 2 lancet

lan'cet n. surgical knife

land n. 1 solid part of earth's surface 2 country or region 3 ground; soil 4 real estate —v. 1 put or go on shore on land 2 catch 3 [Col.] get or secure

land'ing n. 1 a coming to shore 2 pier; dock 3 platform at the end of stairs 4 an alighting

land'lord' n. man who leases land, houses, rooms, etc. to others —**land'la'dy** n.fem.

land'mark' n. 1 identifying feature of a locality 2 important event

land'scape' n. (picture of) natural scenery

land'slide' n. 1 sliding of rocks or earth down a slope 2 overwhelming victory

lane n. narrow path, road, etc.

lan'guage n. 1 speech or writing 2 any means of communicating

lan'guish v. 1 become weak 2 long; pine —**lan'guish·ing** a.

lank'y a. **-i·er, -i·est** awkwardly tall and lean

lan'o·lin n. fatty substance obtained from wool

lan'tern n. transparent case holding a light

lap n. 1 front part from the waist to the knees of a sitting person 2 place in which one is cared for 3 one circuit of a race track 4 overlapping part —v.

lapped 1 fold or wrap 2 lay or extend partly over 3 dip up with the tongue 4 splash lightly

la·pel' n. part folded back at the upper front of a coat

lapse n. 1 small error 2 a falling into a lower condition 3 passing, as of time —v. 1 fall into a certain state 2 deviate from virtue 3 become void

lard n. melted fat of hogs

large a. of great size or amount —adv. in a large way

lar'i·at n. a rope; esp., a lasso

lark n. 1 any of various songbirds 2 merry time

lar'va n., pl. **-vae** (-vē') insect in the earliest stage after hatching

la·sa'gna (-zän'ya) n. wide noodles baked with layers of cheese, ground meat, tomato sauce, etc.

la'ser n. device that concentrates light rays in an intense beam

lash n. 1 striking part of a whip 2 a stroke as with a whip 3 eyelash —v. 1 strike or drive as with a lash 2 swing sharply 3 tie with a rope, etc.

lass n. young woman

las'so n., pl. **-sos'** or **-soes'** rope with a sliding noose, for catching cattle, etc.

last a. 1 after all others 2 only remaining 3 most recent —adv. 1 after all others 2 most recently —n. 1 last one 2 footlike form for making shoes —v. stay in use, etc. —at last finally

latch n. fastening for a door, window, etc., esp. a bar that fits into a notch

late a. 1 after the expected time 2 near the end of a period 3 recent 4 recently dead —adv. 1 after the expected time 2 near the end of a period 3 recently

late'ly adv. recently

lat'er adv. after some time

lat'er·al a. sideways

la'tex n. milky fluid in certain plants and trees

lathe (lāth) n. machine for shaping wood, metal, etc. with a cutting tool

lath'er n. 1 foam formed by soap and water 2 foamy sweat

lat'i·tude n. 1 freedom of opinion, action, etc. 2 distance in degrees from the equator

laugh v. make vocal sounds showing mirth, scorn, etc. —n. act of laughing: also **laugh'ter**

launch v. 1 send into space 2 set afloat 3 begin

laun'der v. wash or wash and iron (clothes, linens, etc.)

laun'dry n., pl. **-dries** 1 place for laundering 2 things (to be) laundered

la·va (lä'və, lav'ə) n. rock from a volcano

lav'a·to'ry n., pl. **-ries** 1 washbowl 2 room with toilet and washbowl

lav'en·der n. pale purple

lav'ish a. very generous

law n. 1 any of the rules of conduct made by a government 2 obedience to these 3 profession of lawyers 4 fundamental rule 5 series of natural events always happening in the same way

lawn n. grass cut short

law'suit' n. case before a court for decision

law'yer n. person licensed to practice law

lax a. 1 not tight 2 not strict

lay v. **laid** 1 put down on something 2 set in place 3 put or place 4 produce (an egg) 5 settle; allay 6 to bet 7 devise 8 to present or assert —n. 1 position; arrangement 2 short poem —a. of or for laymen

lay v. pt. of LIE (recline)

lay'er n. single thickness

lay'man n., pl. **-men** one not belonging to the clergy or to a given profession

la'zy a. **-zi·er, -zi·est** 1 not willing to work 2 sluggish

leach v. extract or lose (a soluble substance)

lead (lēd) v. **led** 1 direct or guide as by going before 2 be at the head of 3 go or pass 4 bring as a result 5 move first in a game, etc. —n. 1 guidance 2 first place 3 distance ahead 4 clue 5 leading role

lead (led) n. 1 heavy, soft metal, a chemical element 2 graphite used in pencils

leaf n., pl. **leaves** 1 flat, thin, usually green part growing from a plant stem 2 sheet of paper, etc. —v. turn the pages of

league n. 1 association of

nations, groups, etc. 2 unit of distance, about 3 miles

leak v. 1 pass or let pass out or in accidentally 2 become known gradually —n. accidental crack that allows leaking

lean v. 1 bend or slant 2 rely (on) 3 tend 4 to rest against something —a. 1 with little or no fat 2 meager —**lean'ness** n.

leap v. **leapt** or **lept** or **leaped** jump (over) —n. a jump

learn v. 1 get knowledge or skill by study 2 hear (of) 3 memorize —**learn'ing** n.

learn'ed a. having or showing much learning

lease n. contract by which property is rented —v. give or get by a lease

leash n. strap or chain for holding a dog, etc. in check

least a. smallest —adv. in the smallest degree —n. smallest in degree, etc.

leath'er n. animal skin that has been tanned —**leath'er·y** a.

leave v. **left** 1 let remain 2 to have remaining behind or after one 3 bequeath 4 go away (from) —n. 1 permission 2 permitted absence from duty

leav'en (lev'-) n. 1 yeast, etc. to make dough rise: also **leav'en·ing**

lec'tern n. reading stand

lec'ture n. 1 informative talk 2 a scolding —v. give a lecture (to)

ledge n. 1 shelf 2 projecting ridge of rocks

ledg'er n. book of final entry for transactions

lee a., n. (on) the side away from the wind —**lee'ward** n., a., adv.

leech n. bloodsucking worm

leek n. onionlike vegetable

left a. of that side toward the west when one faces north —n. 1 left side 2 liberal or radical party, etc. —adv. toward the left

leg n. 1 limb used for standing and walking 2 thing like a leg in shape or use

le'gal a. 1 of, based upon, or permitted by law 2 of lawyers

le·ga·to (li gät'ō) a., adv. Mus. in a smooth, even style

leg'end n. 1 traditional tale 2 inscription, title, etc.

le'gion n. 1 large body of soldiers 2 great number

leg'is·late' v. 1 make laws 2 bring (about) by laws —**leg'is·la'tion** n. —**leg'is·la'tor** n.

leg'is·la·ture n. group of persons who make laws

le·git'i·mate (-mət) a. 1 born of a married couple 2 lawful 3 reasonable

leg'ume' n. plant with pods, as the pea and bean

lei·sure (lē'zhər, lezh'ər) a., n. free (time) for rest, play, etc.

lem'on n. small, sour, yellow citrus fruit

lem'on·ade' n. drink of lemon juice, sugar, and water

lend v. **lent** 1 let another use (a thing) temporarily 2 let out (money) at interest 3 impart

length n. 1 distance from end to end 2 extent in space or time 3 long stretch —**at length** finally —**length'wise'** a., adv.

length'y a. **-i·er**, **-i·est** long; esp., too long

le'ni·ent a. merciful; gentle

lens n. 1 curved piece of glass, plastic, etc. for adjusting light rays passing through it: used in cameras, telescopes, etc. 2 similar part of the eye

leop'ard (lep'-) n. large, black-spotted wildcat of Asia and Africa

lep'er n. one having leprosy

lep're·chaun' (-kôn') n. Irish fairy in the form of a little man who can reveal hidden treasure

lep'ro·sy n. disease with skin ulcers, scaling, etc.

les'bi·an a., n. female homosexual

less a. not so much, so great, etc. —adv. to a smaller extent —n. a smaller amount —prep. minus

less'en v. make or become less

less'er a. smaller, less, etc.

les'son n. 1 exercise for a student to learn 2 something learned by experience

lest con. for fear that

let v. 1 allow; permit 2 leave 3 rent 4 cause to flow, as blood —n. hindrance *Let* is also used as an auxiliary verb

le'thal a. fatal; deadly

let'ter n. 1 a character of the alphabet 2 message sent by mail 3 literal meaning 4 pl. literature —v. mark with letters

let'tuce n. plant with crisp, green leaves used in salads

lev'ee n. river embankment to prevent flooding

lev'el n. 1 instrument for determining the horizontal 2 horizontal plane, line, etc. 3 height 4 position, rank, etc. —a. 1 flat and even 2 even in height (with) —v. 1 make or become level 2 demolish —**lev'el·er** n.

lev'er (or lē'vər) n. bar turning on a fulcrum, used to lift or move weights

lev'y v. **-ied** 1 impose (a tax, etc.) 2 enlist (troops) 3 wage (war)

lewd a. indecent

li'a·ble a. 1 legally responsible 2 subject to 3 likely

li·ai·son (lē ā'zän') n. 1 communication between military units 2 illicit love affair

li'ar n. one who tells lies

lib'er·al a. 1 generous 2 not strict 3 tolerant 4 favoring reform —n. person who favors reform —**lib'er·al·ize'** v.

lib'er·ate' v. set free; release —**lib'er·a'tion** n. —**lib'er·a'tor** n.

lib'er·ty n., pl. **-ties** 1 freedom from slavery, etc. 2 a particular right 3 pl. excessive familiarity

li'brar'y n., pl. **-ies** collection of books or a place for it —**li·brar'i·an** n.

lice n. pl. of LOUSE

li'cense n. 1 legal permit 2 freedom from rules 3 freedom that is abused —v. permit formally

lick v. 1 pass the tongue over 2 [Col.] beat or conquer —n. 1 a licking 2 small quantity

lic·o·rice (lik'ər ish) n. 1 black flavoring from a plant root 2 candy with this flavoring

lid n. 1 movable cover 2 eyelid

lie v. lay, lain 1 be horizontal or rest horizontally 2 be or exist

lie v. lied make a false statement knowingly —n. thing said in lying

lieu (lōō) n. used chiefly in in lieu of, instead of

lieu·ten'ant n. 1 low-ranking commissioned officer 2 deputy

life n., pl. **lives** 1 active existence of plants and animals 2 living things 3 time of being alive 4 way of living 5 a biography 6 liveliness —**life'less** a. —**life'like'** a.

life'boat' n. small rescue boat carried by a ship

life pre·serv'er n. device for keeping a body afloat

lift v. 1 bring higher; raise 2 go up; rise 3 [Sl.] steal —n. 1 a lifting 2 lifting force 3 raising of one's spirits 4 help; aid 5 ride in the direction one is going

light n. 1 radiant energy by which one sees 2 brightness 3 lamp, lantern, etc. 4 daylight 5 thing to ignite something 6 aspect 7 knowledge —a. 1 bright 2 pale; fair 3 not heavy 4 not important 5 easy to bear or do 6 happy 7 dizzy 8 moderate —adv. 1 palely 2 lightly —v. light'ed or lit 1 ignite 2 furnish with light 3 brighten 4 be lighted 5 come to rest 6 happen (on)

light'en v. make or become brighter, less heavy, etc.

light'house' n. tower with a light to guide ships

light'ly adv. 1 gently 2 very little 3 cheerfully 4 carelessly

light'ning n. flash of light in the sky from a discharge of atmospheric electricity

light'-year' n. distance that light travels in a year, about 6 trillion miles

like a. similar; equal —prep. 1 similar(ly) to 2 typical of 3 in the mood for 4 indicative of —con. [Col.] 1 as 2 as if —v. 1 be fond of; enjoy 2 wish —n. 1 an equal 2 pl. preferences

like'ly a. 1 credible 2 probable; expected 3 suitable

lik'en v. compare

like'wise' adv. 1 in the same way 2 also; too

li'lac n. shrub with tiny, pale-purple flower clusters

lil'y n., pl. **-ies** plant with trumpet-shaped flowers

limb (lim) n. 1 arm, leg, or wing 2 large tree branch

lime n. 1 white substance obtained from limestone 2 a green, lemonlike fruit

lime'stone' n. rock used in building, making lime, etc.

lim'it n. 1 point where something ends 2 pl. bounds —v. set a limit to —**lim'i·ta'tion** n.

limp v., n. (walk with) lameness —a. not firm

line n. 1 cord, rope, etc. 2 wire, pipe, etc. 3 long, thin mark 4 boundary 5 outline 6 a row or series 7 conformity 8 transportation system 9 route; course 10 stock of goods 11 short letter —v. 1 mark with lines 2 form a line: with up 3 put, or serve as, a lining in

lin'e·ar a. 1 of a line or lines 2 of length

lin'en n. 1 cloth of flax 2 things of linen or cotton

lin'er n. ship or airplane of a LINE (n. 8)

lin'ger v. 1 continue to stay 2

loiter

lin·ge·rie (län'zhə rā') *n.* women's underwear

lin'ing *n.* material covering an inner surface

link *n.* 1 loop in a chain 2 thing that connects —*v.* join; connect

li·no'le·um *n.* hard, smooth floor covering

lint *n.* bits of thread, fluff, etc. from cloth

li'on *n.* 1 large animal of the cat family, found in Africa and SW Asia 2 very strong, brave person 3 a celebrity —**li'on·ess** *n.fem.*

lip *n.* 1 upper or lower edge of the mouth 2 thing like a lip, as a cup's rim

liq'ue·fy' (lik'wi-) *v.* -**fied'** change to a liquid

li·queur (li kur', -koor') *n.* sweet alcoholic liquor

liq'uid *a.* 1 readily flowing 2 readily changed into cash —*n.* substance that flows easily

liq'uor (-ər) *n.* alcoholic drink, as whiskey

lisp *v.* substitute the sounds "th" and "*th*" for the sounds of "s" and "z" —*n.* act or sound of lisping

list *v.* tilt to one side, as a ship

list *n.* series of names, words, etc. set forth in order —*v.* put in a list

lis'ten (-ən) *v.* 1 try to hear 2 pay attention

li'ter (lē'-) *n.* metric unit of capacity (61.025 cubic inches)

lit'er·al *a.* 1 precise; exact; strict 2 prosaic 3 restricted to fact

lit'er·ar·y *a.* having to do with literature

lit'er·ate *a.* educated; esp., able to read and write —**lit'er·a·cy** *n.*

lit'er·a·ture' *n.* 1 all the valuable writings of a specific time, nation, etc. 2 all writings on some subject

lithe (*lith*) *a.* bending easily

lit'ter *n.* 1 portable couch 2 stretcher 3 young borne at one time by a dog, cat, etc. 4 things lying about in disorder

lit'tle *a.* 1 small in size or amount 2 short; brief 3 not important —*adv.* 1 slightly 2 not at all —*n.* small amount or short time

live (liv) *v.* 1 have life 2 stay alive; endure 3 pass one's life in a certain way 4 have a full life 5 feed (on) 6 reside

live (liv) *a.* 1 having life 2 ener-

getic 3 of interest now 4 still burning 5 unexploded 6 carrying electrical current 7 broadcast while happening

live'ly *a.* -**li·er**, -**li·est** 1 full of life 2 exciting 3 cheerful 4 having much bounce

liv'er *n.* organ in vertebrates that makes bile

live'stock' *n.* animals kept or raised on a farm

liv'ing *a.* 1 having life 2 in active use 3 of persons alive 4 true; lifelike 5 of life 6 enough to live on —*n.* 1 a being alive 2 livelihood 3 way that one lives

liz'ard *n.* reptile with a long tail and four legs

lla'ma (lä'-) *n.* South American camellike animal

load *n.* 1 amount carried 2 burden —*v.* 1 put (a load) in or on 2 burden 3 put ammunition into

loaf *n.*, *pl.* **loaves** bread, etc. baked in one piece —*v.* waste (time) —**loaf'er** *n.*

loam *n.* rich soil

loan *n.* 1 act of lending 2 something lent, esp. money at interest —*v.* lend

loath (lōth) *a.* reluctant

loathe (lō*th*) *v.* abhor

lob'by *n.*, *pl.* -**bies** 1 entrance hall 2 group of lobbyists —*v.* -**bied** act as a lobbyist

lob'by·ist *n.* one who tries to influence legislators

lobe *n.* rounded projection

lob'ster *n.* edible sea animal with large pincers

lo'cal *a.* of or for a particular place or area —**lo'cal·ly** *adv.*

lo'cate' *v.* 1 establish in a certain place 2 find or show the position of

lo·ca'tion *n.* 1 a locating 2 position; place

lock *n.* 1 device for fastening a door, etc. as with a key 2 part of a canal between gates 3 curl of hair —*v.* 1 fasten with a lock 2 shut (*in* or *out*) 3 jam or link together

lode *n.* vein or stratum of metallic ore

lodge *n.* 1 a house for special use 2 chapter of a society —*v.* 1 to house or dwell for a time 2 put in 3 come to rest —**lodg'er** *n.*

lodg'ing *n.* 1 place to live 2 *pl.* rented rooms

loft *n.* 1 space below a roof 2 upper story of a warehouse, etc.

3 gallery

loft'y *a.* **-i·er, -i·est 1** very high **2** noble **3** haughty

log *n.* **1** section cut from a tree trunk **2** daily record of a ship's, etc. progress **3** logarithm —*v.*

logged 1 cut down trees and remove the logs **2** enter in a ship's log —**log on (or off)** enter information to begin (or end) activity on a computer terminal

log'ic *n.* **1** science of reasoning **2** (correct) reasoning

log'i·cal *a.* **1** using or used in logic **2** expected as a result

loin *n.* **1** lower back from ribs to hipbone **2** *pl.* hips and lower abdomen

loi'ter *v.* **1** spend time idly **2** move slowly

lone *a.* by oneself or itself

lone'ly *a.* **-i·er, -i·est 1** alone and unhappy **2** unfrequented

lone'some *a.* having or causing a lonely feeling

long *a.* **1** measuring much **2** in length **3** of great length **4** tedious **5** far-reaching **6** well supplied —*adv.* **1** for a long time **2** for the time of **3** at a remote time —*v.* to wish earnestly; yearn —**as (or so) long as 1** while **2** since **3** provided that

lon'gi·tude' *n.* distance, in degrees, east or west of a line through Greenwich, England

long'shore'man *n., pl.* **-men** one whose work is loading and unloading ships

look *v.* **1** direct the eyes so as to see **2** search **3** seem —*n.* **1** an act of looking **2** appearance **3** [Col.] *pl.* personal appearance —*int.* **1** see! **2** pay attention! —**look after** care for —**look into** investigate

loom *n.* machine for weaving —*v.* come into sight suddenly

loop *n.* line, figure, etc. that curves back to cross itself

loose (lōōs) *a.* **1** free **2** not firm or tight **3** inexact **4** sexually immoral —*v.* **1** to free **2** make less tight, etc. **3** release

loot *n., v.* plunder —**loot'er** *n.*

lop'sid'ed *a.* heavier, lower, etc. on one side

lord *n.* **1** master **2** Br. nobleman —[L-] **1** God **2** Jesus Christ

lose (lōōz) *v.* **lost 1** become unable to find **2** have taken from one by accident, death, etc. **3** fail to keep **4** fail to win

loss *n.* **1** a losing, or damage,

etc. resulting from losing something **2** person, thing, etc. lost

lost *a.* **1** ruined **2** missing or mislaid **3** wasted

lot *n.* **1** deciding of a matter by chance **2** fate **3** piece of land **4** group **5** [Col.] *often pl.* great amount or number: with *a* —*adv.* very much: with *a*

lo'tion *n.* liquid for softening or healing the skin

lot'ter·y *n., pl.* **-ies** game in which numbered chances on prizes are sold

lo'tus *n.* tropical waterlily

loud *a.* **1** strong in sound **2** noisy **3** [Col.] flashy —*adv.* in a loud way —**loud'ly** *adv.*

lounge *v.* **1** sit in a relaxed way **2** to be idle —*n.* **1** room furnished for lounging **2** couch

louse *n., pl.* **lice** small insect parasite

love *n.* **1** strong affection **2** object of this **3** in tennis, a score of zero —*v.* feel love (for) —**in love** feeling love —**make love** woo, embrace, etc. —**lov'a·ble** *a.* —**lov'er** *n.*

love'ly *a.* **-i·er, -i·est 1** beautiful **2** [Col.] very enjoyable

low *a.* **1** not high **2** below others in rank, size, cost, etc. **3** gloomy **4** deep in pitch **5** vulgar **6** not loud —*adv.* in or to a low level, etc. —*n.* **1** low level, degree, etc. **2** gear arrangement giving least speed **3** moo

low'er (lō'-) *a.* below in rank, etc. —*v.* **1** let or put down **2** make or become less in amount, value, etc.

low'er (lou'-) *v.* **1** to scowl **2** appear threatening

low'er-case' *a., n.* (of or in) small, rather than capital, letters

low'ly *a.* **1** of low rank **2** humble —**low'li·ness** *n.*

lox *n.* smoked salmon

loy'al *a.* faithful to one's friends, country, etc. —**loy'al·ly** *adv.* —**loy'al·ty** *n., pl.* **-ties**

lu'bri·cant *a.* that lubricates —*n.* oil, grease, etc.

lu'bri·cate' *v.* apply oil or grease to reduce friction

lu'cid *a.* **1** clear **2** sane **3** shining

luck *n.* **1** chance; fortune **2** good fortune —**luck'less** *a.*

luck'y *a.* **-i·er, -i·est** having, resulting in, or thought to bring good luck —**luck'i·ly** *adv.*

lu'cra·tive *a.* profitable

lug v. **lugged** carry with effort

luge (lōōzh) n. racing sled

lug'gage n. suitcases, trunks, etc.

luke'warm' a. 1 slightly warm 2 lacking enthusiasm

lull v. 1 soothe by gentle sound or motion 2 calm —n. short period of calm

lull'a·by' n., pl. **-bies'** song for lulling a baby to sleep

lum'ber n. wood sawed into beams, boards, etc. —v. move heavily and clumsily

lu'mi·nous a. bright; shining

lump n. 1 a mass of something 2 a swelling —v. to group together —**lump'y** a., **-i·er, -i·est**

lu'nar a. of the moon

lu'na·tic a. 1 insane 2 utterly foolish

lunch n. midday meal

lunch'eon n. formal lunch

lung n. organ in the chest for breathing

lunge n. 1 sudden thrust 2 forward plunge —v. make a lunge

lurch v. sway suddenly to one side —n. 1 lurching movement 2 danger; trouble

lure n. 1 thing that attracts 2 fish bait —v. attract; entice

lu'rid a. 1 shocking 2 glowing strangely

lurk v. 1 to stay or be hidden, ready to attack 2 to move furtively

lus·cious (lush'əs) a. 1 delicious 2 pleasing

lush a. of or having luxuriant growth

lust n. 1 strong sexual desire 2 strong desire, as for power —v. feel an intense desire

lus'ter n. 1 gloss; brightness 2 brilliant fame

lute n. a stringed, guitarlike instrument

lux·u'ri·ous a. 1 giving a feeling of luxury 2 fond of luxury

lux'u·ry n., pl. **-ries** costly comfort(s) or pleasure(s)

lye (lī) n. strong alkaline substance

lynch (linch) v. kill by mob action, without lawful trial, as by hanging

lynx (links) n. North American wildcat

lyre (līr) n. ancient instrument like a small harp

M

ma n. [Col.] mother

mac·a·ro'ni n. tubes of flour paste, cooked for food

mac·a·roon' n. cookie made with almonds or coconut

mace n. 1 heavy, spiked club 2 official's staff 3 spice made from ground nutmeg shell

ma·che'te (-shet'ē) n. large, heavy knife

ma·chine' n. 1 device with moving parts, for doing work 2 group in control of a political party

ma·chin'er·y n. 1 machines 2 working parts

ma'cho a. overly virile, domineering, etc.

mack'er·el n. edible fish of N Atlantic

mac·ra·mé' (-mā') n. coarse yarn, etc. knotted in designs

mad a. **mad'der, mad'dest** 1 insane 2 frantic 3 foolish 4 angry —**mad'ly** adv.

mad'am n. polite title for a woman

ma·dame (ma däm') n., pl. **mes·dames** (mā'däm') married woman: Fr. for **Mrs.**

ma·de·moi·selle (mad'ə mə zel') n. unmarried woman: Fr. for **Miss**

mag·a·zine' n. 1 periodical publication 2 storage place, as for military supplies 3 supply chamber, as in a rifle

ma·gen'ta n. purplish red

mag'got n. wormlike larva

mag'ic n. 1 use of charms, spells, etc. 2 sleight of hand — a. of or as if by magic: also **mag'i·cal** —**mag'i·cal·ly** adv.

ma·gi'cian (-jish'ən) n. one who does magic

mag'is·trate' n. official who administers the law

mag·nan'i·mous a. generous in forgiving; noble

mag'net n. piece of iron, steel, etc. that attracts iron or steel

mag·nif'i·cent a. 1 grand and stately; splendid 2 exalted

mag'ni·fy' v. **-fied'** 1 increase apparent size of, as with a lens 2 exaggerate —**mag·ni·fi'er** n.

mag'ni·tude' n. greatness of size, extent, or importance

ma·ha·ra'jah n. in India, a prince, formerly the ruler of a native state —**ma·ha·ra'ni** n.fem.

ma·hog'a·ny n. reddish-brown wood of a tropical tree

maid n. 1 an unmarried, esp. young, woman 2 woman or girl servant

maid'en *n.* [Now Rare] young unmarried woman —*a.* 1 of or for a maiden 2 unmarried 3 first; earliest

mail *n.* 1 letters, etc. sent by postal service 2 postal system 3 metal mesh armor —*v.* send by mail —**mail'box'** *n.* —**mail'man'** *n., pl.* **-men'**

maim *v.* cripple; disable

main *a.* chief; leading; principal

main'land' *n.* main part of a continent

main'stay' *n.* main support

main'stream' *n.* prevailing trend

main·tain' *v.* 1 keep up; carry on 2 keep in working condition 3 declare to be true 4 support

maize *n.* corn

maj'es·ty *n.* 1 grandeur; dignity 2 [M-] title for a sovereign — **ma·jes'tic** *a.*

ma'jor *a.* 1 greater in size, rank, etc. 2 *Mus.* a semitone higher than the minor —*n.* 1 military officer above a captain 2 main field of study —*v.* specialize (in a subject)

ma·jor'i·ty *n.* 1 more than half 2 full legal age

make *v.* **made** 1 bring into being; build, create, etc. 2 cause to be 3 amount to; equal 4 acquire; earn 5 cause success of 6 execute, do, etc. 7 force; compel 8 [Col.] get a place on (a team) —*n.* 1 act of making 2 style or build —**make believe** pretend —**make over** change —**make up** 1 put together 2 invent 3 compensate 4 stop quarreling —**mak'er** *n.*

make'shift' *a., n.* (as) a temporary substitute

mal'a·dy *n., pl.* **-dies** illness

ma·lar'i·a (-ler'-) *n.* disease with chills and fever, carried by mosquitoes

male *a.* 1 of the sex that fertilizes the ovum 2 of, like, or for men or boys —*n.* a male person, animal, or plant

mal'ice (-is) *n.* ill will; wish to harm —**ma·li'cious** (-lish'əs) *a.*

ma·lign' (-līn') *v.* speak evil of

ma·lig'nant *a.* 1 evil 2 very harmful 3 likely to cause death

mall *n.* 1 shaded public walk 2 enclosed shopping center

mal'lard *n.* wild duck

mal'let *n.* hammer with a wooden head

mal'nu·tri'tion *n.* faulty diet; lack of nourishment

mal·prac'tice *n.* improper practice, as by a doctor

malt *n.* barley, etc. soaked and dried for use in brewing and distilling

ma'ma, mam'ma *n.* mother: child's word

mam'mal *n.* any vertebrate the female of which suckles its offspring

mam'ma·ry *a.* of milk-secreting glands

mam'moth *n.* huge, extinct elephant —*a.* huge

man *n.* 1 human being; person 2 adult male person 3 human race —*v.* **manned** furnish with men for work, etc.

man·age *v.* 1 to control or guide 2 have charge of 3 succeed in doing —**man'age·ment** *n.* — **man'ag·er** *n.*

man'date' *n.* 1 an order; command 2 the will of voters as expressed in elections 3 commission given to a nation to administer a region

man'do·lin' *n.* musical instrument with from 8 to 12 strings

mane *n.* long hair on the neck of a horse, lion, etc.

ma·neu'ver (-nōō'-) *n.* 1 a planned movement of troops, warships, etc. 2 scheme —*v.* 1 perform maneuvers 2 get, etc. by some scheme

man'ger (mān'-) *n.* box from which livestock feed

man'gle *v.* 1 mutilate by hacking, etc. 2 botch

man'go *n., pl.* **-goes** or **-gos** yellow-red tropical fruit

man'hood *n.* 1 time of being a man 2 manly qualities

ma'ni·a *n.* 1 wild insanity 2 obsession —**man'ic** *a.*

man'i·cure' *v., n.* trim, polish, etc. (of) the fingernails

man'i·fest' *a.* obvious —*v.* reveal

ma·nip'u·late' *v.* 1 handle skillfully 2 manage unfairly or dishonestly —**ma·nip'u·la'tion** *n.*

man'kind' *n.* 1 human race 2 all human males

man'ly *a.* **-li·er, -li·est** of, like, or fit for a man —**man'li·ness** *n.*

man'ner *n.* 1 way; style 2 habit 3 *pl.* (polite) ways of behaving 4 kind; sort

man'or *n.* large estate

man'sion *n.* large, imposing house

man'slaugh'ter *n.* unintentional killing of a person

man'tel *n.* frame around or shelf

man'tle *n.* 1 sleeveless cloak 2 thing that covers —*v.* to cover

man'u·al *a.* made or done by hand —*n.* handbook

man'u·fac'ture *n.* making of goods by machinery —*v.* make, esp. by machinery

ma·nure' *n.* animal waste as fertilizer

man'u·script' *n.* written or typed book, article, etc.

man'y *a.* more, most numerous —*n.*, *pron.* large number (of persons or things)

map *n.* drawing of the features of a region, the earth's surface, the sky, etc.

ma'ple *n.* 1 large shade tree 2 its hard wood 3 flavor of syrup or sugar made from its sap

mar *v.* marred damage; spoil

mar'a·thon' *n.* 1 foot race of about 26 miles 2 any endurance contest

mar'ble *n.* hard limestone, white or colored —*a.* of like marble

March *n.* third month

march *v.* 1 walk with regular steps 2 advance steadily —*n.* 1 a marching 2 progress 3 distance marched 4 marching music

mare *n.* female horse, mule, donkey, etc.

mar'ga·rine (-rin) *n.* a spread like butter, of vegetable oil and skim milk

mar'gin *n.* 1 edge, as the blank border of a page 2 extra amount in reserve —**mar'gin·al** *a.*

mar'i·gold' *n.* plant with yellow or orange flowers

mar'i·nate' *v.* soak in spiced vinegar, brine, etc.

ma·rine' *a.* of or in the sea, ships, etc.

mar'i·tal *a.* of marriage

mar'i·time' *a.* 1 on or near the sea 2 of sailing

mark *n.* 1 spot, scratch, etc. 2 sign or label 3 sign of quality 4 grade 5 impression 6 target; goal —*v.* 1 put a mark on 2 show by a mark 3 characterize 4 listen to 5 rate —**mark'er** *n.*

mar'ket *n.* 1 place where goods are sold 2 store selling food 3 buying and selling 4 demand for (goods, etc.) —*v.* buy or sell

ma·roon' *n.*, *a.* dark brownish red

mar·quee' (-kē') *n.* rooflike projection over an entrance

mar'quis (-kwis) *n.* nobleman

---

above an earl or count —**mar·quise'** (-kēz') *n.fem.*

mar'riage (-ij) *n.* 1 married life 2 wedding —**mar'riage·a·ble** *a.*

mar'row *n.* 1 soft core inside bones 2 central part

mar'ry *v.* **-ried** 1 join as husband and wife 2 take as spouse 3 unite

marsh *n.* swamp

mar'shal *n.* 1 highest ranking officer in some armies 2 Federal officer like a sheriff 3 head of a police or fire department

marsh'mal'low *n.* soft, white, spongy candy

mar·su'pi·al *n.* animal with a pouch for carrying its young

mar'tial (-shal) *a.* 1 of war 2 military 3 warlike

mar·ti'ni *n.*, *pl.* **-nis** cocktail

mar'tyr (-tər) *n.* one who suffers or dies for his beliefs

mar'vel *n.* wonderful thing —*v.* be amazed —**mar'vel·ous** *a.*

mas'cu·line *a.* of or like men or boys; male —**mas'cu·lin'i·ty** *n.*

mash *n.* 1 grain crushed in water for brewing, etc. 2 moist feed mixture for horses, etc. —*v.* crush into a soft mass

mask *n.*, *v.* cover to conceal or protect the face

ma'son *n.* construction worker in brick, stone, etc.

mas'quer·ade' (-kər-) *n.* 1 party with masks and costumes 2 disguise —*v.* be disguised

mass *n.* 1 quantity of matter 2 large number 3 size 4 [M-] R.C.Ch. service of the Eucharist

mas'sa·cre *n.* indiscriminate killing

mas·sage (mə säzh') *n.* rubbing and kneading of part of the body

mas'sive *a.* big and heavy

mast *n.* tall, upright pole on a ship, supporting sails

mas·tec'to·my *n.*, *pl.* **-mies** surgical removal of a breast

mas'ter *n.* 1 man who rules others or is in control 2 expert —*v.* 1 control 2 become expert in

mas'ter·piece' *n.* thing made or done with expert skill

mas'tiff *n.* big, strong dog

mas'to·don' *n.* extinct animal like the elephant

mat *n.* 1 flat piece, as of woven straw, for protecting a floor, etc. 2 thick tangled mass 3 border around a picture

match *n.* 1 short sliver with a tip that catches fire by friction

2 person or thing like another **3** contest **4** marriage —v. **1** be equal (to) **2** put in opposition to get an equivalent to

mate n. **1** one of a pair **2** husband or wife **3** lower officer on a ship —v. join, as in marriage

ma·te·ri·al n. **1** what a thing is made of **2** fabric

ma·ter·nal a. of, like, or from a mother

ma·ter·ni·ty n. motherhood

math·e·mat·ics n. science dealing with quantities and forms, their relationships, etc. —**math'e·mat·i·cal** a. —**math·e·ma·ti·cian** (-tish'ən) n.

mat·i·nee (mat'n ā') n. afternoon performance of a play, etc.

mat'ri·mo·ny n. marriage

ma'trix (-triks) n. pl. **-tri·ces'** (-trə sēz') or **-trix·es** that within which a thing develops

ma'tron n. **1** wife or widow **2** woman manager of domestic affairs, as of a prison

mat'ter n. **1** physical substance of a thing **2** thing or affair **3** occasion **4** importance **5** trouble —v. be of importance —**as a matter of fact** really —**no matter** regardless of

mat'ter-of-fact' a. sticking to facts; literal

mat'tress n. casing filled with cotton, springs, etc., for use on a bed

ma·ture' (-toor', -choor') a. **1** fully grown, developed, etc. **2** due for payment —v. make or become mature —**ma·tu'ri·ty** n.

maul v. handle roughly

max'i·mum a., n. greatest possible (quantity or degree)

May n. fifth month

may v. pt. **might** auxiliary verb showing: **1** possibility **2** permission

may'be adv. possibly

may'hem n. **1** crime of maiming a person intentionally **2** deliberate destruction or violence

may'on·naise' (-nāz') n. creamy salad dressing

may'or n. head of a city

maze n. confusing network of paths

me pron. objective case of I

mead·ow (med'ō) n. level field of grass

mea'ger a. **1** poor; scanty **2** thin

meal n. **1** any of the times for eating **2** food served then **3** coarsely ground grain, etc.

mean v. **meant** (ment) **1** intend **2** intend to express **3** signify **4** have a certain importance —a. **1** low in quality or rank **2** poor or shabby **3** ignoble, petty, unkind, etc. **4** stingy **5** halfway between extremes —n. **1** middle point **2** pl. [sing. or pl. v.] that by which a thing is gotten or done **3** pl. wealth

me·an'der v. **1** wind back and forth **2** wander idly

mean'time' adv., n. (during) the intervening time: also **mean'while'**

mea'sles (-zəlz) n. contagious disease, usually of children

meas'ure (mezh'-) v. **1** find out the extent, dimensions, etc. of **2** mark off a certain amount **3** be a thing for measuring **4** be of specified dimensions —n. **1** dimensions, capacity, etc. **2** unit of measuring **3** system of measuring **4** instrument for measuring **5** definite quantity **6** course of action **7** law **8** notes and rests between two bars on a musical staff

meat n. **1** flesh of animals used as food **2** edible part **3** essence

me·chan'ic n. worker who repairs machines

me·chan'i·cal a. **1** of or run by machinery **2** machinelike

mech'a·nism' n. **1** working parts of a machine **2** system of interrelated parts

med'al n. flat, inscribed piece of metal given as an honor or reward

med'dle v. interfere in another's affairs —**med'dler** n.

me'di·an n., a. (number, point, etc.) in the middle

me'di·ate' v. (try to) settle (differences) between two parties

med'i·cal a. having to do with the practice or study of medicine —**med'i·cal·ly** adv.

med'i·cine n. **1** science of treating and preventing disease **2** drug, etc. used in treating disease

medicine man n. among North American Indians, etc., a man supposed to have healing powers

me·di·e'val a. of or like the Middle Ages

med'i·tate' v. **1** think deeply **2** plan —**med·i·ta'tion** n.

me'di·um a. intermediate in amount, degree, etc. —n., pl. **-di·ums** or **-di·a 1** medium thing or state 2 thing through which a force acts 3 means, agency, etc. 4 surrounding substance

med'ley n. 1 mixture of unlike things 2 musical piece made up of several songs

meek a. 1 patient and mild 2 easily imposed on

meet v. met 1 come upon 2 be present at the arrival of 3 be introduced (to) 4 come into contact (with) 5 come together 6 satisfy 7 pay — n. a meeting

meet'ing n. 1 a coming together 2 a gathering of people 3 junction

meg'a·byte' n. million bytes

meg'a·ton' n. explosive force of a million tons of TNT

meld v. to blend; merge

mel'low a. full, rich, gentle, etc.; not harsh

mel'o·dy n., pl. -dies a tune, song, etc. —**me·lod'ic** a.

mel'on n. large, juicy, many-seeded fruit

melt v. 1 change from solid to liquid, as by heat 2 dissolve 3 disappear or merge gradually 4 soften

melt'down' n. dangerous melting of fuel in a nuclear reactor

mem'ber n. 1 distinct part, as an arm 2 person in an organization

mem'brane' n. thin tissue lining an organ or part

me·men'to n., pl. -tos or -toes souvenir

mem'o n., pl. -os memorandum

mem'oirs' (-wärz') n.pl. account of one's past life

mem'o·ran'dum n., pl. -dums or -da short note to remind one of something

me·mo'ri·al n. anything meant to help people remember a person or event

mem'o·rize' v. to commit to memory

mem'o·ry n., pl. -ries 1 power or act of remembering 2 something or everything remembered 3 commemoration 4 device in a computer, etc. that stores information

mend v. 1 repair 2 make or become better —**mend'er** n.

me·no'rah n. Jewish candelabrum

men'stru·ate' v. have a flow of blood monthly from the uterus —**men'stru·al** a.

men'tal a. 1 of or in the mind 2 for the mentally ill —**men'tal·ly** adv.

men'tion n. brief reference —v. refer to briefly

men'u n., pl. -us list of choices of meals, computer functions, etc.

mer'ce·nar'y a. thinking mainly of money —n., pl. -ies soldier paid to serve in a foreign army

mer'chan·dise' (-dīz'; n.: also -dīs') v. buy and sell —n. things bought and sold

mer'chant n. 1 dealer in goods 2 storekeeper

mer'cu·ry n. silvery liquid metal, a chemical element

mer'cy n., pl. -cies 1 kindness; forbearance 2 power to forgive —**mer'ci·ful** a. —**mer'ci·less** a.

mere a. mer'est no more than; only

mere'ly adv. only; simply

merge v. unite or combine so as to lose identity

me·rid'i·an n. 1 highest point 2 circle through the earth's poles

me·ringue' (-raŋ') n. egg whites and sugar beaten stiff

mer'it n. 1 worth; value 2 something deserving praise

mer'maid' n. imaginary creature like a woman with a fish's tail

mer'ry a. -ri·er, -ri·est full of fun —**make merry** have fun —**mer'ri·ly** adv. —**mer'ri·ment** n.

mesh n. (cord or wire of) a net or network —v. 1 to entangle 2 interlock

mess n. 1 a jumble 2 trouble 3 untidy condition 4 communal meal as in the army —v. 1 make dirty, jumbled, etc. 2 meddle —**mess'i·ness** n. —**mess'y** a., -i·er, -i·est

mes'sage n. 1 a communication 2 important idea

mes'sen·ger n. one who carries a message, etc.

Mes·si'ah (-si'-) 1 Judaism expected deliverer of the Jews 2 Christianity Jesus —n. [m—] expected savior or liberator

me·tab'o·lism' n. changing of food by organisms into energy, cells, etc. —**met·a·bol'ic** a.

met'al n. 1 shiny, usually solid, chemical element 2 an alloy —a. of metal —**me·tal'lic** adv.

met'al·lur'gy n. science of refining metals —**met'al·lur'gist** n.

met·a·mor'pho·sis n., pl. -ses' (-sēz') 1 change in form 2 any change

met'a·phor' n. word for one

thing used for another

me·tas'ta·sis *n.*, *pl.* **-ses'** (-sēz') spread of cancer cells through the bloodstream

mete (mēt) *v.* allot

me'te·or *n.* fiery solid body traveling through the earth's atmosphere at high speed

me'te·or·ite' *n.* part of a meteor fallen to earth

me'te·or·ol'o·gy *n.* science of weather, climate, etc. —**me'te·or·ol'o·gist** *n.*

me'ter *n.* 1 rhythmic pattern in verse 2 metric unit of length (39.37 in.) 3 device to measure flow of fluid —**met'ric** *a.* —**met'ri·cal** *a.*

meth'a·done' *n.* synthetic narcotic used in medicine

meth'ane' *n.* colorless, odorless, flammable gas

meth'od *n.* 1 way; process 2 system

me·tic'u·lous *a.* very careful about details; fussy

met'ro·nome' *n.* device that beats time at a set rate

me·trop'o·lis *n.* main or important city —**met'ro·pol'i·tan** *a.*

mi'crobe' *n.* minute organism, esp. one causing disease

mi'cro·com·put'er *n.* small computer for home use, etc.

mi'cro·film' *n.* film on which documents, etc. are recorded in a reduced size

mi'cro·phone' *n.* instrument for changing sound waves into electric impulses

mi'cro·scope' *n.* device for magnifying minute objects

mi'cro·wave' *n.* radio or infrared wave used in radar, cooking, etc.

mid'day' *n.*, *a.* noon

mid'dle *a.* halfway between two points, etc. —*n.* middle point or part

mid'dle-aged' *a.* in the time between youth and old age

midg'et *n.* very small person

mid'night' *n.* twelve o'clock at night

midst *n.* the middle

mid'sum'mer *n.* period about June 21

mid'way' *a.*, *adv.* in the middle; halfway

mid'wife' *n.*, *pl.* **-wives'** woman who helps others in childbirth

mien (mēn) *n.* one's manner

might *v. pt.* of MAY: *might* is also used to show less possibility or permission than *may* —*n.* strength; force

mi'grate' *v.* move from one place or region to another, as with the change in season —**mi'grant** *a.*, *n.* —**mi·gra'tion** *n.*

mil *n.* .001 inch

mild *a.* 1 gentle 2 weak in taste

mil'dew' *n.* whitish fungus on plants, damp cloth, etc.

mile *n.* unit of measure, 5,280 ft.

mile'age *n.* 1 total miles traveled 2 allowance per mile for traveling expenses

mil'i·tant *a.* ready to fight

mil'i·tar'y *a.* of soldiers, war, etc. —*n.* the army

mi·li'tia (-lish'ə) *n.* citizens trained for emergency military service

milk *n.* 1 white liquid secreted by female mammals for suckling their young 2 any liquid like this —*v.* draw milk from (a mammal)

mill *n.* 1 place for grinding grain into flour 2 machine for grinding 3 factory 4 $\frac{1}{10}$ of a cent —*v.* 1 grind by or in a mill 2 move (*around* or *about*) confusedly, as a crowd —**mill'er** *n.*

mil·len'ni·um *n.*, *pl.* **-ni·ums** or **-ni·a** 1 *Theol.* 1,000-year period of Christ's future reign on earth 2 period of peace and joy

mil'li·gram' *n.* one thousandth of a gram

mil'li·li'ter *n.* one thousandth of a liter

mil'li·me'ter *n.* one thousandth of a meter

mil'lion *n.*, *a.* a thousand thousands —**mil'lionth** *a.*, *n.*

mil·lion·aire' *n.* one having at least a million dollars

mim'ic *v.* **-icked** 1 imitate, as to ridicule 2 to copy closely —*n.* one who mimics —**mim'ic·ry** *n.*

mince *v.* 1 cut into small pieces 2 lessen the force (of words)

mind *n.* 1 center of thought, feeling, etc. 2 intellect 3 sanity 4 memory 5 opinion, intention, etc. —*v.* 1 observe 2 obey 3 take care of 4 be careful about 5 object to —**make up one's mind** reach a decision

mine *pron.* that or those belonging to me —*n.* 1 large excavation from which to extract ores, coal, etc. 2 great source of supply 3 explosive device hidden under land or water —*v.* 1 dig (ores, etc.) from a mine 2 hide mines in —**min'er** *n.*

min'er·al *n.* ore, rock, etc. found naturally in the earth —*a.* of or containing minerals

min'gle v. 1 mix or become mixed 2 join with others

min'i·a·ture n. tiny copy, model, painting, etc. —a. minute

min'i·mize' v. reduce to or estimate at a minimum

min'i·mum n. 1 smallest quantity possible 2 lowest degree reached —a. lowest or least possible —**min'i·mal** a.

min'is·cule' a. minuscule: a misspelling

min'is·ter n. 1 head of a governmental department 2 diplomatic official below an ambassador 3 one who conducts religious services

min'is·try n., pl. **-tries** 1 office of a clergyman 2 clergy 3 government department headed by a minister

mink n. 1 weasellike mammal 2 its valuable fur

mi'nor a. 1 lesser in size, rank, etc. 2 Mus. a semitone lower than the major —n. 1 one under full legal age 2 secondary field of study

mi·nor'i·ty n., pl. **-ties** 1 smaller part or number 2 racial, religious, etc. group that differs from the larger groups 3 time of being a minor

mint n. 1 place where the government makes coins 2 large amount 3 aromatic plant with leaves used for flavoring —v. 1 coin (money) 2 invent —a. new —**mint'age** n.

mi'nus prep. less —a. 1 negative 2 less than —n. sign (-) showing subtraction or negative quantity

mi·nus·cule' a. (min'ə skyōōl') a. tiny; minute

min·ute (min'it) n. 1 sixtieth part of an hour 2 moment 3 pl. official record

mi·nute' a. (mī nōōt', -nyōōt') a. very small 2 exact

mir'a·cle n. 1 event that seems to contradict scientific laws 2 remarkable thing

mi·rage' n. (mi räzh') n. optical illusion caused by reflection of light

mire n. deep mud or slush

mir'ror n. coated glass that reflects images

mirth n. gaiety with laughter

mis·be·have' v. behave badly

mis·cal'cu·late' v. misjudge

mis·car'ry v. 1 go wrong 2 lose a fetus before full term —**mis·car'riage** (or mis'kar'ij) n.

mis'cel·la'ne·ous a. of various kinds; mixed

mis'chief (-chif) n. 1 harm or damage 2 prank 3 teasing

mis·con'duct n. wrong conduct

mis·deed' n. crime, sin, etc.

mis·de·mean'or n. Law minor offense

mi'ser n. stingy hoarder of money —**mi'ser·ly** a.

mis'er·a·ble (miz'-) a. 1 in misery 2 causing misery 3 bad, poor, etc. —**mis'er·a·bly** adv.

mis'er·y n., pl. **-ies** pain, poverty, distress, etc.

mis'fit' v. fit improperly —n. 1 improper fit 2 maladjusted person

mis·for'tune n. 1 trouble 2 mishap, calamity, etc.

mis·giv'ings n.pl. feelings of fear, doubt, etc.

mis·hap' n. misfortune

mis·lay' v. **-laid'** put in a place later forgotten

mis·lead' (-lēd') v. **-led'** 1 lead astray 2 deceive

mis·read' (-rēd') v. **-read'** (-red') read wrongly and so misunderstand

miss v. 1 fail to hit, meet, do, see, hear, etc. 2 avoid 3 note or feel the loss of —n. 1 failure to hit, etc. 2 unmarried woman 3 [M-] title used before her name

mis'sal (-əl) n. R.C.Ch. prayer book for Mass for the year

mis'sile (-əl) n. object to be thrown or shot

mis'sion n. 1 special task or duty 2 group or station of missionaries 3 diplomatic delegation

mis'sion·ar'y n., pl. **-ies** person sent by a church to make converts, esp. abroad

mist n. mass of water vapor; thin fog —**mist'y** a., **-i·er, -i·est**

mis·take' v. **-took', -tak'en** understand or perceive wrongly —n. error

mis'ter n. title before a man's name: usually Mr.

mis·treat' v. treat badly

mis'tress n. woman in charge or control

mis·trust' n. lack of trust

mis'un·der·stand' v. **-stood'** understand incorrectly

mis·use' (-yōōz'; n.: -yōōs') v. 1 use improperly 2 abuse —n. incorrect use

mi'ter n. 1 tall cap of a bishop 2 corner joint of two pieces cut at an angle

mit'ten n. glove without separate finger pouches

mix v. **mixed** or **mixt 1** stir or come together in a single mass **2** make by mixing ingredients **3** combine —n. mixture, or its ingredients

mixed a. **1** blended **2** of different kinds **3** of both sexes

mix'ture n. **1** a mixing **2** thing mixed

moat n. low, mournful sound —v. **1** utter (with) a moan **2** complain

moat n. deep, usually water-filled ditch around a castle

mob n. crowd, esp. a disorderly one

mo'bile (-bal, -bil'; n.: -bēl') a. **1** readily movable or adaptable **2** easy in changing social status —n. abstract sculpture suspended to move in the air

moc'ca·sin n. heelless slipper of soft leather

mock v. **1** ridicule **2** mimic and deride —a. false

mod'el n. **1** small copy of something **2** one to be imitated **3** style **4** one who poses for an artist **5** one who displays clothes by wearing them —a. serving as a model

mod'er·ate (-at; v.: -āt') a. avoiding extremes —v. **1** to make or become moderate **2** preside over (a debate, etc.) —**mod'er·a'tion** n. —**mod'er·a'tor** n.

mod'ern a. of recent times; up-to-date —n. modern person —**mod'ern·ize'** v.

mod'est a. **1** not conceited **2** decent **3** moderate

mod'i·fy' v. **-fied'** change or limit slightly —**mod'i·fi·ca'tion** n.

mod·ule (mäj'ōōl') n. detachable section with a special function

moist a. slightly wet

mois'ten (-an) v. make moist

mois'ture n. slight wetness

mo'lar n. back tooth

mo·las'ses n. dark syrup left after sugar is refined

mold n. **1** hollow form in which a thing is shaped **2** thing shaped **3** furry, fungous growth —v. **1** make in a mold **2** shape **3** become moldy

mold'y a. **-i·er, -i·est** of or covered with MOLD (n. 3)

mole n. **1** small, dark, congenital spot on the skin **2** small, burrowing animal

mol'e·cule' n. smallest particle of a substance that can exist alone —**mo·lec'u·lar** a.

mo·lest' v. to trouble or harm

mol'lusk, mol'lusc n. invertebrate with soft body in a shell

mol'ten (mōl'-) a. melted by heat

mom n. [Col.] mother

mo'ment n. brief period of, or certain point in, time

mo·men'tous a. very important

mom'my n., pl. **-mies** mother: child's word

mon'arch n. hereditary ruler

mon'ar·chy n., pl. **-ies** government by a monarch

mon'as·ter'y n., pl. **-ies** residence for monks

Mon'day n. second day of the week

mon'e·tar'y a. **1** of currency **2** of money

mon'ey n., pl. **-eys** or **-ies 1** metal coins or paper notes used as the legal medium of exchange **2** wealth

Mon'gol·oid' n., a. (member) of one of the major groups of human beings, including most of the peoples of Asia

mon'grel n., a. (animal or plant) of mixed breed

mon'i·tor n. **1** student who helps keep order, etc. **2** TV receiver or computer video screen —v. watch, or check on

monk n. man who is a member of an ascetic religious order

mon'key n., pl. **-keys** small, long-tailed primate

mon'o·gram' n. initials of a name, made into a design

mon'o·logue' n. **1** long speech **2** skit for one actor only

mo·nop'o·ly n., pl. **-lies 1** total control of something, esp. of a product or service **2** company having this

mon'o·tone' n. sameness of tone, pitch, color, etc.

mo·not'o·ny n. **1** lack of variety **2** tiresome sameness —**mo·not'o·nous** a.

mon·soon' n. wind bringing rainy season to S Asia

mon'ster n. huge or very abnormal plant or animal

mon'strous a. **1** horrible **2** huge **3** very abnormal

month n. any of the 12 divisions of the year

month'ly a. happening, appearing, etc. every month —adv. every month

mon'u·ment n. **1** memorial statue, building, etc. **2** famous work —**mon'u·men'tal** a.

moo v., n. (make) the vocal sound of a cow

mood n. 1 state of mind 2 verb form to express a fact, wish, or order

mood'y a. **-i·er, -i·est** 1 changing in mood 2 gloomy

moon n. body that revolves around a planet, spec. around the earth —**moon'light'** n.

moor n. open wasteland —v. to secure by cables, ropes, etc.

moose n., pl. **moose** largest animal of the deer family

mop n. rags, sponge, etc. on a stick, as for washing floors —v. **mopped** clean up, as with a mop

mope v. be gloomy

mor'al a. 1 of or dealing with right and wrong 2 good; virtuous 3 giving sympathy, but no active help —n. 1 moral lesson 2 pl. moral rules or standards

mo·rale' (-ral') n. degree of courage, discipline, etc.

mo·ral'i·ty n. 1 moral quality 2 virtue

mor'bid a. 1 diseased 2 gloomy or unwholesome

more a., v. 1 greater (in) amount or degree 2 (something) additional —adv. 1 to a greater degree 2 in addition

morgue (môrg) n. place where bodies of accident victims, etc. are taken, as for autopsy

morn'ing n. first part of the day, till noon

mo'ron n. foolish or stupid person

mor'phine (-fēn') n. opium drug used to relieve pain

mor'sel n. bit, as of food

mor'tal a. 1 that must die 2 causing death 3 very great; extreme —n. human being

mor'tar n. 1 bowl for pulverizing things with a pestle 2 small cannon 3 cement mixture used between bricks, etc.

mort'gage (môr'gij) n. deed pledging property as security for a debt

mo·sa'ic n. design made of colored stones inlaid in mortar

mos·qui'to n., pl. **-toes** or **-tos** small biting insect that sucks blood

moss n. tiny green plant growing in clusters on rocks, etc.

most a. 1 greatest in amount or number 2 almost all —n. the greatest amount or number —adv. to the greatest degree

most'ly adv. 1 mainly; chiefly 2 usually; generally

mo·tel' n. roadside hotel for motorists

moth n. four-winged insect like a butterfly

moth'er n. 1 female parent 2 woman head of a convent: in full **mother superior** —a. 1 of or like a mother 2 native —v. be a mother to —**moth'er·hood'** n. —**moth'er·ly** a.

moth'er-in-law' n., pl. **moth'ers-** mother of one's husband or wife

mo'tion n. 1 a moving; change of position 2 gesture 3 proposal made at a meeting

mo'tive n. reason for doing something —adv. of motion

mo'tor n. 1 machine using electricity to make something work 2 engine; esp., a gasoline engine —a. 1 of or run by a motor 2 of or for motor vehicles 3 producing motion 4 of muscular movements —**mo'tor·ist** n.

mo'tor·cy·cle n. two-wheeled, engine-powered vehicle

mot'to n., pl. **-toes** or **-tos** maxim or phrase, as used on seals, coins, etc., that shows one's ideals, etc.

mound n. heap of earth, etc.

mount v. 1 climb; go up 2 get up on 3 increase in amount 4 fix on or in a mounting —n. 1 act of mounting 2 horse to ride 3 mounting 4 mountain

moun'tain n. very high rise of land on earth's surface

mourn (môrn) v. feel or show grief or sorrow (for) —**mourn'er** n. —**mourn'ful** a.

mourn'ing n. 1 grief at a death 2 mourners' black clothes

mouse n., pl. **mice** 1 small rodent 2 timid person 3 handheld device for controlling images on a computer video screen

mouth n. 1 opening in the face for food 2 any opening

move v. 1 change the place of 2 set or keep in motion 3 change one's residence 4 be active or take action 5 cause 6 stir emotionally 7 propose (a resolution) —n. 1 movement or action 2 Games one's turn —**mov'a·ble, move'a·ble** a.

move'ment n. 1 a moving or way of moving 2 action toward a goal 3 moving parts of a clock, etc. 4 Mus. main division of a composition

mov'ie n. a FILM (n. 3)

mow v. **mowed, mowed** or

mown 1 cut down (grass) 2 kill; knock down —**mow'er** n.

moz'za·rel'la (mät'sə-) n. soft, white cheese with mild flavor

Mr. title used before a man's name

Mrs. title used before a married woman's name

Ms. (miz) title used instead of *Miss* or *Mrs.*

much a. **more, most** great in quantity, degree, etc. —adv. 1 greatly 2 nearly —n. 1 great amount 2 something great

muck n. 1 black earth 2 dirt; filth

mu'cous a. 1 of or secreting mucus 2 slimy

mu'cus n. slimy secretion of mucous membranes

mud n. soft, wet earth

mud'dle v. 1 mix up; confuse 2 act confusedly —n. mess, confusion, etc.

muf'fin n. bread baked in a small cupcake mold

muf'fle v. 1 wrap up warmly 2 deaden (sound), as on an automobile

muf'fler n. 1 thick scarf 2 device to deaden noise, as on an automobile

mug n. 1 heavy drinking cup 2 [Sl.] face

mul'ber'ry n., pl. -ries tree with berrylike fruit

mule n. 1 offspring of a male donkey and a female horse 2 lounging slipper

mul'ti·ple a. having many parts, etc.

mul'ti·ple-choice' a. listing several answers to choose from

mul'ti·ply v. -plied' 1 to increase in number, degree, etc. 2 find the product (of) by adding a certain number a certain number of times —**mul'ti·pli·ca'tion** n. —**mul'ti·pli'er** n.

mum n. [Col.] chrysanthemum

mum'ble v. speak or say indistinctly —n. mumbled utterance

mum'my n., pl. -mies ancient embalmed body

mumps n. disease in which the salivary glands swell

munch v. chew noisily

mu·nic'i·pal a. of a city or town

mu'ral (myoor'əl) a. of or on a wall —n. picture painted on a wall

mur'der v. kill (a person) unlawfully and with malice —n. act of murdering —**mur'der·er** n.

mur'mur n. 1 low, steady sound

2 mumbled complaint —v. 1 make a murmur 2 say in a low voice

mus'cle (-əl) n. 1 tissue forming the fleshy parts that move the body 2 any single part of this tissue 3 strength

mu·se'um n. place for displaying artistic, historical, or scientific objects

mush n. 1 thick, soft mass 2 boiled cornmeal 3 [Col.] maudlin sentimentality

mush'room' n. fleshy, umbrella-shaped fungus, often edible

mu'sic n. 1 songs, symphonies, etc. 2 art of composing or performing these

mu'si·cal a. of, fond of, or set to music —n. play or film with singing and dancing

mu·si'cian (-zish'ən) n. person skilled in music

musk'rat' n. water rodent

Mus'lim (muz'-, mooz'-) n. follower of the religion of Mohammed —a. of Islam or Muslims

must v. auxiliary verb showing: 1 obligation 2 probability 3 certainty —n. [Col.] thing that must be done

mus'tache' n. hair grown out on the upper lip of men

mus'tard n. yellow, spicy powder or paste

mu·ta'tion n. a change, esp. a sudden variation in a plant or animal —**mu'tate'** v.

mute a. 1 silent 2 not able to speak —n. 1 one unable to speak; spec., a deaf-mute 2 device to mute a musical instrument —v. soften the sound of

mu'ti·late' v. cut off or damage part of

mu'ti·ny n., pl. -nies; v. -nied revolt, as against one's military superiors

mut'ter v. 1 speak or say in low, indistinct tones 2 grumble

mut'ton n. flesh of (grown) sheep used as food

mu'tu·al (-chōō-) a. 1 of or for one another 2 in common

muz'zle n. 1 snout 2 device for an animal's mouth to prevent biting 3 front end of a gun barrel

my a. of me

myrrh (mur) n. resin used in incense, perfume, etc.

my·self' pron. intensive or reflexive form of I

mys'ter·y n., pl. -ies 1 unexplained or unknown thing 2

obscurity or secrecy —**mys·te'ri·ous** a.

mys'ti·cism' n. belief that God can be known directly

mys'ti·fy' v. **-fied'** perplex or puzzle —**mys'ti·fi·ca'tion** n.

myth n. **1** traditional story explaining some phenomenon **2** fictitious person or thing

my·thol'o·gy n., pl. **-gies 1** study of myths **2** myths of a certain people

N

nag v. **nagged** scold or urge constantly

nail n. **1** horny layer at the ends of the fingers and toes **2** narrow, pointed piece of metal driven into pieces of wood to hold them

na·ive, na·ïve (nä ēv') a. innocent; simple

na·ked a. **1** without clothing or covering **2** plain

name n. **1** word or words for a person, thing, or place **2** reputation —a. well-known —v. **1** give a name to **2** mention or identify by name **3** appoint

nap v. **napped** sleep briefly —n. **1** short sleep **2** fuzzy surface of fibers on cloth

na'palm' ('-päm') n. jellylike gasoline used in bombs, etc.

nape n. back of the neck

nap'kin n. small piece of paper or cloth to protect clothes while eating

nar·cis'sus n. flowering bulbous plant

nar·cot'ic n. drug that causes deep sleep and lessens pain

nar'rate' v. tell a story

nar'row a. **1** not wide **2** intolerant **3** limited in size, degree, etc.

na'sal (-zəl) a. of or through the nose

nas·tur'tium (-shəm) n. yellowish-red flower

nas'ty a. **-ti·er, -ti·est 1** dirty **2** obscene **3** unpleasant; mean

na'tion n. **1** a people with history, language, etc. in common **2** people under one government

na'tion·al a. of a whole nation

na'tion·al·ism' n. **1** patriotism **2** advocacy of national independence —**na'tion·al·ist** a., n.

na'tion·al'i·ty n., pl. **-ties** nation, esp. of one's birth or citizenship

na'tive a. **1** belonging to a region or country by birth, source, etc.

2 being of the place of one's birth **3** inborn —n. native person, animal, or plant

na·tiv'i·ty n. birth

nat'u·ral a. **1** of or dealing with nature **2** not artificial **3** innate **4** lifelike; usual **5** to be expected **6** Mus. neither sharp nor flat —**nat'u·ral·ly** adv.

nat'u·ral·ize' v. confer citizenship upon (an alien)

na'ture n. **1** basic quality of a thing **2** inborn character **3** kind; sort **4** physical universe or [also N-] its forces **5** natural scenery

naught (nôt) n. **1** nothing **2** zero

naugh'ty a. **-ti·er, -ti·est 1** mischievous **2** not nice or proper

nau'se·a (-shə, -zhə) n. **1** feeling of wanting to vomit **2** disgust

nau'ti·cal a. of sailors, ships, or navigation

na'val a. of or for a navy, its ships, etc.

na'vel n. small abdominal scar where the umbilical cord was attached

nav'i·gate' v. **1** travel through or on (air, sea, etc.) in a ship or aircraft **2** steer (a ship, etc.)

na'vy n., pl. **-vies 1** entire fleet of warships, etc. of a nation **2** very dark blue: also **navy blue**

nay n. **1** denial **2** negative vote or voter

near adv. at a short distance —a. **1** close in distance, time, etc. **2** intimate **3** stingy —v. to draw near to —prep. close to

near'ly adv. almost

near'sight'ed a. seeing only near objects distinctly

neat a. **1** tidy; clean **2** skillful **3** trim in form —**neat'ly** adv.

nec'es·sar'y a. **1** that must be had or done; essential **2** inevitable

ne·ces'si·ty n., pl. **-ties 1** great need **2** something necessary

neck n. **1** part that joins the head to the body **2** narrow part, as of a bottle

neck'lace n. chain of gold, beads, etc. worn around the neck

need n. **1** lack of something required; also, the thing lacking **2** poverty or distress —v. **1** have need of **2** to be obliged —Need is also used as an auxiliary verb

nee'dle n. **1** a very slender, pointed piece, as for sewing, knitting, playing phonograph records, etc. **2** anything needle-shaped —v. [Col.] goad; tease

nee'dle·work' n. sewing, embroidery, crocheting, etc.

need'y a. **-i·er, -i·est** very poor; destitute

neg·a·tive a. **1** saying "no" **2** not positive **3** of the electricity made by friction on resin **4** being less than zero —n. **1** a negative word, reply, etc. **2** battery plate of lower potential **3** photographic plate or film in which light and shadow are reversed

ne·glect' v. **1** fail to do **2** fail to care for properly —n. a neglecting —**ne·glect'ful** a.

ne·go·ti·ate' v. **1** discuss so as to agree on **2** arrange for (a loan, etc.) **3** transfer or sell **4** move across

Ne'groid' n., a. (member) of one of the major groups of human beings, including most of the peoples of central and southern Africa

neigh (nā) v., n. (utter) the cry of a horse

neigh'bor n. **1** one that lives or is near another **2** fellow human being —a. nearby

neigh'bor·hood' n. one part of a city or the people in it

nei'ther (nē'-, nī'-) a., pron. not one or the other (of two) —con. connecting word used with nor

ne'on' n. inert gas used in electric signs, a chemical element

neph'ew n. **1** son of one's brother or sister **2** son of one's brother-in-law or sister-in-law

nerve n. **1** cordlike fiber carrying impulses to and from the brain **2** courage **3** pl. nervousness **4** [Col.] impudence

nerv'ous a. **1** of nerves **2** easily upset; restless **3** fearful

nest n. **1** place where a bird or other animal raises its young **2** cozy place **3** set of things in increasing sizes

net n. **1** openwork fabric as of string, for snaring fish, etc. **2** fine net to hold the hair **3** netlike cloth **4** net amount —a. left over after deductions, etc.

net'work' n. **1** arrangement of wires or threads as in a net **2** system of roads, computers, etc. **3** chain of radio or TV stations

neu'ron' n. nerve cell and its processes

neu'ter a. neither masculine nor

feminine —v. castrate or spay (an animal)

neu'tral a. **1** supporting neither side in a war or quarrel **2** not one or the other **3** having no decided color —n. **1** neutral nation, etc. **2** position of disengaged gears —**neu·tral'i·ty** n.

neu'tron' n. uncharged particle of an atom

nev'er adv. **1** at no time **2** in no way

nev'er·the·less' adv., con. in spite of that; however

new a. **1** appearing, thought of, made, etc. for the first time **2** unfamiliar or foreign **3** fresh **4** unused **5** modern; recent **6** more **7** beginning again

new'ly adv. recently

news n. **1** new information **2** (reports of) recent events

news'cast' n. radio or TV news broadcast —**news'cast'er** n.

news'let·ter n. special group's news bulletin, issued regularly

news'pa·per n. daily or weekly news publication

newt n. small salamander

next a. nearest; closest —adv. in the nearest time, place, etc.

nib'ble v. eat with quick, small bites —n. small bite

nice a. **1** pleasant, kind, good, etc. **2** precise; accurate **3** refined —**nice'ly** adv.

niche (nich) n. **1** recess in a wall for a statue, etc. **2** especially suitable position

nick v. make a small cut, chip, etc. in or on —n. small cut, chip, etc.

nick'el n. **1** rust-resistant metal, a chemical element **2** nickel and copper coin worth five cents

nick'name' n. **1** a substitute name, as "Slim" **2** familiar form of a proper name, as "Bob"

niece n. **1** daughter of one's sister or brother **2** daughter of one's sister-in-law or brother-in-law

night n. period of darkness between sunset and sunrise

night'gown' n. sleeping gown for women and children

night'in·gale' n. a European thrush that sings at night

night'ly a., adv. (done or happening) every night

night'mare' n. frightening dream or experience

nim'ble a. quick in movement or thought —**nim'bly** adv.

nine a., n. one more than eight

—**ninth** *a., n.*

nine'teen' *a., n.* nine more than ten —**nine'teenth'** *a., n.*

nine'ty *a., n., pl.* **-ties** nine times ten —**nine'ti·eth** *a., n.*

nin'ja *n.* in former times, a trained Japanese assassin

nip *v.* **nipped** 1 pinch or bite 2 pinch off 3 spoil, as by frost

nip'ple *n.* 1 protuberance on a breast or udder 2 thing shaped like this

ni'tro·gen *n.* colorless, odorless gas, a chemical element

no *adv.* 1 not at all 2 not so —*a.* not a —*n., pl.* **noes** 1 refusal 2 negative vote

no·bil'i·ty *n., pl.* **-ties** 1 noble state or rank 2 people of noble rank

no'ble *a.* 1 highly moral 2 grand; splendid 3 of high hereditary rank —*n.* person of high rank —**no'ble·man**, *pl.* **-men** —**no'bly** *adv.*

no'bod·y *pron.* no one

nod *v.* **nod'ded** 1 bend the head quickly 2 show (assent) thus 3 let the head fall forward in dozing —*n.* a nodding

No·el (nō el') *n.* Christmas

noise *n.* sound, esp. a loud, unpleasant sound

no'mad *n.* 1 member of a wandering tribe 2 wanderer

nom'i·nal *a.* 1 in name only 2 relatively small

nom'i·nate *v.* 1 appoint; name 2 name as a candidate —**nom'i·na'tion** *n.*

nom'i·nee' *n.* a person who is nominated

non'cha·lant' (-shə länt') *a.* casually indifferent

none (nun) *pron.* 1 no one 2 not any —*adv.* not at all

none'the·less' *adv.* nevertheless

non·fer'rous *a.* of metals other than iron

non·par'ti·san *a.* not of any single party, faction, etc.

non·prof'it *a.* not for profit

non·res'i·dent *n., a.* (person) not living in the locality of his work, etc.

non·sense' *n.* absurd or meaningless words or acts

non·un'ion *a.* not belonging to, or done by, a labor union

non·vi'o·lent *a.* not using violence —**non·vi'o·lence** *n.*

noo'dle *n.* flat strip of dry dough

nook *n.* 1 corner 2 small secluded spot

noon *n.* twelve o'clock in the

daytime; midday: also **noon'day** or **noon'time'**

no one *pron.* no person

noose *n.* loop with a slipknot for tightening it

nor *con.* and not (either)

nor'mal *a.* 1 usual; natural 2 average —*n.* what is normal; usual state

north *n.* direction or region to the right of one facing the sunset —*a., adv.* in, toward, or from the north —**north'er·ly** *a., adv.* —**north'ern** *a.* —**north'ern·er** *n.* —**north'ward** *a., adv.* —**north'wards** *adv.*

north'east' *n.* direction or region between north and east —*a., adv.* in, toward, or from the northeast —**north'east'er·ly** *a., adv.* —**north'east'ern** *a.*

North Star bright star almost directly above the North Pole

north'west' *n.* direction or region between north and west —*a., adv.* in, toward, or from the northwest —**north'west'er·ly** *a., adv.* —**north'west'ern** *a.*

nose *n.* 1 part of the face with two openings for breathing and smelling 2 sense of smell 3 thing like a nose

nos·tal'gi·a *n.* a longing for something past or far away

nos'tril *n.* either of two outer openings of the nose

not *adv.* in no manner, degree, etc.

no'ta·ble *a., n.* remarkable or outstanding (person)

no·ta'tion *n.* 1 (use of) a system of symbols, as in music 2 a note

notch *n.* 1 a V-shaped cut 2 [Col.] a step; degree

note *n.* 1 brief writing, comment, letter, etc. 2 notice; heed 3 written promise to pay 4 musical tone or its symbol 5 importance —*v.* 1 to notice 2 make a note of

note'book' *n.* book for keeping memorandums, etc.

noth'ing *n.* 1 no thing 2 unimportant person or thing 3 zero

no'tice *n.* 1 announcement or warning 2 a short review 3 attention —*v.* observe

no'ti·fy *v.* **-fied** give notice to; inform —**no·ti·fi·ca'tion** *n.*

no'tion *n.* 1 general idea 2 belief; opinion 3 whim 4 *pl.* small wares

no·to'ri·ous *a.* widely known, esp. unfavorably

nought (nôt) *n.* 1 nothing 2

zero

noun n. word that names a person, thing, etc.

nour'ish a. feed to promote life and growth

nov'el a. new and unusual —n. long fictional narrative

nov'el·ist n. writer of novels

nov'el·ty n., pl. **-ties** 1 newness 2 novel thing 3 small, cheap toy, etc.

No·vem'ber n. 11th month

nov'ice n. 1 one in a religious order before taking final vows 2 beginner

now adv. 1 at this moment; at present 2 at that time; then 3 with things as they are —con. since —n. the present time

now'a·days' adv. in these days; at the present time

no'where' adv. not in, at, or to any place

noz'zle n. small spout at the end of a hose, etc.

nu'cle·ar a. of, like, or forming a nucleus or nuclei

nu'cle·us n., pl. **-cle·i'** (-klē ī') or **-cle·us·es** central part, spec. of an atom of a living cell

nude a., n. naked (figure)

nudge v. push gently, as with the elbow to get someone's attention —n. gentle push

nui'sance (nōō'-) n. annoying act, person, etc.

null a. without legal force: also **null and void**

numb (num) a. not able to feel

num'ber n. 1 symbol or word showing how many or what place in a series 2 total 3 often pl. many 4 quantity 5 single issue of a periodical 6 one part of a program of entertainment 7 form of a word showing it to be singular or plural —v. 1 to count 2 give a number to 3 include 4 to total or contain

nu'mer·al n. figure, letter, or word expressing a number

nu'mer·a'tor n. part above the line in a fraction

nu'mer·ous a. 1 very many 2 large in number

nun n. woman living in a convent under vows

nup'tial (-shəl) a. of marriage or a wedding —n. pl. a wedding

nurse n. 1 one trained to care for the sick, help doctors, etc. 2 nursemaid —v. 1 take care of (an invalid, etc.) 2 try to cure; treat 3 suckle 4 protect or conserve 5 nourish

nurs'er·y n., pl. **-ies** 1 room set aside for children 2 place where trees and plants are raised for sale

nur'ture n. training; care

nut n. 1 dry fruit with a kernel inside a hard shell 2 the kernel 3 small metal block for screwing onto a bolt, etc. 4 [Sl.] odd or silly person 5 [Sl.] fan; devotee

nut'meg' n. aromatic seed grated and used as a spice

nu·tri'tion n. 1 process of taking in and assimilating food 2 food —**nu·tri'tious** a.

nuts a. [Sl.] crazy; silly

nuz'zle v. 1 to push against with the nose 2 snuggle

ny'lon n. 1 synthetic material made into thread, etc. 2 pl. stockings of this

O

oaf n. stupid, clumsy fellow

oak n. hardwood tree bearing acorns —**oak'en** a.

oar n. pole with a broad blade at one end, for rowing

o·a'sis n., pl. **-ses** fertile place with water in the desert

oat n. usually pl. 1 a cereal grass 2 its grain —**oat'en** a.

oath n. 1 sworn declaration to tell the truth, etc. 2 word used in cursing

oat'meal' n. ground or rolled oats, cooked as porridge

o·be'di·ent a. obeying or willing to obey —**o·be'di·ence** n.

o·bey' v. 1 carry out orders (of) 2 be guided by

o·bit'u·ar·y (-bich'ōō-) n., pl. **-ies** notice of death, often with a short biography: also **o'bit**

object (v.: əb jekt') n. 1 thing that can be seen or touched 2 person or thing to which action, etc. is directed 3 purpose; goal 4 Gram. word receiving the action of the verb or governed by a preposition —v. feel or express opposition or disapproval —**ob·jec'tor** n.

ob·jec'tion n. 1 expression of disapproval 2 a reason for objecting

ob·jec'tive a. 1 real or actual; not subjective 2 without bias 3 Gram. of the case of an object of a preposition or verb —n. goal

ob'li·gate' v. bind by a promise, sense of duty, etc.

o·blige' v. 1 compel, as by law or duty 2 make indebted; do a favor for

ob·lique (ō blēk´) *a.* 1 slanting 2 not direct —**ob·liq´ui·ty** *n.*

ob·long´ *a.* rectangular and longer than broad —*n.* oblong figure

ob·nox´ious *a.* offensive

o´boe *n.* double-reed woodwind instrument

ob·scene´ *a.* offensive to decency

ob·scure´ *a.* 1 dim 2 not clear or distinct 3 not well-known

ob·serv·a·to´ry *n., pl.* -ries building for astronomical research

ob·serve´ *v.* 1 adhere to (a law, etc.) 2 celebrate (a holiday, etc.) 3 notice; watch 4 to remark —**ob·serv´er** *n.*

ob·sess´ *v.* haunt in mind; preoccupy greatly

ob·so·lete´ (*or* äb´sə lēt´) *a.* no longer used

ob´sta·cle *n.* obstruction

ob·stet´rics *n.* branch of medicine dealing with childbirth —**ob·ste·tri´cian** *n.*

ob´sti·nate *a.* 1 stubborn 2 hard to treat or cure

ob·struct´ *v.* 1 block 2 hinder —**ob·struc´tion** *n.*

ob·tain´ *v.* 1 get by trying 2 prevail; be in effect

ob·tuse´ *a.* 1 more than 90°: said of an angle 2 blunt 3 slow to understand

ob´vi·ous *a.* easy to understand

oc·ca´sion *n.* 1 happening 2 special event 3 opportunity 4 cause —*v.* to cause

oc·ca´sion·al *a.* 1 for special times 2 infrequent —**oc·ca´sion·al·ly** *adv.*

oc·cult´ *a.* 1 secret 2 mysterious 3 magical

oc´cu·pan·cy *n., pl.* -cies an occupying —**oc´cu·pant** *n.*

oc·cu·pa´tion *n.* 1 an occupying 2 work; vocation

oc´cu·py´ *v.* -pied´ 1 take possession of 2 dwell in 3 employ

oc·cur´ *v.* -curred´ 1 exist 2 come to mind 3 happen —**oc·cur´rence** *n.*

o´cean *n.* 1 body of salt water covering much of the earth 2 one of its four main divisions —**o´ce·an´ic** (-shē an´-) *a.*

o´clock´ *adv.* by the clock

oc´ta·gon *n.* figure with eight sides and eight angles

oc´tave (-tiv) *n.* eight full steps of a musical scale

Oc·to´ber *n.* tenth month

oc´to·pus *n.* mollusk with soft body and eight arms

odd *a.* 1 having a remainder of

one when divided by two; not even 2 left over, as from a pair 3 with a few more 4 occasional 5 peculiar; strange

odd´i·ty *n.* 1 odd quality 2 *pl.* -ties odd person or thing

odds *n.pl.* 1 advantage 2 betting ratio based on chances —**at odds** quarreling

ode *n.* lofty poem in praise

o´dor *n.* smell; aroma

o´er (ō´ər) *prep., adv.* [Poet.] over

of *prep.* 1 being or coming from 2 belonging to 3 having or containing 4 concerning; about 5 during

off *adv.* 1 farther away in space or time 2 so as to be no longer on 3 so as to be less —*prep.* 1 not on 2 dependent on 3 away from 4 below the standard of —*a.* 1 not on 2 on the way 3 away from work; absent 4 below standard 5 provided for 6 in error; wrong

of·fend´ *v.* 1 commit an offense 2 make angry; displease

of·fense´ (*or* ō´fens) *n.* 1 sin or crime 2 an offending 3 an attacking —**give offense** make angry; insult —**take offense** become offended

of·fen´sive *a.* 1 attacking 2 disgusting

of´fer *v.* 1 to present or give 2 suggest —*n.* thing offered

off´hand´ *adv.* without preparation —*a.* 1 said offhand 2 rude; curt Also **off´hand´ed**

of´fice *n.* 1 a favor 2 post of authority 3 place for doing business 4 rite

of´fi·cer *n.* 1 one having a position of authority in business, the armed forces, etc. 2 policeman

of·fi´cial *a.* 1 authorized 2 formal —*n.* one holding an office —**of·fi´cial·ly** *adv.*

off´key´ *a.* not harmonious

off´lim´its *a.* not to be gone to

off´shoot´ *n.* anything that comes from a main source

off´spring´ *n.* child or children

of·ten (ōf´ən) *adv.* many times

o´gre (-gər) *n.* 1 *Folklore* maneating giant 2 cruel man

oh (ō) *int., n., pl.* **oh's** or **ohs** exclamation of surprise, fear, wonder, pain, etc.

oil *n.* 1 any greasy liquid 2 petroleum —*v.* lubricate with oil —*a.* of, from, or like oil

oink *v., n.* (make) the vocal sound of a pig

oint'ment *n.* oily cream for healing the skin

OK, O.K. *a., adv., int.* all right —*n.* approval —*v.* **OK'd, O.K.'d** to approve Also sp. **o·kay'**

old *a.* 1 having lived or existed for a long time 2 of a specified age 3 not new 4 former

old'-fash'ioned *a.* of the past; out-of-date

o·le·o·mar'ga·rine *n.* margarine: also **o'le·o'**

ol·fac'to·ry *a.* of the sense of smell

ol'ive *n.* 1 evergreen tree 2 its small, oval fruit 3 yellowish green

om'e·let (äm'lət) *n.* eggs beaten up and cooked as a pancake

o'men *n.* sign of something to come

o·mit' *v.* **o·mit'ted** 1 leave out 2 fail to do

om·nip'o·tent *a.* all-powerful

om·nis'cient (-nish'ənt) *a.* knowing all things

on *prep.* 1 held up by, covering, or attached to 2 near to 3 at the time of 4 connected with 5 in a state of 6 by using 7 concerning 8 [Sl.] using; addicted to —*adv.* 1 in a situation of touching, covering, or being held up 2 toward 3 forward 4 continuously 5 into operation —*a.* in action

once *adv.* 1 one time 2 at any time 3 formerly —*n.* one time —**at once** 1 immediately 2 simultaneously

one *a.* 1 being a single thing 2 united 3 a certain 4 some —*n.* 1 lowest number 2 single person or thing —*pron.* a person or thing —**one by one** individually

one'self' *pron.* one's own self; himself or herself

on·ion (un'yən) *n.* bulblike, sharp-tasting vegetable

on'-line' *a.* connected to a computer's CPU

on'ly *a.* 1 alone of its or their kind 2 best —*adv.* 1 and no other 2 merely

on'set' *n.* 1 attack 2 start

on'to *prep.* to and upon

on'ward *adv.* forward: also **on'wards** —*a.* advancing

on'yx (-iks) *n.* kind of agate

ooze *v.* flow out slowly —*n.* 1 something that oozes 2 soft mud or slime

o'pal *n.* iridescent gem

o·paque' (-pāk') *a.* not transparent —**o·pac'i·ty** (-pas'-) *n.*

o'pen *a.* 1 not closed, covered, etc. 2 not enclosed 3 unfolded 4 free to be entered, used, etc. 5 not restricted 6 available 7 frank —*v.* 1 to cause to be or become open 2 begin 3 start operating

o'pen·ing' *n.* 1 open place 2 beginning 3 favorable chance 4 unfilled job

op'er·a *n.* play set to music and sung with an orchestra

op'er·ate' *v.* 1 be or keep in action 2 have an effect 3 perform an operation 4 manage

op·er·a'tion *n.* 1 act or way of operating 2 a being in action 3 one process in a series 4 surgical treatment for an illness

o·pin'ion *n.* 1 what one thinks true 2 estimation 3 expert judgment

o'pi·um *n.* narcotic drug made from a certain poppy

o·pos'sum *n.* small mammal that lives in trees

op·po'nent *n.* person against one in a fight, etc.

op'por·tu'ni·ty *n., pl.* **-ties** fit time to do something

op·pose' *v.* 1 to place opposite 2 fight or resist

op'po·site *a.* 1 entirely different 2 opposed to —*n.* anything opposed —*prep.* across from

op·press' *v.* 1 weigh down 2 rule in a cruel way

op'ti·cal *a.* 1 of vision 2 aiding sight

op·ti'cian (-tish'ən) *n.* maker or seller of eyeglasses

op'ti·mism' *n.* tendency to be cheerful about life

op'tion *n.* choice or right to choose —**op'tion·al** *a.*

op·tom'e·trist' *n.* one who tests eyes and fits eyeglasses

op'u·lent *a.* 1 wealthy 2 abundant —**op'u·lence** *n.*

o'pus *n., pl.* **o'pe·ra** or **o'pus·es** a work, esp. of music

or *con.* word introducing an alternative, synonym, etc.

o'ral *a.* 1 spoken 2 of the mouth —**o'ral·ly** *adv.*

or'ange *n.* 1 sweet, round, reddish-yellow citrus fruit 2 reddish yellow

o·ra'tion *n.* formal public speech

or'bit *n.* path of one heavenly body around another —*v.* put or go in an orbit

or'chard *n.* grove of fruit trees

or'ches·tra (-kis-) *n.* 1 group of musicians playing together 2 main floor of a theater

or'chid (-kid) *n.* 1 plant having flowers with three petals, one of which is enlarged 2 light bluish red

or·dain' *v.* 1 to decree 2 admit to the ministry

or·deal' *n.* difficult or painful experience

or'der *n.* 1 peaceful, orderly, or proper state 2 monastic or fraternal brotherhood 3 general condition 4 a command 5 (a request for) items to be supplied 6 class; kind —*v.* 1 arrange 2 command 3 request (supplies)

or'der·ly *a.* 1 neatly arranged 2 well-behaved

or'di·nance *n.* statute, esp. of a city government

or'di·nar'y *a.* 1 customary; usual; regular 2 common; average —**or'di·nar'i·ly** *adv.*

ord'nance *n. Mil.* heavy guns, ammunition, etc.

ore *n.* rock or mineral containing metal

or'gan *n.* 1 keyboard musical instrument using pipes, reeds, or electronic tubes 2 animal or plant part with a special function 3 agency or medium

or'gan·ism' *n.* living thing

or'gan·ize' *v.* 1 arrange according to a system 2 form into a group, union, etc.

o'ri·ent *v.* adjust (oneself) to a specific situation —[O-] E Asia —**O'ri·en'tal** *a.*

or·i·gin *n.* 1 beginning 2 parentage 3 source

o·rig'i·nal *a.* 1 first 2 new; novel 3 inventive —*n.* an original work, form, etc.

o·rig'i·nate' *v.* 1 create; invent 2 begin; start —**o·rig'i·na'tor** *n.*

or'na·ment (-mənt; *v.:* -ment') *n.* decoration —*v.* decorate —**or'na·men'tal** *a.*

or·nate' *a.* showy

or'ni·thol'o·gy *n.* study of birds

or'phan *n.* child whose parents are dead —**or'phan·age** *n.*

or'tho·dox' *a.* 1 holding to the usual or fixed beliefs; conventional 2 [O-] of a large eastern Christian church

os·mo'sis *n.* diffusion of fluids through a porous membrane

os'te·op'a·thy *n.* a school of medicine and surgery emphasizing interrelationship of muscles and bones —**os'te·o·path'** *n.*

os'te·o·po·ro'sis *n.* a disorder marked by porous, brittle bones

os'tra·cize' *v.* banish; shut out

os'trich *n.* large, nonflying bird

oth'er *a.* 1 being the one(s) remaining 2 different 3 additional —*pron.* 1 the other one 2 some other one —*adv.* otherwise

oth'er·wise' *adv.* 1 differently 2 in all other ways 3 if not; else

ot'ter *n.* weasellike animal

ouch *int.* cry of pain

ought (ôt) *v.* auxiliary verb showing: 1 duty 2 desirability 3 probability

ounce *n.* 1 unit of weight, $\frac{1}{16}$ pound 2 fluid ounce, $\frac{1}{16}$ pint

our *a.* of us

our·selves' *pron.* intensive or reflexive form of WE

oust *v.* force out; expel

out *adv.* 1 away from a place, etc. 2 outdoors 3 into being or action 4 thoroughly 5 from a group —*a.* 1 not used, working, etc. 2 having lost —*n.* 1 [Sl.] excuse 2 *Baseball* retirement of a batter or runner from play —*v.* become known —*prep.* out of
—**out of** 1 from inside of 2 beyond 3 from (material) 4 because of 5 no longer having 6 so as to deprive

out'break' *n.* a breaking out, as of disease or rioting

out'cast' *a., n.* shunned (person)

out'come' *n.* result

out'do' *v.* do better than

out'door' *a.* in the open

out'doors' *adv.* in or into the open; outside —*n.* the outdoor world

out'er *a.* on or closer to the outside

outer space *n.* space beyond the earth's atmosphere

out'fit' *n.* 1 equipment for some activity 2 group; esp., military unit —*v.* -fit'ted equip

out'growth' *n.* 1 result 2 an offshoot

out'law' *n.* notorious criminal

out'let' *n.* 1 passage or way out 2 market for goods

out'line' *n.* 1 bounding line 2 sketch showing only outer lines 3 general plan

out'live' *v.* live longer than

out'look' *n.* 1 viewpoint 2 prospect

out'num'ber *v.* be greater in number than

out'-of-doors' *a.* outdoor —*n., adv.* outdoors

out'put' *n.* 1 total quantity produced in a given period 2 infor-

out'rage' *n.* 1 shocking act or crime 2 deep insult

out'ra'geous *a.*

out'right' *a.* complete —*adv.* entirely

out'set' *n.* beginning

out'side' *n.* 1 the exterior 2 area beyond —*a.* 1 outer 2 from some other 3 slight —*adv.* on or to the outside —*prep.* on or to the outside of

out'sid'er *n.*

out'skirts' *n.pl.* outlying districts of a city, etc.

out'spo'ken *a.* frank; bold

out'stand'ing *a.* 1 prominent 2 unpaid

out'ward *a.* 1 outer 2 visible —*adv.* toward the outside Also **out'wards** —**out'ward·ly** *adv.*

out·wit' *v.* **-wit'ted** to overcome by cleverness

o'val *a., n.* egg-shaped (thing)

o'va·ry *n., pl.* **-ries** 1 female gland where ova are formed 2 part of a flower where the seeds form —**o·var'i·an** (-ver'-) *a.*

ov'en (uv'-) *n.* compartment for baking, drying, etc.

o'ver *prep.* 1 above 2 on; upon 3 across 4 during 5 more than 6 about —*adv.* 1 above or across 2 more 3 down 4 other side up 5 again —*a.* 1 finished 2 on the other side

o'ver·all' *a.* 1 from end to end 2 total —*n. pl.* work trousers with attached bib

o'ver·board' *adv.* from a ship into the water

o'ver·cast' *a.* cloudy; dark

o'ver·come' *v.* get the better of; master

o'ver·do' *v.* do too much

o'ver·dose' (*n.:* ō'vər dōs') *v., n.* (take) too large a dose

o'ver·draw' *v.* draw in excess of the amount credited to one

o'ver·due' *a.* past the time for payment, arrival, etc.

o'ver·flow' (*n.:* ō'vər flō') *v.* 1 flood; run over 2 fill beyond capacity —*n.* 1 an overflowing 2 vent for overflowing liquids

o'ver·haul' *v.* check thoroughly and make needed repairs

o'ver·head' (*or* ō'vər hed') *a., adv.* above the head

o'ver·hear' *v.* hear a speaker without his knowledge

o'ver·kill' *n.* much more than is needed, suitable, etc.

o'ver·lap' *v.* lap over

o'ver·look' *v.* 1 look down on 2 fail to notice 3 neglect 4 excuse

o'ver·ly *adv.* too much

o'ver·night' *adv.* during the night

o'ver·pow'er *v.* subdue

o'ver·ride' *v.* overrule

o'ver·rule' *v.* 1 set aside 2 prevail over

o'ver·run' *v.* 1 spread out over 2 swarm over

o'ver·seas' *a., adv.* 1 across or beyond the sea 2 foreign

o'ver·see' *v.* supervise

o'ver·shad'ow *v.* be more important than

o'ver·sight' *n.* 1 failure to see 2 careless oversight

o·vert' (*or* ō'vərt') *a.* 1 open; public 2 done openly

o'ver·take' *v.* 1 catch up with 2 come upon suddenly

o'ver·throw' (*n.:* ō'vər thrō') *v., n.* defeat

o'ver·time' *n.* 1 time beyond a set limit 2 pay for overtime work

o'ver·ture *n.* 1 *Mus.* introduction 2 proposal

o'ver·turn' *v.* 1 turn over 2 conquer

o'ver·whelm' *v.* 1 cover over completely 2 crush

o'ver·work' *v.* work too hard

o'ver·wrought' (-rôt') *a.* too nervous or excited

ov'u·late' *v.* make and release ova —**ov'u·la'tion** *n.*

owe *v.* 1 be in debt (to) for a certain sum 2 feel obligated to give

owl *n.* night bird of prey with large eyes —**owl'ish** *a.*

own *a.* belonging to oneself or itself —*n.* what one owns —*v.* 1 possess 2 confess —**own'er** *n.*

ox *n., pl.* **ox'en** 1 a cud-chewing animal, as a cow, bull, etc. 2 castrated bull

ox'y·gen *n.* colorless gas, a chemical element

oys'ter *n.* edible mollusk with hinged shell

P

pa *n.* [Col.] father

pace *n.* 1 a step or stride 2 rate of speed 3 gait —*v.* 1 to walk back and forth across 2 measure by paces 3 set the pace for

pa·cif'ic *a.* peaceful; calm

pac'i·fy' *v.* **-fied'** make calm

pack *n.* 1 bundle of things 2 package of a set number 3 a group of animals, etc. —*v.* 1 put (things) in a box, bundle, etc. 2

crowd; cram 3 fill tightly

pack′age *n.* packed thing

pack′et *n.* small package

pact *n.* compact; agreement

pad *n.* **1** soft stuffing or cushion **2** sole of an animal's foot **3** water lily leaf **4** paper sheets fastened at one edge —*v.* **pad′ded 1** stuff with material **2** walk softly

pad′dle *n.* **1** oar for a canoe **2** similar thing for games, etc.

pad′lock′ *n.* a lock with a U-shaped arm

pa′gan *n., a.* heathen

page *n.* **1** one side of a leaf of a book, etc. **2** the leaf **3** boy attendant —*v.* **1** number the pages of **2** try to find (a person) by calling his or her name

pag′eant (paj′ənt) *n.* elaborate show, parade, play, etc.

pa·go′da *n.* towerlike temple of the Orient

pail *n.* bucket —**pail′ful′** *n.*

pain *n.* **1** hurt felt in body or mind **2** great care —**pain′ful** *a.* —**pain′less** *a.*

paint *n.* pigment mixed with oil, water, etc. —*v.* **1** make pictures (of) with paint **2** cover with paint —**paint′ing** *n.*

pair *n.* two things, persons, etc. that match or make a unit

pa·ja′mas (-jä′-) *n.pl.* matching trousers and top for sleeping

pal *n.* [Col.] close friend

pal′ace *n.* **1** monarch's residence **2** magnificent building —**pa·la′tial** (-shəl) *a.*

pal′ate *n.* **1** roof of the mouth **2** taste

pale *a.* **1** white; colorless **2** not bright or intense

pal′ette *n.* thin board on which artists mix paint

pal′i·sade′ *n.* **1** fence of large pointed stakes for fortification **2** *pl.* steep cliffs

pall (pôl) *v.* **palled** become boring

pall′bear′er *n.* bearer of a coffin at a funeral

pal′let *n.* straw bed

pal′lid *a.* pale —**pal′lor** *n.*

palm (päm) *n.* **1** tall tropical tree topped with a bunch of huge leaves **2** its leaf: symbol of victory **3** inside of the hand

palm′is·try *n.* fortunetelling from the lines, etc. on a person's palm

pal′o·mi′no (-mē′-) *n., pl.* **-nos** pale-yellow horse with white mane and tail

pal′pi·tate′ *v.* to throb

pal′sy (pôl′zē) *n.* paralysis in part of the body, often with tremors —**pal′sied** *a.*

pam′per *v.* to be overindulgent with

pam′phlet *n.* a thin, unbound booklet

pan *n.* broad, shallow container used in cooking, etc. —*v.* **panned 1** move camera to view a panorama **2** [Col.] criticize adversely

pan′cake′ *n.* thin cake of batter fried in a pan

pan′cre·as *n.* gland that secretes a digestive juice

pan′da *n.* white-and-black, bearlike animal of Asia

pan·de·mo′ni·um *n.* wild disorder or noise

pane *n.* sheet of glass

pan′el *n.* **1** flat section set off on a wall, door, etc. **2** group chosen for judging, discussing, etc. —**pan′el·ing** *n.* —**pan′el·ist** *n.*

pang *n.* sudden, sharp pain

pan′ic *n.* sudden, wild fear

pan′o·ram′a *n.* **1** unlimited view **2** constantly changing scene

pan′sy *n., pl.* **-sies** small plant with velvety petals

pant *v.* **1** breathe in pants **2** long (*for*) **3** gasp out —*n.* rapid, heavy breath

pan′ther *n.* **1** cougar **2** jaguar **3** leopard

pant′ies *n.pl.* women's or children's short underpants

pan′to·mime′ *v., n.* (make) use of gestures without words to present a play

pan′try *n., pl.* **-tries** a room for food, pots, etc.

pants *n.pl.* trousers

pa′pa *n.* father: child's word

pa′per *n.* **1** thin material in sheets, used to write or print on, wrap, etc. **2** sheet of this **3** essay **4** newspaper **5** wallpaper **6** *pl.* credentials —*a.* of or like paper —*v.* cover with wallpaper

pa′per·back′ *n.* book bound in paper

Pap test *n.* test for uterine cancer

pa·py′rus *n.* **1** paper made by ancient Egyptians from a water plant **2** this plant

par *n.* **1** equal rank **2** average **3** face value of stocks, etc.

par′a·ble *n.* short, simple story with a moral

par′a·chute′ *n.* umbrellalike device to slow down a person or thing dropping from an aircraft —v. drop by parachute

pa·rade' n. **1** showy display **2** march or procession —v. **1** march in a parade **2** show off

par·a·dise' n. place or state of great happiness

par·a·dox' n. contradictory statement that is or seems false

par'af·fin n. white, waxy substance used for making candles, sealing jars, etc.

par'a·graph' n. distinct section of a piece of writing, begun on a new line and often indented

par·a·keet' n. small parrot

par·a·le'gal a., n. (of) a lawyer's assistant

par·al'lel a. **1** in the same direction and at a fixed distance apart **2** similar —n. **1** parallel line, surface, etc. **2** one like another **3** imaginary line parallel to the equator, representing degrees of latitude

pa·ral'y·sis n. **1** loss of power to move any part of the body **2** a crippling

par'a·lyze' ('-līz) v. **1** to cause paralysis in **2** to make ineffective

par·a·pher·na'li·a n.pl. [sing. or pl. v.] belongings or equipment

par'a·site' n. plant or animal that lives on or in another

par'a·troops' n.pl. unit of soldiers trained to parachute from airplanes behind enemy lines —**par'a·troop'er** n.

par'cel n. **1** package **2** piece (of land)

parch v. **1** make hot and dry **2** make thirsty

parch'ment n. **1** skin of a sheep, etc. prepared as a surface for writing **2** paper resembling this

par'don v. **1** to release from punishment **2** excuse; forgive

pare v. **1** peel **2** reduce gradually

par'ent n. **1** father or mother **2** source —**pa·ren'tal** a.

pa·ren'the·sis n., pl. **-ses'** (-sēz') **1** word of explanation put into a sentence **2** either of the marks ( ) used to set this off

par'ish n. **1** part of a diocese under a priest, etc. **2** church congregation

park n. public land for recreation or rest —v. leave (a vehicle) temporarily

par'ka n. hooded coat

par'lia·ment (-lə-) n. legislative body, spec. [**P-**] of Great Britain, Canada, etc.

par'lor n. **1** living room **2** business establishment, as a shop where hair is styled

pa·ro'chi·al (-kē-) a. **1** of a parish **2** limited; narrow

par'o·dy n., pl. **-dies** (write) a farcical imitation of a work

pa·role' v., n. release from prison on condition of future good behavior

par'rot n. brightly colored bird that can imitate speech

pars'ley n. plant with leaves used to flavor some foods

par'son n. minister or clergyman

part n. **1** portion, piece, element, etc. **2** duty **3** role **4** music for a certain voice or instrument in a composition **5** usually pl. region **6** dividing line formed in combing the hair —v. **1** divide; separate **2** go away from each other —a. less than whole —**part with** give up —**take part** participate

par·take' v. **-took', -tak'en 1** participate (in) **2** eat or drink (of)

par'tial (-shəl) a. **1** favoring one over another **2** not complete

par·tic'i·pate' v. have or take a share with others (in) —**par·tic'i·pant** n.

par'ti·ci·ple n. verb form having the qualities of both a verb and an adjective

par'ti·cle n. **1** tiny fragment **2** preposition, article, or conjunction

par·tic'u·lar a. **1** of one; individual **2** specific **3** hard to please —n. a detail

par·ti'tion (-tish'ən) n. **1** division into parts **2** thing that divides —v. divide into parts

part'ner n. one who undertakes something with another; associate; mate —**part'ner·ship** n.

par'tridge n. game bird, as the pheasant, quail, etc.

par'ty n., pl. **-ties 1** group working together for a political cause, etc. **2** social gathering **3** one involved in a lawsuit, crime, etc.

pass v. **1** go by, beyond, etc. **2** go or change from one form, place, etc. to another **3** cease; end **4** approve or be approved **5** take a test, etc. successfully **6** cause or allow to go, move, qualify, etc. **7** throw **8** spend time **9** happen **10** give as an opinion, judgment, etc. —n. **1** a passing **2** free ticket **3** brief military leave **4** PASSAGE (n. 4)

pas'sage n. 1 a passing 2 right to pass 3 voyage 4 road, opening, etc. 5 part of something written

pas'sen·ger n. one traveling in a train, car, etc.

pas'sion n. 1 strong emotion, as hate, love, etc. 2 an object of strong desire —**pas'sion·ate** a.

pas'sive a. 1 inactive, but acted upon 2 yielding; submissive

pass'port' n. government document identifying a citizen traveling abroad

past a. 1 gone by 2 of a former time —n. 1 history 2 time gone by —prep. beyond in time, space, etc. —adv. to and beyond

pas'ta (päs'-) n. spaghetti, macaroni, etc.

paste n. 1 moist, smooth mixture 2 adhesive mixture with flour, water, etc. —v. make adhere, as with paste

pas·tel' a., n. soft and pale (shade)

pas'teur·ize' (-char-, -tar-) v. kill bacteria (in milk, etc.) by heating —**pas'teur·i·za'tion** n.

pas'time' n. way to spend spare time

pas'tor n. clergyman in charge of a congregation

pas'try (päs'-) n., pl. -tries fancy baked goods

pas'ture n. ground for grazing

pat n. 1 gentle tap with something flat 2 small lump, as of butter —v. **pat'ted** give a gentle pat to —a. suitable

patch n. 1 piece of material used to mend a hole, etc. 2 spot —v. 1 put a patch on 2 to make crudely

pat'ent (pat'-; a. 2: pät'-) n. document granting exclusive rights over an invention —a. 1 protected by patent 2 obvious —v. get a patent for

pa·ter'nal a. 1 fatherly 2 on the father's side —**pa·ter'nal·ism'** n.

path n. 1 way worn by footsteps 2 line of movement 3 course of conduct

pa·thet'ic a. arousing pity

pa·thol'o·gy n. study of the nature and effect of disease

pa'tient (-shant) a. 1 enduring pain, delay, etc. without complaint 2 persevering —n. one receiving medical care —**pa'tience** n. —**pa'tient·ly** adv.

pa'ti·o' n., pl. -os' 1 courtyard 2 paved lounging area next to house

pa'tri·ot n. one who shows love and loyalty to his or her country —**pa'tri·ot'ic** a.

pa·trol' v. -trolled' make trips around in guarding —n. a patrolling, or a group that patrols

pa·trol'man n., pl. -men policeman who patrols a certain area

pa'tron n. 1 a sponsor 2 regular customer

pat'tern n. 1 one worthy of imitation 2 plan used in making things 3 design or decoration 4 usual behavior, procedure, etc.

pause v., n. (make a) temporary stop

pave v. surface (a road, etc.), as with asphalt

pa·vil'ion (-yǝn) n. 1 large tent 2 building for exhibits, etc., as at a fair

paw n. foot of an animal with claws

pawn v. give as security for a loan —n. 1 chessman of lowest value 2 person who is subject to another's will

pay v. **paid** 1 give (money) to (someone) for goods or services 2 settle, as a debt 3 give, as a compliment 4 make, as a visit 5 be profitable (to) —n. wages —a. operated by coins, etc. —**pay'ee** n.

PC n. personal computer, or microcomputer

pea n. plant with pods having round, edible seeds

peace n. 1 freedom from war or strife 2 agreement to end war 3 law and order 4 calm

peace'ful a. 1 not fighting 2 calm 3 of a time of peace

peach n. round, juicy, orange-yellow fruit

peak n. 1 pointed end or top 2 mountain with pointed summit 3 highest point

peak'ed a. thin and drawn

peal n. 1 loud ringing of bell(s) 2 loud, prolonged sound —v. to ring; resound

pea'nut' n. 1 vine with underground pods and edible seeds 2 the pod or a seed

pear n. soft, juicy fruit

pearl (purl) n. 1 smooth, roundish stone formed in oysters, used as a gem 2 mother-of-pearl 3 bluish gray

peas'ant (pez'-) n. farm worker of Europe, etc. —**peas'ant·ry** n.

peat n. decayed plant matter in bogs, dried for fuel

peb'ble n. small, smooth stone

pe·can' n. edible nut with a thin, smooth shell

peck v. strike as with a beak —n. 1 stroke made as with a beak 2 dry measure equal to 8 quarts

pe·cu'liar (-kyōol'yər) a. 1 of only one; exclusive 2 special 3 odd

ped'al n. lever worked by the foot —v. work by pedals

ped'dle v. go from place to place selling —**ped'dler** n.

ped'es·tal n. base, as of a column, statue, etc.

pe·des'tri·an a. 1 going on foot 2 dull and ordinary —n. one who goes on foot; walker

pe'di·at'rics n. medical care and treatment of babies and children

ped'i·gree' n. ancestry; descent

peek v. glance quickly and furtively —n. glance

peel v. 1 cut away (the rind, etc.) of 2 shed skin, bark, etc. come off in layers or flakes —n. rind or skin of fruit

peep v. 1 make the chirping cry of a young bird 2 look through a small opening 3 peek 4 appear partially

peer n. 1 an equal 2 British noble —v. look closely

pee'vish a. irritable

peg n. 1 short pin or bolt 2 step or degree

pel'i·can n. water bird with a pouch in its lower bill

pel'let n. little ball

pelt v. 1 throw things at 2 beat steadily —n. the skin of a fur-bearing animal

pel'vis n. cavity formed by bones of the hip and part of the backbone —**pel'vic** a.

pen n. 1 enclosure for animals 2 device for writing with ink —v. penned, pent 1 enclose as in a pen 2 write with a pen

pe'nal·ize' (or pen'al-) v. punish

pen'al·ty n., pl. **-ties** 1 punishment 2 handicap

pen'ance n. voluntary suffering to show repentance

pen'cil n. device with a core of graphite, etc. for writing, etc.

pend'ant n. hanging object used as an ornament

pend'ing a. not decided —prep. 1 during 2 until

pen'du·lum n. weight hung so as to swing freely

pen'e·trate' v. 1 enter by piercing 2 to affect throughout 3 understand —**pen'e·tra'tion** n.

pen'guin (-gwin) n. flightless bird of the antarctic

pen'i·cil'lin n. antibiotic drug obtained from a mold

pen·in'su·la n. land area almost surrounded by water

pen'i·ten'tia·ry (-shə rē) n., pl. **-ries** prison

pen'knife' n. small pocketknife

pen'man·ship' n. quality of handwriting

pen'nant n. 1 long, narrow flag 2 championship

pen'ny n. 1 pl. **-nies** cent 2 pl. **pence** Br. coin, $\frac{1}{100}$ pound (formerly, $\frac{1}{12}$ shilling)

pen'sion n. regular payment to a retired or disabled person

pent a. shut in; kept in: often with up

pen'ta·gon' n. figure with five angles and five sides

pe·nul'ti·mate a. next to last

pe'on' n. Latin American worker

pe'o·ny n., pl. **-nies** plant with large showy flowers

peo'ple (pē'-) n.pl. 1 human beings 2 a populace 3 one's family —n., pl. **-ples** a nation, race, etc. —v. populate

pep [Col.] n. energy; vigor

pep'per n. 1 plant with a red or green, hot or sweet pod 2 the pod 3 spicy seasoning made from berries (**pep'per·corns'**) of a tropical plant

pep'per·mint' n. mint plant yielding an oily flavoring

per prep. 1 by means of 2 for each

per cap'i·ta a., adv. for each person

per·ceive' v. 1 grasp mentally 2 become aware (of) through the senses

per·cent' adv., a. out of every hundred: also **per cent** —n. [Col.] percentage

per·cent'age n. 1 rate per hundred 2 portion

per·cep'tion n. 1 ability to perceive 2 knowledge gotten by perceiving

perch n. 1 small food fish 2 a pole or branch that birds roost on —v. rest on a perch

per'co·la'tor n. pot in which boiling water filters through ground coffee

per·cus'sion (-kush'ən) n. 1 hitting of one thing against another 2 musical instruments played by striking, as drums

per·di'tion (-dish'ən) n. 1 hell 2

loss of one's soul

per·en'ni·al *a.* 1 lasting a year 2 living more than two years —*n.* plant living more than two years

per'fect (*v.*: pər fekt') *a.* 1 complete 2 excellent 3 completely accurate —*v.* make perfect —**per'fect·ly** *adv.*

per'fo·rate *v.* pierce with a hole or holes —**per'fo·ra'tion** *n.*

per·form' *v.* 1 do; carry out 2 act a role, play music, etc.

per·form'ance *n.* 1 a doing or thing done 2 display of one's skill or talent

per·fume' (*or* pur'fyōōm') *v.* scent with perfume —*n.* 1 fragrance 2 liquid with a pleasing odor

per·haps' *adv.* possibly; probably

per'il *v., n.* (put in) danger or risk —**per'il·ous** *a.*

pe'ri·od *n.* 1 portion of time 2 mark of punctuation (.)

pe'ri·od'ic *a.* recurring at regular intervals

pe'ri·od'i·cal *n.* magazine published every week, month, etc. —*a.* periodic

peri·o·don'tal *a.* around a tooth and affecting the gums

per'i·scope *n.* tube with mirrors, etc., for seeing over or around an obstacle

per·ish *v.* be destroyed; die

per'jure *v.* tell a lie while under oath —**per'ju·ry** *n., pl.* **-ries**

perk *v.* 1 raise or liven (*up*) 2 make stylish or smart 3 [Col.] percolate

perm [Col.] *n.* a permanent

per'ma·nent *a.* lasting indefinitely —*n.* long-lasting hair wave —**per'ma·nence** *n.*

per'me·ate *v.* diffuse; penetrate (through or among)

per·mis'sion *n.* consent

per·mit' (*n.*: pur'mit') *v.* **-mit'ted** allow —*n.* document giving permission

per·pen·dic'u·lar *a.* 1 at right angles to a given line or plane 2 vertical —*n.* perpendicular line

per'pe·trate' *v.* do (something evil, wrong, etc.)

per·pet'u·al (-pech'-) *a.* 1 lasting forever 2 constant

per·plex' *v.* confuse or puzzle

per'se·cute' *v.* torment continuously for one's beliefs, etc.

per·se·vere' *v.* to continue in spite of difficulty

Per'sian (-zhən) *n.* domestic cat with long, thick coat

per·sist' *v.* continue insistently or steadily —**per·sist'ent** *a.*

per'son *n.* 1 human being 2 the body or self 3 *Gram.* any of the three classes of pronouns indicating the identity of the subject, as *I, you, he,* etc.

per'son·al *a.* 1 private; individual 2 of the body 3 of the character, conduct, etc. of a person 4 indicating person in grammar 5 other than real estate: said of property —**per'son·al·ly** *adv.*

personal computer *n.* microcomputer

per·son·al'i·ty *n., pl.* **-ties** 1 distinctive or attractive character of a person 2 notable person

per'son·i·fy' *v.* **-fied'** 1 represent as a person 2 typify

per·son·nel' *n.* persons employed in any work, etc.

per·spec'tive *n.* 1 appearance of objects from their relative distance and positions 2 sense of proportion

per·spire' *v.* to sweat

per·suade' *v.* to cause to do or believe by urging, etc.

per·turb' *v.* alarm; upset

per·verse' *a.* 1 stubbornly contrary 2 erring 3 wicked

per·vert' (*n.*: pur'vurt') *v.* lead astray; corrupt —*n.* perverted person —**per·ver'sion** *n.*

pe'so (pā'-) *n., pl.* **-sos** monetary unit of Mexico, Cuba, etc.

pes'si·mism' *n.* tendency to expect the worst

pest *n.* person or thing that causes trouble, etc.

pes'ter *v.* annoy; vex

pes'ti·cide' *n.* chemical for killing insects, weeds, etc.

pes'tle (-al, -tal) *n.* tool used to pound or grind substances

pet *n.* 1 domesticated animal treated fondly 2 favorite 3 bad humor —*v.* **pet'ted** stroke gently

pet'al *n.* leaflike part of a blossom

pe·ti'tion *n.* solemn, earnest request, esp. in writing —*v.* address a petition to

pet'ri·fy' *v.* **-fied'** 1 change into stony substance 2 stun, as with fear

pe·tro'le·um *n.* oily liquid found in rock strata: it yields kerosene, gasoline, etc.

pet'ty *a.* **-ti·er, -ti·est** 1 of little importance 2 narrow-minded 3 low in rank

pe·tu'ni·a (-tōōn'ya) *n.* plant with funnel-shaped flowers

pew (pyōō) *n.* row of fixed

benches in a church

pew'ter n. alloy of tin with lead, brass, or copper

phan'tom n. 1 ghost; specter 2 illusion —a. unreal

phar'ma·cist n. one whose profession is pharmacy

phar'ma·cy n., pl. **-cies** 1 science of preparing drugs and medicines 2 drugstore

phase n. 1 aspect; side 2 one of a series of changes

pheas'ant (fez'-) n. game bird with a long tail

phe·nom'e·non n., pl. **-na** 1 observable fact or event 2 anything very unusual

phil'o·den'dron n. tropical American climbing plant

phi·los'o·pher n. one who is learned in philosophy

phi·los'o·phy n. 1 study of ultimate reality, ethics, etc. 2 pl. **-phies** system of principles 3 mental calmness —**phil'o·soph'ic, phil'o·soph'i·cal** a.

phlegm (flem) n. mucus in the throat, as during a cold

pho'bi·a n. irrational, persistent fear of something

phoe'nix (fē'-) n. immortal bird of Egyptian mythology

phone n., v. [Col.] telephone

pho'no·graph' n. instrument that reproduces sound from grooved records

pho'ny a., n. **-ni·er, -ni·est** [Col.] fake

phos'pho·res'cent a. giving off light without heat

phos'pho·rus n. phosphorescent, waxy chemical element

pho'to n., pl. **-tos** photograph

pho'to·cop'y n., pl. **-ies** copy made by photographic device (**pho'to·cop'i·er**)

pho'to·graph' n. picture made by photography —v. take a photograph of —**pho·tog'ra·pher** n.

pho·tog'ra·phy n. process of producing images on a surface sensitive to light

pho'ton' n. unit of light or energy

phrase n. 1 a short, colorful expression 2 group of words, not a sentence or clause, conveying a single idea —v. express in words

phys'i·cal adv. 1 of matter 2 of physics 3 of the body —n. physical examination —**phys'i·cal·ly** adv.

phy·si'cian (-zish'ən) n. doctor of medicine

phys'ics n. science that deals with matter and energy —**phys'i·cist** n.

phys·i·ol'o·gy n. science of the functions of living organisms —**phys·i·o·log'i·cal** a.

phy·sique' (-zēk') n. form or build of the body

pi·an'ist (or pē an'ist) n. piano player

pi·an'o (a., adv.: -ä'-) n., pl. **-nos** keyboard instrument with hammers that strike steel wires —a., adv. Mus. soft

pic'co·lo (s), n., pl. **-los'** small flute

pick v. 1 scratch or dig at with something pointed 2 gather, pluck, etc. 3 choose; select 4 provoke (a fight) —n. 1 choice 2 the best 3 pointed tool for breaking up soil, etc. 4 plectrum —**pick on** [Col.] criticize; tease —**pick out** choose —**pick up** 1 lift 2 get, find, etc. 3 gain (speed) 4 improve

pick'et n. 1 pointed stake 2 soldier(s) on guard duty 3 striking union member, etc. stationed outside a factory, etc. —v. place or be a picket at

pick'le v. preserve in vinegar, brine, etc. —n. cucumber, etc. so preserved

pic'nic n. outing with an outdoor meal —v. **-nicked** to hold a picnic —**pic'nick·er** n.

pic·to'ri·al a. of or expressed in pictures

pic'ture n. 1 likeness made by painting, photography, etc. 2 description 3 a FILM (n. 3) —v. 1 make a picture of 2 describe 3 imagine

pic'tur·esque' (-esk') a. 1 having natural beauty 2 quaint 3 vivid

pie n. fruit, meat, etc. baked on or in a crust

piece n. 1 part broken off or separated 2 part complete in itself 3 single thing

pier (pir) n. 1 landing place built out over water 2 heavy, supporting column

pierce v. 1 pass through as a needle does 2 make a hole in 3 sound sharply —**pierc'ing** a.

pig n. 1 fat farm animal; swine 2 greedy or filthy person —**pig'gish** a.

pi·geon (pij'ən) n. plump bird with a small head

pig iron n. molten iron

pig'ment n. coloring matter

pig'pen' n. a pen for pigs: also

pig'sty'

pig'tail' n. braid of hair hanging down the back

pike n. 1 slender, freshwater fish 2 turnpike 3 metal-tipped spear

pile n. 1 mass of things heaped together 2 thick nap, as on a rug 3 heavy, vertical beam —v. 1 heap up 2 accumulate 3 to crowd

pil'grim n. traveler to a holy place —**pil'grim·age** n.

pill n. pellet of medicine to be swallowed whole

pil'lar n. upright support

pil'low n. bag of soft material, to support the head, as in sleeping

pi'lot n. 1 one whose job is steering ships in harbors, etc. 2 one who flies an airplane 3 guide —v. be pilot of, in, etc.

pi·men'to n., pl. **-tos** sweet, bell-shaped red pepper

pim'ple n. small, sore swelling of the skin

pin n. 1 pointed piece of wire to fasten things together 2 thin rod to hold things with 3 thing like a pin 4 ornament with a pin to fasten it 5 club at which a ball is bowled —v. pinned fasten as with a pin

pin'cers n.pl. 1 tool for gripping things 2 claw of a crab, etc.

pinch v. 1 squeeze between two surfaces 2 to make look thin, gaunt, etc. 3 be stingy —n. 1 a squeeze 2 small amount 3 an emergency

pine n. 1 evergreen tree with cones and needle-shaped leaves 2 its wood —v. 1 waste (away) through grief, etc. 2 yearn

pine'ap'ple n. large, juicy tropical fruit

pin'ion (-yən) n. 1 small cogwheel 2 wing or wing feather

pink n. 1 plant with pale-red flowers 2 pale red 3 finest condition

pin'na·cle n. 1 slender spire 2 mountain peak 3 highest point

pi'noch'le (-nuk'-, -näk'-) n. card game using a double deck above the eight

pin'point' v. show the precise location of

pint n. ½ quart

pin'to a., n. piebald (horse)

pinto bean n. mottled, kidney-shaped bean

pi'o·neer' n. early settler, first investigator, etc.

pi'ous a. having, showing, or

pretending religious devotion

pipe n. 1 long tube for conveying water, gas, etc. 2 tube with a bowl at one end, for smoking tobacco 3 tube for making musical sounds —v. 1 utter in a shrill voice 2 convey (water, etc.) by pipes 3 play (a tune) on a pipe —**pip'er** n.

pi·ra·nha (pə rän'ə) n., pl. **-nhas** or **-nha** small fish that hunts in schools

pi'rate n. 1 one who robs ships at sea 2 one who uses a copyrighted or patented work without authorization

pi·ro·gi (pi rō'gē) n.pl. small pastries filled with meat, etc.

pis'til n. seed-bearing organ of a flower

pis'tol n. small firearm held with one hand

pis'ton n. part that moves back and forth in a hollow cylinder from pressure caused by combustion, etc.

pit n. 1 stone of a plum, peach, etc. 2 hole in the ground 3 small hollow in a surface 4 section for the orchestra in front of the stage —v. pit'ted 1 remove the pit from (a fruit) 2 mark with pits 3 set in competition (against)

pi'ta (pē'-) n. round, flat bread of Middle East: also **pita bread**

pitch v. 1 set up (tents) 2 throw 3 plunge forward 4 set at some level, key, etc. 5 rise and fall, as a ship —n. 1 throw 2 point or degree 3 degree of slope 4 highness or lowness of a musical sound 5 black, sticky substance from coal tar, etc.

pitch'er n. 1 container for holding and pouring liquids 2 baseball player who pitches to the batters

pit'i·ful a. 1 arousing or deserving pity 2 contemptible

pit'i·less a. without pity

pi·tu'i·tar'y a. of a small endocrine gland (**pituitary gland**) attached to the brain

pit'y n. 1 sorrow for another's misfortune 2 cause for sorrow or regret —v. **-ied** feel pity (for)

piv'ot n. 1 person or thing on which something turns or depends 2 pivoting motion —v. provide with or turn on a pivot

piz·za (pēt'sə) n. baked dish of thin dough topped with cheese, tomato sauce, etc.

piz·zi·ca·to (pit'si kät'ō) adv., a.

place *n.* 1 space 2 region 3 city or town 4 residence 5 particular building, site, part, position, etc. 6 job or its duties —*v.* 1 put in a certain place 2 identify by some relationship —**in place of** rather than —**take place** occur

pla·gia·rize' (-jǝ rīz') *v.* present another's writings as one's own

plague (plāg) *n.* 1 affliction 2 deadly epidemic disease

plaid (plad) *n., a.* (cloth) with crisscross pattern

plain *a.* 1 clear 2 outspoken 3 obvious 4 simple 5 homely 6 not fancy 7 common —*n.* an extent of flat land —*adv.* clearly

plain'tiff *n.* one who brings a suit into a court of law

plait *v., n.* 1 braid 2 pleat

plan *n.* 1 outline; map 2 way of doing; scheme —*v.* **planned** 1 make a plan of or for 2 intend

plane *a.* flat —*n.* 1 flat surface 2 level or stage 3 airplane 4 carpenter's tool for leveling or smoothing

plan'et *n.* any of nine heavenly bodies revolving around the sun

plank *n.* 1 long, broad, thick board 2 a principle in a political platform —*v.* cover with planks

plant *n.* 1 living thing that cannot move, as a tree, flower, etc. 2 factory —*v.* 1 to put in the ground to grow 2 set firmly in place

plan·ta'tion *n.* estate with its workers living on it

plant'er *n.* container for plants

plaque (plak) *n.* 1 flat, decorative piece of wood or metal 2 thin film of bacteria on teeth

plas'ma *n.* fluid part of blood or lymph

plas'ter *n.* lime, sand, and water, mixed as a coating that hardens on walls

plas'tic *a.* 1 that shapes or can be shaped 2 of plastic —*n.* substance that can be molded and hardened

plate *n.* 1 shallow dish 2 plated dinnerware 3 cast of molded type 4 engraved illustration 5 denture 6 home plate —*v.* coat with metal

pla·teau' (pla tō') *n.* 1 tract of high, level land 2 period of no progress

plat'form' *n.* 1 raised horizontal surface 2 political party's stated aims

pla·toon' *n.* small group, as of soldiers

plat'ter *n.* large serving dish

play *v.* 1 have fun 2 do in fun 3 take part in a game or sport 4 perform on a musical instrument 5 make a tape or disc machine give out sounds or images 6 trifle 7 cause 8 act in a certain way 9 act the part of —*n.* 1 recreation 2 fun 3 motion or freedom for motion 4 move in a game 5 drama

play'ful *a.* full of fun; frisky

playing cards *n.pl.* cards in four suits for playing games

play'wright' *n.* one who writes plays

pla·za (plä'zǝ, plaz'ǝ) *n.* public square

plea *n.* 1 appeal; request 2 statement in defense

plead *v.* 1 beg; entreat 2 argue (a law case) 3 offer as an excuse

pleas'ant *a.* pleasing; agreeable

please *v.* 1 satisfy 2 be the wish of 3 be obliging enough to: used in polite requests —**pleased** *a.*

pleas'ing *a.* giving pleasure

pleas'ure (plezh'-) *n.* 1 delight or satisfaction 2 one's choice

pleat *n.* fold made by doubling cloth —*v.* make pleats in

plec'trum *n., pl.* **-trums** or **-tra** small device for plucking a banjo, etc.

pledge *n.* 1 thing given as security for a contract, etc. 2 promise —*v.* 1 give as security 2 promise

plen'ti·ful *a.* abundant: also **plen'te·ous**

plen'ty *n.* 1 prosperity 2 ample amount

pli'a·ble *a.* easily bent; flexible

pli'ers *n.pl.* small pincers

plight *n.* condition, esp. a bad or dangerous one

plod *v.* **plod'ded** 1 trudge 2 work steadily —**plod'der** *n.*

plop *n.* sound of object falling into water —*v.* **plopped** fall with a plop

plot *n.* 1 piece of ground 2 diagram, plan, etc. 3 plan of action of a play, etc. 4 secret, esp. evil, scheme —*v.* **plot'ted** 1 make a map, plan, etc. of 2 scheme

plow *n.* 1 implement for cutting and turning up soil 2 machine for removing snow —*v.* 1 use a plow (on) 2 make one's way

pluck *v.* 1 pull off or out 2 pull at and release quickly —*n.* 1 a pull 2 courage

plug n. 1 stopper 2 device for making electrical contact —v.

plugged 1 stop up with a plug 2 [Col.] work doggedly

plum n. 1 smooth-skinned, juicy fruit 2 choice thing

plumb (plum) n. weight on a line for checking a vertical wall or sounding a depth —a. perpendicular —adv. 1 straight down 2 [Col.] entirely

plumb′er n. one who fits and repairs water pipes, etc. — **plumb′ing** n.

plume n. feather or tuft of feathers

plump a. full and rounded

plun′der v. rob by force

plunge v. 1 thrust suddenly (into) 2 dive or rush

plu·ral (ploor′əl) a. more than one —n. Gram. word form designating more than one

plus prep. added to —a. 1 designating a sign (+) showing addition 2 positive 3 more than —n. something added

ply n., pl. **plies** one layer in plywood, folded cloth, etc. —v. **plied** 1 work at (a trade) or with (a tool) 2 keep supplying (with) 3 travel back and forth (between)

ply′wood′ n. board made of glued layers of wood

pneu·mat′ic (nōō−) a. 1 of or containing air or gases 2 worked by compressed air

pneu·mo′ni·a n. acute disease of the lungs

poach v. 1 cook (an egg without its shell) in water 2 hunt or fish illegally — **poach′er** n.

pock′et n. 1 little bag or pouch, esp. when sewn into clothing 2 pouchlike cavity or hollow

pock′et·book′ n. purse

pod n. shell of peas, beans, etc. containing the seeds

po′di·um n., pl. **-di·a** platform for an orchestra conductor

po′em n. piece of imaginative writing in rhythm, rhyme, etc.

po′et n. writer of poems

po′et·ry n. 1 writing of poems 2 poems 3 rhythms, deep feelings, etc. of poems — **po·et′ic** a.

point n. 1 a dot 2 specific place or time 3 a stage or degree reached 4 item; detail 5 special feature 6 unit, as of a game score 7 sharp end 8 cape (land) 9 purpose; object 10 essential idea 11 mark showing direction on a compass —v. 1 sharpen to

a point 2 call attention (to) 3 show 4 aim

point′er n. 1 long, tapered rod for pointing 2 indicator 3 large hunting dog 4 [Col.] hint; suggestion

poise (poiz) n. 1 balance 2 ease and dignity of manner

poi′son n. substance which can cause illness or death —v. 1 harm or kill with poison 2 put poison into

poison ivy n. plant that can cause severe skin rash

poke v. 1 prod, as with a stick 2 search (about or around) 3 move slowly (along)

pok′er n. 1 gambling game with cards 2 iron bar for stirring a fire

po′lar a. 1 having opposite magnetic poles 2 opposite in character, nature, etc.

pole n. 1 long, slender piece of wood, metal, etc. 2 end of an axis, as of the earth 3 either of two opposed forces, as the ends of a magnet

po·lice′ n. 1 department of a city, etc. for keeping law and order 2 [with pl. v.] members of such a department

po·lice′man n., pl. **-men** member of a police force — **po·lice′wom′an** n.fem., pl. **-wom′en**

pol′i·cy n., pl. **-cies** 1 governing principle, plan, etc. 2 insurance contract

pol′ish v. 1 smooth and brighten, as by rubbing 2 refine (manners, etc.) —n. 1 surface gloss 2 elegance 3 substance used to polish

po·lite′ a. 1 showing good manners; courteous 2 refined

po·lit′i·cal a. of government, politics, etc. — **po·lit′i·cize′** v.

pol′i·ti′cian (-tish′ən) n. one active in politics

pol′i·tics n.pl. [sing. or pl. v.] 1 science of government 2 political affairs, methods, opinions, scheming, etc.

poll n. 1 a counting or listing as of voters 2 number of votes recorded 3 pl. voting place 4 survey of opinion

pol′len n. powderlike sex cells in flower stamens

pol′li·nate′ v. put pollen on the pistil of — **pol′li·na′tion** n.

pol·lute′ v. make unclean or impure — **pol·lu′tant** n.

po′lo n. team game played on horseback

pol'y·graph' *n.* device measuring bodily changes, used on one suspected of lying

pol'y·mer *n.* substance of giant molecules formed from smaller molecules of same kind

pol'yp (-ip) *n.* 1 slender water animal with tentacles 2 growth on a mucous membrane

pom'mel (pum'-) *n.* 1 rounded, upward-projecting front part of a saddle —*v.* pummel

pomp *n.* stately or ostentatious display

pom'pous *a.* pretentious

pon'cho *n., pl.* **-chos** cloak like a blanket

pond *n.* small lake

pon'der *v.* think deeply (about)

po'ny *n., pl.* **-nies** small horse

poo'dle *n.* curly-haired dog

pool *n.* 1 small pond 2 puddle 3 tank for swimming 4 billiards on a table with pockets 5 common fund of money, etc.

poor *a.* 1 having little money 2 below average; inferior 3 worthy of pity —**poor'ly** *adv.*

pop *n.* 1 light, explosive sound 2 flavored soda water —*v.* **popped** 1 make, or burst with, a pop 2 cause to pop 3 move, go, etc. suddenly 4 bulge —*adv.* like a pop —*a.* 1 of music popular with many people 2 intended for popular taste

pop'corn' *n.* corn with kernels that pop when heated

Pope *n.* head of the Roman Catholic Church

pop'lar *n.* tall tree

pop'py *n., pl.* **-pies** plant with showy flowers

pop'u·lar *a.* 1 of, by, or for people generally 2 very well liked

pop'u·la'tion *n.* total number of inhabitants

por'ce·lain (-lin) *n.* hard, fine, glazed earthenware

porch *n.* open or screen-enclosed room on the outside of a building

por'cu·pine' *n.* gnawing animal with long, sharp spines in its coat

pore *v.* study or ponder (over) —*n.* tiny opening, as in the skin, for absorbing or discharging fluids

pork *n.* flesh of a pig used as food

por·nog'ra·phy *n.* writings, pictures, etc. intended to arouse sexual desire

por'poise (-pəs) *n.* 1 sea mammal with a blunt snout 2 dolphin

por'ridge *n.* cereal or meal boiled in water or milk

port *n.* 1 harbor 2 city with a harbor 3 sweet, dark-red wine 4 left side of a ship as one faces the bow 5 porthole 6 opening, as in a valve face

port'a·ble *a.* that can be carried

por'tage *n.* 1 carrying of boats and supplies overland between waterways 2 route so used

por'ter *n.* 1 doorman 2 attendant who carries luggage, sweeps up, etc.

port'hole' *n.* window in a ship's side

por'tion *n.* part; share

por'trait (-trit) *n.* a painting, photograph, etc. of a person

por·tray' *v.* 1 make a portrait of 2 describe 3 represent on the stage —**por·tray'al** *n.*

pose *v.* 1 present, as a question 2 assume a bodily posture, a false role, etc. —*n.* assumed posture, etc.

po·si'tion *n.* 1 way of being placed 2 opinion 3 place; location 4 status 5 job —*v.* to place

pos'i·tive *a.* 1 explicit; definite 2 sure or too sure 3 affirmative 4 real; absolute 5 of the electricity made by friction on glass 6 *Gram.* of an adjective, etc. in its uncompared degree 7 *Math.* greater than zero —*n.* 1 anything positive 2 battery plate of higher potential

pos·sess' *v.* 1 own 2 have as a quality, etc. 3 control

pos'si·ble *a.* that can be, can happen, etc. —**pos'si·bil'i·ty** *n., pl.* **-ties** —**pos'si·bly** *adv.*

post *n.* 1 piece of wood, etc. set upright as a support 2 place where a soldier or soldiers are stationed 3 job; position 4 mail —*v.* 1 put up (a notice, etc.) 2 assign to a post 3 to mail 4 inform

post'age *n.* amount charged for mailing a letter, etc.

post'al *a.* of (the) mail

post'card *n.* card, often a picture card, sent by mail

post'er *n.* large sign or notice posted publicly

post'man *n., pl.* **-men** mailman

post office *n.* place where mail is sorted, etc.

post·pone' *v.* put off; delay

post'script' *n.* note added at the end of a letter, etc.

pos'ture n. way one holds the body

pot n. round container for cooking, etc.

po·ta'to n., pl. **-toes** starchy tuber of a common plant, used as a vegetable

po'tent a. 1 powerful 2 effective

po·ten'tial (-shəl) a. that can be; possible; latent —n. 1 something potential 2 voltage at a given point in a circuit

po'tion n. a drink, esp. of medicine or poison

pot'ter n. one who makes pots, dishes, etc. of clay

pot'ter·y n. earthenware

pouch n. 1 small sack or bag 2 baglike part

poul'try (pōl'-) n. domestic fowls

pounce v. leap or swoop down, as if to seize —n. a pouncing

pound n. 1 unit of weight, 16 ounces 2 British monetary unit 3 enclosure for stray animals —v. 1 hit hard 2 beat to pulp, powder, etc. 3 throb

pour (pôr) v. 1 flow or make flow steadily 2 rain heavily

pout v. 1 push out the lips, as in sullenness 2 sulk —n. a pouting

pov'er·ty n. 1 a being poor; need 2 inadequacy

pow'der n. dry substance of fine particles —v. 1 put powder on 2 make into powder

pow'er n. 1 ability to do or act 2 strength or energy 3 authority 4 powerful person, nation, etc. 5 result of multiplying a number by itself —a. operated by electricity, fuel engine, etc.

prac'ti·cal a. 1 of or obtained through practice 2 useful 3 sensible 4 virtual

prac'tice v. 1 do repeatedly so as to gain skill 2 make a habit of 3 work at as a profession —n. 1 a practicing 2 acquired skill 3 the work or business of a professional

prai'rie (prer'ē) n. large area of grassy land

praise v. 1 to say good things about 2 worship —n. a praising

prance v. 1 move along on the hind legs, as a horse 2 strut

prank n. mischievous trick

pray v. 1 implore 2 ask for by prayer 3 say prayers

prayer n. 1 a praying 2 words of worship or entreaty to God 3 thing prayed for —**pray'ful** a.

preach v. 1 give a (sermon) 2 urge or advise as by preaching —**preach'er** n.

pre·am'ble n. introduction

pre·cau'tion n. care taken beforehand, as against danger

pre·cede' v. go or come before

prec'e·dent n. earlier case that sets an example

pre'cinct (-siŋkt') n. 1 subdivision of a city, ward, etc. 2 pl. grounds or environs

pre'cious (presh'əs) a. 1 of great value 2 beloved 3 too refined

pre·cip'i·ta'tion n. 1 a precipitating 2 (amount of) rain, snow, etc.

pre·cise' a. 1 exact; definite; accurate 2 strict; scrupulous —**pre·cise'ly** adv. —**pre·ci'sion** (-sizh' ən) n.

pred'a·to·ry a. 1 plundering 2 preying on other animals

pre·dic'a·ment n. difficult situation

pred'i·cate (-kāt'; a., n.: -kət) v. base upon facts, conditions, etc. —a., n. Gram. (of) the word or words that make a statement about the subject

pre·dict' v. tell about in advance

pre·dom'i·nate v. be greater in amount, power, etc.; prevail

pre·empt', pre·empt' v. 1 to seize beforehand for anyone else can 2 to replace a scheduled radio or TV program

preen v. 1 groom (its feathers): said of a bird 2 groom (oneself)

pre·fab'ri·cat'ed a. made in sections ready for quick assembly, as a house

pref'ace n. introduction to a book, speech, etc.

pre·fer' v. **-ferred'** 1 like better 2 bring (charges) before a court

pref'er·ence n. 1 a preferring 2 thing preferred 3 advantage given to one over others

pre'fix n. syllable(s) added to the beginning of a word to alter its meaning

preg'nant a. 1 bearing a fetus in the uterus 2 filled (with) —**preg'nan·cy** n., pl. **-cies**

pre·his·tor'ic a. of times before recorded history

pre·judge' v. judge beforehand

prej'u·dice (-dis) n. 1 preconceived idea 2 hatred or intolerance of other races, etc. 3 disadvantage

pre·lim'i·nar'y a. leading up to the main action

prel·ude (prel'yood', prā'lood') n. preliminary part, as of a musical piece

pre·mar'i·tal a. before marriage

pre'ma·ture' a. before the proper or usual time

pre·mier (-mir') a. foremost —n. prime minister

pre·mière, pre·miere (-mir') n. first performance of a play, etc.

prem'ise n. 1 a basic assumption 2 pl. piece of real estate

pre'mi·um n. 1 prize 2 extra charge 3 a payment 4 high value

pre·na'tal a. before birth

pre·oc'cu·py v. -pied; engross; absorb —**pre·oc'cu·pa'tion** n.

prep a. preparatory

preparatory school n. private school preparing students for college

pre·pare' v. 1 make or get ready 2 equip 3 to put together —**prep'a·ra'tion** n.

prep'o·si'tion (-zish'ən) n. word that connects a noun or pronoun to another word

pre·re·cord'ed a. of a magnetic tape on which sound, etc. has been recorded before its sale

pre'school' a. younger than school age

pre·scribe' v. 1 to order 2 order to take a certain medicine or treatment

pre·scrip'tion n. 1 a prescribing, esp. by a doctor 2 medicine prescribed

pres'ence n. 1 a being present 2 one's appearance

pres'ent (v.: prē zent') a. 1 being at a certain place or time 2 of this time —n. 1 present time 2 gift —v. 1 introduce 2 show 3 offer for consideration 4 give (to)

pres'ent·ly adv. 1 soon 2 now

pre·serve' v. 1 keep from harm, spoiling, etc. 2 maintain —n. pl. fruit cooked with sugar

pre·set' v. set (controls) beforehand

pre·side' (-zīd') v. 1 act as chairman 2 have control

pres'i·dent n. chief executive of a republic, company, etc. —**pres'i·den·cy**, pl. -cies —**pres'i·den'tial** (-shəl) a.

press v. 1 push against; squeeze 2 iron, as clothes 3 force 4 entreat 5 urge on 6 keep moving 7 crowd —n. 1 pressure 2 crowd 3 machine for crushing, printing, etc. 4 newspapers 5 journalists

press'ing a. urgent

pres·sure (presh'ər) n. 1 a pressing 2 distress 3 strong influence 4 urgency 5 force of weight —v. try to influence

pres·tige' (-tēzh') n. earned fame and respect

pres'to adv., a. fast

pre·sume' v. 1 dare 2 suppose 3 take liberties

pre·teen' n. child nearly a teenager

pre·tend' v. 1 claim falsely 2 make believe 3 lay claim: with to

pret'ty a. -ti·er, -ti·est attractive and dainty —adv. somewhat —**pret'ti·ly** adv. —**pret'ti·ness** n.

pret'zel n. hard, salted biscuit, twisted in a knot

pre·vail' v. 1 win out or be successful 2 become more common

prev'a·lent a. common; general

pre·vent' v. stop or keep from doing or happening —**pre·vent'a·ble** a. —**pre·ven'tion** n.

pre'view' n. advance showing of (scenes from) a movie

pre'vi·ous a. coming before; prior —**pre'vi·ous·ly** adv.

prey (prā) n. 1 animal seized by another for food 2 victim

price n. 1 sum asked or paid for a thing 2 value —v. get or put a price on

prick v. 1 pierce with a sharp point 2 pain sharply 3 raise (the ears) —n. 1 a pricking 2 sharp pain

prick'le n. thorn or spiny point —v. tingle

pride n. 1 too high opinion of oneself 2 self-respect 3 satisfaction in one's achievements 4 person or thing one is proud of

priest n. one who conducts religious rites —**priest'ess** n.fem. —**priest'hood** n. —**priest'ly** a.

pri'ma·ry a. 1 most important 2 basic 3 first in order —n., pl. -ies preliminary election

pri'mate' n. 1 archbishop 2 member of the order of mammals having hands and feet with five digits; human, ape, etc.

prime a. first in rank, importance, or quality —n. best period or part —v. make ready

prime minister n. chief official in some countries

prim'er (prim-) n. 1 explosive used to set off a larger explosive 2 preliminary coat of paint, etc.

prim'i·tive a. 1 of earliest times 2 crude; simple

prince n. 1 monarch's son 2 ruler of a principality —

prince'ly a. —**prin'cess** n.fem.

prin'ci·pal a. chief; main —n. 1 principal person or thing 2 head of a school 3 sum owed, etc. aside from interest

prin'ci·ple n. 1 basic truth, rule, action, etc. 2 rule of conduct 3 integrity

print n. 1 cloth stamped with a design 2 impression made by inked type, plates, etc. 3 photograph —v. 1 to impress inked type, etc. on paper 2 publish in print 3 write in letters like printed ones —**print'er** n. —**print'ing** n., a.

print'out' n. printed or typed computer output

pri'or a. preceding in time, order, or importance

pris'on n. place of confinement

pri'vate a. 1 of or for a particular person or group; not public 2 secret —n. Mil. lowest rank of enlisted man —**pri'va·cy** n.

priv'i·lege (-lij) n. special right, favor, etc.

prize v. value highly —n. 1 thing given to the winner of a contest, etc. 2 valued possession

pro adv. on the affirmative side —n. 1 pl. **pros** reason or vote for 2 professional

prob'a·ble a. likely to occur or to be so —**prob'a·bly** adv.

pro'bate' v. establish the validity of (a will) —a. of such action

pro·ba'tion n. 1 trial of ability, etc. 2 conditional suspension of a jail sentence

probe n. 1 a slender surgical instrument for exploring a wound 2 investigation 3 spacecraft, etc. used to get information about an environment —v. 1 explore with a probe 2 investigate —**prob'er** n.

prob'lem n. 1 question to be solved 2 difficult matter, etc.

pro·ce'dure (-jər) n. act or way of doing something

pro·ceed' v. 1 go on after stopping 2 carry on an action 3 come forth

pro·ceed'ing n. 1 course of action 2 pl. transactions 3 pl. legal action

pro'ceeds' n.pl. money from a business deal

proc'ess' n. 1 series of changes in developing 2 act or way of doing something 3 court summons 4 projecting part

pro·ces'sion n. group moving

forward, as in a parade

pro·claim' v. announce officially

pro·cras'ti·nate' v. put off; delay

proc'tor n. one supervising students, as during a test

pro·cure' v. obtain; get

prod n., v. **prod'ded** goad or jab

prod'i·gal a. very wasteful or generous —n. spendthrift

prod'i·gy n., pl. **-gies** remarkable person or thing

pro·duce' (-dōōs') v. 1 show 2 bring forth 3 manufacture 4 cause 5 get (a play, etc.) ready for the public —n. farm products —**pro·duc'tion** n.

prod'uct' n. 1 thing produced 2 result 3 result of multiplying numbers

pro·fane' a. 1 not religious 2 scornful of sacred things

pro·fess' v. 1 declare openly 2 claim to have or be 3 declare one's belief in

pro·fes'sion n. 1 occupation requiring special study 2 its members 3 avowal

pro·fes'sion·al n., a. (one) of a profession, or (one) paid to play in games, etc.

pro·fes'sor n. college teacher

pro·fi'cient (-fish'ənt) a. skilled

pro'file' n. 1 side view of the face 2 outline

prof'it n. 1 gain; benefit 2 net income from business —v. benefit —**prof'it·a·ble** a.

pro·found' a. 1 very deep 2 complete

pro'gram' n. 1 list of things to be performed 2 plan or procedure 3 scheduled radio or TV broadcast 4 logical sequence of operations for electronic computer —v. 1 schedule in a program 2 plan a computer program for 3 furnish with a program

prog·ress (prō gres'; n.: präg'res) v. advance, develop, or improve —n. a progressing

pro·gres'sive a. 1 progressing 2 favoring progress, reform, etc. —n. progressive person

pro·hib'it v. 1 forbid, as by law 2 prevent

proj·ect' (v.: prə jekt') n. 1 scheme 2 undertaking —v. 1 propose 2 stick out 3 cause (a light, etc.) to fall upon a surface —**pro·jec'tor** n.

pro'logue' (-lôg) n. introduction to a poem, play, etc.

pro·long' v. lengthen

prom'e·nade' (-näd', -nād') n. 1 walk for pleasure 2 public place for walking

prom'i·nent *a.* 1 projecting 2 conspicuous; very noticeable 3 famous —**prom'i·nence** *n.*

prom'ise *n.* 1 agreement to do or not do something 2 sign as of future success —*v.* 1 to make a promise of or to 2 to cause to expect

pro·mote' *v.* 1 raise in rank 2 further the growth or sale of —**pro·mo'tion** *n.* —**pro·mot'er** *n.*

prompt *a.* ready; quick —*v.* 1 help with a cue 2 inspire or urge —**prompt'ly** *adv.*

prone *a.* 1 lying face downward 2 apt or likely

prong *n.* projecting point, as of a fork —**pronged** *a.*

pro'noun' *n.* word used in place of a noun —**pro·nom'i·nal** *a.*

pro·nounce' *v.* 1 declare officially 2 utter the sounds of

pro·nounced' *a.* definite; unmistakable

pro·nun'ci·a'tion *n.* act or way of pronouncing words

proof *n.* 1 convincing evidence 2 a test 3 strength of a liquor

prop *n.* 1 a support or aid 2 propeller —*v.* **propped** to support or lean against

prop'a·gan'da *n.* 1 systematic spreading of ideas 2 ideas so spread —**prop'a·gan'dist** *a., n.*

prop'a·gate' *v.* 1 produce offspring 2 raise; breed 3 spread (ideas) —**prop'a·ga'tion** *n.*

pro'pane' *n.* a gas used as a fuel

pro·pel' *v.* **-pelled'** drive forward

pro·pel'ler *n.* blades on end of a revolving shaft for propelling a ship or aircraft

prop'er *a.* 1 suitable; fit 2 correct 3 genteel; respectable 4 belonging (*to*) 5 actual

prop'er·ty *n.*, *pl.* **-ties** 1 thing owned 2 characteristic

proph'e·cy *n.*, *pl.* **-cies** prediction

proph'e·sy' *v.* **-sied'** to predict; foretell —**pro·phet'ic** *a.*

proph'et *n.* 1 leader regarded as divinely inspired 2 one who predicts

pro·po'nent *n.* supporter

pro·por'tion *n.* 1 part in relation to the whole 2 ratio 3 symmetry 4 *pl.* dimensions

pro·pose' *v.* 1 suggest for considering 2 plan 3 offer marriage —**pro·pos'al** *n.*

prop'o·si'tion *n.* 1 a plan 2 subject for debate

pro·pri'e·tor *n.* owner

pro·pul'sion *n.* a propelling or a force that propels

prose *n.* nonpoetic language

pros'e·cute' *v.* 1 engage in 2 take legal action against

pros'pect' *n.* 1 outlook 2 likely customer, etc. 3 apparent chance for success —*v.* search (*for*) —**pros'pec·tor** *n.*

pro·spec'tive *a.* expected

pros'per *v.* thrive

pros·per'i·ty *n.* wealth —**pros'per·ous** *a.*

pros·the'sis *n.*, *pl.* **-ses'** (-sēz') (use) of artificial body part(s)

pros'ti·tute' *n.* one who engages in sexual intercourse for pay

pros'trate' *a.* 1 lying flat, esp. face downward 2 overcome —*v.* 1 lay flat 2 overcome

pro·tect' *v.* shield from harm —**pro·tec'tive** *a.* —**pro·tec'tor** *n.*

pro·tec'tor·ate *n.* territory controlled and protected by a strong state

pro'te·in' (-tēn') *n.* nitrogenous substance essential to diet

pro·test' (*n.*: prō'test') *v.* 1 to object 2 assert —*n.* objection —**pro·test'er, pro·tes'tor** *n.*

pro'ton' *n.* positive particle in the nucleus of an atom

pro'to·plasm' *n.* essential matter in all living cells

pro'to·type' *n.* first thing of its kind

pro·tract' *v.* draw out; prolong

pro·trac'tor *n.* device for drawing and measuring angles

pro·trude' *v.* jut out

proud *a.* 1 haughty 2 feeling or causing pride 3 splendid

prove *v.* **proved, proved** or **prov'en** 1 test by experiment 2 establish as true

prov'erb' *n.* wise saying

pro·vide' *v.* 1 supply; furnish (with) 2 prepare (*for* or *against*)

pro·vid'ed *con.* on condition (*that*): also **pro·vid'ing**

prov'i·dence *n.* 1 prudent foresight 2 guidance of God or Nature —[P-] God

prov'ince *n.* 1 division of a country 2 *pl.* parts of a country outside major cities 3 sphere; field

pro·vin'cial (-shəl) *a.* 1 of a province 2 narrow-minded

pro·vi'sion (-vizh'ən) *n.* 1 a providing 2 *pl.* stock of food 3 stipulation

pro·voke' *v.* 1 anger 2 stir up or evoke

prow (prou) *n.* forward part of a ship

prowl *v.* roam or stalk furtively

prox'y *n., pl.* **-ies** (one with) authority to act for another

prude *n.* one overly modest or proper —**prud'ish** *a.*

pru'dent *a.* wisely careful

prune *n.* dried plum —*v.* trim twigs, etc. from

pry *n., pl.* **pries** lever —*v.* **pried** 1 raise with a lever 2 look closely or inquisitively

psalm (säm) *n.* sacred song or poem —**psalm'ist** *n.*

psy·chi'a·try (sī kī'-) *n.* branch of medicine dealing with mental illness —**psy·chi'a·trist** *n.*

psy'chic (-kik) *a.* 1 of the mind 2 supernatural —*n.* one sensitive to psychic phenomena

psy'cho·a·nal'y·sis (-kō-) *n.* method of treating neuroses —**psy'cho·an'a·lyst** *n.*

psy·chol'o·gy (-käl'-) *n.* science dealing with the mind and behavior —**psy'cho·log'i·cal** *a.* —**psy·chol'o·gist** *n.*

psy·cho'sis (-kō'-) *n., pl.* **-ses'** (-sēz') severe mental illness

pto'maine (tō'-) *n.* a substance in decaying matter

pu'ber·ty *n.* time of maturing sexually

pu'bic *a.* of or in the region of the groin

pub'lic *a.* 1 of people as a whole 2 for everyone 3 known by all —*n.* the people

pub'li·ca'tion *n.* 1 printing and selling of books, etc. 2 thing published

pub·lic'i·ty *n.* 1 public attention 2 information meant to bring one this —**pub'li·cize'** *v.*

pub'lish *v.* 1 issue (a printed work) for sale 2 announce

puck *n.* hard rubber disk used in ice hockey

puck'er *n., v.* wrinkle

pud'ding (pood'-) *n.* soft food of flour, milk, eggs, etc.

pud'dle *n.* small pool of water

puff *n.* 1 brief burst of wind, etc. 2 a draw at a cigarette 3 light pastry shell 4 soft pad —*v.* 1 blow in puffs 2 breathe rapidly 3 smoke 4 swell

pull *v.* 1 to make (something) move toward one 2 pluck out 3 rip 4 strain 5 [Col.] do; perform 6 move (*away, ahead,* etc.) —*n.* 1 act or effort of pulling 2 handle, etc. 3 [Col.] influence —**pull off** accomplish —**pull out** 1 depart 2 quit or withdraw —**pull through** [Col.] get over (an illness, etc.)

pul'ley (pool'-) *n., pl.* **-leys** wheel with a grooved rim in which a rope runs, for raising weights

pull'o·ver *n.* sweater, etc. to be pulled over the head

pulp *n.* 1 soft, inside part, as of fruit 2 moist wood fiber, ground to make paper

pul'pit *n.* clergyman's platform for preaching

pul'sate *v.* throb

pulse *n.* regular beat, as of blood in the arteries

pul'ver·ize' *v.* grind or crush into powder

pu'ma (pyōō'-, pōō'-) *n.* cougar

pum'ice *n.* light, spongy rock, used for cleaning, etc.

pump *n.* 1 machine that forces fluids in or out 2 low-cut, strapless shoe —*v.* 1 move or empty (fluids) with a pump 2 move like a pump 3 question persistently

pump'kin *n.* large, round, orange-yellow gourd

pun *n.* humorous use of different words that sound alike

punch *n.* 1 tool for piercing, etc. 2 fruit drink 3 blow with the fist —*v.* 1 pierce, etc. with a punch 2 hit with the fist

punc'tu·al (-chōō-) *a.* on time

punc'tu·ate' *v.* use periods, commas, etc. in (writing) —**punc'tu·a'tion** *n.*

punc'ture *n.* hole made by a sharp point —*v.* pierce as with a point

pun'gent *a.* 1 sharp in taste or smell 2 keen and direct

pun'ish *v.* make suffer pain, loss, etc. as for a crime or offense

punt *v.* 1 kick a dropped football before it touches the ground 2 move (a boat) using a long pole

pu'ny *a.* **-ni·er, -ni·est** small or weak

pup *n.* young dog, wolf, etc.

pu'pa *n., pl.* **-pae** (-pē) or **-pas** insect just before the adult stage

pu'pil *n.* 1 person being taught 2 contracting opening in iris of the eye

pup'pet *n.* 1 doll moved manually by strings, etc. 2 person controlled by another —**pup'pet·eer'** *n.*

pup'py *n., pl.* **-pies** young dog

pur'chase *v.* buy —*n.* 1 thing bought 2 act of buying

pure *a.* 1 unmixed 2 clean 3 mere 4 faultless 5 chaste 6 abstract —**pure'ly** *adv.* —**pu'ri·fy'** *v.* —**pu'ri·ty** *n.*

pu·rée, pu·ree (pyoō rā´) *n.* 1 mashed, strained food 2 thick soup

purge *v.* 1 cleanse; make pure 2 move (the bowels) 3 get rid of —*n.* 1 a purging 2 a laxative

pu´ri·tan *n.* one very strict in morals and religion

pur´ple *n., a.* bluish red

pur·port´ *v.* seem or claim to mean or be

pur·pose *n.* 1 intention; aim 2 determination —**on purpose** intentionally —**pur´pose·ful** *a.* —**pur´pose·less** *a.*

purr *v., n.* (make) the sound of a cat at ease

purse *n.* 1 small bag for money 2 woman's handbag 3 prize money —*v.* to pucker (the lips)

pur·sue´ *v.* 1 try to overtake; chase 2 go on with 3 seek

pur·suit´ *n.* 1 a pursuing 2 occupation

pus *n.* yellowish matter forming in infections

push *v.* 1 to move by pressing against 2 urge on —*n.* 1 a pushing 2 an enterprise

put *v.* **put** 1 make be in some place, state, relation, etc. 2 impose or assign 3 express 4 go (*in, out,* etc.) —**put down** 1 repress [Sl.] belittle or humiliate —**put off** 1 postpone 2 perturb —**put on** 1 pretend 2 [Sl.] to hoax —**put out** 1 extinguish 2 inconvenience —**put up** 1 preserve (fruits, etc.) 2 give lodgings 3 provide (money) —**put upon** impose on —**put up with** tolerate —**stay put** [Col.] remain; stay

putt *v., n. Golf* (make) a stroke to roll the ball into the hole

put´ter *v.* busy oneself aimlessly

put´ty *n.* pliable substance to fill cracks, etc.

puz´zle *v.* perplex —*n.* 1 thing that puzzles 2 problem to test cleverness

pyg´my (pig´-) *n., pl.* **-mies** dwarf

pyr´a·mid (pir´-) *n.* solid figure or structure with triangular sides meeting at a point —*v.* build up

py´thon´ *n.* large snake that crushes its prey to death

Q

quack *v.* utter the cry of a duck —*n.* 1 this cry 2 one who practices medicine fraudulently

quad´ran´gle *n.* plane figure with four angles and four sides

quad´rant *n.* quarter section of a circle

quad´ri·lat´er·al *a., n.* four-sided (figure)

quad´ru·ped´ *n.* four-footed animal

quad·ru´ple *a., adv.* four times as much

quad·ru´plet *n.* any of four children born at one birth

quail *v.* draw back in fear —*n.* game bird

quaint *a.* pleasingly odd or old-fashioned —**quaint´ly** *adv.*

quake *v.* shake —*n.* 1 a quaking 2 earthquake

qual´i·fy *v.* **-fied´** 1 make or be fit for a job, etc. 2 modify; restrict 3 moderate

qual´i·ty *n., pl.* **-ties** 1 characteristic 2 kind 3 degree of (excellence) —**qual´i·ta´tive** *a.*

qualm (kwäm) *n.* scruple; misgiving

quan´ti·ty *n., pl.* **-ties** 1 amount 2 large amount 3 number or symbol expressing measure

quar´an·tine´ (-tēn´) *n.* isolation to keep contagious disease from spreading

quar´rel *v., n.* (have) an argument or disagreement

quar´ry *n., pl.* **-ries** 1 animal, etc. being hunted down 2 place where stone is excavated

quart *n.* ¼ gallon

quar´ter *n.* 1 any of four equal parts; ¼ 2 25-cent coin 3 district 4 *pl.* lodgings 5 mercy —*v.* 1 divide into quarters 2 provide lodgings for

quar´ter·ly *a.* occurring regularly four times a year —*adv.* once every quarter of the year —*n., pl.* **-lies** publication issued quarterly

quar·tet´, quar·tette´ *n.* musical composition for four performers

quartz *n.* bright mineral

qua·si (kwā´zī´, kwä´zē´) *a., adv.* seeming(ly)

qua´ver *v.* 1 tremble 2 be tremulous: said of the voice

quay (kē) *n.* wharf

queen *n.* 1 wife of a king 2 woman monarch 3 female in an insect colony 4 playing card with a queen's picture 5 most powerful chess piece

queer *a.* 1 odd 2 [Col.] eccentric —**queer´ly** *adv.*

quell *v.* subdue or quiet

quench *v.* 1 extinguish 2 satisfy —**quench´less** *a.*

que·ry (kwir'ē) *n., pl.* **-ries;** *v.* **-ried** question

quest *n.* a seeking —*v.* seek

ques'tion **1** inquiry **2** thing asked **3** doubt **4** problem **5** point being debated —*v.* **1** inquire **2** doubt **3** challenge

question mark *n.* mark of punctuation (?)

ques'tion·naire' *n.* list of questions for gathering information

queue (kyoo) *n.* **1** pigtail **2** line of persons

quiche (kēsh) *n.* hot custard pie made with cheese, spinach, etc.

quick *a.* **1** swift **2** prompt — *adv.* rapidly

quick'en *v.* **1** enliven **2** hasten

quick'-wit'ted *a.* alert

qui'et *a.* **1** still **2** silent **3** gentle —*n.* **1** stillness **2** silence —*v.* make or become quiet

quill *n.* **1** large feather **2** pen made from this **3** spine of a porcupine

quilt *v., n.* (make) a bedcover stitched in layers

quin·tet', quin·tette' *n.* musical composition for five performers

quin·tu'plet (-tup'lət) *n.* any of five children born at one birth

quit *v.* **quit, quit'ted 1** give up **2** leave **3** stop

quite *adv.* **1** completely **2** really **3** very or fairly —**quite a few** [Col.] many

quiv'er *v.* tremble —*n.* **1** tremor **2** case for arrows

quiz *n., pl.* **quiz'zes** test of knowledge

quo'rum (kwôr'əm) *n.* minimum number needed to transact business at an assembly

quo'ta *n., pl.* **-tas** share assigned to each one

quo·ta'tion *n.* **1** a quoting **2** words quoted **3** current price of a stock or bond

quote *v.* **1** repeat (the words of) **2** state (the price of)

quo'tient (-shənt) *n.* number got by dividing one number into another

R

rab'bi (-ī) *n., pl.* **-bis** ordained teacher of the Jewish law

rab'bit *n.* burrowing rodent with soft fur and long ears

ra'bies *n.* disease of dogs, etc., transmitted by biting

rac·coon' *n.* small, furry mammal with black-ringed tail

race *n.* **1** a competition, esp. of

---

speed **2** swift current **3** division of mankind, esp. based on skin color **4** any group or class —*v.* **1** be in a race **2** move swiftly or swiftly

rac'er *n.* —**ra'cial** (-shəl) *a.*

rac'ism' *n.* racial discrimination or persecution —**rac'ist** *a., n.*

rack *n.* **1** framework for holding things **2** ancient torture device **3** great torment **4** toothed bar meshing with a gearwheel

rack'et *n.* **1** noisy confusion **2** dishonest scheme **3** netted frame used as a bat in tennis

ra'dar *n.* device for locating objects by their reflection of radio waves

ra'di·ant *a.* **1** beaming **2** shining bright **3** issuing in rays

ra'di·ate' *v.* **1** send out rays, as of heat or light **2** branch out as from a center

ra'di·a'tion *n.* **1** a radiating **2** rays sent out **3** nuclear particles

ra'di·a'tor *n.* device for radiating heat

rad'i·cal *a.* **1** basic **2** favoring extreme change —*n.* **1** one with radical views **2** *Chem.* group of atoms acting as one

ra'di·o' *n., pl.* **-os' 1** way of sending sounds through space by electromagnetic waves **2** set for receiving radio waves **3** broadcasting by radio

ra'di·o·ac'tive *a.* emitting radiant energy by the disintegration of atomic nuclei

rad'ish *n.* edible pungent root of certain plant

ra'di·us *n., pl.* **-di·i'** (-dē ī') or **-di·us·es** straight line from the center to the outside of a circle or sphere

ra'don *n.* radioactive gas, a chemical element

raf'fle *n.* lottery

raft *n.* floating platform of logs fastened together

raf'ter *n.* beam in a roof

rag *n.* **1** piece of torn or waste cloth **2** *pl.* tattered clothes

rage *n.* **1** furious anger **2** craze; fad —*v.* **1** show violent anger **2** be unchecked

raid *n.* sudden attack or invasion

rail *n.* **1** bar put between posts as a guard or support **2** either of the bars of a railroad track **3** railroad **4** small wading bird

rail'road' *n.* **1** road with steel rails for trains **2** system of such roads

rail'way' *n.* railroad

rain *n.* water falling in drops

from the clouds —v. fall as or like rain —**rain'drop'** n. —**rain'fall'** n. —**rain'storm'** n.

rain'bow' n. arc of colors formed by sunshine on rain

raise v. 1 lift up 2 increase in amount, degree, etc. 3 build or put up 4 bring up 5 collect 6 make grow —n. a pay increase

rai'sin n. sweet, dried grape

rake n. long-handled tool with teeth at one end 2 debauched man —v. 1 gather (leaves, etc.) with a rake 2 search carefully

ral'ly v. -**lied** 1 regroup to set in order 2 gather for a common aim 3 revive —n., pl. -**lies** 1 a rallying 2 mass meeting

ram n. 1 male sheep 2 battering ram —v. **rammed** 1 strike against with force 2 force into place

ram'ble v. 1 stroll; roam 2 talk or write aimlessly 3 spread, as vines —n. a stroll —**ram'bler** n.

ramp n. sloping passage joining different levels

ranch n. large farm for raising livestock

ran'cid a. stale, as oil or fat; spoiled

ran'dom a. haphazard

range v. 1 set in rows 2 roam about 3 extend —n. 1 row or line, esp. of mountains 2 effective distance 3 extent 4 open land 5 place for shooting practice 6 cooking stove

rang'er n. 1 trooper who patrols a region 2 warden who patrols forests

rank n. 1 row; line 2 class or grade 3 pl. enlisted soldiers —v. 1 to place in, or hold, a certain rank 2 outrank —a. 1 growing wildly 2 bad in taste or smell 3 utter

ran'som n. 1 the freeing of a captive by paying money 2 price asked

rap v. **rapped** 1 strike or knock sharply 2 [Sl.] to chat; talk —n. quick, sharp knock

rape n. 1 crime of attacking sexually 2 plant whose leaves are used as fodder —v. commit rape (on) —**rap'ist** n.

rap'id a. swift —**ra·pid'i·ty** n.

rare a. 1 scarce; uncommon 2 very good 3 not dense 4 partly raw —**rare'ness** n.

ras'cal n. 1 rogue 2 mischievous child —**ras·cal'i·ty** n.

rash a. too hasty; reckless —n. red spots on the skin

rasp v. 1 scrape harshly 2 irritate —n. 1 rough file 2 grating sound

rasp'ber'ry n., pl. -**ries** 1 shrub with red or black berries 2 the berry

rat n. long-tailed rodent, larger than a mouse

rate n. 1 relative amount or degree 2 price per unit 3 rank —v. 1 estimate the value of 2 deserve

rath'er adv. 1 preferably 2 with more reason 3 more truly 4 on the contrary 5 somewhat

rat'i·fy' v. -**fied'** approve formally

ra'tio (-shō, -shē ō') n., pl. -**tios** relation of one thing to another in size, etc.

ra'tion (rash'ən, rā'shən) n. fixed share, as of food

ra'tion·al (rash'-) a. 1 able to reason 2 reasonable

rat'tle v. 1 make or cause to make a series of sharp, short sounds 2 chatter 3 [Col.] upset —n. 1 a rattling 2 baby's toy that rattles

rat'tle·snake' n. snake with a tail that rattles: also **rat'tler**

rav'age v., n. ruin

rave v. 1 talk wildly 2 praise greatly

rav'el v. untwist; fray

ra'ven n. large black crow

ra·vine' (-vēn') n. long, deep hollow in the earth

raw a. 1 uncooked 2 unprocessed 3 inexperienced 4 sore and inflamed 5 cold and damp

ray n. 1 thin beam of light 2 stream of radiant energy 3 tiny amount 4 broad, flat fish

ray'on n. fabric made from cellulose

raze v. demolish

ra'zor n. sharp-edged instrument for shaving

reach v. 1 extend the hand, etc. 2 touch 3 get to 4 influence 5 get in touch with 6 try to get —n. act or extent of reaching

re·act' v. 1 respond to stimulus 2 return to an earlier state 3 act with another substance in a chemical change —**re·ac'tion** n.

re·ac'tor n. device for producing atomic energy

read (rēd) v. **read** (red) 1 understand or utter (written or printed matter) 2 to study 3 to register, as a gauge 4 access computer data —**read'er** n.

read'ing n. 1 act of one that reads 2 thing to be read 3 interpretation

read'y a. -**i·er**, -**i·est** 1 prepared

to act 2 willing 3 available

re'al a. 1 actual; true 2 genuine —adv. [Col.] very —**re'al·ly** adv.

real estate n. land, including buildings, etc., on it

re'al·ism' n. awareness of things as they really are —**re'al·ist** n.

re·al'i·ty n., pl. -ties 1 state of being real 2 real thing; fact

re'al·ize' v. 1 achieve 2 understand fully 3 make real 4 gain —**re'al·i·za'tion** n.

realm (relm) n. 1 kingdom 2 region; sphere

ream n. quantity of 480 to 516 sheets of paper

reap v. cut and gather (grain, etc.) —**reap'er** n.

rear n. back part or place —a. of or at the rear —v. 1 bring up; raise 2 rise on the hind legs

rea'son n. 1 explanation 2 cause 3 power to think 4 good sense —**rea'son·ing** n.

rea'son·a·ble a. 1 fair 2 sensible 3 not expensive

re·as·sure' v. restore to confidence —**re'as·sur'ance** n.

re'bate' v., n. return (of) part of a payment

reb'el (v.: rē bel') n. one who openly resists authority —v. **re·bel'**, **-belled'** resist authority —**re·bel'lion** n. —**re·bel'lious** a.

re·call' v. 1 call back 2 remember 3 revoke

re·cede' v. move or slope backward

re·ceipt' (-sēt') n. 1 a receiving 2 written acknowledgment of sum received 3 pl. amount received

re·ceive' v. 1 get; be given 2 greet (guests) 3 react to

re·ceiv'er n. 1 one who receives 2 one holding in trust property in bankruptcy, etc. 3 apparatus that converts electrical signals into sound or light, as in radio and TV

re'cent a. of a short time ago

re'cess (or rē ses') n. 1 hollow in a wall 2 break from work

re·ces'sion n. temporary falling off of business

rec'i·pe' (-pē') n. directions for preparing dish or drink

re·cit'al (-sīt'-) n. 1 account told 2 musical program

re·cite' v. 1 repeat something memorized 2 narrate

reck'less a. heedless; rash

reck'on v. 1 count 2 estimate 3 [Col.] suppose

reck'on·ing n. 1 a figuring out 2 settlement of accounts

re·claim' v. restore for use

re·cline' v. lie down or lean back

rec'og·nize' v. 1 to identify as known before 2 to perceive 3 acknowledge; notice formally —**rec'og·ni'tion** n.

re·coil' v. pull back

re·col·lect' v. remember

rec'om·mend' v. 1 suggest as fit or worthy 2 advise

rec'on·cile' v. 1 make friendly again 2 settle (a quarrel) 3 make agree or fit 4 to make acquiescent (to) —**rec'on·cil'i·a'tion** n.

rec'ord (n., a.: rek'ərd) v. 1 keep a written account of 2 show on a dial, etc. 3 put (sound, images, etc.) on a disc, tape, etc. —n. 1 official account 2 known facts 3 a disc with recorded sound 4 the best yet done —a. best

re·cord'ing n. 1 what is recorded on a disc, tape, etc. 2 the record itself

re·count' v. narrate

re·count' v. narrate

re·cov'er v. 1 get back; regain 2 become normal 3 keep from a fall 4 reclaim

rec're·a'tion n. refreshing play

re·cruit' n. new member, soldier, etc. —v. enlist (recruits)

rec'tan'gle n. four-sided figure with four right angles —**rec·tan'gu·lar** a.

rec'tor n. head of some schools or parishes

rec'tum n. lowest part of intestine —**rec'tal** a.

re·cu'per·ate' v. recover health, losses, etc. —**re·cu'per·a'tion** n.

re·cur' v. -curred' 1 occur again 2 return in talk, etc.

re·cy'cle v. 1 pass through a cycle again 2 use (metal, paper, etc.) again (and again)

red n. color of blood —a. red'der, red'dest of the color red —**red'dish** a. —**red'ness** n.

re·deem' v. 1 buy back 2 pay off 3 turn in for a prize 4 free, as from sin 5 atone for —**re·deem'er** n. —**re·demp'tion** n.

re·doubt' (-dout') n. stronghold

re·duce' v. 1 lessen; decrease 2 change the form of 3 lower 4 lose weight —**re·duc'tion** n.

red'wood' n. 1 giant evergreen 2 its reddish wood

reed n. 1 a hollow-stemmed grass 2 musical pipe made of this 3 vibrating strip in some musical instruments

reef n. ridge of land near the surface of water

reel n. 1 spool or frame on which thread, film, etc. is wound 2 amount wound on it 3 lively dance —v. 1 to wind (in or out) on a reel 2 tell fluently: with off 3 stagger

re-fer' v. -ferred' 1 go to, or direct someone to, for aid, information, etc. 2 allude to

ref-er-ee' n. 1 one chosen to decide something 2 a judge in sports —v. act as referee in

ref'er-ence n. 1 a referring 2 relation or connection 3 mention of a source of information 4 recommendation, or person giving it

re-fine' v. free from impurities, coarseness, etc.

re-flect' v. 1 throw back, as an image or sound 2 result in (credit, etc.) —**re-flec'tion** n. —**re-flec'tive** a. —**re-flec'tor** n.

re'flex' a., n. (designating or of) an involuntary reaction to a stimulus

re-flex'ive a. 1 designating a verb whose subject and object are the same 2 designating a pronoun used as object of such a verb

re-form' v. 1 improve 2 behave or make behave better —n. improvement —**re-form'er** n.

re-frain' v. hold back (from) —n. repeated verse of a song

re-fresh' v. make fresh or stronger; renew or revive

re-frig'er-ate' v. make cold, as to preserve

ref'uge n. protection from danger or pursuit

ref'u-gee' n. one who flees to seek refuge

re-fund' v. give back (money, etc.) —n. amount refunded

re-fuse' (rē fyooz'; n.: ref'yoos) v. 1 reject 2 decline (to do, etc.) —n. rubbish —**re-fus'al** n.

re'gal a. royal

re-gard' n. 1 concern 2 affection and respect 3 reference 4 pl. good wishes —v. 1 to gaze upon 2 think of; consider 3 concern —**re-gard'ing** a., adv.

re-gard'ing prep. about

reg-gae (reg'ā) n. type of popular Jamaican music

re-gime (rā zhēm') n. political or ruling system

reg'i-ment n. section of an army division

re'gion n. area, division, or part

reg'is-ter n. 1 list of names, etc. 2 recording device, as for cash transactions 3 a device for adjusting passage of air 4 musical range —v. 1 enter in a list 2 show 3 make an impression

reg'is-trar' n. keeper of records, as in a college

re-gret' v. -gret'ted be sorry for (a mistake, etc.) —n. a being sorry —**re-gret'ta-ble** a.

reg'u-lar a. 1 according to rule; orderly 2 usual 3 unchanging —**reg'u-lar'i-ty** n.

reg'u-late' v. 1 control 2 adjust to a standard, etc. —**reg'u-la'tor** n. —**reg'u-la-to'ry** a.

reg'u-la'tion n. 1 a regulating 2 a rule —a. usual

re'ha-bil'i-tate' v. restore to earlier state —**re'ha-bil'i-ta'tion** n.

re-hearse' (-hurs') v. 1 recite 2 practice for a performance —**re-hears'al** n.

reign (rān) n. (period of) a sovereign's rule —v. rule as sovereign

re'im-burse' v. pay back

rein (rān) n. 1 strap hooked to a bit for controlling a horse 2 pl. means of controlling

re'in-car-na'tion n. rebirth (of the soul) —**re'in-car'nate** v.

rein'deer n., pl. -deer large northern deer

re'in-force' v. strengthen

re-ject' (n.: rē'jekt) v. 1 refuse to accept 2 discard —n. thing rejected —**re-jec'tion** n.

re-joice' v. be or make happy

re-lapse' (n.: also rē'laps) v., n. fall back into a past state

re-late' v. 1 narrate 2 connect, as in meaning 3 have reference (to)

re-lat'ed a. of the same family or kind

re-la'tion n. 1 a relating or being related 2 kinship 3 a relative 4 pl. dealings, as between people

rel'a-tive a. 1 related 2 relevant 3 comparative —n. related person

re-lax' v. 1 loosen up 2 rest, as from work —**re'lax-a'tion** n.

re'lay n. fresh group of workers, runners, etc. —v. get and pass on

re-lease' v. 1 set free 2 allow to be issued —n. 1 a releasing 2 device to release a catch

re-lent' v. become less stern

rel'e-vant a. pertinent

re-li'a-ble a. that can be relied on

rel'ic n. 1 something from the past 2 sacred object

re·lief' *n.* 1 a relieving 2 thing that relieves 3 public aid, as to the poor 4 sculpted figures projecting from a flat surface

re·lieve' *v.* 1 to ease; comfort 2 give aid to 3 to free by replacing 4 bring a pleasant change to

re·li'gion *n.* 1 belief in God or gods 2 system of worship

rel'ish *n.* 1 pleasing flavor 2 enjoyment 3 pickles, etc. served with a meal —*v.* enjoy

re·live' *v.* experience again

re·luc'tant *a.* unwilling

re·ly' *v.* -lied' to trust; depend on or upon

re·main' *v.* 1 be left when part is gone 2 stay 3 continue

re·mains' *n.pl.* 1 part left 2 dead body

re·mark' *v., n.* (make) a brief comment or observation

re·mark'a·ble *a.* unusual

rem'e·dy *n., pl.* -dies thing that corrects, etc.

re·mem'ber *v.* 1 think of again 2 to bear in mind

re·mind' *v.* cause to remember

rem'nant *n.* part left over

re·mod'el *v.* rebuild

re·morse' *n.* deep sense of guilt

re·mote' *a.* 1 distant 2 slight

re·move' *v.* 1 take away 2 dismiss 3 get rid of —**re·mov'a·ble** *a.* —**re·mov'al** *n.*

ren'ais·sance' (-ə säns') *n.* rebirth; revival: also **re·nas'cence** —**the Renaissance** period in Europe, 14th-16th c.

rend *v.* rent tear; split apart

ren'der *v.* 1 submit 2 give in return 3 cause to be 4 perform 5 translate 6 melt (fat)

ren'e·gade *n.* traitor

re·nege' (-nig') *v.* go back on a promise

re·new' *v.* 1 make new again 2 begin again 3 replenish (a supply) —**re·new'al** *n.*

re·nounce' *v.* 1 give up (a claim, etc.) 2 disown

ren'o·vate' *v.* make like new; restore —**ren'o·va'tion** *n.*

re·nown' *n.* fame

rent *n.* 1 payment for the use of property 2 a rip —*v.* get or give rent (for)

re·pair' *v.* 1 fix; mend 2 make amends for 3 go (*to*) —*n.* a repairing or being repaired

re·pay' *v.* -paid' pay back —**re·pay'ment** *n.*

re·peal' *v.* revoke; annul (a law) —*n.* revocation

re·peat' *v.* say or do again —*n.* 1 a repeating 2 thing repeated

re·pel' *v.* -pelled' 1 force back 2 disgust —**re·pel'lent** *a., n.*

re·pent' *v.* feel sorry for (a sin, etc.) —**re·pent'ance** *n.*

rep'e·ti'tion (-tish'ən) *n.* 1 a repeating 2 thing repeated

re·place' *v.* 1 put back 2 take the place of 3 put another in place of —**re·place'ment** *n.*

re·plen'ish *v.* fill again

rep'li·ca *n.* exact copy

re·ply' *v.* -plied'; *n., pl.* -plies' answer

re·port' *v.* 1 give an account of 2 tell as news; announce 3 denounce (an offender, etc.) to someone in authority 4 present oneself —*n.* 1 statement or account 2 rumor 3 explosive noise —**re·port'ed·ly** *adv.*

re·port'er *n.* one who gathers and reports news

re·pose' *v., n.* rest

rep're·sent' *v.* 1 to portray or describe 2 symbolize 3 act in place of 4 be an example of

rep're·sent'a·tive *a.* 1 representing 2 typical —*n.* 1 typical example 2 one chosen to act for others 3 [R-] Congressional or State legislator

re·press' *v.* 1 hold back 2 subdue 3 force (painful ideas, etc.) into the unconscious

re·prieve' *n., v.* delay (in) the execution of (one sentenced to die)

re·proach' *v.* blame; rebuke —*n.* 1 disgrace 2 a scolding or blaming —**re·proach'ful** *a.*

re·pro·duce' *v.* 1 produce copies, offspring, etc. —**re'pro·duc'tion** *n.* —**re'pro·duc'tive** *a.*

re·proof' *n.* a reproving; rebuke

re·prove' *v.* find fault with

rep'tile *n.* coldblooded, creeping vertebrate, as a snake, lizard, etc. —**rep·til'i·an** *a.*

re·pub'lic *n.* government by elected representatives —**re·pub'li·can** *a., n.*

re·pulse' *v.* 1 repel 2 rebuff

re·pul'sive *a.* disgusting

rep'u·ta'tion *n.* 1 others' opinion of one 2 good character 3 fame

re·pute' *v.* consider to be —*n.* reputation —**re·put'ed** *a.*

re·quest' *n.* 1 an asking for 2 thing asked for —*v.* ask for

re·quire' *v.* 1 demand 2 need

re'run *n.* showing of a movie, etc. after the first showing

res'cue *v.* free or save —*n.* a rescuing —res'cu·er n.

re'search' (or rē surch') v., n. (do) careful study in a subject

re·sem'ble v. be like

re·sent' v. feel anger at —re·sent'ful a. —re·sent'ment n.

res'er·va'tion n. 1 a reserving, as of a hotel room 2 public land set aside, as for North American Indians

re·serve' v. keep back; set aside —n. 1 thing reserved 2 limitation 3 reticence 4 pl. troops subject to call —re·served' a.

res'er·voir' (-vwär', -vôr') n. 1 place for storing water 2 large supply

re·side' v. 1 live (in or at) 2 be present (in)

res'i·dence n. 1 a residing 2 home —res'i·dent a., n.

res'i·due n. part that is left

re·sign' v. 1 give up, as a claim, position, etc. 2 be submissive —res'ig·na'tion n.

re·sil'ient a. bouncing back; elastic —re·sil'ience n.

res'in n. 1 substance from trees used in varnish, etc. 2 rosin

re·sist' v. 1 withstand 2 to fight against

re·sist'ance n. 1 power to resist 2 opposition to another force

res'o·lu'tion n. 1 a resolving 2 formal statement 3 determination

re·solve' v. 1 decide 2 solve 3 change —n. fixed purpose

re·sort' v. 1 go often 2 turn for help (to) —n. 1 place for a vacation, etc. 2 source of help

re·sound' (-zound') v. make an echoing sound

re'source' (or ri sôrs') n. 1 emergency supply 2 pl. wealth

re·spect' v. 1 think highly of 2 show concern for —n. 1 honor 2 concern 3 pl. regards 4 reference —re·spect'ful a.

re·spect'a·ble a. 1 of good reputation 2 good enough

res'pi·ra'tion n. act or process of breathing —res'pi·ra·to'ry a.

res'pite (-pit) n. 1 a delay 2 period of relief or rest

re·spond' v. 1 to answer 2 react

re·spon'si·ble a. 1 obliged to do or answer for 2 involving duties 3 dependable

rest n. 1 ease or inactivity 2 peace 3 a support 4 a pause 5 remainder —v. 1 get, or be at, ease 2 become still 3 lie or lay 4 depend —rest'ful a.

res'tau·rant (-ta ränt', -tränt) n. place for buying and eating meals

rest'less a. 1 uneasy 2 disturbed 3 active

re·store' v. 1 give back 2 return to a former position, condition, etc. —res'to·ra'tion n.

re·strain' v. to hold back from action; suppress

re·straint' n. 1 a restraining 2 thing that restrains 3 self-control

re·strict' v. limit; confine —re·stric'tion n. —re·stric'tive a.

re·struc'ture v. plan or provide a new structure, etc. for

re·sult' v. 1 happen as an effect 2 to end (in) —n. 1 what is caused; outcome 2 mathematical answer —re·sult'ant a.

re·sume' v. 1 take again 2 continue after interrupting

ré'su·mé' n. summary

res'ur·rect' v. bring back to life, use, etc. —res'ur·rec'tion n.

re'tail' n. sale of goods in small amounts to consumers —a. of such a sale —v. sell at retail

re·tain' v. 1 keep in possession, use, etc. 2 keep in mind 3 hire (a lawyer)

re·tard' v. slow down; delay

re·tard'ant n. substance delaying chemical reaction

re·tard'ed v. slowed in development, esp. mentally

retch v. strain to vomit

ret'i·na n. cells lining the interior of the eyeball, on which images are formed

re·tire' v. 1 withdraw or retreat 2 withdraw from one's career, etc. 3 go to bed

re·tir'ee' n. one who has retired from work, business, etc.

re·tort' v. reply sharply or cleverly —n. 1 sharp or clever reply 2 container for distilling, etc.

re·trace' v. go back over

re·tract' v. 1 draw back or in 2 withdraw, as a charge

re·trieve' v. 1 get back or bring back 2 make good (a loss or error)

re·turn' v. 1 go or come back 2 bring or send back 3 repay (a visit, etc.) 4 yield (profit) —n. 1 a going or coming back 2 something returned 3 recurrence 4 requital 5 often pl. yield or profit 6 official report

re·un'ion n. a coming together again

re·veal' v. 1 make known, as a secret 2 show

rev'el v. 1 make merry 2 take

rev·e·la'tion n. 1 a revealing 2 striking disclosure

re·venge' v., n. harm in retaliation —**re·venge'ful** a.

rev'e·nue' n. a government's income from taxes, etc.

re·vere' v. show deep respect or love for —**rev'er·ence** n.

rev'er·end a. respected: [R-] used with the for a member of the clergy

re·verse' a. opposite —n. 1 the opposite 2 the back of a coin, etc. 3 change for the worse 4 gear for reversing —v. 1 turn about or inside out 2 revoke 3 go or make go in the opposite direction —**re·ver'sal** n.

re·vert' v. go back to a former state, owner, etc.

re·view' n. 1 general survey 2 reexamination 3 a criticism of a book, play, etc. 4 formal inspection —v. 1 survey 2 study again 3 to inspect formally 4 write a review of (a book, etc.) —**re·view'er** n.

re·vile' v. use abusive language (to or about)

re·vise' v. change, esp. after reading —**re·vi'sion** n.

re·viv'al n. 1 a reviving 2 meeting to stir up religious feeling

re·vive' v. return to life, health, use, etc.

re·voke' v. put an end to; cancel

re·volt' v. 1 to rebel 2 disgust or be disgusted —n. a rebellion

rev·o·lu'tion n. 1 movement in an orbit 2 complete cycle 3 complete change 4 overthrow of a government, etc. —**rev·o·lu'tion·ar'y** a.; n., pl. **-ies**

re·volve' v. 1 rotate 2 move in an orbit 3 think about

re·volv'er n. pistol with a revolving cylinder for bullets

re·ward' n. thing given in return for something done —v. give a reward to or for

re·wind' v. **-wound'** wind (film or tape) back on reel

re·write' v. **-wrote', -writ'ten** revise

rhet'o·ric (ret'-) n. effective or showy use of words —**rhe·tor'i·cal** a.

rheu·ma'tism (rōō'-) n. painful condition of the joints, etc.

rhine'stone' (rīn'-) n. artificial gem of glass, etc.

rhi·noc'er·os (rī-) n. large mammal with one or two horns on the snout

rho·do·den'dron (rō'-) n. shrub with showy flowers

rhu'barb' (rōō'-) n. plant with edible leafstalks

rhyme (rīm) n. 1 likeness of end sounds in words 2 verse using this —v. make (a) rhyme

rhythm (rith'əm) n. pattern of regular beat, accent, etc. —**rhyth'mi·cal, rhyth'mic** a.

rib n. 1 any of the curved bones around the chest 2 anything riblike —v. **ribbed** 1 form with ribs 2 [Sl.] tease

rib'bon n. 1 narrow strip, as of silk, etc. 2 pl. shreds

rice n. food grain grown in warm climates

rich a. 1 wealthy 2 well supplied 3 costly 4 full of fats or sugar 5 full and deep 6 producing much

rich'es n.pl. wealth

rick'et·y a. weak; shaky

ri·cot'ta (ri-) n. soft Italian cheese

rid v. **rid** or **rid'ded** to free or relieve of —**get rid of** dispose of

rid'dle n. puzzling question, thing, etc. —v. perforate

ride v. **rode, rid'den** 1 sit on and make go 2 move along, as in a car 3 be carried along on or by 4 dominate 5 [Col.] tease —n. 1 a riding 2 thing to ride in at an amusement park

ridge n. 1 crest 2 narrow, raised strip —v. form into ridges

rid'i·cule' n. remarks meant to make fun of another

ri·dic'u·lous a. foolish; absurd

ri'fle n. gun with spiral grooves in the barrel —v. rob

rig v. **rigged** 1 equip 2 arrange dishonestly —n. 1 equipment 2 arrangement of sails

rig'ging n. ropes, etc. to work the sails of a ship

right a. 1 straight 2 just and good 3 correct 4 suitable 5 normal 6 of that side toward the east when one faces north —n. 1 what is right 2 right side 3 power or privilege 4 conservative party, etc. —adv. 1 directly 2 properly 3 completely 4 toward the right —v. set right

right·eous (rī'chəs) a. 1 virtuous 2 morally hard

right'ist n., a. conservative or reactionary

rig'id a. 1 stiff and firm 2 severe; strict —**ri·gid'i·ty** n.

rim n. edge, esp. of something round

rind n. firm outer layer

ring v. **rang, rung 1** make, or cause to make, the sound of a bell **2** seem **3** resound **4** encircle —n. **1** sound of a bell **2** band for the finger **3** hollow circle **4** group with selfish aims **5** enclosed area —**ring'er** n.

rink n. smooth area for skating

rinse v. **1** wash lightly **2** wash soap from

ri'ot v., n. (take part in) mob violence —**ri'ot·er** n. —**ri'ot·ous** a.

rip v. **ripped 1** tear apart roughly **2** become torn

ripe a. **1** ready to be harvested, eaten, etc. **2** ready —**rip'en** v.

rip'ple v. to form small surface waves —n. small wave

rise v. **rose, ris'en 1** stand up **2** come or go up **3** increase **4** begin **5** revolt —n. **1** ascent **2** upward slope **3** an increase **4** origin

risk n. chance of harm, loss, etc. —v. **1** put in danger **2** take the chance of

rite n. ceremony —a.

ri'val n. competitor —a. competing —**ri'val·ry** n., pl. **-ries**

riv'er n. large stream

riv'et n. metal bolt used to fasten by hammering the ends into heads —v. fasten firmly

roach n. cockroach

road n. **1** way made for traveling **2** way; path —**road'side'** n., a.

roam v. wander about; rove

roar v., n. **1** (make) a loud, deep, rumbling sound **2** (burst out in) loud laughter

roast v. cook (meat, etc.) in an oven or over an open fire —n. roasted meat —a. roasted

rob v. **robbed** take property from unlawfully by force —**rob'ber** n. —**rob'ber·y** n., pl. **-ies**

robe n. **1** long, loose, outer garment **2** covering

rob'in n. red-breasted North American thrush

ro·bust' a. strong and healthy

rock n. **1** mass or pieces of stone **2** popular music based on jazz, folk music, etc. —v. move back and forth

rock'-and-roll' n. popular music with a strong rhythm

rock'er n. chair mounted on curved pieces of stone for rocking: also **rock'ing chair**

rock'et n. projectile propelled by the thrust of escaping gases

rod n. **1** straight stick or bar **2** linear measure, 5½ yd.

ro'dent n. gnawing mammal, as

a rat, rabbit, etc.

rogue (rōg) n. **1** scoundrel **2** mischievous person

role, rôle n. **1** part played by an actor **2** function taken on by someone

roll v. **1** move by turning **2** move on wheels **3** wind into a ball or cylinder **4** flatten with a roller **5** rock **6** trill —n. **1** a rolling **2** scroll **3** list of names **4** small cake of bread **5** a swaying motion **6** loud, echoing sound —**roll'er** n.

ROM n. computer memory that can be read but not altered

ro·maine' n. type of lettuce having long leaves

ro·mance' a. [R-] of any language derived from Latin —n. **1** tale of love, adventure, etc. **2** exciting quality **3** love affair

ro·man'tic a. **1** of romance **2** visionary **3** full of feelings of romance —n. a romantic person

romp v. play boisterously —n. romping

roof n., pl. **roofs** outside top covering of a building

room n. **1** enough space **2** space set off by walls **3** pl. living quarters; apartment —**room'ful'** n. —**room'mate'** n.

roost'er n. male chicken

root (rōōt, root) n. **1** underground part of a plant **2** embedded part, as of a tooth **3** cause **4** quantity multiplied by itself —v. **1** take root **2** place firmly **3** dig (up or out) with snout **4** rummage about

rope n. strong cord of twisted strands

rose n. **1** sweet-smelling flower that has a prickly stem **2** pinkish red —**rose'bud'** n. —**rose' bush'** n. —**rose'-col'ored** a.

rose'ma·ry n. fragrant herb used in cooking

ros'ter n. list; roll

ros'y a. **-i·er, -i·est 1** rose red or pink **2** bright or promising

rot v. **rot'ted** decay; spoil —n. **1** a rotting **2** plant disease

ro'ta·ry a. **1** rotating **2** having rotating parts

ro'tate v. **1** turn around, as a wheel **2** alternate

rot'ten a. **1** decayed **2** corrupt

rough a. **1** not smooth; uneven **2** disorderly **3** harsh **4** not perfected **5** [Col.] difficult —adv. in a rough way —n. rough part —v. **1** treat roughly: with up **2** shape roughly —**rough'en** v.

round a. 1 that forms a circle or curve 2 complete 3 that is a whole number 4 vigorous —n. 1 thigh of beef 2 a course or series 3 often pl. regular circuit 4 single gun shot 5 outburst 6 period of action or time 7 simple song for three or four voices —v. 1 make round 2 finish 3 turn 4 pass around —adv. 1 in a circle 2 through a cycle 3 from one to another 4 in the opposite direction —prep. 1 so as to encircle 2 near 3 in a circuit through

rouse (rouz) v. 1 excite 2 wake

rout (rout) n. 1 confused flight 2 crushing defeat —v. 1 make flee 2 defeat 3 force out

route (rōōt, rout) n. course traveled, as to make deliveries

rou·tine' n. regular procedure — a. regular; customary —**rou·tine'ly** adv.

rove v. roam —**rov'er** n.

row (rō) n. 1 line of people, seats, etc. 2 a trip by rowboat —v. move (in) a boat with oars

row (rou) n., v. quarrel; brawl

row'dy a. -**di·er**, -**di·est** rough, disorderly, etc.

roy'al a. of a monarch, kingdom, etc. —**roy'al·ly** adv.

roy'al·ty n., pl. -**ties** 1 royal rank, person, or persons 2 set payment for use of copyright or patent

rub v. **rubbed** 1 move over a surface with pressure and friction 2 spread on, erase, injure, etc. by rubbing

rub'ber n. 1 elastic substance 2 an overshoe —**rub'ber·y** a.

rub'bish n. 1 trash; worthless material 2 nonsense

ru'by n., pl. -**bies** deep-red precious stone

rud'der n. steering piece at ship's stern or aircraft's tail

rud'dy a. -**di·er**, -**di·est** 1 healthily red 2 reddish

rude a. 1 coarse; crude 2 impolite —**rude'ly** adv.

ruf'fle v. 1 to ripple 2 make ruffles in or on 3 make (feathers, etc.) stand up 4 disturb —n. 1 narrow, pleated cloth trimming

rug n. floor covering of thick fabric in one piece

rug'ged a. 1 uneven; rough 2 harsh; severe 3 strong

ru'in n. 1 anything destroyed, etc. 2 pl. remains of this 3 downfall; destruction —v. bring or come to ruin —**ru'in·ous** a.

rule n. 1 set guide for conduct, etc. 2 custom; usage 3 government 4 RULER (n. 2) 5 straight line —v. 1 guide 2 govern 3 decide officially 4 mark lines on

rul'er n. 1 one who governs 2 straight-edged strip for drawing lines, measuring, etc.

rum n. alcoholic liquor made from molasses, etc.

rum'ble v., n. (make) a deep rolling sound

ru'mor n. unconfirmed report or story —v. spread as a rumor

rump n. animal's hind part buttocks

run v. **ran**, **run** 1 go by moving the legs fast 2 make a quick trip 3 compete (in) 4 unravel 5 spread (over) 6 continue 7 operate 8 follow (a course) 9 undergo 10 cause to run —n. 1 act or period of running 2 journey; trip 3 brook 4 a kind 5 enclosed area 6 freedom 7 unraveled part in a fabric 8 Baseball point scored by a circuit of the bases —**run out** expire —**run out of** use up —**run over** 1 ride over 2 overflow

run'a·way' n. person or animal that has run away or fled

rung v. pp. of RING —n. rodlike step of a ladder, etc.

run'ner n. 1 one that runs 2 long, narrow rug 3 unraveled part 4 either of the pieces on which a sled slides

run'ning a. 1 that runs 2 measured straight 3 continuous — adv. in succession —n. act of one that runs

runt n. stunted animal or plant

rup'ture n. 1 a breaking apart 2 hernia —v. 1 burst 2 induce a hernia

ru'ral a. of or living in the country

ruse (rōōz) n. artful trick

rush v. 1 move, push, attack, etc. swiftly 2 hurry —n. 1 a rushing 2 busyness 3 grassy marsh plant

rust n. 1 reddish-brown coating formed on iron, etc. 2 plant disease —v. 1 form rust on 2 deteriorate, as through disuse —**rust'y** a., -**i·er**, -**i·est**

rus'tle (-al) v. 1 steal cattle 2 make soft sounds of slight motion, as stirring leaves

rut n. 1 groove as made by wheels 2 fixed routine 3 sexual excitement in animals

ruth'less a. without pity

rye (ri) *n.* **1** cereal grass **2** its grain, used for flour

S

Sab'bath *n.* day of rest and worship; Saturday for Jews, Sunday for many Christians

sa'ber, sa'bre (-bər) *n.* cavalry sword

sab'o·tage' (-täzh') *n.* destruction of factories, etc. by enemy agents, strikers, etc. —*v.* destroy by sabotage

sac *n.* pouchlike part

sac'cha·rin (sak'ə-) *n.* sugar substitute

sack *n.* **1** bag **2** large, coarse bag **3** plunder **4** [Sl.] bed —*v.* **1** put in sacks **2** plunder **3** [Sl.] dismiss from a job

sac'ra·ment *n.* sacred Christian rite, as Communion

sa'cred *a.* **1** consecrated to a god or God **2** venerated **3** inviolate

sac'ri·fice' *v.* **1** offer (something) to a deity **2** give up something for another **3** take a loss in selling —*n.* a sacrificing

sad *a.* **sad'der, sad'dest** showing or causing sorrow; unhappy —**sad'den** *v.* —**sad'ly** *adv.*

sad'dle *n.* seat for a rider on a horse, etc. —*v.* **1** put a saddle on **2** burden

safe *a.* **1** free from danger **2** unharmed **3** trustworthy **4** cautious —*n.* metal box with a lock —**safe'ly** *adv.* —**safe'ty** *n.*

safe'guard' *n.* protection; precaution —*v.* protect

sag *v.* **sagged 1** sink in the middle **2** hang unevenly **3** lose strength —*n.* place that sags

sa'ga (sä'-) *n.* long story of heroic deeds

sage *a.* very wise —*n.* **1** very wise old man **2** herb used as seasoning **3** sagebrush

sage'brush' *n.* shrub of the western plains of the U.S.

sail *n.* **1** canvas sheet to catch the wind and move a vessel **2** boat trip —*v.* **1** move by means of sails **2** travel on water **3** glide —**sail'boat'** *n.*

sail'or *n.* **1** enlisted man in the navy **2** one who sails

saint *n.* holy person —**saint'ly** *a.*, **-li·er, -li·est** —**saint'li·ness** *n.*

sake *n.* **1** motive; cause **2** behalf

sal'ad *n.* mixture of vegetables, fruit, etc., with salad dressing

sal'a·man'der *n.* amphibian resembling a lizard

sa·la'mi *n.* spiced, salted sausage

sal'a·ry *n.*, *pl.* **-ries** fixed payment at regular intervals for work —**sal'a·ried** *a.*

sale *n.* **1** a selling **2** special selling of goods at reduced prices —**for sale** to be sold —**on sale** for sale at a reduced price

sales'man *n.*, *pl.* **-men** employed to sell goods or services —**sales'wom'an** *n.fem.*, *pl.* **-wom·en** —**sales'man·ship'** *n.*

sa·li'va *n.* watery fluid secreted by glands in the mouth

sal'low *a.* sickly yellow

salm·on (sam'-) *n.* large, edible ocean fish

sa·lon' *n.* **1** parlor **2** gathering of notables

sa·loon' *n.* **1** public place where liquor is sold and drunk **2** large public room

sal'sa (säl'-) *n.* sauce made with chilies, tomatoes, etc.

salt *n.* **1** white substance found in the earth, sea water, etc., used to flavor food **2** a compound formed from an acid **3** [Col.] sailor —*a.* containing salt —*v.* add salt to —**salt'wa'ter** *a.* of salt water, or of the sea

sa·lute' *n.* formal gesture, act, etc. expressing respect —*v.* to greet with a salute

sal'vage (-vij) *n.* **1** rescue of a ship, etc. from shipwreck **2** reclaimed property or goods —*v.* **1** save from shipwreck, etc. **2** utilize (damaged goods, etc.)

sal·va'tion *n.* **1** a saving or being saved **2** one that saves **3** saving of the soul

salve (sav) *n.* soothing ointment

sal'vo *n.*, *pl.* **-vos** or **-voes** discharge of a number of guns together

same *a.* **1** being the very one **2** alike **3** unchanged **4** before-mentioned —*pron.* the same person or thing —*adv.* in like manner

sam'ple *n.* **1** part typical of a whole **2** example

sam'u·rai' (-ə ri') *n.*, *pl.* **-rai'** member of a military class in feudal Japan

sanc'tion *n.* **1** authorization **2** approval **3** punitive measure against a nation: *often used in pl.* —*v.* **1** authorize **2** approve

sanc'tu·ar'y (-choō-) *n.*, *pl.* **-ies 1** holy place, as a church **2** place of refuge

sand *n.* **1** loose grains of disinte-

san'dal *n.* open shoe with sole tied to the foot by straps

sand'stone' *n.* kind of rock much used in building

sand'wich' *n.* slices of bread with meat, etc. between them

sand'y *a.* -i·er, -i·est 1 of or like sand 2 dull yellow

sane *a.* 1 mentally healthy 2 sensible —**sane'ly** *adv.*

san'i·tar'i·um *n.* institution for invalids, etc.

san'i·tar'y *a.* 1 of health 2 clean and healthful —**san'i·tize'** *v.*

san'i·ty *n.* soundness of mind or judgment

sap *n.* 1 juice of a plant 2 vigor 3 [Sl.] a fool

sap'phire (saf'īr) *n.* deep-blue precious stone

sar'casm' *n.* taunting, ironic remark(s) —**sar·cas'tic** *a.*

sar·dine' (-dēn') *n.* small herring preserved in oil

sash *n.* 1 band worn over the shoulder or around the waist 2 sliding frame for glass in a window

Sa'tan the Devil —**sa·tan'ic** *a.*

sate *v.* 1 satisfy fully 2 satiate

sat'el·lite' *n.* 1 small planet revolving around a larger one 2 man-made object orbiting in space 3 small state dependent on a larger one

sat'in *n.* smooth and glossy silk, nylon, or rayon cloth

sat'ire' *n.* 1 use of ridicule, irony, etc. to attack vice or folly 2 literary work in which this is done

sat'is·fy' *v.* -fied' 1 fulfill the needs and desires of 2 fulfill the requirements of 3 convince 4 pay in full —**sat'is·fac'to·ry** *a.*

sat'u·rate' (sach'-) *v.* 1 soak thoroughly 2 fill completely —**sat'u·rat'ed** *a.* —**sat'u·ra'tion** *n.*

Sat'ur·day *n.* seventh day of the week

sauce *n.* 1 tasty, liquid or soft dressing for food 2 mashed, stewed fruit 3 flavored syrup

sau'cer *n.* shallow dish, esp. one for holding a cup

sau'cy *a.* -ci·er, -ci·est 1 impudent 2 lively and bold

sau'sage *n.* chopped, seasoned pork, etc., often stuffed into a casing

sau·té (sō tā') *v.* fry quickly in a little fat

sav'age *a.* 1 fierce; untamed 2 primitive; barbarous —*n.* an

uncivilized or brutal person

save *v.* 1 rescue; keep safe 2 keep or store (*up*) for future use 3 avoid waste (of) —*prep., con.* except; but

sav'ing *a.* that saves —*n.* 1 reduction in time, cost, etc. 2 *pl.* money saved

sav'ior, sav'iour (-yər) *n.* one who saves or rescues

sa'vor *v., n.* (have) a special taste, smell, or quality

sa'vor·y *a.* -i·er, -i·est tasting or smelling good

saw *n.* 1 thin, metal blade with sharp teeth, for cutting 2 proverb —*v.* 1 pt. of SEE 2 cut with a saw —**saw'yer** *n.*

say *v.* **said** 1 speak 2 to state 3 suppose —*n.* 1 chance to speak 2 power to decide

say'ing *n.* proverb

scab *n.* 1 crust over a healing sore 2 worker who rejects union or breaks a strike

scald (skôld) *v.* 1 burn with hot liquid or steam 2 heat almost to a boil

scale *n.* 1 series of gradations or degrees 2 ratio of a map, etc. to the thing represented 3 any of the thin, hard plates on a fish, snake, etc. 4 flake 5 either pan of a balance 6 *often pl.* balance or weighing machine 7 *Mus.* series of consecutive tones —*v.* 1 climb up 2 set according to a scale 3 scrape scales from —scale off in scales

scal'lop *n.* 1 edible mollusk 2 any of the curves forming a fancy edge —*v.* 1 to edge in scallops 2 to bake with a milk sauce, etc.

scalp *n.* skin on top of the head —*v.* [Inf.] to sell (tickets, etc.) at a price higher than the established one

scam *n.* [Sl.] a trick or swindle

scamp *n.* rascal

scam'per *v.* run quickly

scan *v.* **scanned** 1 look at quickly 2 examine 3 analyze the meter in verse

scan'dal *n.* 1 disgrace or thing that disgraces 2 gossip

scant *a.* not enough

scape'goat' *n.* one who is blamed for others' mistakes

scar *n.* mark left after a wound has healed —*v.* **scarred** to mark with or form a scar

scarce *a.* 1 not common 2 hard to get —*adv.* scarcely

scarce'ly *adv.* hardly

scare *v.* frighten —*n.* sudden fear

scarf *n., pl.* **scarfs** or **scarves** long

or broad cloth piece for the neck, etc.

scar'let *n.* bright red

scat'ter *v.* 1 throw about 2 move in several directions

scene *n.* 1 place; setting 2 view 3 division of a play, film, etc. 4 show of emotion

scen'er·y *n.*, *pl.* **-ies** 1 painted backdrops for a stage play 2 outdoor views

sce'nic *a.* 1 of scenery 2 picturesque

scent *v.* 1 to suspect 2 to perfume —*n.* 1 odor 2 perfume 3 sense of smell

scep'ter (sep'-) *n.* a staff as symbol of a ruler's power

sched'ule (skej'-) *n.* 1 timetable 2 timed plan 3 list of details

scheme *n.* 1 plan; system 2 plot; intrigue 3 diagram — **sche·mat'ic** *a.*

schol'ar *n.* 1 learned person 2 student —**schol'ar·ly** *a.*

schol'ar·ship' *n.* 1 academic knowledge; learning 2 money given to help a student

scho·las'tic *a.* of schools, students, teachers, etc.

school *n.* 1 place for teaching and learning 2 its students and teachers 3 education 4 group with the same beliefs 5 group of fish —*v.* train; teach —*a.* of, in, or for school —**school'mate'** *n.*

schoon'er *n.* ship with two or more masts

sci'ence *n.* systematized knowledge or a branch of it —**sci'en·tif'ic** *a.* —**sci·en·tif'i·cal·ly** *adv.*

science fiction *n.* imaginative fiction involving scientific phenomena

sci'en·tist *n.* expert in science

scis'sors *n.pl.* cutting tool with two opposing blades that move on a pivot

scoff *v.* mock or jeer (at)

scold *v.* find fault with angrily

scoop *n.* 1 small, shovellike utensil 2 bucket of a dredge, etc. 3 a scooping —*v.* 1 take up with a scoop 2 hollow out

scoot *v.* [Col.] scurry off

scope *n.* 1 range of understanding, action, etc. 2 chance

scorch *v.* 1 burn slightly 2 parch *n.* surface burn

score *n.* 1 points made in a game, etc. 2 grade on a test 3 piece of music showing all parts 4 scratch or mark 5 twenty 6 *pl.* very many 7 debt —*v.* 1 make a score or scores 2 evalu-

ate 3 achieve 4 keep score

scorn *n.* contempt; disdain —*v.* 1 treat with scorn 2 refuse

scor'pi·on *n.* arachnid with a poisonous sting

scoun'drel *n.* villain

scour *v.* 1 to clean by rubbing with abrasives 2 go through thoroughly, as in search

scout *n., v.* (one sent ahead) to spy, search, etc.

scowl *v., n.* (to have) an angry frown

scram'ble *v.* 1 climb, crawl, etc. hurriedly 2 struggle for something 3 to mix; jumble 4 stir and cook (eggs) 5 make (signals) unclear —*n.* a scrambling

scrap *n.* 1 fragment 2 discarded material 3 *pl.* bits of food —*a.* discarded —*v.* **scrapped** 1 discard 2 [Col.] fight

scrape *v.* 1 rub smooth or rub away 2 scratch 3 gather bit by bit —*n.* 1 scraped place 2 harsh sound 3 predicament

scratch *v.* 1 cut the surface 2 scrape or dig with one's nails 3 scrape noisily 4 cross out —*n.* mark from scratching —*a.* for hasty notes, etc. —**from scratch** from nothing

scrawl *v.* write carelessly —*n.* poor handwriting

scraw'ny *a.* **-ni·er, -ni·est** lean; thin

scream *v., n.* (make) a loud, shrill cry or noise

screech *v., n.* (give) a harsh, high shriek

screen *n.* 1 thing used to shield, conceal, etc. 2 wire mesh in a frame 3 surface for showing video images, films, etc. —*v.* 1 conceal or shelter 2 sift or sift out

screw *n.* 1 naillike fastener with a spiral groove 2 propeller

screw'driv'er *n.* tool for turning screws

scrib'ble *v.* 1 write carelessly 2 draw marks

scribe *n.* writer; author

scrimp *v.* spend or use as little as possible

script *n.* 1 handwriting 2 working copy of a play

Scrip'ture *n.* 1 *often pl.* the Bible 2 [s-] any sacred writing —**Scrip'tur·al** *a.*

scrod *n.* young cod or haddock

scroll *n.* 1 roll of paper, etc. with writing on it 2 coiled or spiral design

scrub *v.* **scrubbed** rub hard, as in

washing

scruff *n.* back of the neck; nape

scruff'y *a.* **-i·er, -i·est** shabby or unkempt

scru'ple *n.* a doubt as to what is right, proper, etc.

scru'pu·lous *a.* **1** showing or having scruples **2** precise

scu'ba *n.* equipment, as an air tank, for breathing underwater

scuff *v.* **1** scrape with the feet **2** wear a rough place on

scuf'fle *n.* rough, confused fight

sculp'ture *n.* statues, etc. carved from wood, stone, etc.

scum *n.* **1** surface impurities on a liquid **2** [Col.] vile person or people

scythe (sīth) *n.* long-bladed tool to cut grass, etc.

sea *n.* **1** the ocean **2** a smaller body of salt water **3** large body of fresh water **4** heavy wave

sea'board' *n.* land along the sea: also **sea'coast'**

seal *n.* **1** sea mammal with flippers **2** official design stamped on a letter, etc. **3** thing that seals —*v.* **1** certify as with a seal **2** close tight **3** settle finally

sea level *n.* mean level of the sea's surface

seam *n.* **1** line where two pieces are sewn or welded together **2** layer of ore or coal

sea'man *n., pl.* **-men 1** sailor **2** navy enlisted man

seam'stress *n.* woman whose work is sewing

sea'port' *n.* port for ocean ships

sear *a.* withered —*v.* **1** wither **2** burn the surface of

search *v.* look through or examine to find something —*n.* a searching

sea'shore' *n.* land along the sea

sea'son *n.* **1** any of the four divisions of the year **2** special time —*v.* **1** to flavor **2** age

sea'son·ing *n.* flavoring for food

seat *n.* **1** place to sit **2** thing or part one sits on **3** right to sit as a member **4** chief location

sea'weed' *n.* any sea plant(s)

se·cede' *v.* withdraw formally from a group, etc.

sec'ond *a.* **1** next after the first **2** another, like the first —*n.* **1** one that is second **2** ⁶⁰ part of a minute —*v.* support (a suggestion, motion, etc.) —*adv.* in the second place, etc.

sec'ond·ar·y *a.* **1** second in order **2** less important **3** derivative

secondary school *n.* high school

sec'ond-class' *a.* **1** of the class, rank, etc. next below the highest **2** inferior

sec'ond-hand' *a.* **1** not from the original source **2** used before

se'cret *a.* **1** kept from being known by others **2** hidden —*n.* secret fact, etc. —**se'cre·cy** *n.*

sec're·tar'y *n., pl.* **-ies 1** one who keeps records, writes letters, etc. for a person or group **2** head of a department of government **3** tall desk

se·crete' *v.* **1** to hide **2** make (a body substance), as a gland

sect *n.* group having the same beliefs, esp. in religion

sec'tion *n.* distinct part

sec'tor *n.* **1** part of a circle like a pie slice **2** district for military operations

sec'u·lar *a.* not connected with church or religion

se·cure' *a.* **1** free from danger, care, etc. **2** firm; stable **3** sure

se·cu'ri·ty *n., pl.* **-ties 1** secure state or feeling **2** protection **3** thing given as a pledge of repayment, etc. **4** *pl.* stocks, bonds, etc.

se·date' *a.* quiet and dignified

sed'a·tive *a.* making one calmer —*n.* sedative medicine

sed'i·ment *n.* matter that settles from a liquid

se·duce' *v.* **1** to lead astray **2** entice into sexual intercourse, esp. for the first time

see *v.* **saw, seen 1** look at **2** understand **3** find out **4** make sure **5** escort **6** meet; visit with **7** consult **8** have the power of sight —**see to** attend to

seed *n., pl.* **seeds** or **seed 1** the part of a plant from which a new one will grow **2** source **3** sperm —*v.* **1** plant with seed **2** take the seeds from —**seed'less** *a.*

seed'ling *n.* young plant grown from a seed

seek *v.* **sought 1** search for **2** try to get

seem *v.* look, feel, etc. (to be)

seep *v.* leak through; ooze

seer (sir) *n.* prophet

seethe (sēth) *v.* boil

seg'ment *n.* section

seg're·gate *v.* set apart

seize (sēz) *v.* **1** take suddenly or by force **2** attack **3** capture

sel'dom *adv.* rarely

se·lect' *a.* **1** chosen with care **2** exclusive —*v.* choose; pick out

self *n., pl.* **selves** one's own person, welfare, etc.

self-con'fi·dent a. sure of oneself —**self'-con'fi·dence** n.

self'-con'scious a. ill at ease

self-con·trol' n. control of one's emotions, actions, etc.

self'-im'age n. one's idea of oneself, one's worth, etc.

self'ish a. caring too much about oneself —**self'ish·ly** adv.

self'less a. unselfish

self-pos·ses'sion n. full control over one's actions, etc.

self-re·straint' n. self-control

self-right'eous a. feeling more righteous than others

self-serv'ice n. practice of serving oneself in a store, cafeteria, etc.

self-suf·fi'cient a. independent

self-willed' a. stubborn

sell v. **sold** 1 exchange for money 2 offer for sale 3 be sold (for) —**sell out** 1 sell completely 2 [Col.] betray

se·mes'ter n. either of the terms in a school year

sem'i·cir'cle n. half circle

sem'i·co'lon n. mark of punctuation (;)

sem'i·fi'nal n., a. (contest) just before the finals

sem'i-skilled' a. of manual work requiring little training

sem'i·tone' n. Mus. half of a whole tone

sem'i·trail'er n. detachable trailer attached to a TRACTOR (n. 2)

sen'ate n. 1 lawmaking assembly 2 [S-] upper branch of Congress or a State legislature —**sen'a·tor** n. —**sen'a·to'ri·al** a.

send v. **sent** 1 cause to go or be carried 2 impel; drive —**send for** summon —**send'er** n.

se'nile a. 1 of old age 2 weak in mind and body —**se·nil'i·ty** n.

sen'ior a. 1 the older: written Sr. 2 of higher rank, etc. —n. high school or college student in the last year

sen·ior'i·ty (-yôr'-) n. status gained by length of service

sen·sa'tion n. 1 sense impression or the power to receive it 2 exciting thing

sen·sa'tion·al a. shocking

sense n. 1 power to see, hear, taste, feel, etc. 2 sound judgment 3 meaning —v. perceive

sense'less a. 1 unconscious 2 foolish or stupid

sen'si·ble a. 1 reasonable; wise 2 aware 3 noticeable

sen'si·tive' a. 1 quick to feel, notice, etc. 2 susceptible to stimuli 3 tender or sore 4 touchy —**sen'si·tiv'i·ty** n.

sen'sor n. device for detecting heat, light, etc.

sen'so·ry a. of the senses

sen'su·al (-shoo-) a. of or enjoying the pleasures of the body —**sen'su·al·ly** adv.

sen'su·ous a. having to do with the senses

sen'tence n. 1 group of words stating something 2 court decision 3 punishment

sen'ti·ment n. 1 a feeling 2 opinion 3 tender feelings 4 maudlin emotion —**sen'ti·men'tal** a. —**sen'ti·men·tal'i·ty** n.

sep'a·rate' (-rāt'; a.: -rat) v. 1 divide; set apart 2 keep apart 3 go apart —a. set apart; distinct —**sep'a·ra'tion** n.

Sep·tem'ber n. ninth month

sep'ul·cher (-kər) n. tomb

se'quel n. 1 result 2 book, etc. that continues an earlier one

se'quence n. 1 succession or the order of this 2 series 3 scene; episode

se'quin n. small, shiny disk for decorating cloth

se·quoi'a (-kwoi'-) n. giant evergreen tree

ser'e·nade' v., n. (perform) music sung or played at night, esp. by a lover

se·rene' a. undisturbed; calm

serf n. feudal farmer, almost a slave —**serf'dom** n.

ser'geant n. 1 low-ranking police officer 2 noncommissioned officer above a corporal

se'ri·al a. of, in, or published in a series —n. serial story —**se'ri·al·ize'** v.

se'ries n., pl. **se'ries** number of similar things coming one after another

se'ri·ous a. 1 earnest 2 important 3 dangerous

ser'mon n. 1 religious speech by a clergyman 2 serious talk on duty, etc.

ser'pent n. snake

serv'ant n. one hired to work in another's home

serve v. 1 be a servant to 2 aid 3 do official service 4 spend a prison term 5 offer (food, etc.) to 6 be used by 7 deliver 8 hit a ball to start play —n. a hitting of a ball in tennis, etc.

serv'ice n. 1 a serving 2 governmental work 3 armed forces 4 religious ceremony 5 set of silverware, etc. 6 aid

serv'ice·man' *n., pl.* **-men'** member of the armed forces

ses'sion *n.* meeting of a court, legislature, class, etc.

set *v.* set 1 put; place 2 put in the proper condition, position, or fixed 3 make or become firm or fixed 4 establish; fix 5 sit on eggs, as a hen 6 start 7 mount (gems) 8 furnish (an example) 9 sink below the horizon 10 fit (words) to music —*a.* 1 fixed 2 obstinate 3 ready —*n.* 1 way in which a thing is set 2 scenery for a play 3 group of like persons or things 4 assembled parts, as of a radio

set'ting *n.* 1 that in which a thing is set 2 time, place, etc., as of a story 3 surroundings

set'tle *v.* 1 put in order 2 set in place firmly or comfortably 3 go to live in 4 deposit sediment, etc. 5 calm 6 decide 7 pay, as a debt 8 come to rest 9 sink

set'tle·ment *n.* 1 a settling 2 a colonizing of new land 3 colony 4 village 5 an agreement 6 payment

sev'en *a., n.* one more than six —**sev'enth** *a., n.*

sev'en·teen' *a., n.* seven more than ten —**sev'en·teenth'** *a., n.*

sev'en·ty *a.; n., pl.* **-ties** seven times ten —**sev'en·ti·eth** *a., n.*

sev'er *v.* cut off; separate

sev'er·al *a.* 1 more than two but not many 2 separate

se·vere' *a.* 1 harsh; strict 2 grave 3 very plain 4 intense

sew (sō) *v.* **sewed, sewn** or **sewed** fasten, make, etc. by means of needle and thread

sew'age (sōō'-) *n.* waste matter carried off by sewers

sew'er *n.* underground drain for water and waste matter

sex *n.* 1 either of the two divisions of organisms, male or female 2 character of being male or female 3 attraction between the sexes 4 sexual intercourse —**sex'u·al** *a.*

sex'ism' *n.* unfair treatment of one sex by the other, esp. of women by men —**sex'ist** *a.*

sex'y *a.* **-i·er, -i·est** [Col.] exciting sexual desire

shab'by *a.* **-bi·er, -bi·est** 1 worn out 2 clothed poorly 3 mean

shack *n.* shanty

shade *n.* 1 partial darkness caused by cutting off light rays

2 device to cut off light 3 degree of darkness of a color 4 small difference

shad'ow *n.* 1 shade cast by a body blocking light rays 2 sadness 3 small amount

shaft *n.* 1 arrow or spear, or its stem 2 long, slender part or thing 3 vertical opening 4 bar that transmits motion to a mechanical part

shag'gy *a.* **-gi·er, -gi·est** 1 having long, coarse hair 2 unkempt

shake *v.* **shook, shak'en** 1 move quickly up and down, back and forth, etc. 2 tremble 3 weaken, disturb, upset, etc. 4 clasp (another's hand), as in greeting —*n.* a shaking

shale *n.* rock of hard clay

shall *v. pt.* **should** auxiliary verb showing: 1 future time 2 determination or obligation

shal'low *a.* not deep —*n.* shoal

shame *n.* 1 guilt, embarrassment, etc. felt for a wrong act 2 dishonor 3 a misfortune —*v.* 1 make ashamed 2 dishonor 3 force by a sense of shame

sham·poo' *v.* wash (the hair, etc.) —*n.* a shampooing, or soap, etc. used for this

shan'ty *n., pl.* **-ties** small, shabby dwelling

shape *n.* 1 outer form 2 definite form 3 [Col.] condition —*v.* form or adapt

share *n.* 1 part each gets or has 2 equal part of stock in a corporation —*v.* 1 give in shares 2 have a share (in) 3 use in common (with)

shark *n.* a large, fierce fish

sharp *a.* 1 having a fine point or cutting edge 2 abrupt 3 distinct 4 clever or shrewd 5 vigilant 6 harsh or intense 7 *Mus.* above the true pitch —*n. Mus.* a note one half step above another: symbol (#) —*adv.* 1 in a sharp way 2 precisely

shat'ter *v.* 1 break into pieces 2 damage badly

shave *v.* **shaved, shaved** or **shav'en** 1 cut into slices from 2 cut the hair or beard (of) or the skin —*n.* act of shaving

shawl *n.* cloth covering for the head and shoulders

she *pron.* the female mentioned

sheaf *n., pl.* **sheaves** bundle of stalks, papers, etc.

shear *v.* **sheared, sheared** or **shorn** 1 cut or cut off as with shears 2 clip hair from —*n. pl.*

large scissors

sheath (shēth) *n.* **1** case for a knife blade, etc. **2** any covering like this

sheathe (shēth) *v.* put into or cover with a sheath

shed *n.* small shelter or storage place —*v.* **shed 1** make flow **2** radiate **3** throw or cast off

sheep *n., pl.* **sheep** cud-chewing animal with heavy wool

sheer *v.* to swerve —*a.* **1** very thin **2** absolute **3** very steep

sheet *n.* **1** large cloth of cotton, etc. used on beds **2** piece of paper **3** broad, thin piece of glass, etc. **4** rope to control a sail

shelf *n., pl.* **shelves 1** thin, flat board for holding things **2** ledge or reef

shell *n.* **1** hard outer covering, as of an egg **2** narrow rowboat for racing **3** missile from a large gun **4** cartridge —*v.* **1** remove the shell from **2** bombard

shel·lac, shel·lack *n.* thin varnish of resin and alcohol

shell'fish *n.* aquatic animal with a shell

shel'ter *n.* something that covers or protects —*v.* give shelter to

shelve *v.* **1** put on a shelf **2** lay aside

shep'herd (-ərd) *n.* **1** one who herds sheep **2** religious leader

sher'bet *n.* frozen dessert of fruit juice, milk, etc.

sher'iff *n.* chief law officer of a county

sher'ry *n., pl.* **-ries** a strong wine

shield *n.* **1** armor carried on the arm **2** thing that protects —*v.* protect

shift *v.* **1** move or change from one person, place, direction, etc. to another **2** get along —*n.* **1** a shifting **2** time at work **3** trick

shim'mer *v., n.* (shine with) a wavering light

shin *n.* front of the leg between knee and ankle

shine *v.* **shone** or (esp. for *v.* 3) **shined 1** be or make be bright **2** excel **3** make shiny by polishing —*n.* **1** brightness **2** polish

shin'gle *n.* **1** piece of wood, slate, etc. for roofing **2** [Col.] small signboard

shin'y *a.* **-i·er, -i·est** bright; shining

ship *n.* **1** large watercraft **2** aircraft —*v.* **shipped 1** put or go in a ship **2** transport —**ship'ment** *n.* —**ship'per** *n.*

shirk *v.* to neglect (a duty)

shirt *n.* **1** upper garment for men **2** undershirt

shiv'er *v.* **1** shake or tremble **2** shatter —*n.* **1** a trembling **2** sliver

shoal *n.* **1** school of fish **2** shallow place in water

shock *n.* **1** sudden blow or jar **2** sudden emotional upset **3** effect of electric current on the body **4** bundle of grain **5** thick mass of hair —*v.* **1** astonish; horrify **2** give an electric shock to

shoe *n.* **1** outer covering for the foot **2** horseshoe **3** part of a brake that presses on the wheel

shoot *v.* **shot 1** send out, or move, with force, speed, etc. **2** send a bullet, etc. from **3** wound or kill with a bullet, etc. **4** to photograph **5** to score (a point, etc.) in sports **6** grow rapidly **7** to mark in spots, etc. (*with* color) —*n.* new growth; sprout

shop *n.* **1** place where things are sold **2** manufacturing place —*v.* **shopped** look at or buy goods in shops —**shop'per** *n.*

shore *n.* **1** land next to water **2** prop; support —*v.* prop (*up*)

short *a.* **1** not measuring much **2** not tall **3** brief **4** brusque **5** less than enough —*n.* **1** short movie **2** *pl.* short pants —*adv.* **1** abruptly or briefly —**in short** briefly —**short'en** *v.*

short'age *n.* **1** lack; deficiency **2** deficit

short'com'ing *n.* defect

short'cut' *n.* **1** shorter route **2** way of saving time, etc.

short'en·ing *n.* fat used to make baked goods flaky

short'ly *adv.* **1** briefly **2** soon **3** curtly

short'sight'ed *a.* lacking in foresight

short'stop' *n. Baseball* infielder between second and third basemen

short'-term' *a.* for a short time

shot *v. pt. & pp.* of SHOOT —*n.* **1** act of shooting **2** range; scope **3** attempt **4** throw, etc., as of a ball **5** projectile(s) for a gun **6** marksman **7** photograph **8** dose or drink —**shot'gun'** *n.*

should *v. pt.* of SHALL: *should* is used to express obligation, probability, etc.

shoul'der *n.* **1** part of the body to which an arm or foreleg is connected **2** edge of a road

shout *v., n.* (utter) a loud, sudden cry or call

shove v. 1 push along a surface 2 push roughly —n. a push

shov'el n. tool with a broad scoop and a handle

show v. **showed, shown** or **showed** 1 bring into sight; reveal 2 appear 3 be noticeable 4 guide 5 point out 6 prove; explain —n. 1 a display, performance, etc. 2 pompous display 3 pretense

show'down' n. [Col.] disclosure of facts to force a settlement

show'er n. 1 brief fall of rain 2 any sudden fall or flow 3 party with gifts for a bride, etc. 4 bath of fine water spray —v. 1 to spray with water 2 give, or fall, abundantly 3 bathe under a shower —**show'er·y** a.

show'y a. **-i·er, -i·est** 1 of striking appearance 2 gaudy; flashy

shrap'nel n. fragments of an exploded artillery shell

shred n. 1 torn strip 2 fragment —v. **shred'ded** or **shred** cut or tear into shreds

shrewd a. clever or sharp in practical affairs —**shrewd'ly** adv. —**shrewd'ness** n.

shriek v., n. (utter) a loud, piercing cry

shrill a. high-pitched and piercing in sound —**shrill'ness** n.

shrimp n. 1 small, long-tailed, edible shellfish 2 [Col.] small person

shrine n. saint's tomb or other sacred place

shrink v. **shrank** or **shrunk, shrunk** or **shrunk'en** 1 lessen in size; contract 2 draw back

shriv'el v. dry up; wither

shroud n. 1 cloth used to wrap a corpse 2 cover; veil 3 pl. ropes supporting ship's masts

shrub n. bush —**shrub'ber·y** n.

shrug v. **shrugged**; n. (draw up the shoulders in) a gesture of doubt, indifference, etc.

shud'der v. shake, as in horror —n. a shuddering

shuf'fle v. 1 walk with feet dragging 2 mix or jumble together

shun v. **shunned** keep away from

shunt v. 1 move to one side 2 switch or shift

shut v. **shut** 1 close (a door, etc.) 2 prevent entrance to —a. closed —**shut down** cease operating —**shut off** prevent passage of or on

shut'ter n. 1 movable window cover 2 light-controlling device

on a camera lens

shut'tle n. device to carry thread back and forth in weaving

shy a. **shy'er** or **shi'er, shy'est** or **shi'est** 1 timid 2 bashful 3 distrustful 4 [Sl.] lacking —v. **shied** 1 be startled 2 hesitate

sic v. **sicked** to urge to attack

sick a. 1 having disease; ill 2 nauseated 3 of or for sick people 4 disgusted 5 [Col.] morbid

sick'en v. make or become sick

sick'le n. curved blade with a short handle, for cutting light grass

sick'ly a. **-li·er, -li·est** 1 in poor health 2 faint or weak

side n. 1 right or left half 2 a bounding line 3 a surface 4 aspect 5 relative position 6 party; faction —a. 1 of, at, or to a side 2 secondary —**take sides** support one faction

side'burns' n.pl. hair on the cheeks, beside the ears

side'step' v. avoid as by stepping aside

side'walk' n. path for pedestrians alongside a street

side'ways' a., adv. 1 to or from one side 2 side first

sid'ing n. 1 outside boards, etc. on a building 2 short railroad track off the main track

si'dle v. move sideways cautiously

siege (sēj) n. 1 encircling of a place to effect its capture 2 persistent attack

si·es'ta n. brief rest or nap, esp. in the afternoon

sieve (siv) n. strainer with many small holes

sift v. 1 pass through a sieve, as to separate 2 examine with care, as evidence

sigh (sī) v. 1 let out a deep breath, as in sorrow 2 long (for) —n. a sighing

sight n. 1 something seen 2 act or power of seeing 3 range of vision 4 aiming device —v. 1 to see 2 aim (a gun, etc.)

sign n. 1 mark or symbol 2 meaningful gesture 3 signboard, road marker, etc. 4 trace; vestige —v. write one's name (on)

sig'nal n. 1 gesture, device, etc. to warn, order, etc. 2 radio wave —v. make signals (to)

sig'na·ture n. one's name written by oneself

sig·nif'i·cance n. 1 meaning 2 importance —**sig·nif'i·cant** a.

sig'ni·fy' v. **-fied'** 1 to mean 2

make known, as by a sign

si'lence n. absence of sound —v. 1 make silent 2 repress

si'lent a. 1 not speaking 2 still; quiet 3 inactive

sil'hou·ette' (-ōō-) v., n. (make) a dark shape against a light background

silk n. thread or fabric of soft fiber made by silkworms

silk'worm' n. moth caterpillar that spins silk fiber

sill n. bottom of a door frame or window frame

sil'ly a. -li·er, -li·est foolish; absurd —**sil'li·ness** n.

si'lo n., pl. -los tower for storing green fodder

silt n. fine particles of soil floating in or left by water

sil'ver n. 1 white, precious metal, a chemical element 2 silver coins 3 silverware 4 grayish white —a. of silver

sil'ver·ware' n. tableware of or plated with silver

sim'i·lar a. nearly alike

sim'mer v., n. (keep at or near) a gentle boiling

sim'per v. smile in a silly way

sim'ple a. 1 having only one or a few parts 2 easy to do or understand 3 plain 4 natural 5 common 6 foolish

sim'pli·fy' v. -fied' make easier

sim'ply adv. 1 in a simple way 2 merely 3 completely

sim'u·late' v. pretend

si'mul·ta'ne·ous a. done, etc. at the same time

sin n. breaking of religious or moral law —v. **sinned** commit a sin —**sin'ful** a. —**sin'ner** n.

since adv., prep. 1 from then until now 2 at some time between then and now —con. 1 after that time 2 because

sin·cere' a. 1 without deceit 2 genuine —**sin·cer'i·ty** n.

sing v. **sang, sung** 1 make musical sounds with the voice, etc. 2 perform by singing 3 hum, buzz, etc. 4 tell in song —n. [Col.] group singing —**sing'er** n.

singe v. **singed** burn superficially

sin'gle a. 1 one only 2 of or for one person or family 3 unmarried —v. select from others: with out —n. 1 single person or thing 2 pl. tennis game with only two players 3 Baseball hit on which the batter reaches first base —**sin'gle·ness** n.

sin'gle-hand'ed a. without help

sin'gly adv. 1 alone 2 one by one

sin'gu·lar a. 1 unique 2 separate 3 exceptional 4 unusual —n. Gram. word form designating only one —**sin'gu·lar'i·ty** n.

sin'is·ter a. 1 threatening 2 wicked or evil

sink v. **sank** or **sunk, sunk** 1 go or put beneath the surface of water, etc. 2 go down slowly 3 become lower 4 pass gradually (into sleep, etc.) 5 invest 6 defeat —n. basin with a drain pipe

si'nus n., pl. -nus·es any air cavity in the skull opening into the nasal cavities

sip v. **sipped** drink a little at a time —n. a small amount sipped

si'phon n. tube for causing liquid from one container to another below it

sir n. 1 polite title for a man 2 [S-] title for a knight or baronet

sire n. male parent

si'ren n. warning device with a wailing sound

sir'loin' n. choice cut of beef from the loin

sis'ter n. 1 female related to one by having the same parents 2 female fellow member 3 nun

sis'ter-in-law' n., pl. **sis'ters-in-law'** 1 sister of one's spouse 2 brother's wife

sit v. **sat** rest on one's buttocks or haunches 2 perch 3 be in session 4 pose, as for a portrait 5 be located 6 baby-sit

site n. location; scene

sit·u·a'tion n. 1 location 2 condition 3 job

six a., n. one more than five —**sixth** a., n.

six·teen' a., n. six more than ten —**six'teenth'** a., n.

sixth sense n. intuitive power

six'ty a., n., pl. -ties six times ten —**six'ti·eth** a., n.

size n. 1 dimensions 2 any of a series of measures, often numbered 2 pasty glaze: also **siz'ing** —v. to make according to size

siz'zle v. to hiss when hot

skate n. 1 ice skate 2 roller skate —v. glide or roll on skates

skel'e·ton n. framework, as of the bones of a body

skep'tic n. one who questions matters generally accepted

sketch n. 1 rough drawing or design 2 outline —v. make a sketch (of)

ski n., pl. **skis** long, flat runner fastened to the shoe for snow travel —v. travel on skis —

ski'er n.

skid n. 1 plank, log, etc. on which to support or slide something heavy 2 act of skidding — v. **skid'ded** slide sideways

skill n. 1 great ability 2 art or craft involving use of the hands or body —**skill'ful** a.

skil'let n. frying pan

skim v. **skimmed** 1 take floating matter from a liquid 2 read quickly 3 glide lightly

skin n. 1 tissue covering the body 2 pelt 3 covering like skin, as fruit rind —v. **skinned** remove the skin from

skin'ny a. **-ni-er, -ni-est** very thin —**skin'ni-ness** n.

skip v. **skipped** 1 move by hopping on alternate feet 2 leap lightly (over) 3 bounce 4 omit

skirt n. 1 part of a dress, coat, etc. below the waist 2 woman's garment that hangs from the waist —v. go along the edge of

skit n. short, funny play

skull n. bony framework of the head

skunk n. small mammal that ejects a smelly liquid

sky n., pl. **skies** often pl. upper atmosphere or space around the earth

sky'scrap'er n. very tall building

slab n. flat, thick piece

slack a. 1 loose 2 not busy 3 slow; sluggish

slacks n.pl. trousers

slag n. smelting refuse

slam v. **slammed** shut, hit, etc. with force —n. heavy impact

slan'der n. spoken falsehood harmful to another —v. speak slander against

slang n. vigorous, short-lived, informal language

slant v., n. 1 incline; slope 2 (show) a special attitude

slap n. a blow with something flat —v. **slapped** strike with a slap

slash v. 1 cut at with a knife 2 cut slits in 3 reduce

slat n. narrow strip

slate n. 1 bluish-gray rock in thin layers 2 tile, etc. of slate 3 list of candidates —v. designate

slaugh'ter v. 1 kill (animals) for food 2 kill (people) brutally —n. a slaughtering

slave n. human being owned by another —v. to toil —**slav'ish** a.

slav'er·y n. 1 condition of slaves 2 ownership of slaves 3 drudgery

slay v. **slew, slain** kill by violent means —**slay'er** n.

sled n. vehicle with runners, for snow —v. **sled'ded** ride a sled

sledge n. 1 long, heavy hammer 2 heavy sled

sleep n. natural regular rest, as at night —v. **slept** to be in a state of sleep —**sleep'less** a.

sleet n. partly frozen rain

sleeve n. 1 part of a garment covering the arm 2 protective cover —**sleeve'less** a.

sleigh (slā) n. vehicle on runners for travel on snow

slen'der a. 1 long and thin 2 small in size or force

slice n. 1 thin, broad piece cut off 2 share —v. cut into slices or as a slice —**slic'er** n.

slick v. make smooth —a. 1 smooth 2 slippery 3 clever

slide v. **slid** 1 move along a smooth surface 2 glide 3 slip —n. 1 a sliding 2 inclined surface to slide on 3 picture for projection on a screen

slight a. 1 slender 2 unimportant 3 small or weak —v., n. neglect or snub —**slight'ly** adv.

slim a. **slim'mer, slim'mest** 1 long and thin 2 small

slime n. soft, wet, sticky matter

sling n. 1 device for hurling stones 2 band or looped cloth for raising or supporting

slip v. **slipped** 1 go quietly or pass smoothly or quickly 2 slide accidentally 4 escape from 5 become worse 6 err —n. 1 dock for ships 2 woman's undergarment 3 a falling down 4 error: also [Col.] **slip'-up'** 5 plant stem or root, for planting, etc. 6 small piece of paper

slip'per n. light, low shoe

slip'per·y a. **-i-er, -i-est** 1 that can cause slipping 2 tending to slip 3 tricky

slit v. **slit** cut or split open —n. a straight, narrow opening

sliv'er n. thin, pointed piece cut or split off

slob'ber v., n. drool

slop n. 1 spilled liquid 2 slush 3 watery food 4 often pl. liquid waste —v. **slopped** splash

slope n. 1 rising or falling surface, line, etc. 2 amount of this

slop'py a. **-pi-er, -pi-est** 1 slushy 2 careless

slot n. narrow opening

sloth (slôth, slōth) n. 1 laziness 2 South American mammal living in trees —**sloth'ful** a.

slouch n. 1 a lazy person 2 drooping posture —v. have a drooping posture

slow a. 1 taking longer than usual 2 low in speed 3 behind the right time 4 stupid 5 sluggish —adv. in a slow way —**slow'ly** adv. —**slow'ness** n.

slug n. 1 small mollusk 2 bullet 3 false coin —v. [Col.] hit hard —**slug'ger** n.

slug'gish a. slow-moving

slum n. populous area with very poor living conditions

slum'ber v., n. sleep

slump v. 1 fall suddenly 2 to slouch —n. sudden fall

slur v. **slurred** 1 pass over quickly 2 pronounce indistinctly 3 insult —n. 1 a slurring 2 insult

sly a. **sli'er** or **sly'er, sli'est** or **sly'est** 1 cunning; crafty 2 playfully mischievous —**sly'ly** adv.

smack n. 1 slight taste 2 sharp noise made by parting the lips suddenly 3 sharp slap 4 loud kiss 5 fishing boat —v. 1 have a trace 2 make a smack with one's lips 3 slap loudly

small a. 1 little in size, extent, etc. 2 trivial 3 mean; petty

smart v. 1 cause or feel stinging pain 2 suffer —a. 1 that smarts 2 brisk; lively 3 bright; clever 4 neat 5 stylish —**smart'ly** adv.

smash v. 1 break violently 2 crash 3 to destroy

smear v. 1 make greasy, dirty, etc. 2 spread 3 slander

smell v. **smelled** or [Br.] **smelt** 1 catch the odor of 2 sniff 3 have an odor —n. 1 power to smell 2 thing smelled; odor

smelt n. small, silvery food fish —v. melt (ore or metal) so as to remove the impurities

smile v. 1 to show pleasure, amusement, etc. by curving the mouth upward 2 show with a smile —n. act of smiling

smirk v. to smile in a conceited or annoyingly complacent way

smite v. **smote, smit'ten** 1 hit or strike hard 2 affect strongly

smith n. one who makes or repairs metal objects

smock n. loose, protective outer garment

smog n. fog and smoke

smoke n. vapor, as from something burning —v. 1 give off smoke 2 use cigarettes, a pipe, etc. 3 cure (meats, etc.) with smoke

smol'der v. 1 burn without flame 2 exist suppressed

smooth a. 1 having no roughness or bumps; even 2 with no trouble 3 ingratiating —v. to make smooth

smoth'er v. 1 suffocate 2 cover thickly

smudge n. 1 dirty spot 2 fire with dense smoke —v. to smear

smug a. smug'ger, smug'gest too self-satisfied —**smug'ly** adv.

smug'gle v. bring in or take out secretly or illegally

snag n. 1 sharp projection 2 tear made by this 3 hidden difficulty —v. **snagged** 1 tear on a snag 2 hinder

snail n. mollusk with a spiral shell

snake n. long, legless reptile

snap v. **snapped** 1 bite or grasp suddenly 2 shout (at) 3 break suddenly 4 make a cracking sound 5 move quickly 6 take a snapshot of —n. 1 sharp sound 2 fastening that clicks shut 3 [Sl.] easy job —a. quick

snap'shot' n. picture taken with a hand camera

snare n. 1 trap for small animals 2 dangerous lure 3 string across the bottom of a drum —v. to trap

snarl v. 1 growl, baring the teeth 2 speak sharply 3 tangle —n. 1 a snarling 2 tangle; disorder

snatch v. seize; grab

sneak v. move, do, etc. secretly —n. one who sneaks

sneer v. show scorn —n. sneering look or remark

sneeze v. expel breath from the nose and mouth in a sudden, uncontrolled way —n. act of sneezing

snick'er v., n. (give) a silly, partly stifled laugh

sniff v. inhale forcibly through the nose, as in smelling

snif'fle v., n. sniff to check mucus flow

snip v. **snipped** cut in a quick stroke —n. small piece cut off

snipe n. wading bird —v. shoot at from a hidden place

snoop [Col.] v. pry in a sneaky way —n. one who snoops

snooze v., n. (take) a nap

snore v. breathe noisily while asleep —n. a snoring

snort v. force breath audibly from the nose —n. a snorting

snout n. projecting nose and jaws of an animal

snow n. flakes of frozen water vapor from the sky —v. 1 fall as snow 2 cover with snow 3 [Sl.] deceive —**snow'drift'** n. — **snow'fall'** n. —**snow'flake'** n. —**snow'y** a., -i·er, -i·est

snub v. snubbed 1 treat with scorn 2 stop abruptly

snuff v. put out (a candle, etc.)

snug a. snug'ger, snug'gest 1 cozy 2 compact 3 tight in fit

snug'gle v. cuddle; nestle

so adv. 1 in such a way 2 to such a degree 3 very 4 therefore 5 more or less 6 also 7 then 8 [Col.] very much —con. 1 in order (that) 2 [Col.] with the result (that) —**and so on** (or **forth**) and the rest

soak v. 1 make wet 2 stay in liquid —**soak up** absorb

soap n. substance that makes suds in water for washing

soar v. fly high in the air

sob v. sobbed weep aloud with short gasps —n. act of sobbing

so'ber a. 1 not drunk 2 serious; sedate 3 plain

so'cia·ble (-sha-) a. friendly; agreeable —**so·cia·bil'i·ty** n.

so'cial a. 1 of society 2 living in groups 3 sociable 4 of social work —n. a party

so'cial·ism' n. public ownership of the means of production — **so'cial·ist** n., a. —**so'cial·is'tic** a.

so'cial·ize' v. 1 put under public ownership 2 take part in social affairs

social science n. field of study dealing with society

so·ci'e·ty n., pl. -ties 1 community of people 2 all people 3 companionship 4 organized group 5 the fashionable class

so·ci·ol'o·gy (-sē-) n. study of the organization, problems, etc. of society —**so·ci·ol'o·gist** n.

sock n. 1 short stocking 2 [Sl.] a blow —v. [Sl.] hit with force

sock'et n. hollow part into which something fits

sod n. earth surface with grass

so'da n. 1 substance containing sodium 2 soda water 3 beverage of soda water and ice cream

soda water n. carbonated water

soft a. 1 not hard; easy to crush, cut etc. 2 not harsh; mild, gentle, etc. 3 without minerals that hinder lathering 4 weak 5 nonalcoholic —adv. gently

soft'ball' n. game like baseball played with a larger and softer ball

soft'en (sôf'-) v. make or become soft —**soft'en·er** n.

soft'ware' n. programs, etc. for a computer or other electronic equipment

sog'gy a. -gi·er, -gi·est very wet and heavy; soaked

soil n. earth or ground, esp. the surface layer

so'lar a. of or having to do with the sun

sol'der (säd'ər) n. metal alloy for joining metal parts —v. join with solder

sol'dier n. member of an army, esp. one who is not an officer — v. be a soldier

sole n. 1 bottom of the foot, or of a shoe 2 sea flatfish —a. one and only

sol'emn (-əm) a. 1 formal 2 serious —**sol'emn·ly** adv.

sol'id a. 1 firm or hard 2 not hollow 3 three-dimensional 4 of one piece, solid, etc. —n. 1 firm or hard substance 2 three-dimensional object

sol'i·tar'y a. 1 alone; lonely 2 single

so'lo n., a. (piece of music) for one performer —**so'lo·ist** n.

so·lu'tion n. 1 solving of a problem 2 explanation or answer 3 liquid with something dissolved in it

solve v. find the answer to

som'ber a. 1 dark and gloomy 2 sad

some a. 1 certain but unspecified 2 of indefinite quantity 3 about —pron. indefinite quantity —adv. 1 approximately 2 [Col.] somewhat 3 [Col.] to a great extent

some'bod'y n., pl. -ies important person —pron. person not named or known

some'day' adv. sometime

some'how' adv. in some way

some'one' pron. somebody

some'thing' n. thing not named or known

some'time' adv. at some unspecified time —a. former

some'times adv. at times

some'what' n. some part, amount, etc. —adv. a little

some'where' adv. in, to, or at some unnamed place

son n. male in relation to his parents

song n. 1 music, or poem, to be sung 2 singing sound

son'ic a. of or having to do with sound

son'-in-law' *n., pl.* **sons'-** husband of one's daughter

son'net *n.* 14-line poem

soon *adv.* 1 in a short time 2 early 3 readily

soot *n.* black particles in smoke

soothe (sᴏᴏᵗʰ) *v.* 1 make calm, as by kindness 2 ease, as pain

sop *v.* sopped soak (up)

so·phis'ti·cat'ed *a.* 1 knowledgeable, subtle, etc. 2 highly complex; advanced

soph'o·more' *n.* second-year student in high school or college

sop'ping *a.* very wet

so·pra'no (-pran'ō, -prä'nō) *n., pl.* **-nos** highest female voice

sor'cer·y *n.* witchcraft —**sor'cer·er** *n.* —**sor'cer·ess** *n.fem.*

sor'did *a.* 1 dirty; filthy 2 mean; selfish

sore *a.* 1 painful 2 sad 3 [Col.] angry —*n.* injured body tissue

so·ror'i·ty *n., pl.* **-ties** social club for women

sor'row *v., n.* (feel) sadness

sor'ry *a.* **-ri·er, -ri·est** 1 full of sorrow, regret, etc. 2 pitiful; wretched

sort *n.* kind; class —*v.* arrange according to kind —**sort of** [Col.] somewhat

so'-so' *a., adv.* fair or fairly well

soul *n.* 1 spiritual part of a person 2 vital part 3 person

sound *n.* 1 that which is heard 2 strait or inlet of the sea —*v.* 1 (cause) to make a sound 2 seem 3 measure the depth of water 4 seek the opinion of: often with **out** —*a.* 1 free from defect; healthy, secure, wise, etc. 2 deep or thorough —*adv.* in a sound way —**sound'ly** *adv.*

soup *n.* liquid food with meat, vegetables, etc. in it

sour *a.* 1 having an acid taste 2 fermented 3 unpleasant

source *n.* 1 starting point 2 place of origin

south *n.* direction or region to the left of one facing the sunset —*a., adv.* in, toward, or from the south —**south'er·ly** *a., adv.* —**south'ern** *a.* —**south'ern·er** *n.* —**south'ward** *a., adv.* —**south'wards** *adv.*

south'east' *n.* direction or region between south and east —*a., adv.* in, toward, or from the southeast —**south'east'er·ly** *a., adv.* —**south'east'ern** *a.*

south'west' *n.* direction or region between south and west —*a., adv.* in, toward, or from

the southwest —**south'west'er·ly** *a., adv.* —**south'west'ern** *a.*

sou've·nir' *n.* thing kept as a reminder

sov'er·eign (säv'rən) *a.* 1 chief; supreme 2 independent

sow (sou) *n.* adult female pig

sow (sō) *v.* **sowed, sown** or **sowed** scatter, or plant with, seed for growing

space *n.* 1 limitless expanse containing all things 2 distance or area 3 interval of time

space'craft' *n., pl.* **-craft'** vehicle or satellite for outer-space travel, exploration, etc.

spa'cious (-shəs) *a.* having much space; vast

spade *n.* 1 flat-bladed digging tool 2 playing card marked with a ♠ —*v.* dig with a spade

spa·ghet'ti *n.* (cooked) strings of dried flour paste

span *n.* 1 extent 2 period of time

span'iel (-yəl) *n.* dog with large drooping ears

spank *v., n.* slap on the buttocks

spare *v.* 1 save or free from something 2 avoid using 3 give up, as time or money —*a.* 1 extra 2 lean; meager —*n.* extra thing

spark *n.* 1 small glowing piece from a fire 2 particle 3 flash from an electrical discharge across a gap

spar·kle *v.* 1 give off sparks 2 glitter 3 effervesce —*n.* glitter

spar'row *n.* small songbird

sparse *a.* thinly spread

spasm (spaz'əm) *n.* 1 involuntary muscular contraction 2 short, sudden burst of activity

spa'tial (-shəl) *a.* of, or existing in, space

spat'ter *v.* 1 spurt out in drops 2 splash

spat'u·la (spach'ə-) *n.* tool with a broad, flexible blade

spawn *n.* 1 eggs of fishes, etc. 2 offspring —*v.* produce (spawn)

spay *v.* sterilize (a female animal)

speak *v.* **spoke, spo'ken** 1 utter words 2 tell; express 3 make a speech 4 use (a language) in speaking —**speak for** ask for

speak'er *n.* 1 one who speaks 2 loudspeaker

spear *n.* long, slender sharp-pointed weapon

spe'cial *a.* 1 distinctive 2 unusual 3 main; chief 4 for a certain use

spe'cial·ize' v. concentrate on a certain type of study, work, etc.

spe'cial·ty n., pl. **-ties** 1 special feature, interest, etc. 2 special article

spe'cies n., pl. **-cies** distinct kind of plant or animal

spe·cif'ic a. definite; explicit

spec'i·fy' v. **-fied'** state explicitly

spec'i·men n. sample

spec'ta·cle n. 1 unusual sight 2 public show 3 pl. eyeglasses

spec·ta'tor n. one who watches

spec'ter n. ghost

spec'trum n., pl. **-tra** or **-trums** row of colors formed by diffraction

spec'u·late' v. 1 ponder 2 take risky chances in business

speech n. 1 act or way of speaking 2 power to speak 3 something said 4 public talk

speed n. 1 rapid motion 2 rate of movement

spell n. 1 supposedly magic words 2 fascination; charm 3 period of work, duty, etc. —v. 1 give in order the letters of (a word) 2 mean 3 [Col.] relieve (another)

spell'ing n. 1 a forming words from letters 2 way a word is spelled

spend v. **spent** 1 use up 2 pay out (money) 3 pass (time)

spend'thrift' n. one who wastes money —a. wasteful

sphere (sfir) n. 1 globe; ball 2 place or range of action

spice n. 1 any aromatic seasoning 2 stimulating quality

spi'der n. arachnid that spins webs

spig'ot n. faucet or tap

spike n. 1 sharp-pointed projection 2 long, heavy nail 3 ear of grain 4 long flower cluster

spill v. **spilled** or **spilt** 1 let run over 2 overflow 3 shed (blood) 4 [Col.] make fall —n. a fall

spin v. **spun** 1 twist fibers into thread 2 make a web, cocoon, etc. 3 tell (a story) 4 to whirl 5 move fast —n. 1 whirling movement 2 fast ride

spin'ach n. plant with dark-green, edible leaves

spi'nal a. of the spine

spin'dle n. 1 rod used in spinning thread 2 rod that acts as an axis

spine n. 1 thorn, quill, etc. 2 spinal column

spi'ral a. circling around a center —n. spiral curve or coil

spire n. tapering, pointed part, as of a steeple

spir'it n. 1 soul 2 ghost, angel, etc. 3 pl. mood 4 courage 5 enthusiasm and loyalty 6 essential quality 7 pl. alcoholic liquor

spir'it·u·al a. 1 of the soul 2 religious; sacred —n. religious song originally of U.S. blacks

spit n. 1 thin rod to roast meat on 2 shoreline narrowed to a point 3 saliva —v. **spit'ted** or (v. 2) **spit** or [Br.] **spat** 1 fix as on a spit 2 eject (saliva, etc.) from the mouth

spite n. malice —v. annoy; hurt —**in spite of** regardless of

splash v. dash liquid, etc. (on) —n. 1 a splashing 2 a spot made by splashing

spleen n. 1 large abdominal organ 2 malice; spite

splen'did a. magnificent; grand —**splen'dor** n.

splice v., n. (make) a joint with ends overlapped

splint n. stiff strip to hold a broken bone in place

splin'ter n. thin, sharp piece —v. split in splinters

split v. split separate into parts —n. break; crack —a. divided

spoil v. **spoiled** or **spoilt** to damage, ruin, decay, etc.

spoke v. pt. of SPEAK —n. rod from hub to rim of a wheel

spo'ken v. pp. of SPEAK —a. oral; voiced

spokes'man n., pl. **-men** one who speaks for another — **spokes'per·son** n.

sponge n. 1 absorbent substance made from a sea animal, plastic, etc. 2 the animal —v. 1 clean, etc. with a sponge 2 [Col.] live off others

spon'sor n. 1 promoter; supporter 2 advertiser who pays for a radio or TV program —v. be sponsor for

spon·ta'ne·ous a. 1 without effort 2 within or by itself

spook n. [Col.] ghost

spool n. cylinder upon which thread, etc. is wound

spoon n. small bowl with a handle, used in eating

spore n. tiny reproductive cell of mosses, ferns, etc.

sport n. 1 athletic game 2 fun —v. 1 [Col.] display 2 play

spot n. 1 stain; mark 2 place —v. **spot'ted** 1 mark with spots 2 see —**spot'less** a.

spouse n. husband or wife

spout n. 1 pipe, etc. by which a liquid pours 2 stream of liquid —v. 1 shoot out with force 2 talk loudly and on and on

sprain v. twist a muscle or ligament in a joint —n. injury caused by this

spray n. 1 mist or stream of tiny liquid drops 2 branch with leaves, flowers, etc. 3 spray gun —v. apply, or emit in, a spray

spread v. 1 open out 2 extend in time or space 3 make known 4 go or make go —n. 1 act or extent of spreading 2 a cloth cover 3 butter, jam, etc.

spring v. sprang or sprung, sprung 1 leap 2 grow; develop 3 snap back or shut 4 make or become bent, split, etc. 5 make known —n. 1 a leap 2 resilience 3 resilient coil of wire, etc. 4 flow of water from the ground 5 source 6 season after winter —a. of, for, or in the season of spring —spring'y a., -i-er, -i-est

sprin'kle v. 1 scatter drops of or on 2 rain lightly

sprint v., n. race at full speed for a short distance

sprout v. begin to grow —n. new growth; shoot

spruce n. evergreen tree

spunk [Col.] n. courage

spur n. 1 pointed device on a shoe to prick a horse 2 stimulus 3 projecting part

spurt v. 1 shoot forth; squirt 2 make a sudden effort

sput'ter v. 1 speak in a fast, confused way 2 spit out bits 3 make hissing sounds

spy v. spied 1 watch closely and secretly 2 see —n., pl. spies one who spies, esp. to get another country's secrets

squab'ble v., n. quarrel over a small matter

squad n. small group

squad'ron n. unit of warships, aircraft, etc.

squall n. 1 brief, violent windstorm 2 harsh, loud cry

squan'der v. spend or use wastefully

square n. 1 rectangle with all sides equal 2 area with streets on four sides 3 tool for making right angles 4 product of a number multiplied by itself —v. 1 make square 2 make straight, even, etc. 3 settle; adjust 4 multiply by itself —a. 1 shaped like a square 2 forming a right

angle 3 straight, level, or even 4 just; fair 5 [Col.] filling, as a meal —adv. in a square way

square root n. quantity that when squared produces another, given quantity

squash v. 1 press into a soft, flat mass 2 to suppress —n. 1 a squashing 2 game played with rackets in a walled court 3 fleshy vegetable growing on a vine

squat v. squat'ted 1 crouch 2 settle on land without title to it —a. short and heavy —n. position of squatting —squat'ter n.

squawk v. 1 utter a loud, harsh cry 2 [Col.] complain

squeak v. make a sharp, high-pitched sound —n. such a sound

squeal v., n. (utter) a long, shrill cry

squeeze v. 1 press hard 2 extract by pressure 3 force by pressing 4 hug —n. a squeezing

squint v. 1 peer with eyes partly closed 2 be cross-eyed

squire n. English country gentleman —v. escort

squirm v. twist and turn

squir'rel n. tree-dwelling rodent with a bushy tail

squirt v., n. (shoot out in) a jet or spurt

stab v. stabbed pierce or wound as with a knife —n. 1 a thrust, as with a knife 2 [Col.] a try

sta'bi·lize v. 1 make stable, or firm 2 keep from changing

sta'ble a. not apt to change; firm —n. building for horses or cattle

stack n. 1 orderly pile 2 smokestack 3 set of bookshelves —v. to pile in a stack

sta'di·um n. place for outdoor games, surrounded by tiers of seats

staff n., pl. (in 1, 2, 3) **staffs** or (in 1 & 3) **staves** 1 stick or rod used for support, etc. 2 group of people assisting a leader 3 the five lines on and between which music is written —v. provide with workers

stag n. full-grown male deer

stage n. 1 platform, esp. one on which plays are presented 2 the theater 3 part of a journey 4 period in growth or development

stage'coach' n. horse-drawn public coach for long trips

stag'ger v. 1 (cause to) totter, reel, etc. 2 shock 3 arrange alternately —n. a staggering

stain v. 1 discolor; spot 2 dishonor 3 color (wood, etc.) with a dye —n. 1 a spot; mark 2 dishonor 3 dye for wood, etc.

stair n. 1 one of a series of steps between levels 2 usually pl. flight of stairs: also **stair'case'** or **stair'way'**

stake n. 1 pointed stick to be driven into the ground 2 often pl. money risked as a wager —v. 1 mark the boundaries of 2 wager —**at stake** being risked

stale a. 1 no longer fresh 2 trite

stalk v. 1 stride haughtily 2 track secretly —n. 1 a stalking 2 plant stem —**stalk'er** n.

stall n. 1 section for one animal in a stable 2 market booth —v. 1 put in a stall 2 stop 3 delay by evading

stal'lion (-yən) n. uncastrated male horse

sta'men n. pollen-bearing part of a flower

stam'mer v., n. pause or halt in speaking

stamp v. 1 put the foot down hard 2 pound with the foot 3 cut out with a die 4 impress a design on 5 put a stamp on —n. 1 a stamping 2 gummed piece of paper, as for postage 3 a stamped mark 4 stamping device

stam·pede' n. sudden, headlong rush, as of a herd

stanch (stônch, stanch) v. check the flow of blood from a wound

stand v. **stood** 1 be or get in an upright position 2 place or be placed 3 hold a certain opinion 4 halt 5 endure or resist —n. 1 a halt 2 position 3 platform, rack, counter, etc. 4 a growth (of trees) —**stand by** be ready to help —**stand out** to project, be prominent, etc.

stand'ard n. 1 flag, banner, etc. 2 thing set up as a rule or model 3 upright support —a. 1 that is a standard or rule 2 proper

stan'za n. group of lines making a section of a poem

sta'ple n. 1 main product, part, etc. 2 basic trade item, as flour 3 U-shaped metal fastener

star n. 1 celestial body seen as a point of light at night 2 flat figure with five or more points 3 asterisk 4 one who excels or plays a leading role in acting

star'board (-bərd) n. right side of a ship, etc. as one faces the bow

starch n. 1 white food substance in potatoes, etc. 2 powdered form of this

stare v. gaze steadily —n. long steady look

star'fish' n. small, star-shaped sea animal

stark a. 1 bleak 2 complete; utter —adv. entirely

start v. 1 begin to go, do, etc. 2 set in motion 3 jump or jerk —n. 1 a starting 2 a jump or jerk 3 place or time of beginning 4 lead; advantage

star'tle v. 1 frighten suddenly 2 surprise —**startling** a.

starve v. 1 suffer or die from lack of food 2 cause to starve

state n. 1 the way a person or thing is 2 formal style 3 nation 4 [often S–] a unit of a federal government —v. to express in words

state'ly a. **-li·er, -li·est** grand or dignified

state'ment n. 1 a stating 2 something stated 3 report, as of money owed

states'man n., pl. **-men** person skillful in government

stat'ic a. 1 at rest 2 of electricity caused by friction —n. electrical disturbances in radio reception

sta'tion n. 1 assigned place 2 stopping place 3 place for radio or TV transmission 4 social rank —v. assign to a station

sta'tion·ar'y a. not moving or changing

sta'tion·er'y n. writing materials

sta·tis'tics n. analysis of numerical data —n.pl. the data —**statis'ti·cal** a.

stat'ue n. likeness done in stone, metal, etc.

stat'ure n. 1 rank 2 condition

stat'ute n. a law

staunch (stônch) a. firm, loyal, etc. —v. stanch

stave n. 1 any of the wooden side strips of a barrel 2 staff —v. 1 stay 1 remain 2 dwell 3 stop or delay 4 to support —n. 1 a staying 2 prop

stead'y a. **-i·er, -i·est** 1 firm 2 regular 3 calm 4 reliable

steak n. slice of meat or fish

steal v. **stole, stol'en** 1 take dishonestly and secretly 2 move stealthily

steam n. water changed to a vapor by boiling: source of heat and power —a. using steam —v. 1 expose to steam 2 cook with steam 3 give off steam —

steam'y *a*. **-i·er, -i·est**

steel *n*. hard alloy of iron with carbon —*a*. of steel

steep *a*. having a sharp rise or slope —*v*. soak or saturate

stee'ple *n*. high tower

steer *v*. guide; direct —*n*. male of beef cattle; ox

stem *n*. **1** stalk of a plant, flower, etc. **2** stemlike part **3** prow of a ship **4** root of a word —*v*. **stemmed 1** remove the stem of **2** advance against **3** stop **4** derive

sten'cil *n*. sheet cut with letters, etc. to print when inked over

step *n*. **1** one foot movement, as in walking **2** footstep **3** way of stepping **4** stair tread **5** degree; rank **6** act in a series —*v*. **1** move with a step **2** press the foot down

step'broth'er *n*. stepparent's son

step'child' *n*. spouse's child (**step'daugh'ter** or **step'son**) by a former marriage

step'lad'der *n*. four-legged ladder with flat steps

step'par'ent *n*. the spouse (**step'fa'ther** or **step'moth'er**) of one's remarried parent

step'sis'ter *n*. a stepparent's daughter

ster'e·o·phon'ic *a*. of a blend of sounds reproduced through separate speakers

ster'e·o·type *v., n*. (express or conceive in) a set, trite form

ster'ile (-əl) *a*. **1** not able to reproduce itself or oneself **2** free of germs —**ste·ril'i·ty** *n*.

ster'i·lize' *v*. to make sterile

ster'ling *a*. **1** (made) of silver at least 92.5% pure **2** of British money **3** excellent

stern *a*. severe; unyielding —*n*. rear end of a ship, etc.

steth'o·scope' *n*. instrument for hearing chest sounds

stew *v*. cook by boiling slowly —*n*. meat with vegetables, cooked in this way

stick *n*. **1** small branch broken or cut off **2** long, thin piece, as of wood —*v*. **stuck 1** pierce **2** attach or be attached as by pinning or gluing **3** extend **4** become fixed, jammed, etc. **5** persevere **6** hesitate **7** be puzzled

stick'y *a*. **-i·er, -i·est** adhesive

stiff *a*. **1** hard to bend or move **2** thick; dense **3** strong, as a wind **4** difficult **5** tense —**stiff'en** *v*.

sti'fle *v*. **1** suffocate **2** suppress; restrain

still *a*. **1** quiet **2** motionless **3** calm —*adv*. **1** until then or now **2** even; yet **3** nevertheless —*con*. nevertheless

still'born' *a*. dead at birth

stim'u·late' *v*. make (more) active —**stim'u·la'tion** *n*.

sting *v*. **stung 1** hurt with a sting **2** cause or feel sharp pain —*n*. **1** a stinging, or pain from it **2** sharp part in some plants, bees, etc. that pricks: also **sting'er**

stin'gy (-jē) *a*. **-gi·er, -gi·est** miserly; grudging

stink *v*. **stank** or **stunk, stunk;** *n*. (have) a strong, unpleasant smell

stint *v*. restrict to a small amount —*n*. **1** limit **2** assigned task

stir *v*. **stirred 1** move, esp. slightly **2** move around as with a spoon **3** excite

stir-fry' *v*. fry (vegetables, meat, etc.) quickly while stirring

stir'rup *n*. ring hung from a saddle as a footrest

stitch *n*. **1** single movement or loop made by a needle in sewing, knitting, etc. **2** sudden pain —*v*. sew

stock *n*. **1** tree trunk **2** ancestry **3** biological breed **4** rifle part holding the barrel **5** broth from meat or fish **6** livestock **7** goods on hand **8** shares in a business —*v*. supply or keep in stock —*a*. **1** kept in stock **2** common —**in** (or **out of**) **stock** (not) available

stock'hold'er *n*. one owning stock in a company

stock'ing *n*. knitted covering for the leg and foot

stock'y *a*. **-i·er, -i·est** short and heavy

stoke *v*. stir up and feed fuel to a (fire) —**stok'er** *n*.

stole *v*. pt. of STEAL —*n*. long fur piece worn by women around the shoulders

stom'ach *n*. **1** digestive organ into which food passes **2** abdomen **3** appetite

stone *n*. **1** solid nonmetallic mineral matter **2** piece of this **3** seed of certain fruits **4** abnormal stony mass in the kidney, etc. —*v*. throw stones at

stool *n*. **1** single seat with no back or arms **2** feces

stoop *v*. **1** bend the body forward **2** lower one's dignity —*n*. **1** position of stooping **2** small porch

stop v. **stopped** 1 close by filling, shutting off, etc. 2 cease; end; halt 3 to block; obstruct 4 stay —n. 1 a stopping 2 a place stopped at 3 obstruction, plug, etc. —**stop off** stop for a while

stor'age n. 1 a storing 2 place for, or cost of, storing goods

store n. 1 supply; stock 2 establishment where goods are sold —v. put aside for future use

stork n. large, long-legged wading bird

storm n. 1 strong wind with rain, snow, etc. 2 any strong disturbance 3 strong attack —v. 1 blow violently, rain, etc. 2 rage 3 rush or attack violently

sto'ry n., pl. **-ries** 1 a telling of an event 2 fictitious narrative 3 one level of a building 4 [Col.] a falsehood —**sto'ried** a.

stout a. 1 brave 2 firm; strong 3 fat —n. strong, dark beer

stove n. apparatus for heating, cooking, etc.

stow (stō) v. pack or store away

straight a. 1 not crooked, bent, etc. 2 direct 3 in order 4 honest or frank 5 undiluted 6 [Sl.] conventional 7 [Sl.] heterosexual —adv. 1 in a straight line 2 directly 3 without delay —**straight'en** v.

straight'for'ward a. 1 direct 2 honest

strain v. 1 stretch tight or to the utmost 2 strive hard 3 sprain 4 filter —n. 1 a straining or being strained 2 excessive demand on one's emotions, etc. 3 ancestry 4 inherited tendency 5 trace; streak 6 often pl. tune

strait n. often pl. 1 narrow waterway 2 distress

strand n. 1 any of the threads, wires, etc. that form a string, cable, etc. 2 string, as of pearls 3 shore

strange a. 1 unfamiliar 2 unusual 3 peculiar; odd

stran'ger n. 1 newcomer 2 person not known to one

stran'gle v. 1 choke to death 2 stifle —**stran'gler** n.

strap n. narrow strip of leather, etc., as for binding things

strat'e-gy n., pl. **-gies** 1 science of military operations 2 artful managing 3 plan

straw n. 1 grain stalk or stalks after threshing 2 tube for sucking a drink

straw'ber'ry n., pl. **-ries** small, red, juicy fruit of a vinelike

plant

stray v. 1 wander; roam 2 deviate —a. 1 lost 2 isolated

streak n. 1 long, thin mark 2 layer 3 tendency in behavior 4 spell, as of luck

stream n. 1 small river 2 steady flow, as of air —v. 1 flow in a stream 2 move swiftly

stream'lined' a. 1 shaped to move easily in air, etc. 2 made more efficient

street n. road in a city

street'car' n. passenger car on rails along streets

strength n. 1 force; power; vigor 2 durability 3 intensity 4 potency

stress n. 1 strain; pressure 2 importance; emphasis 3 special force on a syllable, etc. —v. 1 to strain 2 accent 3 emphasize

stretch v. 1 reach out 2 draw out to full extent 3 strain 4 exaggerate —n. 1 a stretching 2 ability to be stretched 3 extent

strew v. **strewed**, **strewed** or **strewn** 1 scatter 2 cover as by scattering

strick'en a. struck, wounded, afflicted, etc.

strict a. 1 exact or absolute 2 rigidly enforced or enforcing

stride v. **strode**, **strid'den** with long steps —n. 1 long step 2 pl. progress

strife n. a quarrel(ing)

strike v. **struck**, **struck** or **strick'en** 1 hit 2 sound by hitting some part 3 ignite (a match) 4 make by stamping 5 attack 6 reach or find 7 occur to 8 assume (a pose) 9 take down or apart 10 stop working until demands are met —n. 1 a striking 2 Baseball a pitched ball struck at but missed, etc. 3 Bowling a knocking down of all the pins at once

string n. 1 thick thread, etc. used as for tying 2 numbers of things on a string or in a row 3 thin cord bowed, etc. to make music, as on a violin 4 pl. condition attached to a plan, offer, etc. —v. **strung** 1 provide with strings 2 put on a string 3 extend

strip v. **stripped** 1 take off clothing, covering, etc. (of) 2 make bare 3 break the teeth of (a gear, etc.) —n. long, narrow piece

stripe n. 1 narrow band of different color or material 2 kind; sort —v. mark with stripes

strive v. **strove** or **strived**, **striv'en** or **strived** 1 try very hard 2 struggle

stroke n. 1 sudden blow, attack, action, etc. 2 a single movement of the arm, a tool, etc. 3 striking sound —v. draw one's hand, etc. gently over

stroll n. leisurely walk —v. 1 take a stroll 2 wander

strong a. 1 powerful 2 healthy 3 durable 4 intense

struc'ture n. 1 thing built 2 plan, design, etc.

strug'gle v. 1 fight 2 strive —n. a struggling

strut v. **strut'ted** walk arrogantly —n. 1 strutting walk 2 rod used as a support

stub n. short, leftover, or blunt part —v. **stubbed** bump (one's toe)

stub'ble n. 1 short grain stumps 2 short growth

stub'born a. obstinate

stuc'co v. **-coed**; n. (cover with) rough plaster

stud n. 1 decorative nail 2 removable button 3 upright support in a wall 4 breeding stallion

stu'dent n. one who studies

stu'di·o n., pl. **-os'** 1 artist's work area 2 place for producing movies, radio or TV programs, etc.

stud'y v. **-ied** 1 learn by reading, thinking, etc. 2 investigate —n., pl. **-ies** 1 act of studying 2 pl. education 3 deep thought 4 place to study

stuff n. 1 material; substance 2 (worthless) objects —v. 1 fill 2 cram —**stuff'ing** n.

stum'ble v. 1 walk unsteadily; trip 2 speak confusedly 3 come by chance —n. a stumbling

stump n. part left after cutting off the rest

stun v. **stunned** 1 make unconscious, as by a blow 2 shock deeply

stunt v. keep from growing —n. daring show of skill

stu·pen'dous a. overwhelming

stu'pid a. 1 not intelligent 2 foolish 3 dull

stu'por n. dazed condition

stur'dy a. **-di·er**, **-di·est** 1 firm 2 strong

stur'geon (-jən) n. food fish

stut'ter n., v. stammer

sty n., pl. **sties** pigpen

sty, stye n., pl. **sties** swelling on the rim of the eyelid

style n. 1 way of making, writing, etc. 2 fine style 3 fashion

styl'ish a. fashionable

styp'tic (stip'-) a. that halts bleeding; astringent

suave (swäv) a. smoothly polite

sub'a·tom'ic a. smaller than an atom

sub·con'scious a., n. (of) one's feelings, wishes, etc. of which one is unaware

sub·due' v. 1 get control over 2 make less intense

sub·ject' (v.: səb jekt') a. 1 that is a subject 2 liable 3 contingent upon —n. 1 one controlled by another 2 topic of discussion or study 3 Gram. word or words about which something is said —v. 1 bring under the control of 2 make undergo

sub·jec'tive a. of one's feelings rather than from facts

sub·lime' a. noble; lofty

sub'ma·rine' n. warship operating under water

sub·merge' v. put or go under water —**sub·mer'gence** n.

sub·merse' v. submerge

sub·mis'sion n. 1 a submitting 2 obedience —**sub·mis'sive** a.

sub·mit' v. **-mit'ted** 1 to present for consideration, etc. 2 surrender

sub·or'di·nate (-nət; v.: -nāt') a. lower in rank; secondary —n. subordinate person —v. to make subordinate

sub·poe'na, sub·pe'na (sə pē'nə) n. legal paper ordering one to appear in court —v. to order with a subpoena

sub·scribe' v. 1 give support or consent (to) 2 promise to contribute (money) 3 agree to take and pay for a periodical, etc.: with to —**sub·scrip'tion** n.

sub'se·quent' a. following

sub·side' v. 1 to sink lower 2 become quieter

sub·sid'i·ar'y a. helping in a lesser way

sub'si·dy n., pl. **-dies** (government) grant of money

sub·sist' v. continue to live or exist

sub'stance n. 1 essence 2 physical matter 3 central meaning 4 wealth

sub·stand'ard a. below standard

sub·stan'tial (-shəl) a. 1 material 2 strong 3 large 4 wealthy 5 in essentials

sub'sti·tute' n. one that takes the place of another —v. use as or be a substitute

sub'ti·tle n. 1 secondary title 2 line translating dialogue, etc. as at the bottom of a film image

sub·tle (sut''l) a. 1 keen; acute 2 crafty 3 delicate 4 not obvious —**sub'tle·ty** n., pl. **-ties** —**sub'tly** adv.

sub·tract' v. take away, as one number from another —**sub·trac'tion** n.

sub'tra·hend' n. quantity to be subtracted from another

sub'urb n. district, town, etc. on the outskirts of a city —**sub·ur'ban** a. —**sub·ur'ban·ite'** n.

sub'way' n. underground electric railroad in a city

suc·ceed' v. 1 come next after 2 have success

suc·cess' n. 1 favorable result 2 the gaining of wealth, fame, etc. 3 successful one —**suc·cess'ful** a. —**suc·cess'ful·ly** adv.

suc·ces'sor n. one who succeeds another, as in office

such a. 1 of this or that kind 2 whatever 3 so much —pron. such a one —**such as** for example

suck v. 1 draw into the mouth 2 suck liquid from 3 dissolve in the mouth —n. act of sucking

suck'er n. 1 one that sucks or clings 2 sprout 3 lollipop

suck'le v. give or get milk from the breast or udder

suc'tion n. creation of a vacuum that sucks up fluid, etc.

sud'den a. 1 unexpected 2 hasty —**sud'den·ly** adv.

suds n.pl. foam on soapy water

sue v. 1 begin a lawsuit against 2 petition

suede (swād) n. 1 leather with one side buffed into a nap 2 cloth like this

suf'fer v. 1 undergo or endure (pain, loss, etc.) 2 tolerate

suf·fi'cient (-fish'ənt) a. enough

suf'fix n. syllable(s) added at the end of a word to alter its meaning, etc.

suf'fo·cate' v. 1 kill by cutting off air 2 die from lack of air 3 stifle —**suf·fo·ca'tion** n.

suf'frage n. right to vote

sug'ar n. sweet carbohydrate found in sugar cane, etc.

sug·gest' v. 1 bring to mind 2 propose as a possibility 3 imply —**sug·ges'tion** n.

su'i·cide' n. 1 act of killing oneself intentionally 2 one who commits suicide —**su'i·cid'al** a.

suit n. 1 coat and trousers (or skirt) 2 any of the four sets of playing cards 3 lawsuit 4 suing, pleading, etc. —v. 1 be suitable for 2 make suitable 3 please

suit'a·ble a. appropriate; fitting

suit'case' n. traveling bag

suite (swēt) n. 1 group of connected rooms 2 set of matched furniture

sul'fa a. of a family of drugs used in combating certain bacterial infections

sul'fur n. yellow solid substance, a chemical element

sul'len a. 1 showing ill-humor by morose withdrawal 2 gloomy

sul'ly v. **-lied** soil, stain, defile, etc.

sul'tan n. Muslim ruler

sum n. 1 amount of money 2 summary 3 total

su'mac, su'mach (shoo'- soo'-) n. plant with lance-shaped leaves and red fruit

sum'ma·rize' v. make or be a summary of

sum'ma·ry n., pl. **-ries** brief report; digest —a. 1 concise 2 prompt —**sum·mar'i·ly** adv.

sum'mer n. warmest season of the year —a. of or for summer

sum'mit n. highest point

sum'mon v. 1 call together 2 send for 3 rouse

sum'mons n. official order to appear in court

sun n. 1 incandescent body about which (the) planets revolve 2 heat or light of the sun

sun'beam' n. beam of sunlight

sun'dae n. ice cream covered with syrup, nuts, etc.

Sun'day first day of the week

sun'down' n. sunset

sun'dry a. various

sun'flow'er n. tall plant with big, daisylike flowers

sun'glass·es n.pl. eyeglasses with tinted lenses

sunk'en a. 1 sunk in liquid 2 depressed; hollow

sun'light' n. light of the sun

sun'lit' a. lighted by the sun

sun'ny a. **-ni·er, -ni·est** 1 full of sunshine 2 cheerful

sun'rise' n. daily rising of the sun in the east

sun'set' n. daily setting of the sun in the west

sun'shine' n. 1 shining of the

sun 2 light from the sun

sun'stroke' *n.* illness from over-exposure to the sun

sun'tan' *n.* skin darkened by exposure to the sun

sup *v.* **supped** had supper

su'per *a.* [Col.] outstanding

su·perb' *a.* excellent

su·per·fi'cial (-fish'əl) *a.* 1 of or on the surface 2 shallow; hasty —**su'per·fi'cial·ly** *adv.*

su'per·hu'man *a.* 1 divine 2 greater than normal

su'per·in·tend' *v.* direct or manage —**su'per·in·tend'ent** *n.*

su·pe'ri·or *a.* 1 higher in rank, etc. 2 above average 3 haughty —*n.* one that is superior

su·per'la·tive *a.* of the highest degree; supreme —*n.* 1 highest degree 2 third degree in the comparison of adjectives and adverbs

su'per·mar'ket *n.* large, self-service food store

su'per·nat'u·ral *a.* beyond known laws of nature

su'per·script' *n.* figure, letter, etc. written above and to the side of another

su'per·star' *n.* famous athlete, entertainer, etc.

su'per·sti'tion *n.* belief or practice based on fear or ignorance —**su'per·sti'tious** *a.*

su'per·tank'er *n.* extremely large oil tanker

su'per·vise' *v.* oversee or direct —**su'per·vi'sion** *n.* —**su'per·vi'sor** *n.* —**su'per·vi'so·ry** *a.*

sup'per *n.* evening meal

sup'ple *a.* flexible

sup'ple·ment *n.* something added —*v.* add to

sup'pli·cate' *v.* implore

sup·ply' *v.* **-plied'** 1 furnish; provide 2 make up for —*n.*, *pl.* **-plies'** 1 amount available 2 *pl.* materials —**sup·pli'er** *n.*

sup·port' *v.* 1 hold up 2 help 3 provide for 4 help prove —*n.* 1 a supporting 2 that which supports

sup·pose' *v.* 1 take as true; assume 2 guess; think 3 expect

sup·press' *v.* 1 put down by force 2 keep back; conceal

su·preme' *a.* highest in rank, power, or degree

sure *a.* 1 reliable; certain 2 without doubt 3 bound to happen or do —*adv.* [Col.] surely

sure'-foot'ed *a.* not likely to stumble, err, etc.

sure'ly *adv.* 1 with confidence 2 without doubt

surf *n.* ocean waves breaking on a shore or reef

sur'face *n.* 1 outside of a thing 2 any face of a solid 3 outward look —*a.* superficial

surge *v.*, *n.* (move in) a large wave or sudden rush

sur'geon *n.* doctor who practices surgery

sur'ger·y *n.* 1 treatment of disease or injury by operations 2 a room for this —**sur'gi·cal** *a.*

sur·mount' *v.* 1 to overcome 2 climb over 3 top

sur'name' *n.* family name

sur·pass' *v.* 1 excel 2 go beyond the limit of

sur'plus' *n.*, *a.* (quantity) over what is needed or used

sur·prise' *v.* 1 come upon unexpectedly 2 astonish —*n.* 1 a surprising or being surprised 2 thing that surprises

sur·ren'der *v.* 1 give oneself up 2 give up; abandon —*n.* act of surrendering

sur'ro·gate (-gət) *n.*, *a.* (a) substitute

sur·round' *v.* encircle on all sides

sur'tax' *n.* extra tax on top of the regular tax

sur·veil'lance (-vā'-) *n.* watch kept over a person

sur·vey' (*n.:* sur'vā') *v.* 1 examine in detail 2 determine the form, boundaries, etc. of a piece of land —*n.* 1 general or comprehensive study 2 act of surveying an area —**sur·vey'or** *n.*

sur·vive' *v.* 1 outlive 2 continue to live —**sur·vi'vor** *n.*

su'shi *n.* Japanese dish of rice cakes, raw fish, etc.

sus·pect' *v.* (*n.:* sus'pekt') *v.* 1 believe to be guilty on little evidence 2 distrust 3 surmise —*n.* one suspected

sus·pend' *v.* 1 exclude, stop, etc. for a time 2 hold back (judgment, etc.) 3 hang —**sus·pen'sion** *n.*

sus·pend'ers *n.pl.* shoulder straps to hold up trousers

sus·pense' *n.* tense uncertainty

sus·pi'cion *n.* 1 a suspecting or being suspected 2 feeling of one who suspects 3 trace —**sus·pi'cious** *a.*

sus·tain' *v.* 1 maintain; prolong 2 provide for 3 support 4 suffer 5 uphold as valid 6 confirm

swab *n.* 1 a mop 2 piece of cotton, etc. used to medicate or clean the throat, etc.

swag'ger *v.* 1 walk with a bold

stride 2 brag loudly

swal'low v. 1 pass (food, etc.) from the mouth into the stomach 2 take in; absorb 3 tolerate 4 suppress —n. 1 act of swallowing 2 amount swallowed 3 small, swift-flying bird

swamp n. piece of wet, spongy ground —v. 1 flood with water 2 overwhelm

swan n. large water bird with a long graceful neck

swap n., v. **swapped** [Col.] trade

swarm n. 1 colony of bees 2 large, moving mass of insects, etc. —v. move in a swarm

swat v., n. **swat'ted** (hit with) a quick, sharp blow —**swat'ter** n.

sway v. 1 swing from side to side or to and fro 2 incline 3 influence

swear v. **swore, sworn** 1 make a solemn declaration or promise 2 curse 3 make take an oath

sweat n. 1 salty liquid given off through the skin 2 moisture collected on a surface —v. **sweat** or **sweat'ed** 1 give forth sweat 2 work so hard as to cause sweating

sweat'er n. knitted garment for the upper body

sweep v. **swept** 1 clean, or clear away, with a broom 2 carry away or pass over swiftly 3 extend in a long line —n. 1 a sweeping 2 range or extent

sweet a. 1 tasting of sugar 2 pleasant 3 fresh —n. a candy

sweet'en·er n. sugar substitute

sweet'heart n. loved one

sweet potato n. thick, yellow root of a tropical vine

swell v. **swelled, swelled** or **swol'len** 1 bulge 2 increase in size, force, etc. 3 fill, as with pride —n. 1 a swelling 2 large wave —a. [Sl.] excellent

swerve v. n. (make) a quick turn aside

swift a. 1 moving fast 2 prompt —n. swallowlike bird

swim v. **swam, swum** 1 move in water by moving the limbs, fins, etc. 2 float on a liquid 3 overflow 4 be dizzy —n. a swimming —**swim'mer** n.

swin'dle v. defraud; cheat —n. a swindling

swine n., pl. **swine** pig or hog

swing v. **swung** 1 sway back and forth 2 turn, as on a hinge 3 manage to get, win, etc. 4 to strike (at) —n. 1 a swinging or a sweeping blow 3 musical

rhythm 4 seat hanging from ropes

swirl v., n. whirl; twist

swish v., n. (move with) a hissing or rustling sound

Swiss (cheese) n. pale-yellow cheese with large holes

switch n. 1 thin stick used for whipping 2 control device for an electric circuit 3 movable section of railroad track 4 shift; change —v. 1 to whip 2 jerk 3 turn a light, etc. on or off 4 move a train to another track 5 shift

swiv'el n. fastening with free-turning parts —v. turn as on a swivel

swoop v. sweep down or pounce upon —n. a swooping

sword (sôrd) n. weapon with a handle and a long blade

syc'a·more (sik'-) n. shade tree with shedding bark

syl'la·ble n. 1 vocal sound with one main vowel 2 written form of this

sym'bol n. object, mark, etc. that represents another object, an idea, etc. —**sym'bol·ize'** v.

sym'me·try n. balance of opposite parts in position or size —**sym·met'ri·cal** a.

sym·pa·thet'ic a. of, in, or feeling sympathy

sym'pa·thy n., pl. **-thies** 1 sameness of feeling 2 agreement 3 compassion

sym·pho·ny n., pl. **-nies** full orchestra or composition for it

symp'tom n. indication or sign, as of disease

syn'a·gogue' ('-gäg') n. building where Jews worship

syn'chro·nize' v. 1 move or occur at the same time or rate 2 make agree in time or rate

syn'o·nym (-nim) n. word meaning the same as another

syn·the·sis n., pl. **-ses'** (-sēz') combining of parts into a whole

syn·thet'ic a. 1 of or using synthesis 2 artificial; not natural

syph'i·lis (sif'-) n. infectious venereal disease

sy·ringe' n. ball with a tube, for ejecting fluids

syr'up n. sweet, thick liquid, as of sugar boiled in water —**syr'up·y** a.

sys'tem n. 1 whole formed of related things set of organized facts, rules, etc. 3 orderly way of doing things

sys·tem·at'ic a. orderly; methodi-

tab 159 **taps**

T

tab *n.* small flap or tag

tab·er·na·cle (-nak'əl) *n.* large place of worship

ta'ble *n.* 1 flat surface set on legs 2 table set with food 3 orderly list or arrangement

ta'ble·spoon' *n.* spoon holding ½ fluid ounce —**ta'ble·spoon'ful** *n., pl.* **-fuls**

tab'let *n.* 1 flat, inscribed piece of stone, metal, etc. 2 writing pad 3 flat, hard cake of medicine

ta·boo' *n.* sacred or social prohibition —*v.* prohibit

tac'it (tas'-) *a.* not expressed openly, but implied

tack *n.* 1 short, flat-headed nail 2 a course of action 3 ship's direction relative to position of sails —*v.* 1 fasten with tacks 2 add 3 change course

tack'le *n.* 1 equipment 2 set of ropes and pulleys 3 a tackling —*v.* 1 undertake 2 *Football* bring down (the ball carrier)

tack'y *a.* **-i·er, -i·est** 1 slightly sticky [Col.] in poor taste

ta'co *n., pl.* **-cos** folded, fried tortilla, filled with meat, etc.

tact *n.* skill in dealing with people —**tact'ful** *a.* —**tact'less** *a.*

tac'tics *n.* science of battle maneuvers —**tac'ti·cal** *a.*

tad'pole' *n.* frog or toad in an early stage

taf'fy *n.* a chewy candy

tag *n.* 1 hanging end 2 card, etc. attached as a label 3 children's chasing game —*v.* 1 provide with a tag 2 touch as in game of tag 3 [Col.] follow closely: with *along, after,* etc.

tail *n.* 1 appendage at rear end of an animal's body 2 hind or end part

tai'lor *n.* one who makes or alters clothes —*v.* 1 make by a tailor's work 2 form, alter, etc. to suit

taint *v.* 1 spoil; rot 2 make corrupt or depraved

take *v.* **took, tak'en** 1 grasp 2 capture, seize, win, etc. 3 obtain, select, assume, etc. 4 use, consume, etc. 5 buy; rent 6 travel by 7 deal with 8 occupy 9 derive from 10 write down 11 make (a photograph) 12 require 13 engage in 14 understand 15 have or feel 16 carry, lead, etc. 17 remove 18 sub-

tract —*n.* amount taken —**take after** act or look like —**take in** 1 admit; receive 2 make smaller 3 understand 4 trick —**take over** begin managing

tale *n.* 1 story 2 lie 3 gossip

tal'ent *n.* special, natural ability

talk *v.* 1 say words; speak 2 gossip 3 confer 4 discuss —*n.* 1 a talking 2 conversation 3 speech 4 conference 5 gossip

tall *a.* high, as in stature

tal'low *n.* hard animal fat used in candles and soap

tal'ly *n., pl.* **-lies** record, account, etc. —*v.* 1 record; score 2 add 3 agree

Tal·mud (täl'mood) body of early Jewish law

tal'on *n.* claw of a bird of prey

ta·ma'le *n.* peppery chopped meat rolled in corn meal

tame *a.* 1 trained from a wild state 2 gentle 3 not lively; dull

tamp *v.* pack down by tapping

tam'per *v.* interfere (*with*)

tan *n.* yellowish brown —*a.* **tan'ner, tan'nest** yellowish-brown —*v.* **tanned** 1 make (hide) into leather by soaking in tannic acid 2 brown by sun's rays

tan'gent *a.* touching a curve at one point —*n.* a tangent curve, line, etc. —**go off at** (or **on**) **a tangent** change suddenly to another line of action

tan'ge·rine' *n.* small, loose-skinned orange

tan'gi·ble *a.* 1 real or solid 2 definite

tan'gle *v.* 1 make or become knotted, confused, etc. 2 catch, as in a snare —*n.* tangled mass or condition

tank *n.* 1 large container for liquid or gas 2 armored vehicle carrying guns

tank'er *n.* ship for transporting liquids, esp. oil

tan'trum *n.* fit of rage

tap *v.* **tapped** 1 hit lightly 2 make a hole in 3 draw off, as liquid 4 connect into —*n.* 1 light blow 2 faucet or spigot 3 plug or cork 4 place for connection

tape *n.* narrow strip of cloth, paper, etc. —*v.* 1 to bind with a tape 2 record on tape

ta'per *v.* decrease or lessen gradually in thickness, loudness, etc.

tap'es·try *n., pl.* **-tries** cloth with woven designs

taps *n.* bugle call for funerals and

the end of the day

tar *n.* 1 black liquid distilled from wood or coal 2 [Col.] sailor —*v.* tarred cover with tar

ta·ran'tu·la (-chə lə) *n.* large, hairy spider

tar'dy *a.* **-di·er, -di·est** 1 slow 2 late

tar'get *n.* thing aimed at, shot at, or attacked

tar'iff *n.* 1 tax on exports or imports 2 list of prices, charges, etc.

tar'nish *v.* stain; discolor —*n.* dullness; stain

tart *a.* 1 sour; acid 2 sharp in meaning —*n.* pastry filled with jam, etc. —**tart'ly** *adv.*

tar'tar *n.* hard deposit forming on the teeth

task *n.* work that must be done

tas'sel *n.* 1 bunch of threads hanging from a knob 2 tuft of corn silk

taste *v.* 1 notice or test the flavor of in one's mouth 2 eat or drink sparingly 3 have a certain flavor —*n.* 1 sense for telling flavor 2 flavor 3 small amount 4 sense of the beautiful, proper, etc. 5 liking —**taste'ful** *a.*

tat'ter *n.* 1 rag; shred 2 *pl.* ragged clothes —**tat'tered** *a.*

tat'tle *v.* 1 tell secrets 2 gossip

tat·too' *v.* **-tooed'** make designs on the skin —*n.*, *pl.* **-toos'** 1 tattooed design 2 steady beating, as on a drum

taunt *v.* mock; tease

taut *a.* 1 tightly stretched 2 tense

tav'ern *n.* saloon or inn

taw'ny *a.* **-ni·er, -ni·est** dark yellow or tan

tax *n.* 1 compulsory payment to a government 2 burden; strain —*v.* 1 levy, or make pay, a tax 2 burden 3 accuse; charge —**tax·a'tion** *n.* —**tax'pay·er** *n.*

tax'i *n.*, *pl.* **-is** taxicab —*v.* **-ied** 1 go in a taxicab 2 move along the ground or water, as an airplane

tax'i·cab' *n.* automobile for passengers who pay

tea *n.* 1 leaves of an Asian shrub 2 drink made from these 3 similar drink made from other plants, etc. 4 afternoon party with tea —**tea'cup'** *n.*

teach *v.* **taught** give lessons (in)

team *n.* 1 two or more animals harnessed together 2 group working or playing together

tear (ter) *v.* **tore, torn** 1 pull apart, up, etc. by force 2 make by tearing 3 move fast —*n.* 1 a tearing 2 torn place

tear (tir) *n.* drop of liquid from the eye: also **tear'drop'** —**tear'ful, tear'y** *a.*

tease *v.* 1 annoy by poking fun at, etc. 2 fluff up, as hair

tea'spoon' *n.* small spoon —**tea'spoon·ful'** *n.*, *pl.* **-fuls'**

teat *n.* nipple on a breast or udder

tech'ni·cal *a.* 1 dealing with industrial arts or skills 2 of a specific art, science, etc. 3 of technique

tech·ni'cian (-nish'ən) *n.* one skilled in a technique or in a technical area

tech·nique' (-nēk') *n.* method of procedure, as in art

tech·nol'o·gy *n.* study of applied arts and sciences

te'di·ous *a.* tiring; boring

tee *Golf n.* 1 small peg to rest the ball on 2 starting place for each hole —*v.* **teed** hit a ball from a tee: with *off*

teem *v.* abound; swarm

teen *n.* 1 *pl.* numbers or years from 13 through 19 2 teenager —*a.* teenage

teen'age' *a.* 1 in one's teens 2 of or for those in their teens —**teen'ag·er** *n.*

tel'e·cast' *v.* **-cast'** or **-cast'ed**; *n.* broadcast over television

tel'e·gram' *n.* message sent by telegraph

tel'e·graph' *n.* device or system for sending messages by electric signals through a wire

te·lep'a·thy *n.* supposed communication without help of speech, sight, etc.

tel'e·phone' *n.* device or system for talking over distances through wires

tel'e·scope' *n.* device with lenses that magnify distant objects

tel'e·vise' *v.* transmit by television

tel'e·vi'sion *n.* 1 way of sending pictures through space by radio waves to a receiving set 2 such a set

tell *v.* **told** 1 report; narrate 2 put into words 3 show 4 inform 5 recognize 6 order

tem'per *v.* 1 make less intense 2 make hard, as steel —*n.* 1 state of mind 2 self-control 3 rage 4 tendency to become angry

tem'per·a *n.* painting with pigments mixed with egg, etc.

tem′per·a·ment (-prə mənt, -pər mənt) *n.* (moody or excitable) disposition

tem′per·ate *a.* 1 moderate; self-restrained 2 neither very hot nor very cold

tem′per·a·ture (-prə chər) *n.* 1 degree of hotness or coldness 2 fever

tem′pest *n.* wild storm

tem′ple *n.* 1 a building for worship service or for some special purpose 2 area between the eye and ear

tem′po *n., pl.* **-pos** or **-pi** (-pē) rate of speed, esp. for playing music

tem′po·ral *a.* 1 worldly 2 of time

tem′po·rar′y *a.* lasting only a while —**tem′po·rar′i·ly** *adv.*

tempt *v.* 1 entice, esp. to an immoral act 2 provoke 3 to incline strongly

ten *a., n.* one more than nine — **tenth** *a., n.*

ten′ant *n.* occupant (who pays rent) —**ten′an·cy** *n.*

tend *v.* 1 take care of 2 be apt; incline 3 lead

tend′en·cy *n., pl.* **-cies** a being likely to move or act in a certain way

ten′e·ment *n.* apartment house, esp. an old one

ten′et *n.* opinion or belief

ten′nis *n.* game played by hitting a ball over a net with a racket

ten′or *n.* 1 highest male voice 2 general course 3 meaning

tense *a.* 1 taut 2 anxious —*v.* make or become tense —*n.* verb form showing time

ten′sion *n.* 1 a stretching 2 stress from this 3 nervous strain 4 voltage

tent *n.* shelter of canvas, nylon, etc. supported by poles and stakes

ten′ta·cle *n.* slender growth on an animal's head, for feeling, grasping, etc.

ten′ure (-yər) *n.* right or duration of holding a position, etc.

te′pee *n.* cone-shaped tent

tep′id *a.* lukewarm

term *n.* 1 fixed time period 2 *pl.* conditions of a contract, etc. 3 *pl.* personal relationship 4 word or phrase 5 either part of a fraction, etc. —*v.* name

ter′mi·nal *a.* 1 of or at the end 2 final —*n.* 1 end (part) 2 main station, as for buses 3 keyboard

and video screen connected to a computer

ter′mi·nate′ *v.* 1 stop; end 2 form the end of

ter′mite′ *n.* antlike insect that eats wood

ter′race *n.* 1 patio 2 flat mound with sloping side 3 row of houses on this

ter·rar′i·um (-rer′-) *n., pl.* **-i·ums** or **-i·a** glass enclosure for small plants, etc.

ter′ri·ble *a.* 1 causing terror 2 extreme 3 [Col.] very bad

ter′ri·er *n.* breed of small, lively dog

ter·rif′ic *a.* 1 terrifying 2 [Col.] very great, etc.

ter′ri·fy′ *v.* **-fied′** fill with terror

ter′ri·to′ry *n., pl.* **-ries** 1 land ruled by a nation 2 national region not yet a State 3 region —**ter′ri·to′ri·al** *a.*

ter′ror *n.* great fear, or cause of this

ter′ror·ism′ *n.* use of force and threats to intimidate —**ter′ror·ist** *n., a.*

terse *a.* concise; to the point

test *n.* examination or trial to determine a thing's value, a person's knowledge, etc. —*v.* subject to a test

tes′ti·fy′ *v.* **-fied′** 1 give evidence in court 2 indicate

teth′er *n.* rope or chain tied to an animal to confine it

text *n.* 1 author's words 2 main part of a printed page 3 textbook 4 Biblical passage 5 topic

tex′tile (-til′, təl) *n.* woven fabric —*a.* 1 of weaving 2 woven

tex′ture *n.* 1 look and feel of a fabric 2 structure

than *con.* compared to

thank *v.* give thanks to —**thank you** I thank you

thank′ful *a.* showing thanks

thank′less *a.* ungrateful or unappreciated

thanks *n.pl.* expression of gratitude —*int.* I thank you

thanks′giv′ing *n.* 1 thanks to God 2 [T-] U.S. holiday: fourth Thursday in November

that *pron., pl.* **those** 1 the one mentioned 2 the farther one or other one 3 who, whom, or which 4 when —*a., pl.* **those** being that one —*con. That* is used to introduce certain dependent clauses —*adv.* to that extent —**that is** 1 to be specific 2 in other words

thatch *v., n.* (cover with) a roof of straw, etc.

thaw v. melt or become so warm that ice melts

the a., *definite article* that of this one in particular or of a certain kind —adv. that much or by that much

the·a·ter, the·a·tre n. 1 place where plays, movies, etc. are shown 2 scene of events 3 dramatic art —**the·at′ri·cal** a.

theft n. act of stealing

their a. of them

theirs pron. that or those belonging to them

them pron. objective case of THEY

theme n. 1 topic 2 short essay 3 main melody

them·selves′ pron. intensive or reflexive form of THEY

then adv. 1 at that time 2 next 3 in that case 4 besides —n. that time

thence adv. from that place

the·ol·o·gy n. study of God and of religious beliefs

the·o·ry n., pl. **-ries** 1 explanation based on scientific study and reasoning 2 principles of an art or science 3 guess, conjecture, etc. —**the·o·rize′** v.

ther·a·py n., pl. **-pies** method of treating disease or disorders

there adv. 1 at, in, or to that place 2 at that point 3 in that respect —n. that place

there·af′ter adv. after that

there′fore′ adv., con. for this or that reason

there·in′ adv. in that place, matter, writing, etc.

there·of′ adv. 1 of that 2 from that as a cause

ther·mom′e·ter n. device for measuring temperature

ther′mo·stat′ n. device for regulating temperature

these pron., a. pl. of THIS

the·sis n., pl. **-ses′** (-sēz′) 1 statement to be defended 2 essay written to obtain an academic degree

they pron. 1 the ones mentioned 2 people

thick a. 1 great in extent from side to side 2 as measured from side to side 3 dense 4 not clear

thief n., pl. **thieves** one who steals

thigh n. the leg between the knee and the hip

thin a. **thin′ner, thin′nest** 1 small in extent from side to side 2 lean; slender 3 sparse 4 watery 5 weak 6 transparent; flimsy

thing n. 1 real object or substance 2 a happening, act, event, etc. 3 matter or affair 4 pl. belongings

think v. **thought** 1 form in or use the mind 2 consider 3 believe 4 remember: with *of* or *about* 5 have an opinion of: with *of* or *about* 6 consider: with *about* 7 conceive (*of*)

third a. preceded by two others —n. 1 third one 2 one of three equal parts

thirst n. 1 need or craving for water 2 strong desire

thir′teen′ a., n. three more than ten —**thir′teenth′** a., n.

thir′ty a., n., pl. **-ties** three times ten —**thir′ti·eth** a., n.

this a., pron., pl. **these** (being) the one mentioned or nearer —adv. to this extent

this′tle (-əl) n. prickly plant

thith′er (thith′-) adv. there

thorn n. short, sharp point on a plant stem —**thorn′y** a.

thor·ough (thur′ō) a. 1 complete 2 very exact

those a., pron. pl. of THAT

thou pron. [Ar.] you (sing. subject of v.)

though (thō) con. 1 although 2 yet 3 even if —adv. however

thought n. 1 act or way of thinking 2 idea, plan, etc.

thought′ful a. 1 full of thought 2 considerate

thought′less a. 1 careless 2 inconsiderate

thou′sand a., n. ten hundred —**thou′sandth** a., n.

thrash v. 1 thresh 2 beat 3 toss about violently

thread n. 1 fine cord of spun cotton, silk, etc. 2 spiral ridge of a screw, etc. —v. 1 put a thread through (a needle) 2 make one's way

threat n. 1 warning of plan to harm 2 sign of danger

threat′en v. make or be a threat

three a., n. one more than two

thresh v. beat out (grain) from its husk —**thresh′er** n.

thrice adv. three times

thrift n. careful managing of money, etc. —**thrift′i·ly** adv. —**thrift′y** a., **-i·er, -i·est**

thrill v., n. (feel or make feel) great excitement

thrive v. **throve** or **thrived, thrived** or **thriv′en** 1 be successful 2 grow luxuriantly

throat n. 1 front of the neck 2

upper passage from mouth to stomach or lungs

throb v. **throbbed** beat or vibrate strongly —n. a throbbing

throne n. 1 official chair, as of a king 2 his power

throng n., v. crowd

through (thrōō) prep. 1 from end to end of 2 by way of 3 to places in 4 throughout 5 by means of 6 because of —adv. 1 in and out of 2 all the way 3 entirely —a. 1 open; free 2 to the end without stops 3 finished

through-out' adv., prep. in every part (of)

throw v. **threw, thrown** 1 send through the air from the hand 2 make fall 3 put suddenly 4 move, as a switch 5 direct, cast, etc. —n. 1 a throwing 2 distance thrown

thrush n. any of a large group of songbirds

thrust v. **thrust** push with sudden force —n. 1 sudden push 2 stab 3 forward force

thumb n. short, thick finger nearest the wrist

thun'der n. loud noise after lightning —v. 1 cause thunder 2 shout loudly

Thurs'day n. fifth day of the week

thus adv. 1 in this way 2 to this or that degree 3 therefore

tick n. 1 light clicking sound 2 blood-sucking insect —v. make a ticking sound

tick'et n. 1 printed card entitling one to a theater seat, etc. 2 tag, label, etc. 3 list of a party's candidates —v. put a ticket on

tick'le v. 1 stroke lightly and make twitch or laugh 2 feel tickled 3 amuse; delight

tid'al a. of, having, or caused by a tide

tide n. 1 rise and fall of the ocean twice a day 2 trend

tide'wa'ter n. 1 water affected by tide 2 seaboard

ti'dings n.pl. news

ti'dy a. **-di-er, -di-est** 1 neat; orderly 2 [Col.] quite large

tie v. **tied** 1 fasten with string, rope, etc. 2 make (a knot) 3 bind in any way 4 to equal, as in a score —n. 1 thing that ties or joins 2 necktie 3 contest with equal scores

tier (tir) n. any of a series of rows, one above another

ti'ger n. large, striped jungle cat

tight a. 1 made to keep water, air, etc. out or in 2 fitting closely or too closely 3 taut 4 difficult 5 [Col.] stingy —adv. closely —**tight'en** v.

tights n.pl. tight garment from the waist to the feet

tile n. thin piece of baked clay, stone, plastic, etc. for roofing, flooring, etc.

till prep., con. until —v. cultivate land for crops —n. drawer for money

till'er n. bar or handle to turn a boat's rudder

tilt v., n. 1 slope; tip 2 joust

tim'ber n. 1 wood for building houses, etc. 2 wooden beam 3 trees

time n. 1 period; duration 2 the right instant, hour, etc. 3 the passing hours, day, etc.; or, system of measuring them 4 an occasion 5 set period of work, or pay for this 6 tempo or rhythm —v. 1 choose a right time for 2 measure the speed of —a. 1 of time 2 set to work at a given time —**at times** sometimes —**in time** 1 eventually 2 before it is too late —**on time** 1 not late 2 by installment payments —**tim'er** n.

time'less a. eternal

time'ly a. **-li-er, -li-est** at the right time

times prep. multiplied by

time'ta'ble n. schedule of arrivals and departures

tim'id a. shy; easily frightened

tim'ing n. regulation of speed, etc. to improve performance

tin n. soft, silvery metal, a chemical element

tinc'ture n. solution of medicine in alcohol —v. tinge

tin'der n. any dry, easily ignited material

tinge n. 1 tint 2 slight trace —v. give a tinge to

tin'gle v. sting slightly; prickle

tin'ker v. 1 mend clumsily 2 to putter

tin'kle n. ring of a small bell —v. make a tinkle

tint n. 1 light color 2 a shading of a color —v. give a tint to

ti'ny a. **-ni-er, -ni-est** very small

tip n. 1 a point or end 2 thing fitted to an end 3 light blow; tap 4 secret information 5 a warning 6 gratuity 7 slant —v. 1 make or put a tip on 2 give a tip 3 overturn 4 slant

tipped 1 make or put a tip on 2 give a tip 3 overturn 4 slant

tip'toe' n. tip of the toes —v.

–toed' walk stealthily on one's toes

tire v. make or become weary, bored, etc. —n. hoop or rubber tube around a wheel

tired a. weary; exhausted

tis'sue n. 1 tissue paper 2 cellular material of organisms 3 thin cloth

tithe (tith) v., n. (pay) a tenth part of one's income

ti'tle n. 1 name of a book, picture, etc. 2 word showing rank or occupation 3 legal right 4 championship —v. name

TNT n. an explosive

to prep. 1 toward 2 as far as 3 on, onto, or against 4 until 5 causing 6 with 7 in each To may indicate an infinitive or a receiver of action —adv. 1 forward 2 shut

toad n. froglike land animal

toast v. 1 brown by heating, as bread 2 warm 3 drink in honor of —n. 1 toasted bread 2 a toasting

to·bac'co n., pl. **-cos** plant with leaves dried for smoking, chewing, etc.

to·bog'gan v., n. (coast on) a flat, runnerless sled

to·day' adv. 1 during this day 2 nowadays —n. this day or time

toe n. any of five end parts of the foot —**toe'nail'** n.

to'fu n. Japanese cheeselike food made from soybeans

to·geth'er adv. 1 in one group or place 2 at the same time 3 so as to meet, agree, etc.

toil v. 1 work hard 2 go with effort —n. hard work

toi'let n. 1 fixture to receive body waste 2 bathroom

to'ken n. 1 sign or symbol 2 keepsake 3 metal disk, as for fare —a. pretended

tol'er·ance n. 1 a tolerating, as of another's ways 2 power to resist a drug's effect 3 deviation allowed —**tol'er·ant** a.

tol'er·ate' v. 1 to put up with; endure 2 permit

toll n. 1 charge on a turnpike, for a long-distance phone call, etc. 2 the number lost, etc. —v. ring with slow, regular strokes, as a bell

tom'a·hawk' n. light ax used by North American Indians

to·ma'to n., pl. **-toes** red, round, juicy vegetable

tomb (tōōm) n. vault or grave for the dead

to·mor'row adv., n. (on) the day after today

ton n. 2,000 pounds

tone n. 1 vocal or musical sound; spec., a full interval of a diatonic scale 2 style, character, feeling, etc. 3 shade or tint 4 healthy condition, as of muscles

tongs n.pl. device for seizing, lifting, etc., made of two long, hinged arms

tongue (tuŋ) n. 1 movable muscle in the mouth, used in eating and speaking 2 act or manner of speaking 3 language 4 tonguelike part

ton'ic n. medicine, etc. that invigorates

to·night' adv., n. (on) this night

too adv. 1 also 2 more than enough 3 very

tool n. 1 instrument, implement, etc. used for some work 2 stooge

toot v., n. (make) a short blast on a horn, etc.

tooth n., pl. **teeth** 1 any of a set of bony structures in the jaws, used for biting and chewing 2 toothlike part, as of a saw, gear, etc. —**tooth'ache'** n. —**tooth'brush'** n.

tooth'paste' n. paste for brushing the teeth

top n. 1 highest point or surface 2 uppermost part or covering 3 highest degree or rank 4 toy that spins round —a. of, at, or being the top —v. topped 1 provide with a top 2 be at the top of 3 surpass; exceed

top'ic n. subject of an essay, speech, etc.

top'most' a. uppermost

top'ple v. (make) fall over

torch n. 1 portable flaming light 2 device that makes a very hot flame, as in welding

tor·ment' (v.: tôr ment') n. great pain —v. make suffer

tor·na'do n., pl. **-does** violent wind with a whirling, funnel-shaped cloud

tor·pe'do n., pl. **-does** large, cigar-shaped, underwater projectile

tor'rent n. swift, violent stream

tor'rid a. very hot

tor'so n., pl. **-sos** human body minus head and limbs

tort n. Law wrongful act, injury, etc.

torte n. rich cake

tor'toise (-təs) n. turtle, esp. one living on land

tor'ture *n.* 1 inflicting of great pain 2 great pain —*v.* 1 subject to torture 2 twist

toss *v.* tossed 1 throw lightly from the hand 2 fling or be flung about 3 jerk upward —*n.* a tossing

to'tal *n.* the whole amount; sum —*a.* 1 entire; whole 2 complete —*v.* add (up to) —**to'tal·ly** *adv.*

to·tal·i·tar'i·an *a.* of a dictatorship

touch *v.* 1 put the hand, etc. on so as to feel 2 bring or come into contact 3 tap lightly 4 handle; use 5 concern 6 arouse pity, etc. in 7 treat in passing: with *on* or *upon* —*n.* 1 a touching 2 way things feel 3 sense of this 4 small bit 5 contact —**in touch** in contact —**touch up** improve by additions

touch'down' *n.* 1 goal scored in football, for six points 2 moment when an aircraft lands

touch'y *a.* -i·er, -i·est 1 irritable 2 difficult

tough *a.* 1 hard to chew, cut, break, etc. 2 strong or rough 3 very difficult —*n.* ruffian

tour *n.* long trip, as to see sights, put on plays, etc. —*v.* go on a tour (through) —**tour'ist** *n., a.*

tour'na·ment *n.* 1 series of contests for a championship 2 knights' jousting contest

tow *v.* pull by a rope or chain

to·ward (tôrd, tword) *prep.* 1 in the direction of 2 concerning 3 near 4 for Also **towards**

tow'el *n.* piece of cloth or paper to wipe things dry

tow'er *n.* high structure, often part of another building

town *n.* 1 small city 2 business center

town'ship *n.* 1 part of a county 2 U.S. land unit 6 miles square

tox'in *n.* poison, esp. from bacteria, viruses, etc.

toy *n.* thing to play with —*a.* small —*v.* play (*with*)

trace *n.* 1 mark or track left 2 small bit 3 harness strap connecting to vehicle —*v.* 1 follow (the trail or course of) 2 draw, outline, etc. —**trac'er** *n.*

track *n.* 1 footprint, wheel rut, etc. 2 path, trail, or course 3 running sports, etc. 4 pair of rails a train runs on —*v.* 1 follow the track of 2 leave footprints on

tract *n.* 1 large stretch of land 2 system of bodily organs 3 book-

let

trac'tor *n.* 1 motor vehicle to pull farm machines, etc. 2 truck to haul a trailer

trade *n.* 1 skilled work 2 buying and selling 3 an exchange —*v.* 1 buy and sell 2 exchange

trade'mark' *n.* special mark or name (**trade name**) put on a product

tra·di'tion *n.* 1 custom, etc. handed down from the past 2 such handing down

traf'fic *n.* 1 vehicles moving along streets, etc. 2 amount of business done 3 TRADE (*n.* 2)

trag'e·dy *n., pl.* -dies 1 serious play with a sad ending 2 tragic event

trail *v.* 1 drag or lag behind 2 follow or drift behind 3 dwindle —*n.* 1 thing trailing behind 2 beaten path

trail'er *n.* wagon or van pulled by a car or truck, sometimes used as a home

train *n.* 1 a thing that drags behind 2 procession 3 connected series 4 locomotive with cars —*v.* 1 guide the development of 2 instruct or prepare 3 aim —**train·ee'** *n.*

trait *n.* characteristic

trai'tor *n.* disloyal person

tramp *v.* 1 walk, or step, heavily 2 roam about —*n.* 1 vagrant 2 a tramping

tram'ple *v.* step hard on or crush underfoot

trance *n.* state of shock, hypnosis, or deep thought

tran'quil *a.* calm; quiet

tran·scend' ('-send') *v.* exceed

tran'script' *n.* written or typewritten copy

trans·fer' (*v.:* also trans fur') *v.* -ferred move or change from one person, place, etc. to another —*n.* 1 a transferring 2 ticket letting one change to another bus, etc.

trans·form' *v.* change the form or condition of —**trans·for·ma'tion** *n.*

trans·form'er *n.* device that changes voltage

tran'si·ent (-shənt, -sē ənt) *a.* temporary

tran·sis'tor *n.* small electronic device that controls current flow

tran'sit *n.* 1 passage across 2 a conveying

tran·si'tion *n.* a passing from one condition, place, etc. to another

tran'si·tive *a.* taking a direct

translate	166	trip

object, as some verbs

trans·late' v. put into another language, form, etc. —**trans·la'tion** n. —**trans·la'tor** n.

trans·lu'cent a. letting light pass through but not transparent

trans·mit' v. -**mit'ted** 1 transfer 2 pass or convey 3 send out radio or TV signals

trans·par'ent a. that can be seen through; clear

trans·plant' (n.: trans'plant') v. 1 dig up and plant in another place 2 to transfer (tissue or organ) from one to another; graft —n. something transplanted

trans·port' v. 1 carry from one place to another 2 carry away with emotion —**trans·por·ta'tion** n.

trans·verse' a. situated, placed, etc. across

trap n. 1 device for catching animals 2 tricky ruse 3 bend in a drainpipe —v. **trapped** 1 catch in a trap 2 set traps for animals —**trap'per** n.

trap'pings n.pl. adornments

trash n. rubbish

trau'ma n. emotional shock with lasting psychic effects

trav'el v. 1 make a journey (through) 2 move or pass —n. 1 a traveling 2 pl. journeys —**trav'el·er** n.

tra·verse' v. to cross

trav'es·ty n., pl. -ties farcical imitation

tray n. flat, low-sided server to carry things

treach'er·ous a. 1 disloyal 2 not safe or reliable

tread v. **trod, trod'den** or **trod** 1 walk on, along, over, etc. 2 trample —n. 1 way or amount of treading 2 part for treading or moving on

trea'son n. betrayal of one's country

treas'ure n. 1 accumulated money, jewels, etc. 2 valued person or thing

treas·ur·y n., pl. -ies 1 place where money is kept 2 funds of a state, corporation, etc.

treat v. 1 deal with or act toward 2 pay for the food, etc. of 3 subject to a process, medical care, etc. —n. 1 food, etc. paid for by another 2 thing giving pleasure —**treat'ment** n.

trea'ty n., pl. -ties agreement between nations

tre'ble a. 1 triple 2 of or for the

treble —n. 1 Mus. highest part 2 high-pitched voice or sound —v. to triple

tree n. large, woody plant with one main trunk and many branches

trel'lis n. lattice on which vines, etc. are grown

trem'ble v. 1 shake from cold, fear, etc. 2 quiver or vibrate

tre·men'dous a. 1 very large 2 [Col.] wonderful

trem'or n. a trembling, shaking, etc.

trench n. ditch, esp. one dug for cover in battle

trend v., n. (have) a general direction or tendency

tres'pass v. 1 enter another's property unlawfully 2 sin —n. a trespassing —**tres'pass·er** n.

tri'al n. 1 hearing and deciding of a case in a law court 2 attempt 3 test 4 pain, trouble, etc.

tri'an·gle n. three-sided figure with three angles —**tri·an'gu·lar** a.

tribe n. 1 group of people living together under a chief 2 group or class —**trib'al** a.

trib·u·tar·y (-ter'-) n., pl. -ies river that flows into a larger one

trib'ute n. 1 forced payment, as by a weak nation to a stronger 2 gift, speech, etc. showing respect

trick n. 1 something done to fool, cheat, etc. 2 prank 3 clever act or skillful way 4 turn at work 5 personal habit 6 cards played in one round —v. fool or cheat —**trick'er·y** n.

trick'le v. 1 flow in drops or a thin stream 2 move slowly —n. slow flow

tri'cy·cle n. three-wheeled vehicle

trig'ger n. lever pressed in firing a gun

trig·o·nom'e·try n. mathematics dealing with relations between sides and angles of triangles

tril'lion n., a. thousand billions —**tril'lionth** a., n.

trim v. **trimmed** 1 clip, lop, etc. 2 decorate 3 put (sails) in order —n. 1 good condition 2 decoration —**trim'mer** n.

trin'ket n. small ornament

tri'o n., pl. -os musical composition for three performers

trip v. **tripped** 1 move with light, rapid steps 2 stumble or make stumble 3 err or cause to err —n. a journey

tri'ple *a.* **1** of or for three **2** three times as much or as many —*n.* Baseball hit putting the batter on third —*v.* to make or become triple

tri'plet *n.* any of three children born at one birth

tri'pod' *n.* three-legged stool, support, etc.

trite *a.* worn-out; stale

tri'umph *n.* victory; success

triv'i-al *a.* unimportant

troll (trōl) *v.* **1** fish with a moving line **2** sing loudly —*n.* Folklore cave-dwelling giant

trol'ley *n.*, *pl.* **-leys 1** overhead device that sends electric current to a streetcar **2** electric streetcar: also **trolley car**

trom'bone' *n.* brass instrument with a sliding tube

troop *n.* **1** group of persons **2** *pl.* soldiers **3** cavalry unit

tro'phy *n.*, *pl.* **-phies** souvenir of victory, etc.

trop'ic *n.* **1** either of two parallels of latitude (**Tropic of Cancer** and **Tropic of Capricorn**) N and S of the equator **2** [also T-] *pl.* hot region between these latitudes —**trop'i-cal** *a.*

trot *v.* **trot'ted** go at a trot —*n.* **1** running gait of a horse **2** slow, jogging run —**trot'ter** *n.*

trou'ble *n.* **1** worry, distress, bother, etc. **2** disturbance **3** difficulty

trough (trôf) *n.* **1** long, narrow, open container, as for feeding animals **2** long, narrow hollow

trou'sers *n.pl.* two-legged outer garment, esp. for men and boys

trout *n.* freshwater food fish related to the salmon

trow'el (trou'-) *n.* **1** flat tool for smoothing **2** scooplike tool for digging

tru'ant *n.* **1** pupil who stays away from school without leave **2** one who shirks his or her duties —**tru'an-cy** *n.*

truce *n.* cessation of fighting by mutual agreement

truck *n.* **1** large motor vehicle for carrying loads **2** wheeled frame **3** vegetables raised for market **4** [Col.] dealings

trudge *v.* walk wearily

true *a.* **1** loyal **2** not false **3** accurate **4** real; genuine —*adv.* exactly —*n.* that which is true —**tru'ly** *adv.*

trump *n.* (playing card of) a suit ranked highest

trum'pet *n.* brass instrument

with a flared end

trunk *n.* **1** main stem of a tree **2** body, not including the head and limbs **3** long snout of an elephant **4** large box for clothes, etc. **5** main line **6** *pl.* very short pants worn for sports

truss *v.* tie, fasten, or tighten

trust *n.* **1** belief in the honesty, reliability, etc. of another **2** one trusted **3** responsibility **4** custody **5** CREDIT (*n.* **4**) **6** property managed for another **7** a monopolistic group of corporations —*v.* **1** have trust in **2** put in the care of **3** believe **4** hope **5** let buy on credit —**trust'ful** *a.* —**trust'wor'thy** *a.*

trust-ee' *n.* **1** one put in charge of another's property **2** member of a controlling board

truth *n.* **1** a being true, honest, etc. **2** that which is true **3** established fact —**truth'ful** *a.*

try *v.* **tried 1** conduct the trial of **2** test **3** afflict **4** attempt —*n.*, *pl.* **tries** attempt; effort

tub *n.* **1** large, open container **2** bathtub

tu'ba *n.* large, deep-toned brass instrument

tube *n.* **1** slender pipe for fluids **2** tubelike, sealed container **3** electron tube —**tu'bu-lar** *a.*

tu-ber-cu-lo'sis *n.* wasting disease, esp. of the lungs

tuck *v.* **1** gather up in folds **2** push the edges of something under **3** cover snugly **4** press into a small space —*n.* sewn fold

Tues'day *n.* third day of the week

tuft *n.* bunch of hairs, grass, etc. growing or tied together

tug *v.* **tugged** pull; drag —*n.* **1** hard pull **2** tugboat

tug'boat' *n.* small boat for towing or pushing ships

tu-i'tion (-ish'ən) *n.* charge for instruction

tu'lip *n.* bulb plant with cup-shaped flower

tum'ble *v.* **1** fall or move suddenly or clumsily **2** toss about **3** do acrobatics —*n.* a fall

tu'mor *n.* abnormal growth in or on the body

tu'na (**fish**) *n.* large ocean fish with oily flesh

tune *n.* **1** melody **2** *Mus.* right pitch **3** agreement —*v.* **1** put in TUNE (*n.* **2**) **2** adjust to proper performance

tu'nic *n.* **1** loose gown worn in ancient Greece and Rome **2**

long, belted blouse

tun'nel n. underground passageway —v. make a tunnel

tur'ban n. scarf wound round the head, as in the Middle East

tur'bine (-bin, -bin') n. engine driven by the pressure of air, steam, or water on the vanes of a wheel

turf n. top layer of earth with grass

tur'key n. 1 large bird with a spreading tail 2 its flesh, used as food

tur'moil' n. noisy, excited condition

turn v. 1 revolve or rotate 2 change in position or direction 3 make or perform 4 reverse 5 change in feelings, etc. 6 change in form, etc. 7 drive, set, etc. 8 to wrench or twist 9 divert; deflect 10 upset 11 depend 12 reach or pass 13 become 14 become sour —n. 1 a turning around 2 change in position or direction 3 short walk, ride, etc. 4 bend; twist 5 chance; try 6 deed 7 turning point 8 style; form 9 sudden shock —**in** (or **out of**) **turn** in (or not in) proper order —**turn off** 1 shut off 2 [Sl.] cause to be bored, etc. —**turn on** 1 make go on 2 [Sl.] make or become elated, etc. —**turn out** 1 shut off 2 come 3 make 4 result —**turn to** rely on

tur'nip n. plant with an edible, round root

turn'pike' n. highway, esp. one on which a toll is paid

tur'pen·tine' n. oil from trees, used in paints, etc.

tur'quoise' (-kwoiz', -koiz') n. greenish-blue gem

tur'ret n. 1 small tower on a building 2 armored dome, as on a tank

tur'tle n. hard-shelled land and water reptile

tusk n. long, projecting tooth, as of an elephant

tus'sle n., v. struggle

tu'tor n. private teacher —v. teach —**tu·to'ri·al** (-tôr'ē-) a.

tux·e'do n., pl. **-dos** man's semi-formal suit

TV n. 1 television 2 pl. **TVs** or **TV's** television set

'twas [Poet.] it was

tweed n. 1 rough wool fabric 2 pl. clothes of tweed

tweez'ers n.pl. small pincers for plucking hairs

twelve a., n. two more than ten

—**twelfth** a., n.

twen'ty a., n., pl. **-ties** two times ten —**twen'ti·eth** a., n.

twice adv. 1 two times 2 two times as much

twig n. small branch

twi'light' n. 1 dim light after sunset 2 gradual decline

twin n. 1 either of two born at the same birth 2 either of two very much alike

twine n. strong cord made of twisted strands —v. 1 interweave 2 wind around

twin'kle v. 1 sparkle 2 light up —n. a sparkle; twinkling

twirl v., n. spin; twist

twist v. 1 to wind together or around something 2 force out of shape 3 pervert meaning of 4 sprain 5 rotate 6 curve —n. 1 something twisted 2 a twisting

twitch v. pull or move with a sudden jerk —n. sudden, spasmodic motion

two a., n. one more than one —**in two** in two parts

two'fold' a. 1 having two parts 2 having twice as much or as many —adv. twice as much or as many

type n. 1 kind or sort 2 model; example 3 metal piece or pieces for printing 4 printed letters, etc. —v. 1 classify 2 use a typewriter

type'writ'er n. a keyboard machine for making printed letters on paper

ty·phoon' n. cyclonic storm, esp. in the W Pacific

typ'i·cal (tip'-) a. 1 being a true example of its kind 2 characteristic —**typ'i·cal·ly** adv.

typ'ist n. one who operates a typewriter

ty·ran'no·saur' n. huge, two-footed dinosaur

tyr·an'ny (tir'-) n. 1 government of a tyrant 2 cruel and unjust use of power —**ty·ran'ni·cal** a. —**tyr'an·nize'** v.

ty'rant (tī'-) n. 1 absolute ruler 2 cruel, unjust ruler

U

ud'der n. large, milk-secreting gland of cows, etc.

UFO n., pl. **UFOs** or **UFO's** unidentified flying object

ug'ly a. **-li·er, -li·est** 1 unpleasant to see 2 bad 3 dangerous

u·ku·le·le (yōō'kə lā'lē) n. small, four-stringed guitar

ul'cer n. open sore, as on the skin —**ul'cer·ous** a.

ul'ti·mate a. 1 farthest 2 final 3 basic —n. final point or result —**ul'ti·mate·ly** adv.

um·brel'la n. cloth screen on a folding frame, carried for protection against rain

um'pire n. 1 one who judges a dispute 2 an official in certain sports —v. act as umpire

un·a·bridged' a. not abridged; complete

un·ac·cus'tomed a. 1 not accustomed (to) 2 unusual

u·nan'i·mous a. without dissent —**u'na·nim'i·ty** n.

un·armed' a. having no weapon

un·a·ware' a. not aware —adv. unawares

un·a·wares' adv. 1 unintentionally 2 by surprise

un·be·com'ing a. 1 not suited 2 not proper

un·bend' v. -bent' or -bend'ed 1 relax 2 straighten

un·bend'ing a. 1 rigid; stiff 2 firm; unyielding

un·bound'ed a. not restrained

un·bri'dled a. 1 with no bridle on 2 uncontrolled

un·bur'den v. relieve by disclosing (guilt, etc.)

un·called'-for' a. unnecessary and out of place

un'cle n. 1 brother of one's father or mother 2 husband of one's aunt

un'con·cern' n. lack of interest or worry; indifference

un'con·di'tion·al a. without conditions or limits

un·con'scious a. 1 not conscious 2 not aware (of) 3 unintentional

un·couth' (-kōōth') a. rude; crude

un·cut' a. 1 not shaped: said of a gem 2 not abridged

un·daunt'ed a. not hesitating because of fear

un'der prep. 1 lower than; below; beneath 2 covered by 3 less than 4 below and across 5 subject to 6 undergoing —adv. 1 in or to a lower position 2 so as to be covered —a. lower

un'der·a·chieve' v. fail to do as well as expected

un'der·age' a. below the legal age

un'der·brush' n. small trees, bushes, etc. in a forest

un'der·cov'er a. secret

un'der·cur'rent n. underlying tendency, opinion, etc.

un'der·dog' n. one that is expected to lose

un'der·foot' adv., a. 1 under feet 2 in the way

un'der·gar'ment n. piece of underwear

un'der·go' v. -went', -gone' experience; endure

un'der·grad'u·ate n. college student who does not yet have a degree

un'der·ground' a., adv. 1 beneath the earth's surface 2 secret 3 unconventional, radical, etc.

un'der·hand' a. 1 with the hand held below the elbow 2 underhanded; sly —adv. 1 with an underhand motion 2 in an underhanded way

un'der·hand'ed a. sly, deceitful, etc.

un'der·lie' v. 1 lie beneath 2 to support

un'der·line' v. 1 to draw a line under 2 to stress

un'der·mine' v. 1 dig beneath 2 weaken gradually

un'der·neath' adv., prep. under; below

un'der·pants' n.pl. undergarment of short pants

un'der·priv'i·leged a. needy; poor

un'der·score' v. underline

un'der·sell' v. sell for less than

un'der·shirt' n. undergarment worn under a shirt

un'der·stand' v. -stood' 1 get the meaning (of) 2 take as a fact 3 know or perceive the nature, etc. of 4 sympathize with —**un'der·stand'a·ble** a.

un'der·stand'ing n. 1 comprehension 2 intelligence 3 mutual agreement

un'der·state' v. say with little or no emphasis

un'der·take' v. -took', -tak'en 1 begin (a task, etc.) 2 promise

un'der·tak'er n. funeral director

un'der·tone' n. subdued tone

un'der·wa'ter a., adv. beneath the surface of the water

un'der·wear' n. clothes worn next to the skin

un'der·write' v. -wrote', -writ'ten 1 agree to finance 2 write insurance for

un·do' v. -did', -done' 1 open, untie, etc. 2 cancel or destroy

un·doubt'ed a. certain

un·dress' v. take the clothes off

un·due' a. more than is proper

un·earth' v. 1 dig up from the

earth 2 find

un·earth'ly a. 1 supernatural 2 weird

un·eas'y a. **-i·er, -i·est** uncomfortable —**un·eas'i·ness** n.

un·ex·pect'ed a. not expected; sudden —**un·ex·pect'ed·ly** adv.

un·fa·mil'iar a. 1 not well-known 2 not acquainted (with)

un·fin'ished a. 1 incomplete 2 not painted, etc.

un·fold' v. 1 spread out 2 make or become known

un·furl' v. unfold

un·hap'py a. **-pi·er, -pi·est** 1 unlucky 2 sad; wretched

un·health'y a. **-i·er, -i·est** 1 not well 2 harmful to health

un·heard'-of' a. never known or done before

un·ho'ly a. **-li·er, -li·est** 1 not sacred 2 wicked; sinful

u'ni·form' a. 1 never changing 2 all alike —n. special clothes for some group —v. dress in a uniform —**u'ni·form'i·ty** n.

u'ni·fy' v. **-fied'** make into one

un'ion n. 1 a uniting 2 group of nations or states united 3 marriage 4 a labor union

u·nique' (-nēk') a. 1 one and only 2 without equal 3 unusual

u'ni·sex' a. not differentiated for the sexes

u'ni·son n. 1 Mus. sameness of pitch 2 agreement

u'nit n. 1 single part of a whole 2 a special part 3 a standard measure 4 one

u·nite' v. 1 put together as one; combine 2 join together (in)

u'ni·ty n., pl. **-ties** 1 a being united 2 harmony; agreement

u'ni·ver'sal a. 1 of or for all 2 present everywhere

u'ni·verse' n. 1 space and all things in it 2 the world

u'ni·ver'si·ty n., pl. **-ties** school made up of college and, often, graduate schools

un·kempt' a. untidy; messy

un·known' a., n. unfamiliar or unidentified (person or thing)

un·lead'ed a. not containing lead compounds, as gasoline

un·like'ly a. not likely to happen, be true, succeed, etc.

un'mis·tak'a·ble a. that cannot be mistaken; clear

un·nat'u·ral a. 1 abnormal 2 artificial

un·pack' v. take things out of a trunk, box, etc.

un'quote' int. that ends the quotation

un·rav'el v. 1 undo the threads of 2 make clear

un·read' (-red') a. 1 not having been read 2 having read little

un·re'al a. fantastic

un·rea'son·a·ble a. 1 not reasonable 2 excessive

un·rest' n. 1 restlessness 2 angry discontent

un·ru'ly a. **-i·er, -i·est** not obedient or orderly

un·seem'ly a. improper

un·set'tle v. disturb, displace, or disorder

un'so·phis'ti·cat'ed a. simple, naive, etc.

un·speak'a·ble a. so bad, evil, etc. that description is impossible

un·sta'ble a. 1 not fixed, firm, etc. 2 changeable 3 emotionally unsettled

un·stead'y a. unstable

un·sung' a. not honored

un·think'ing a. thoughtless

un·til' prep. 1 up to the time of 2 before —con. 1 up to the point, degree, etc. that 2 before

un·time'ly a. 1 premature 2 at the wrong time —adv. too soon

un·told' a. 1 not told or revealed 2 very great

un·truth' n. lie; falsehood

un·used' a. 1 not in use 2 unaccustomed (to) 3 never used before

un·u'su·al a. not usual; rare

un·well' a. not well; sick

un·wield'y a. **-i·er, -i·est** 1 hard to handle because of size, etc. 2 clumsy —**un·wield'i·ness** n.

un·wind' v. 1 make or become undone or uncoiled 2 relax

un·writ'ten a. 1 not in writing 2 observed through custom, as some rules

up adv. 1 to, in, or on a higher place, level, etc. 2 to a later time 3 upright 4 into action, discussion, etc. 5 aside; away 6 so as to be even 7 completely 8 apiece —prep. up along, on, in, etc. —a. 1 put, brought, going, or gone up 2 at an end —**up to** [Col.] 1 doing or scheming 2 capable of 3 as many as 4 as far as 5 dependent upon

up'bring'ing n. training received as a child

up'com'ing a. coming soon

up·date' (n.: up'dāt') v. make conform to most recent facts, etc. —n. updated information

up'grade' n. upward slope —v. raise in grade or rank

up·heav'al n. 1 a heaving up 2 quick, violent change

up·hill' a., adv. 1 upward 2 with difficulty

up·hol'ster v. fit out (furniture) with coverings, etc.

up·on' prep., adv. on, or up and on

up'per a. higher in place, rank, etc.

up'per·case' a., n. (of or in) capital letters

up'per·most' a. highest in place, power, etc. —adv. in the highest place; first

up'right' a. 1 standing up; erect 2 honest; just —adv. in an upright position —n. upright pole, beam, etc.

up·ris'ing n. a revolt

up'roar' n. loud, confused noise or condition

up·set' (n.: up'set') v. -set' 1 overturn 2 disturb or distress 3 defeat unexpectedly —n. an upsetting —a. 1 overturned 2 disturbed

up'side' down' adv. 1 with the top part underneath 2 in disorder —**up'side-down'** a.

up'stairs' adv., a. to or on an upper floor —n. upper floor or floors

up'stream' adv., a. against the current of a stream

up'-to-date' a. 1 having the latest facts, ideas, etc. 2 of the newest or latest kind

up'town' n. part of city away from the business district

up'ward adv., a. toward a higher place, position, etc.

ur'ban a. of or in a city

ur·bane' a. suave; refined

ur'chin n. small mischievous child, esp. a boy

urge v. 1 insist on 2 to force onward 3 plead with 4 incite —n. impulse

ur'gent a. 1 needing quick action 2 insistent

urn n. 1 footed vase 2 container with a faucet

us pron. the objective case of WE

us'a·ble a. that can be used

us'age n. 1 treatment 2 custom; habit

use (yōōz; n.: yōōs) v. 1 put into action 2 treat 3 consume —n. 1 a using or being used 2 power or right to use 3 need to use 4 utility or function —**used to** 1 did once 2 familiar with

used a. not new; secondhand

use'ful a. that can be used; help-

ful —**use'ful·ness** n.

use'less a. worthless

us'er n. one that uses something; spec., a) drug addict b) computer operator

us'er-friend'ly a. easy to use or understand, as a computer program

ush'er v. show the way to or bring in —n. one who ushers

u'su·al a. in common use; ordinary —**u'su·al·ly** adv.

u·surp' v. take by force and without right —**u·surp'er** n.

u·su·ry (yōō'zhar ē) n. lending of money at an excessive interest rate —**u'su·rer** n.

u·ten'sil n. container or tool for a special purpose

u'ter·us n. hollow female organ in which a fetus grows

u·til'i·ty n., pl. -ties 1 usefulness 2 water, gas, etc. for public use 3 company providing this

u'ti·lize' v. put to use

ut'most' a. 1 most distant 2 greatest or highest —n. the most possible

ut'ter a. complete; absolute —v. express with the voice

V

va'cant a. 1 empty; unoccupied 2 free from work 3 stupid —**va' can·cy** n., pl. -cies

va·ca'tion v., n. rest from work, study, etc.

vac·cine' n. preparation injected for immunity to a disease —**vac' ci·nate'** v.

vac'u·um (-yōō əm, -yōōm') n. 1 completely empty space 2 space with most of the air or gas taken out —a. of, having, or working by a vacuum

va'grant n. homeless wanderer; tramp —**va'gran·cy** n.

vague (vāg) a. indefinite; unclear

vain a. 1 conceited 2 futile 3 worthless —**in vain** 1 without success 2 profanely

val·e·dic'to·ry n. farewell speech, as at graduation —**val'e·dic'to' ri·an** n.

val'en·tine' n. sweetheart or card for St. Valentine's Day

val'et (val'ət, va lā') n. servant to another man

val'iant (-yənt) a. brave

val'id a. 1 true or sound 2 having legal force —**val'i·date'** v.

val'ley n., pl. -leys 1 low land between hills 2 land drained by a river system

val'or n. courage; bravery

val'u·a·ble a. 1 having value 2 worth much money —n. valuable thing: usually used in pl.

val'ue n. 1 importance, desirability, utility, etc. 2 worth in money 3 buying power 4 pl. standards —v. 1 set the value of 2 think highly of

valve n. 1 device in a pipe, etc. to control the flow of a gas or liquid 2 body membrane like this

van n. large closed truck

van'dal n. one who destroys another's property on purpose

vane n. 1 device that swings to show wind direction 2 blade of a windmill, etc.

va·nil'la n. flavoring made from the pods of an orchid

van'ish v. disappear

van'i·ty n., pl. **-ties** 1 a being vain, or conceited 2 futility 3 low table with mirror

van'tage n. 1 advantage 2 position allowing a clear view, etc.: also **vantage point**

va'por n. 1 thick mist, as fog or steam 2 gas formed by heating a liquid or solid —**va'por·ous** a.

var'i·a·ble a. that varies or can be varied —n. variable thing

var·i·a'tion n. 1 change in form, etc. 2 amount of change

var'i·cose' a. swollen, as veins

var'ied a. 1 of different kinds 2 changed

va·ri'e·ty n., pl. **-ties** 1 change 2 kind; sort 3 a number of different kinds

var'i·ous a. 1 of several kinds 2 several or many

var'nish n. resinous liquid forming a hard, glossy surface —v. cover with this

var'si·ty n., pl. **-ties** school's main team in contests, esp. in athletic events

var'y v. **-ied** 1 make or become different; change 2 differ

vase n. open container for flowers, etc.

vas'sal n. 1 feudal tenant 2 subject, servant, etc.

vast a. very great in size, degree, etc. —**vast'ly** adv.

vat n. large tank or cask

vault n. 1 arched roof or ceiling 2 arched room 3 burial chamber 4 room for keeping money, etc. as in a bank 5 a vaulting or leap —v. 1 provide with a vault 2 leap over, balancing on a pole or the hands —**vault'er** n.

vaunt n., v. boast

VCR n. videocassette recorder

VDT n. video display terminal

veal n. meat from a calf

veer v., n. shift; turn

veg'e·ta·ble n. 1 plant eaten raw or cooked 2 any plant

veg'e·tar'i·an n. one who eats no meat —a. 1 of vegetarians 2 of vegetables only

ve'hi·cle n. means of conveying, esp. a device on wheels

veil (vāl) n. 1 piece of thin fabric worn by women over the face or head 2 thing that conceals

vein (vān) n. 1 blood vessel going to the heart 2 line in a leaf or an insect's wing 3 body of minerals in a fissure or zone of rock 4 colored streak 5 trace or quality

ve·loc'i·ty n. speed

vel'vet n. fabric of silk, rayon, etc. with a soft, thick pile

vel'vet·een' n. cotton cloth with a nap like velvet

ve·neer' n. thin, covering layer, as of fine wood

ven'er·ate' v. show deep respect for —**ven'er·a'tion** n.

ve·ne're·al (-nir'ē-) a. of or passed on by sexual intercourse

venge'ance n. revenge —**with a vengeance** 1 with great force 2 very much

ven'i·son n. flesh of deer

ven'om n. 1 poison of some snakes, spiders, etc. 2 malice

vent n. 1 outlet 2 opening to let gas, etc. out —v. let out

ven'ti·late' v. circulate fresh air in —**ven'ti·la'tion** n.

ven'tri·cle n. either lower chamber of the heart

ven'ture n. risky undertaking —v. 1 place in danger 2 dare to do, say, etc.

ve·ran'da n. open, roofed porch

verb n. word expressing action or being

ver'bal a. 1 of or in words 2 in speech 3 like or derived from a verb —n. derivative of a verb, as a gerund —**ver'bal·ly** adv.

ver'dict n. decision, as of a jury in a law case

verge v., n. (be on) the edge or border

ver'i·fy' v. **-fied'** 1 prove to be true 2 test the accuracy of —**ver'i·fi'a·ble** a.; true; real

ver·mil'ion n. bright yellowish red

ver'min n., pl. **-min** small, destructive animal, as a fly or

ver'sa·tile (-tǝl) *a.* able to do many things well

verse *n.* 1 poetry 2 stanza 3 short division of a Bible chapter

ver'sion *n.* 1 translation 2 report showing one point of view

ver'sus *prep.* against

ver'te·bra *n., pl.* **-brae** (-brē´, -brā´) or **-bras** any single bone of the spinal column

ver'te·brate *n., a.* (animal) having a spinal column

ver'ti·cal *n., a.* (line, plane, etc.) that is straight up and down

verve *n.* vigor; enthusiasm

ver'y *a.* 1 complete; absolute 2 same; identical 3 actual —*adv.* 1 extremely 2 truly

ves'sel *n.* 1 container 2 ship or boat 3 tube of the body, as a vein

vest *n.* 1 man's sleeveless garment 2 undershirt —*v.* 1 to clothe 2 give power over or right to

vest'ment *n.* garment, esp. one for a clergyman

vet'er·an *a.* experienced —*n.* 1 former member of the armed forces 2 longtime employee, etc.

vet'er·i·nar'i·an *n.* doctor for animals

ve'to *n., pl.* **-toes** 1 power, or right, to prohibit or reject 2 use of this —*v.* **-toed** use a veto on

vex *v.* annoy; disturb

vi·a (vī'ǝ, vē'ǝ) *prep.* by way of

vi'a·duct *n.* bridge held up by a series of towers

vi'al *n.* small bottle

vi'brate *v.* move rapidly back and forth; quiver

vic'ar *n.* 1 Church of England priest 2 *R.C.Ch.* deputy of a bishop, etc.

vice *n.* 1 bad or evil conduct 2 bad or evil habit

vice'-pres'i·dent *n.* officer next in rank to a president

vi'ce ver'sa (vī'sǝ-, vīs'-) *adv.* the other way around

vi·cin'i·ty *n., pl.* **-ties** 1 nearness 2 nearby area

vi'cious (vish'ǝs) *a.* 1 evil 2 unruly 3 malicious

vic'tim *n.* 1 one killed, hurt, etc. 2 one cheated, tricked, etc.

vic'to·ry *n., pl.* **-ries** success in war or any struggle

vict'uals (vit'lz) *n.pl.* [Dial. or Col.] food

vid'e·o *a., n.* 1 (of) television 2 (of) performance on videocas-

sette, etc.

vid'e·o·cas·sette' *n.* cassette containing videotape, recorded on and played back esp. by using a **videocassette recorder**

vid'e·o·tape' *n.* magnetic tape for recording and playing back images and sounds

vie *v.* **vied** to compete as in a contest

view *n.* 1 a looking 2 range of vision 3 idea or thought 4 scene 5 opinion 6 aim; goal —*v.* 1 look at or see 2 consider

view'point' *n.* 1 place of observation 2 attitude

vig'il *n.* 1 watchful staying awake 2 watch kept 3 eve of a religious festival

vig'or *n.* active force; strength and energy —**vig'or·ous** *a.*

vile *a.* 1 evil; wicked 2 disgusting 3 lowly and bad

vil'lage *n.* small town

vil'lain (-ǝn) *n.* evil or wicked person —**vil'lain·ous** *a.*

vin'ai·grette' (-ǝ-) *n.* dressing of vinegar, oil, herbs, etc.

vine *n.* plant with a stem that grows along the ground or climbs a support

vin'e·gar *n.* sour liquid made by fermenting cider, wine, etc.

vine'yard (vin'yǝrd) *n.* land where grapevines are grown

vin'tage *n.* wine of a certain region and year

vi'nyl (-nǝl) *a.* of a group of chemical compounds used in making plastics

vi·o'la (vē-) *n.* instrument like, but larger than, the violin

vi'o·late' *v.* 1 break (a law, etc.) 2 rape 3 desecrate 4 disturb —**vi'o·la'tion** *n.* —**vi'o·la'tor** *n.*

vi'o·lent *a.* 1 showing or acting with wild force or feeling 2 intense —**vi'o·lence** *n.*

vi'o·let *n.* delicate spring flower, usually bluish-purple

vi'o·lin' *n.* four-stringed instrument played with a bow

vi'per *n.* 1 venomous snake 2 treacherous person

vir'gin *n.* person, esp. a woman, who has not had sexual intercourse —**vir·gin'i·ty** *n.*

vir'ile (-ǝl) *a.* 1 masculine 2 strong, vigorous, etc.

vir'tu·al *a.* being so in effect if not in fact

vir'tue *n.* 1 moral excellence 2 good quality, esp. a moral one 3 chastity —**vir'tu·ous** *a.*

vi'rus *n.* 1 infective agent that

causes disease 3 harmful influence 3 unauthorized computer program instructions added as a joke or to sabotage —**vi'ral** a.

vi·sa (vē'zə) n. endorsement on a passport, granting entry into a country

vise n. device with adjustable jaws for holding an object firmly

vis'i·ble a. that can be seen; evident —**vis'i·bly** adv.

vi'sion n. 1 power of seeing 2 something seen in a dream, trance, etc. 3 mental image 4 foresight

vis'it v. 1 go or come to see 2 stay with as a guest 3 afflict —n. a visiting —**vis'i·tor** n.

vi'sor n. 1 movable part of a helmet, covering the face 2 brim on a cap for shading the eyes

vis'u·al a. 1 of or used in seeing 2 visible

vi'tal a. 1 of life 2 essential to life 3 very important 4 full of life —**vi'tal·ly** adv.

vi'ta·min n. any of certain substances vital to good health: vitamins A and D are found in fish-liver oil, eggs, etc.; vitamin B (complex), in liver, yeast, etc.; vitamin C, in citrus fruits

viv'id a. 1 full of life 2 bright; intense 3 strong; active

vo·cab'u·lar'y n., pl. **-ies** all the words used by a person, group, etc. or listed in a dictionary, etc.

vo'cal a. 1 of or by the voice 2 speaking freely —**vo'cal·ly** adv.

vo·ca'tion n. one's profession, trade, or career

vogue (vōg) n. 1 current fashion 2 popularity

voice n. 1 sound made through the mouth 2 ability to make such sound 3 sound like this 4 right to express one's opinion, etc. 5 expression

voice mail n. electronic storage and delivery of telephone messages

void a. 1 empty; vacant 2 lacking 3 of no legal force —n. empty space —v. 1 to empty 2 cancel

vol·ca'no n., pl. **-noes** or **-nos** mountain formed by erupting molten rock —**vol·can'ic** a.

vol'ley n., v., pl. **-leys** 1 discharge (of) a number of weapons together 2 return (of) a tennis ball before it hits the ground

volt n. unit of electrical force

volt'age n. electrical force,

shown in volts

vol'ume n. 1 a book 2 cubic measure 3 amount 4 loudness of sound

vol'un·tar'y a. 1 by choice; of one's own free will 2 controlled by the will —**vol·un·tar'i·ly** adv.

vol'un·teer' v. offer, give, etc. of one's own free will —n. one who volunteers

vom'it v., n. (have) matter from the stomach ejected through the mouth

vote n. 1 a decision or choice shown on a ballot, etc. 2 all the votes 3 the right to vote —v. 1 cast a vote 2 decide by vote —**vot'er** n.

vouch v. give or be a guarantee (for)

vow v., n. (make) a solemn promise or statement

vow'el n. speech sound of the letters a, e, i, o, u

voy'age n., v. journey by ship

vul'gar a. 1 popular 2 lacking culture; crude —**vul·gar'i·ty** adv.

vul·gar'i·ty n. 1 vulgar state or quality 2 pl. **-ties** vulgar act, etc.

vul'ner·a·ble a. 1 that can be hurt, attacked, etc. 2 easily hurt; sensitive

vul'ture n. 1 large bird of prey 2 greedy, ruthless person

W

wad n. 1 small, soft mass 2 small lump

wad'dle v., n. walk with short steps, swaying from side to side

wade v. 1 walk through water, mud, etc. 2 proceed with difficulty 3 cross by wading

wa'fer n. 1 thin, crisp cracker 2 disklike thing

waf'fle n. crisp cake baked between two flat, studded plates (**waffle iron**)

wag v. **wagged** move rapidly back and forth or up and down

wage v. take part in —n. pl. money paid for work done

wa'ger n., v. bet

wag'on n. four-wheeled vehicle, esp. for hauling

waif n. homeless child

wail v., n. 1 (make) a loud, sad cry 2 lament

waist n. 1 body part between the ribs and the hips 2 waistline

waist'line' n. middle or narrow part of the waist

wait v. 1 remain until something

occurs 2 remain undone 4
serve food at 4 await —*n.* act or
time of waiting

wait'er *n.* man who serves food
at table —**wait'ress** *n.fem.*

waive *v.* 1 give up, as a right 2
postpone

wake *v.* **woke** or **waked, waked**
or **wok'en** 1 come or bring out
of a sleep 2 become alert (*to*) 3
stir up —*n.* 1 all-night vigil
over a corpse 2 track or trail
left behind

wak'en *v.* to wake

walk *v.* 1 go on foot at moderate
speed 2 walk along, over, with,
etc. 3 *Baseball* advance to first
base by a walk —*n.* 1 way of
walking 2 stroll; hike 3 path
for walking 4 *Baseball* advance-
ment by batter to first base on
four pitches not strikes

wall *n.* upright structure that
encloses, divides, etc.

wal'let *n.* flat case for carrying
money, cards, etc.

wal'low *v.* 1 roll around in mud
or filth, as pigs do 2 live self-
ishly

wal'nut' *n.* 1 tree bearing an
edible nut in a hard shell 2 its
nut 3 its wood

wal'rus *n.* large seallike animal
with two tusks

waltz *n.* ballroom dance in 3/4
time —*v.* dance a waltz

wand *n.* slender rod, as one of
supposed magic power

wan'der *v.* 1 roam idly about 2
go astray; stray —**wan'der-er** *n.*

wane *v.* 1 get smaller, weaker,
etc. 2 approach the end —*n.* a
waning

want *v.* 1 wish for; desire 2
need 3 lack —*n.* 1 lack; need 2
poverty 3 desire

war *n.* 1 armed conflict, as
between nations 2 any fight

war'ble *v.* sing with trills, runs,
etc. —**war'bler** *n.*

ward *n.* 1 one under the care of
a guardian 2 division of a hospital 3 voting district of a city

war'den *n.* 1 one who takes care
of something 2 head official of a
prison

ward'robe' *n.* 1 a closet for
clothes 2 all one's clothes

ware'house' *n.* building where
goods are stored

war'fare' *n.* war or any conflict

warm *a.* 1 moderately hot 2
enthusiastic 3 kind and loving
—*v.* make or become warm

warmth *n.* 1 a being warm 2

strong feeling

warn *v.* 1 tell of danger; advise
to be careful 2 inform; let know
—**warn'ing** *n., a.*

warp *v.* 1 bend or twist out of
shape 2 distort —*n.* 1 a warp-
ing or twist 2 long threads in a
loom

war'rant *n.* 1 justification 2
legal writ authorizing an arrest,
search, etc.

war'ran·ty *n., pl.* **-ties** GUARAN-
TEE (*n.* 1)

war'ri·or *n.* soldier

wart *n.* small, hard growth on
the skin

war·y (wer'ē) *a.* **-i·er, -i·est** on
guard; cautious

was *v. pt.* of BE: used with *he,
she,* or *it*

wash *v.* 1 clean with water 2
wash clothes 3 flow over or
against 4 remove by washing 5
coat thinly —*n.* 1 a washing 2
clothes (to be) washed 3 rush of
water 4 eddy from propeller,
oars, etc. —**wash'a·ble** *a.*

wash'er *n.* 1 machine for washing 2 flat ring used to make a
bolt, nut, etc. fit tight 3 one
who washes

wasp *n.* flying insect: some have
a sharp sting

waste *v.* 1 use up needlessly 2
fail to take advantage of 3 wear
away 4 lose strength or weaken
5 destroy —*a.* 1 barren or wild,
as land 2 left over —*n.* 1 a
wasting 2 wasted matter;
refuse, etc. 3 wasteland —**lay
waste (to)** devastate —**waste'-
ful** *a.*

watch *n.* 1 act of guarding or
observing 2 guard(s), or period
of guard duty 3 small clock for
wrist or pocket 4 *Naut.* period
of duty, or crew on duty —*v.* 1
keep vigil 2 observe 3 guard or
tend 4 be alert (*for*) —**watch'-
ful** *a.*

watch'man *n., pl.* **-men** person
hired to guard

wa'ter *n.* 1 colorless liquid of
rivers, lakes, etc. 2 water solution 3 body secretion, as urine
—*v.* 1 to supply with water 2
dilute with water 3 fill with
tears 4 secrete saliva —*a.* of,
for, in, or by water

wa'ter-col'or *n.* 1 paint made by
mixing pigment and water 2
picture painted with such paints

wa'ter-craft' *n., pl.* **-craft'** boat,
ship, or other water vehicle

wa'ter-fall' *n.* steep fall of water,

wa'ter·front' n. land or docks at the edge of a river, harbor, etc.

wa'ter·mel'on n. large melon with juicy, red pulp

wa'ter·proof' v., a. (to make) impervious to water

wa'ter·shed' n. 1 area a river system drains 2 ridge between two such areas

water table n. level below which the ground is saturated with water

wa'ter·way' n. navigable river, lake, canal, etc.

watt n. unit of electric power

wave v. 1 move to and fro 2 wave the hand, etc., or signal thus 3 arrange in curves —n. 1 curving swell moving along on the ocean, etc. 2 wavelike vibration 3 curve(s), as in the hair 4 a waving, as of the hand

wa'ver v. 1 flutter, falter, flicker, etc. 2 show indecision

wax n. 1 plastic substance secreted by bees 2 substance like this, as paraffin —v. 1 put polish or wax on 2 get larger, stronger, etc. 3 to become

way n. 1 road or route 2 movement forward 3 method, manner, etc. 4 distance 5 direction 6 particular 7 wish; will 8 pl. framework from which a ship is built —adv. [Col.] far —**by the way** incidentally

we pron. persons speaking or writing

weak a. lacking strength, power, etc.; not strong effective, etc. —**weak'en** v.

weak'ly adv. in a weak way

wealth n. 1 riches 2 large amount —**wealth'y** a., -i·er, -i·est

weap'on n. 1 thing used for fighting 2 means of attack or defense

wear v. wore, worn 1 have on the body as clothes 2 make or become damaged by use 3 endure in use 4 to tire or exhaust

wea·ry (wir'ē) a. -ri·er, -ri·est 1 tired 2 bored

wea'sel n. small, flesh-eating mammal

weath'er n. condition outside as to temperature, humidity, etc. —v. 1 to pass through safely 2 wear, discolor, etc. by exposure to sun, rain, etc.

weath'er·proof' v., a. (make) able to withstand exposure to the weather

weave v. wove, wo'ven 1 make cloth by interlacing threads, as on a loom 2 twist or move from side to side or in and out

web n. 1 network, esp. one spun by a spider 2 skin joining the toes of a duck, frog, etc.

wed v. wed'ded, wed'ded or wed 1 marry 2 unite

wed'ding n. ceremony of marrying

wedge n. piece of wood, etc. tapering to a thin edge

Wednes'day (wenz'-) n. fourth day of the week

wee a. very small; tiny

weed n. unwanted plant, as in a lawn

week n. 1 period of seven days, esp. Sunday through Saturday 2 the hours or days one works each week

week'day' n. any day of the week except Sunday and, often, Saturday

week'end', week'-end' n. Saturday and Sunday

week'ly a. 1 lasting a week 2 done, etc. once a week —adv. once a week —n., pl. -lies periodical coming out weekly

weep v. wept 1 shed tears 2 mourn (for)

wee'vil n. beetle larva that destroys cotton, grain, etc.

weigh v. 1 determine the heaviness of, as on a scale 2 have a certain weight 3 consider well 4 burden: with down 5 hoist (an anchor)

weight n. 1 (amount of) heaviness 2 unit of heaviness 3 solid mass 4 burden 5 importance or influence —v. to burden

weight'less a. having little or no apparent weight

weird (wird) a. 1 mysterious 2 bizarre

wel'come a. 1 gladly received 2 freely permitted 3 under no obligation —n. a welcoming —v. greet with pleasure

weld v. unite by melting together —n. welded joint

wel'fare' n. health, happiness, and comfort —**on welfare** receiving government aid because of poverty, etc.

well n. 1 natural spring 2 hole dug in the earth to get water, oil, etc. 3 hollow shaft 4 source —v. gush or flow —adv. bet'ter, best 1 in a pleasing, good, or right way 2 prosperously 3 much 4 thoroughly —a. in good health —**as well (as)** 1 in addition (to) 2 equally (with)

well'-be'ing n. welfare

well'-bred' a. showing good manners; courteous

well'-off' a. 1 fortunate 2 prosperous

well'-read' (-red') a. having read much

well'-to-do' a. wealthy

went v. pt. of GO

were v. pt. of BE: used with *you, we,* or *they*

west n. 1 direction in which sunset occurs 2 region in this direction 3 [W-] Europe and North and South America —a., adv. in, toward, or from the west —**west'er·ly** a., adv. —**west'ern** a. —**west'ern·er** n. —**west'ward** a., adv. —**west'wards** adv.

wet a. **wet'ter, wet'test** 1 covered or soaked with water 2 rainy 3 not dry yet

whack v., n. hit or slap with a sharp sound

whale n. huge, fishlike sea mammal —v. hunt for whales

wharf n., pl. **wharves** or **wharfs** platform at which ships dock to load, etc.

what pron. 1 which thing, event, etc.? 2 that which —a. 1 which or which kind of 2 as much or as many as 3 how great! —adv. 1 how 2 partly —int. exclamation of surprise, etc. —**what for?** why? —**what if** suppose

what·ev'er pron. 1 anything that 2 no matter what 3 what —a. 1 of any kind 2 no matter what

wheat n. cereal grass with seed ground for flour, etc.

wheel n. round disk turning on an axle

wheeze v., n. (make) a whistling, breathy sound

when adv. at what time? —con. 1 at what time 2 at which 3 at the time that 4 if —pron. what or which time

whence adv. from what place

when·ev'er adv. [Col.] when —con. at whatever time

where adv. 1 in or to what place? 2 in what way? 3 from what source? —con. 1 in or at what place 2 in or at which place 3 to the place that —pron. 1 what place? 2 the place at which

where'a·bouts' n. location

where·as' con. 1 because 2 while on the contrary

where·in' con. in which

wher·ev'er adv. [Col.] where? —con. in or to whatever place

whet v. **whet'ted** 1 sharpen, as by grinding 2 to stimulate

wheth'er con. 1 if it is true or likely that 2 in either case that

whey n. watery part of curdled milk

which pron. 1 what one or ones of several 2 the one or ones that 3 that —a. 1 what one or ones 2 whatever

while n. period of time —con. 1 during the time that 2 although

whim n. sudden notion

whim'per v., n. (make) a low, broken cry

whine v., n. (make) a long, high cry, as in complaining

whip v. **whipped** 1 move suddenly 2 strike, as with a strap 3 beat (cream, etc.) into a froth 4 [Col.] defeat —n. 1 rod with a lash at one end 2 dessert of whipped cream, fruit, etc.

whirl v. 1 move or spin rapidly 2 seem to spin —n. 1 a whirling 2 confused condition

whirl'pool' n. water in violent, whirling motion

whisk v. move, pull, etc. with a quick, sweeping motion

whisk'er n. 1 pl. the hair on a man's face 2 long hair, as on a cat's upper lip

whis'per v. 1 say very softly —n. a whispering

whis'tle (-al) v. 1 make, or move with, a high, shrill sound 2 blow a whistle —n. 1 device for making whistling sounds 2 a whistling

white a. 1 of the color of snow 2 pale 3 pure; innocent 4 having light skin —n. 1 color of pure snow 2 a white thing, as egg albumen —**white'ness** n.

white'wash' n. mixture of lime, water, etc. as for whitening walls

whith'er adv. where

whit'tle v. 1 cut shavings from wood with a knife 2 reduce gradually

who pron. 1 what person? 2 which person 3 that

who·ev'er pron. 1 any person that 2 no matter who

whole a. 1 not broken, damaged, etc. 2 complete 3 not divided up 4 healthy —n. 1 entire amount 2 thing complete in itself —**whole'ness** n.

whole'sale' n. sale of goods in

large amounts, as to retailers —
a. 1 of such sale 2 extensive —
v. to sell at wholesale

whole'some *a.* 1 healthful 2
improving one's morals 3
healthy —**whole'some·ness** *n.*

whol'ly *adv.* completely

whom *pron.* objective case of
WHO

whore *n.* prostitute

whose *pron.* that or those
belonging to whom —*a.* of
whom or of which

why *adv.* for what reason? —
con. 1 because of which 2 reason for which —*n., pl.* whys the
reason

wick *n.* piece of cord, etc. for
burning, as in a candle

wick'ed *a.* 1 evil 2 unpleasant
3 naughty

wide *a.* 1 great in width,
amount, degree, etc. 2 of a
specified width 3 far from the
goal —*adv.* 1 over or to a large
extent 2 so as to be wide

wide'spread' *a.* occurring over a
wide area

wid'ow *n.* woman whose husband has died

wid'ow·er *n.* man whose wife
has died

width *n.* 1 distance side to side
2 a piece so wide

wield (wēld) *v.* 1 handle with
skill 2 use (power, etc.)

wie'ner *n.* frankfurter

wife *n., pl.* wives married woman

wig *n.* false covering of hair for
the head

wig'gle *v., n.* twist and turn from
side to side

wig'wam *n.* cone-shaped tent of
North American Indians

wild *a.* 1 in its natural state 2
not civilized 3 unruly 4 stormy
5 enthusiastic 6 reckless 7
missing the target —*adv.* in a
wild way —*n. pl.* wilderness

wil'der·ness *n.* wild region

wild'life' *n.* wild animals

wile *v., n.* trick; lure

will *n.* 1 wish; desire 2 strong
purpose 3 power of choice 4
attitude 5 legal document dis-
posing of one's property after
death —*v.* 1 decide 2 control
by the will 3 bequeath

will *v. pt.* would auxiliary verb
showing: 1 future time 2 determination or obligation 3 ability
or capacity

wil'low *n.* a tree with narrow
leaves

wilt *v.* 1 make or become limp 2

make or become weak

win *v.* won 1 gain a victory 2
get by work, effort, etc. 3 persuade —*n.* [Col.] victory

wince *v.* draw back; flinch

winch *n.* machine for hoisting by
a cable, etc. wound on a drum

wind (wind) *n.* 1 air in motion
2 gales 3 breath 4 smell

wind (wīnd) *v.* wound 1 turn,
coil, or twine around 2 cover, or
tighten, by winding 3 move or
go indirectly —*n.* a turn

wind instrument *n.* Mus. instrument played by blowing air, esp.
breath, through it

wind'mill' *n.* machine operated
by the wind's rotation of a wheel
of vanes

win'dow *n.* 1 opening for light
and air in a building, car, etc. 2
glass in a frame set in this

wind'ward *a., adv., n.* (in or
toward) the direction from
which the wind blows

wine *n.* fermented juice of
grapes or other fruits

wing *n.* 1 organ used by a bird,
insect, etc. in flying 2 thing like
a wing in use or position 3
political faction —*v.* 1 to fly 2
send swiftly 3 wound in the
wing or arm —**on the wing** in
flight —**under one's wing**
under one's protection, etc.

wink *v.* 1 close and open the
eyelids quickly 2 do this with
one eye, as a signal 3 twinkle —
n. 1 a winking 2 an instant

win'ning *a.* 1 victorious 2
charming

win'ter *n.* coldest season of the
year —*a.* of or for winter

wipe *v.* 1 clean or dry by rubbing 2 rub (a cloth, etc.) over
something —*n.* a wiping

wire *n.* 1 metal drawn into a
long thread 2 telegraph 3 telegram —*v.* 1 furnish or fasten
with wire(s) 2 telegraph

wir'ing *n.* system of wires, as for
carrying electricity

wis'dom *n.* 1 a being wise; good
judgment 2 knowledge

wise *a.* 1 having good judgment
2 informed or learned

wish *v.* 1 to want; desire 2
express a desire concerning 3
request —*n.* 1 a wishing 2
something wished for 3 request

wisp *n.* slight thing or bit

wit *n.* 1 (one with) the ability to
make clever remarks 2 *pl.* powers of thinking —**to wit** namely

witch *n.* woman supposed to

have evil, magic power

with *prep.* **1** against **2** near to; in the care or company of **3** into **4** as a member of **5** concerning **6** compared to **7** as well as **8** in the opinion of **9** as a result of **10** by means of **11** having or showing **12** to; onto **13** from **14** after

with·draw' *v.* **-drew', -drawn' 1** take back **2** move back **3** leave

with·er *v.* wilt

with·hold' *v.* **-held' 1** keep back; restrain **2** refrain from granting

with·in' *adv.* in or to the inside —*prep.* **1** inside **2** not beyond

with·out' *adv.* on the outside —*prep.* **1** outside **2** lacking **3** avoiding

with·stand' *v.* **-stood'** resist; endure

wit·ness *n.* **1** one who saw and can testify to a thing **2** testimony; evidence **3** an attesting signer —*v.* **1** see **2** act as a witness of **3** be proof of

wit·ty *a.* **-ti·er, -ti·est** cleverly amusing

wiz·ard *n.* magician

wob·ble *v.* move unsteadily from side to side —*n.* a wobbling

woe *n.* grief or trouble

wok *n.* bowl-shaped frying pan

wolf *n., pl.* **wolves 1** wild, doglike animal **2** cruel or greedy person —*v.* eat greedily

wom·an *n., pl.* **wom·en** adult female person

womb (wōōm) *n.* uterus

won·der *n.* **1** amazing thing; marvel **2** feeling caused by this —*v.* **1** feel wonder **2** be curious about

won·der·ful *a.* **1** causing wonder **2** [Col.] excellent

wont (wänt, wōnt) *n.* habit

wood *n.* **1** hard substance under a tree's bark **2** lumber **3** *pl.* forest —*a.* **1** of wood **2** of the woods —**wood'ed** *a.*

wood'chuck' *n.* North American burrowing animal

wood'en *a.* **1** made of wood **2** lifeless, dull, etc.

wood'peck'er *n.* bird that pecks holes in bark

wood'work' *n.* wooden doors, frames, moldings, etc.

wood'y *a.* **-i·er, -i·est 1** tree-covered **2** of or like wood

woof *n.* weft

wool *n.* **1** soft curly hair of sheep, goats, etc. **2** yarn or cloth made of this

wool'ly *a.* **-li·er, -li·est** of, like, or covered with wool

word *n.* **1** a sound or sounds as a speech unit **2** letter or letters standing for this **3** brief remark **4** news **5** promise **6** *pl.* quarrel —*v.* put into words —**word'ing** *n.* choice and arrangement of words

work *n.* **1** effort of doing or making; labor **2** occupation, trade, etc. **3** task; duty **4** thing made, done, etc. **5** *pl.* factory **6** *pl.* engineering structures, as bridges **7** workmanship —*v.* **1** do work; toil **2** to function **3** cause to work **4** be employed **5** bring about **6** come or bring to some condition **7** solve (a problem) —**at work** working —**work off** get rid of —**work on 1** influence **2** try to persuade —**work out 1** develop or result **2** to exercise

work'man·ship' *n.* worker's skill or product

world *n.* **1** the earth **2** the universe **3** all people **4** any sphere or domain **5** secular life **6** *often pl.* great deal

worm *n.* **1** long, slender creeping animal **2** thing like a worm

wor·ry *v.* **-ried 1** make, or be, troubled or uneasy **2** annoy **3** shake with the teeth —*n.*, *pl.* **-ries 1** troubled feeling **2** cause of this —**wor'ri·some** *a.*

worse *a.* **1** more evil, bad, etc. **2** more ill —*adv.* in a worse way —*n.* that which is worse

wors·en *v.* make or become worse

wor'ship *n.* **1** prayer, service, etc. in reverence to a deity **2** intense love or admiration —*v.* **1** show reverence for **2** take part in worship service

worst *a.* most evil, bad, etc. —*adv.* in the worst way —*n.* that which is worst

worth *n.* **1** value or merit **2** equivalent in money —*a.* **1** deserving **2** equal in value to

worth'while' *a.* worth the time or effort spent

wor'thy *a.* **-thi·er, -thi·est 1** having worth or value **2** deserving —*n.* worthy person

would *v.* pt. of WILL: *would* is used to express a condition, a wish, a request, etc.

wound (wōōnd) *n.* **1** injury to the body tissue **2** scar **3** injury to the feelings, etc. —*v.* injure; hurt

wrap v. **wrapped** or **wrapt** 1 wind or fold (a covering) around 2 enclose in paper, etc.

wrath n. great anger; rage

wreak (rēk) v. 1 inflict (vengeance, etc.) 2 give vent to (anger, etc.)

wreath (rēth) n., pl. **wreaths** twisted ring of leaves, etc.

wreathe (rēth) v. 1 encircle 2 decorate with wreaths

wreck n. 1 remains of a thing, destroyed 2 rundown person 3 a wrecking —v. 1 destroy or ruin 2 tear down

wren n. small songbird

wrench n. 1 sudden, sharp twist 2 injury caused by a twist 3 tool for turning nuts, bolts, etc. —v. 1 twist or jerk sharply 2 injure with a twist

wrest v. take by force

wres'tle (-əl) v. 1 struggle with (an opponent) trying to throw him 2 contend (with)

wretch n. 1 very unhappy person 2 person despised

wretch'ed a. 1 very unhappy 2 distressing 3 unsatisfactory

wring v. **wrung** 1 squeeze and twist 2 force out by this means 3 get by force —**wring'er** n.

wrin'kle n. 1 small crease or fold 2 [Col.] clever idea, etc. — v. form wrinkles (in)

wrist n. joint between the hand and forearm

writ n. formal court order

write v. **wrote, writ'ten** 1 form (words, letters, etc.) 2 produce (writing or music) 3 write a letter —**write off** cancel, as a debt

writhe (rīth) v. twist and turn, as in pain

wrong a. 1 not right or just 2 not true or correct 3 not suitable 4 mistaken 5 out of order 6 not meant to be seen —adv. incorrectly —n. something wrong —v. treat unjustly

wrought (rôt) a. 1 made 2 shaped by hammering

wry (ri) a. **wri'er, wri'est** twisted or distorted —**wry'ly** adv. — **wry'ness** n.

X

X'-ray' n. 1 ray that can penetrate solid matter 2 photograph made with X-rays —a. of or by X-rays —v. photograph, treat, or examine with X-rays

xy'lo·phone' (zī'-) n. musical instrument of a row of wooden

bars struck with hammers

Y

yacht (yät) n. small ship

yam n. 1 starchy, edible root of a tropical plant 2 [Dial.] sweet potato

yard n. 1 measure of length, three feet 2 ground around a building 3 enclosed place

yarn n. 1 spun strand of wool, cotton, etc. 2 [Col.] tale or story

yawn v. open the mouth widely, as when one is sleepy —n. a yawning

ye (yē; a.: thə) [Ar.] pron. you — a. the

yea (yā) adv. 1 yes 2 truly —n. vote of "yes"

yeah (ya, ye) adv. [Col.] yes

year n. 1 period of 365 days (366 in leap year) or 12 months 2 pl. age 3 pl. a long time

year'ly a. 1 every year 2 of a year —adv. every year

yearn v. feel longing

yeast n. frothy substance causing fermentation

yell v., n. scream; shout

yel'low a. 1 of the color of ripe lemons 2 [Col.] cowardly —n. yellow color —v. to make or become yellow —**yel'low·ish** a.

yes adv. it is so —n., pl. **yes'es** 1 consent 2 affirmative vote

yes'ter·day' n. 1 day before today 2 recent time —adv. on the day before today

yet adv. 1 up to now 2 now 3 still; even now 4 nevertheless —con. nevertheless

yield v. 1 produce; give 2 surrender 3 concede; grant 4 give way to force —n. amount produced

yo'ga n. Hindu discipline for uniting self with supreme spirit through various exercises

yoke n. 1 frame for harnessing together a pair of oxen, etc. 2 thing that binds or unites 3 servitude 4 part of a garment at the shoulders

yolk (yōk) n. yellow part of an egg

yon'der a., adv. over there

you pron. [sing. or pl. v.] 1 the person(s) spoken to 2 person(s) generally

young a. 1 in an early stage of life or growth 2 fresh —n. young offspring

your a. of you

yours pron. that or those belonging to you

your·self' *pron.*, *pl.* **-selves'** intensive or reflexive form of YOU

youth *n.* 1 state or quality of being young 2 adolescence 3 young people 4 young man

yule *n.* [*often* Y-] Christmas

yup'pie *n.* [Col.] affluent, ambitious, young professional

Z

zeal *n.* eager endeavor or devotion

ze'bra *n.* striped African animal similar to the horse

Zen *n.* form of Buddhism seeking intuitive knowledge through meditation

ze'nith *n.* 1 point in the sky directly overhead 2 the highest point

ze'ro *n.*, *pl.* **-ros** or **-roes** 1 the symbol 0 2 point marked 0 in a scale 3 nothing —*a.* of or at zero

zest *n.* 1 stimulating quality 2 keen enjoyment —**zest'ful** *a.*

zig'zag' *n.* line with sharp turns back and forth

zip *v.* **zipped** 1 make a short, sharp hissing sound 2 [Col.] move fast 3 fasten with a zipper

zip'per *n.* fastener with interlocking tabs worked by a sliding part

zo'di·ac' *n.* imaginary belt along the sun's path divided into 12 parts named for constellations

zone *n.* 1 any of the five areas into which the earth is divided according to climate 2 area set apart in some way

zoo *n.* place with wild animals on exhibition

zo·ol'o·gy (zō-) *n.* science of animal life —**zo·ol'o·gist** *n.*

zoom *v.* 1 make a loud, buzzing sound 2 speed upward or forward —*n.* a zooming

ABBREVIATIONS

Many abbreviations can be written in various ways (p.m., P.M., pm, PM). The most commonly used forms are listed here.

a. adjective
A *Sports* assist(s)
AA, A.A. Associate in Arts
AB, A.B. Bachelor of Arts
abbr., abbrev. abbreviated; abbreviation
AC air conditioning; alternating current
acct. account
A.D. in the year of our Lord
adj. adjective
Adm. Admiral
admn. administration
adv. adverb
AFDC Aid to Families with Dependent Children
agcy. agency
Ala. Alabama
Alas. Alaska
alt. alternate; altitude
a.m., A.M. before noon
AM, A.M. Master of Arts
Am. America(n)
anon. anonymous
Apr. April
apt. apartment
Ariz. Arizona
Ark. Arkansas
assn. association
assoc. associate
asst. assistant
Attn. attention
atty. attorney
Aug. August
av. average (also **avg.**); avoirdupois
Av(e). Avenue
b. born
BA, B.A. Bachelor of Arts
bbl. barrel(s)
B.C. before Christ
biol. biology
bldg. building
Blvd. Boulevard
Br., Brit. Britain; British
Bros. Brothers
BS, B.S. Bachelor of Science
Btu British thermal units
bu. bushel(s)
bur. bureau
c centimeter; copyright
c. century
C Celsius (or centigrade)
C cup(s)
c(a). circa (about)
Cal., Calif. California
cal. calorie(s)
Can. Canada; Canadian (also **Cdn.**)
cap. capacity; capital(ize)
Capt. Captain
cc carbon copy; cubic centimeter(s)

cent. century; centuries
cert. certificate; certified
cf. compare
cg centigram(s)
Ch. Church
ch., chap. chapter(s)
chem. chemistry
chg(d). charge(d)
CIA Central Intelligence Agency
cm centimeter(s)
Cmdr. Commander
CO Commanding Officer
C/O, c/o care of
Co. Company; County
COD collect on delivery
Col. Colonel
Colo. Colorado
Cong. Congress
Conn. Connecticut
cont. continued
Corp. Corporal; Corporation
CPA Certified Public Accountant
CST Central Standard Time
cu. cubic
d. degree(s); diameter; died
DA, D.A. District Attorney
dba doing business as
D.C. District of Columbia
DC direct current
DD, D.D. Doctor of Divinity
DDS, D.D.S. Doctor of Dental Surgery
dec. deceased
Dec. December
Del. Delaware
Dem. Democrat(ic)
dept. department; deputy
dlr. director
dist. district
div. division
d(o)z. dozen(s)
Dr. Doctor; Drive
DST Daylight Saving(s) Time
DWI driving while intoxicated
E *Baseball* error(s)
E, E. east(ern)
ea. each
econ. economics
ed. edited (by); edition; editor; education
e.g. for example
EKG electrocardiogram
elem. elementary
enc(l). enclosure
Eng. England; English
EPA Environmental Protection Agency
ERA earned run average; Equal Rights Amendment
ESP extrasensory perception
esp. especially
Esq. Esquire
EST Eastern Standard Time

ABBREVIATIONS

est. established (also **estab.**); estimate(d)
ETA estimated time of arrival
et al. and (the) others
et seq. and the following
ex. example; exchange
exec. executive; executor
ext. extension
f. folio
F Fahrenheit; female
FBI Federal Bureau of Investigation
FCC Federal Communications Commission
FDA Food and Drug Administration
Feb. February
Fed. Federal; Federation
fem. feminine
ff. folios; following (pages, etc.)
FG *Sports* field goal(s)
FICA Federal Insurance Contributions Act
fig. figuratively; figure(s)
fl. flourished; fluid
Fla. Florida
Fr. Father; French
Fri. Friday
FT *Basketball* free throw(s)
ft. foot; feet
Ft. Fort
FTC Federal Trade Commission
g *Sports* goal(s); gram(s)
Ga. Georgia
gal. gallon(s)
Gen. General
gen., genl. general
Ger. German(y)
GM General Manager
GOP Grand Old (Republican) Party
Gov. Governor
gov., govt. government
GP, G.P. general practitioner
Gr. Greece; Greek
Gr. Brit. Great Britain
grad. graduate(d)
gram. grammar
guar. guaranteed
H *Baseball* hit(s)
hdqrs. headquarters
hist. history
H.J. here lies
HMO health maintenance organization
HP horsepower
HQ headquarters
HR *Baseball* home run(s)
HR, H.R. House of Representatives
hr. hour
HS, H.S. high school
ht. height
hwy. highway
Hz, hz hertz
ia. Iowa
ib., ibid. in the same place
ICC Interstate Commerce Commission

Id. the same
Ida. Idaho
i.e. that is (to say)
Ill. Illinois
illus. illustrated; illustration; illustrator
in. inch(es)
Inc., inc. incorporated
incl. including; inclusive
Ind. Indiana
ins. insurance
Inst. Institute; Institution
int. interest; interjection; international (also **intl.**)
IRA Independent Retirement Account
IRS Internal Revenue Service
It., Ital. Italian; Italy
ital. italic type
IV intravenous
Jan. January
JD, J.D. Doctor of Laws
JP, J.P. Justice of the Peace
Jpn. Japan(ese)
Jr. Junior
Jul. July
Jun. June
k karat(s); kilogram(s); kilometer(s)
K karat(s); kilobyte(s); kilometer(s); *Baseball* strikeout(s)
Kans. Kansas
KB kilobyte(s)
kc kilocycle(s)
kg kilogram(s)
kHz, khz kilohertz
km kilometer(s)
KO *Boxing* knockout
Ky. Kentucky
l. line
L *Sports* loss(es)
L, l liter(s)
L. Lake; Latin
LA, L.A. Los Angeles
La. Louisiana
Lat. Latin
lat. latitude
lb. pound(s)
l.c. in the place cited; lower case
Lieut. Lieutenant
lit. literal(ly); literature
ll. lines
LLB, LL.B. Bachelor of Laws
LLD, LL.D. Doctor of Laws
loc. cit. in the place cited
long. longitude
LPN, L.P.N. Licensed Practical Nurse
Lt. Lieutenant
Ltd., ltd. limited
m meter(s); mile(s) (also **m.**)
M male
M. Monsieur
MA, M.A. Master of Arts
Maj. Major
Mar. March
masc. masculine
Mass. Massachusetts

ABBREVIATIONS

math. mathematics
max. maximum
MB megabyte(s)
MC Master of Ceremonies
MD, M.D. Doctor of Medicine
Md. Maryland
mdse. merchandise
Me. Maine
med. medical; medicine; medium
met. metropolitan
Mex. Mexican; Mexico
mfg. manufacturing
mfr. manufacture(r)
mg milligram(s)
mgr. manager
MHz, Mhz megahertz
mi. mile(s)
Mich. Michigan
mil. military
min. minimum; minute(s)
Minn. Minnesota
misc. miscellaneous
Miss. Mississippi
mkt. market
ml milliliter(s)
Mlle. Mademoiselle
mm millimeter(s)
Mme. Madame
MO mode of operation; money order
Mo. Missouri
mo. month
Mon. Monday
Mont. Montana
MP Member of Parliament (also M.P.); Military Police
mpg miles per gallon
mph miles per hour
MS, M.S. Master of Science
MS manuscript; multiple sclerosis
MST Mountain Standard Time
Mt., mt. mount; mountain
mtg. meeting; mortgage
mun. municipal
mus. museum; music
myth. mythology
n. noun
N, N. north(ern)
N.A. North America
NASA National Aeronautics and Space Administration
NATO North Atlantic Treaty Organization
naut. nautical
n.b. note well
N.C. North Carolina
NCO noncommissioned officer
N.D., N.Dak. North Dakota
NE, N.E. northeast(ern)
Neb., Nebr. Nebraska
neg. negative
Nev. Nevada
N.H. New Hampshire
N.J. New Jersey
N.M., N.Mex. New Mexico
no. number
non seq. it does not follow
Nov. November

nt. wt. net weight
NW, N.W. northwest(ern)
N.Y. New York
NYC, N.Y.C. New York City
O *Baseball* out(s)
O. Ohio
Oct. October
off. office; officer; official
Okla. Oklahoma
op. cit. in the work cited
Oreg. Oregon
orig. origin(al)(ly)
OT overtime
oz. ounce(s)
p. page; participle; past
PA public address (system)
Pa. Pennsylvania
PAC political action committee
pat. patent(ed)
pc. piece
pct. percent
pd. paid
Penn., Penna. Pennsylvania
pg. page
PhD, Ph.D. Doctor of Philosophy
phys. physical; physician; physics
pk. pack; park; peck
pkg. package(s)
pl. place; plate; plural
PM, P.M. Postmaster; Prime Minister
p.m., P.M. after noon
PO, P.O. Post Office (box)
pop. popularly; population
pos. positive
POW prisoner of war
PP parcel post
pp. pages; past participle
ppd. postpaid
ppr. present participle
P.R. public relations (also PR); Puerto Rico
pr. pair(s); price
prec. preceding
pref. preferred; prefix
prelim. preliminary
prep. preparatory; preposition
Pres. President
pres. present
prim. primary
prob. probably; problem
Prof. Professor
pron. pronoun; pronunciation
prop. proper(ly); property; proprietor
P.S. postscript
PST Pacific Standard Time
pt. part; past tense; pint; point
pub. public; published; publisher
Pvt. Private
Q question
qb *Football* quarterback
Q.E.D. which was to be demonstrated
qt. quart(s)
qty. quantity
quot. quotation
q.v. which see

184

ABBREVIATIONS

R *Baseball* run(s)

rbi, RBI *Baseball* runs batted in

R.C. Roman Catholic

Rd. Road

recd., rec'd. received

ref. referee; reference; reformed; refund

reg. registered; regular; regulation

rel. relative(ly); religion

Rep. Representative; Republic(an)

rep. report(ed)

rept. report

res. reserve; residence; resigned

ret. retired; return(ed)

Rev. Reverend

rev. revenue; revise(d); revolution

R.I. Rhode Island

R.I.P., RIP may he (she) rest in peace

RN, R.N. Registered Nurse

Rom. Roman

ROTC Reserve Officers Training Corps

rpm revolutions per minute

RR railroad; rural route

R.S.V.P. please reply

Rte. Route

S, S. south(ern)

Sat. Saturday

S.C. South Carolina

ScD, Sc.D. Doctor of Science

S.D., S.Dak. South Dakota

SE, S.E. southeast(ern)

sec. second(s); secondary; secretary (also **secy.**); section(s) (also **sect.**)

Sen. Senate; Senator

Sept. September

seq(q). the following one(s)

Sgt. Sergeant

shpt. shipment

sing. singular

soc. social; society

Sp. Spain; Spanish

sp. special; spelling

spec. special; specifically (also **specif.**); specification

sq. square

SST supersonic transport

St. Saint; Strait; Street

STD sexually transmitted disease

Sun. Sunday

Supt. Superintendent

SW, S.W. southwest(ern)

t. teaspoon(s); tense; ton

T. tablespoon(s)

TB tuberculosis

tbs. tablespoon(s)

TD *Football* touchdown

tech. technical; technology

tel. telegram; telephone

temp. temperature; temporary

Tenn. Tennessee

Tex. Texas

theol. theology

Thur., Thurs. Thursday

TKO *Boxing* technical knockout

TM trademark

tr. translated (by); translation; translator; transpose

trans. translated (by); translation; translator; transportation

treas. treasurer; treasury

tsp. teaspoon(s)

Tue., Tues. Tuesday

U. Union; United; University

u.c. upper case

UHF ultrahigh frequency

UK, U.K. United Kingdom

UN United Nations

Univ. University

U.S., US United States of America

USA United States of America (also **U.S.A.**); United States Army

USAF United States Air Force

USDA United States Department of Agriculture

USMC United States Marine Corps

USN United States Navy

U.S.S.R., USSR Union of Soviet Socialist Republics

Ut. Utah

v. verb; verse; versus; very

V, v vanadium

VA Veterans Administration

Va. Virginia

VD venereal disease

vet. veteran; veterinary

VHF very high frequency

viz. namely

vol. volume

vs. versus

VP, V.P. Vice President

Vt. Vermont

W watt(s) (also **w**); west(ern) (also **W.**); *Sports* win(s)

Wash. Washington

Wed. Wednesday

Wis., Wisc. Wisconsin

wk. week

wt. weight

W.Va. West Virginia

Wyo. Wyoming

yd. yard(s)

YMCA Young Men's Christian Association

yr. year

YWCA Young Women's Christian Association

UNITED STATES AND CANADA

State	Capital	Postal Abbrev.
Alabama	Montgomery	AL
Alaska	Juneau	AK
Arizona	Phoenix	AZ
Arkansas	Little Rock	AR
California	Sacramento	CA
Colorado	Denver	CO
Connecticut	Hartford	CT
Delaware	Dover	DE
[District of Columbia]	–	DC
Florida	Tallahassee	FL
Georgia	Atlanta	GA
Hawaii	Honolulu	HI
Idaho	Boise	ID
Illinois	Springfield	IL
Indiana	Indianapolis	IN
Iowa	Des Moines	IA
Kansas	Topeka	KS
Kentucky	Frankfort	KY
Louisiana	Baton Rouge	LA
Maine	Augusta	ME
Maryland	Annapolis	MD
Massachusetts	Boston	MA
Michigan	Lansing	MI
Minnesota	St. Paul	MN
Mississippi	Jackson	MS
Missouri	Jefferson City	MO
Montana	Helena	MT
Nebraska	Lincoln	NE
Nevada	Carson City	NV
New Hampshire	Concord	NH
New Jersey	Trenton	NJ
New Mexico	Santa Fe	NM
New York	Albany	NY
North Carolina	Raleigh	NC
North Dakota	Bismarck	ND
Ohio	Columbus	OH
Oklahoma	Oklahoma City	OK
Oregon	Salem	OR
Pennsylvania	Harrisburg	PA
Rhode Island	Providence	RI
South Carolina	Columbia	SC
South Dakota	Pierre	SD
Tennessee	Nashville	TN
Texas	Austin	TX
Utah	Salt Lake City	UT
Vermont	Montpelier	VT
Virginia	Richmond	VA
Washington	Olympia	WA
West Virginia	Charleston	WV
Wisconsin	Madison	WI
Wyoming	Cheyenne	WY

UNITED STATES AND CANADA

U.S. Territory	Capital	Postal Abbrev.
American Samoa	Pago Pago	AS
Belau	Koror	PW
Guam	Agana	GU
Northern Marianas	Saipan	MP
Puerto Rico	San Juan	PR
Virgin Islands	Charlotte Amalie	VI

CANADIAN PROVINCES AND TERRITORIES

Province

Alberta	Edmonton	AB
British Columbia	Victoria	BC
Manitoba	Winnipeg	MB
New Brunswick	Fredericton	NB
Newfoundland	St. John's	NF
Nova Scotia	Halifax	NS
Ontario	Toronto	ON
Prince Edward Island	Charlottetown	PE
Quebec	Quebec	PQ
Saskatchewan	Regina	SK

Territory

Northwest Territories	Yellowknife	NT
Yukon Territory	Whitehorse	YT

DICTIONARY STAFF

Executive Editor: Michael Agnes
Managing Editor: James J. Heaney
Senior Editors: Andrew N. Sparks, Jonathan L. Goldman
Editor and Database Administrator: Donald Stewart
Editors: Laura J. Borovac, Andra I. Kalnins,
    James E. Naso, Katherine Soltis, Stephen P. Teresi
Administrative and Data Processing Staff:
    Alisa Murray Davis, Cynthia M. Sadonick,
    Betty Thompson
Citation Readers: Joan Felice, Batya Jundef,
    Patricia Nash

KEY TO PRONUNCIATION

	as in		*as in*
a	cat	ou	out
ā	ape	u	up
ä	cot	u	fur
e	ten	ə	a *in* ago
ē	me		o *in* atom
i	fit	'	fertile (furt''l)
ī	ice	ch	chin
ō	go	ŋ	ring
ô	fall	sh	she
oi	oil	th	thin
oo	look	*th*	then
ōō	tool	zh	measure

ABBREVIATIONS USED

a.	adjective	Mil.	military
abbrev.	abbreviated;	Mus.	music
	abbreviation	myth.	mythology
adv.	adverb	n.	noun
Ar.	archaic	Naut.	nautical
Biol.	biology	Obs.	obsolete
Br.	British	orig.	originally
c.	century	pl.	plural
Chem.	chemistry	Poet.	poetic
Col.	colloquial	prep.	preposition
con.	conjunction	pres.	present
Dial.	dialectal	pron.	pronoun
esp.	especially	pt.	past tense
etc.	et cetera	R.C.Ch.	Roman Catholic
fem.	feminine		Church
Fr.	French	Rom.	Roman
ft.	foot; feet	sing.	singular
Gr.	Greek	Sl.	slang
Gram.	grammar	Sp.	Spanish
in.	inch(es)	sp.	spelling; spelled
int.	interjection	spec.	specifically
L.	Latin	t.	tense
Math.	mathematics	Theol.	theology
mi.	mile(s)	v.	verb

Other abbreviations will be found on pages 182-185.